INUBAKA
CRAZY FOR DOGS

17

D1245545

CHASE BRANCH LIBRARY
17731 W. SEVEN MILE RD.
DETROIT, MI 48235

YUKIYA SAKURAGI

Contents

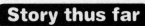

Story thus far

Teppei is the manager of the recently opened pet shop Woofles. He intended to breed his black Labrador Noa with a champion dog, but instead Noa was "taken advantage of" by an unknown and unfixed male dog!

The unknown dog's owner was Suguri Miyauchi, and her dog was a mutt named Lupin. Suguri is now working at Woofles to make up for her dog's actions.

Suguri's enthusiasm is more than a little unique. She has eaten dog food (and said it was tasty), caught dog poop with her bare hands and caused dogs to have "happy pee" in her presence. Teppei is starting to realize that Suguri is indeed a very special girl.

Chizuru, a regular customer at Woofles, brings her friend Serina to the shop. Serina buys a puppy so she can practice for taking care of a baby sometime in the future. Unfortunately, she soon gets fed up with the playful puppy, and Suguri visits her to offer some advice. About the time Serina is getting used to living with a puppy, her "hubby," a professional baseball player, comes back from away games and begins spoiling Milk. Serina gets sick of the way Milk likes her husband more than her—even though she's the one who spends the most time with the puppy—and decides she doesn't want a dog anymore! She shows up at Woofles to give Milk back, but...

CHARACTERS

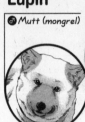

Suguri Miyauchi

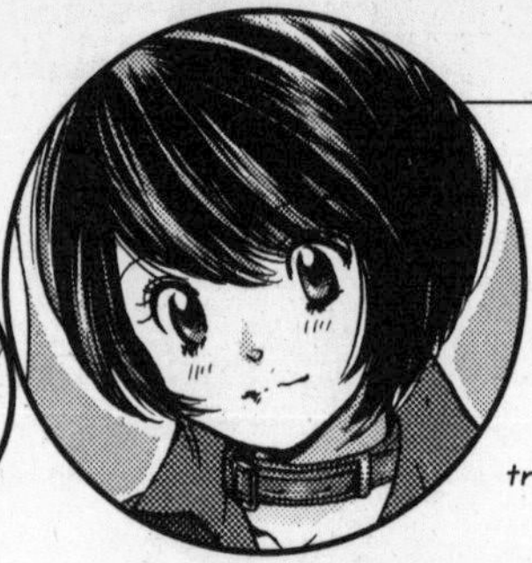

Seems to possess an almost supernatural connection with dogs. When she approaches them they often urinate with great excitement! She is crazy for dogs and can catch their droppings with her bare hands. She is currently a trainee at the Woofles Pet Shop.

Lupin

♂ Mutt (mongrel)

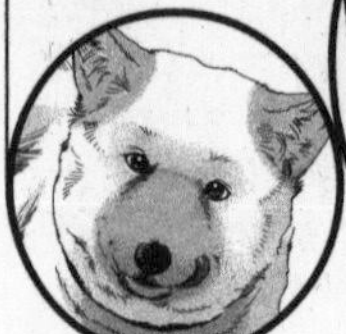

Teppei Iida

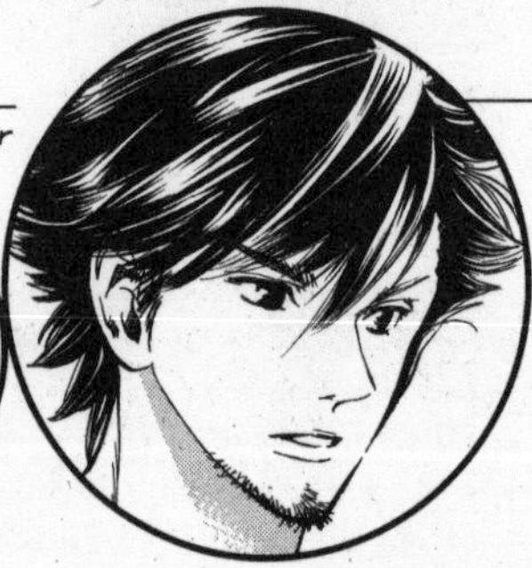

Manager of the recently opened pet shop Woofles. He is aware of Suguri's special ability and has hired her to work in his shop.

Noa

♀ Labrador retriever

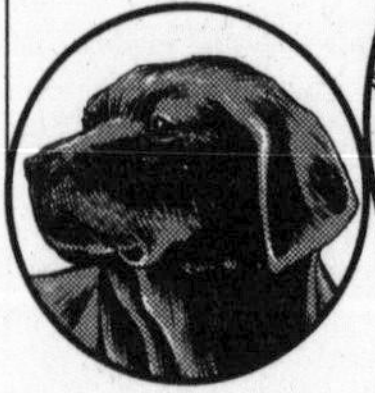

Mel

♀ Toy poodle

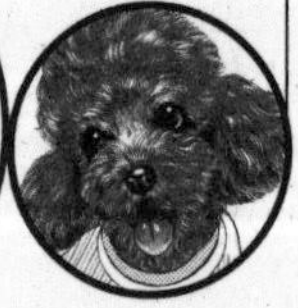

Momoko Takeuchi

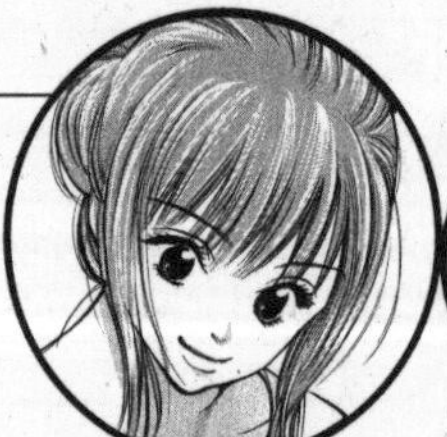

The Woofles Pet Shop (second location) pet groomer. At first she had many problems and rarely smiled. But after meeting Suguri she's changed, and the two are now best friends.

Show Kaneko

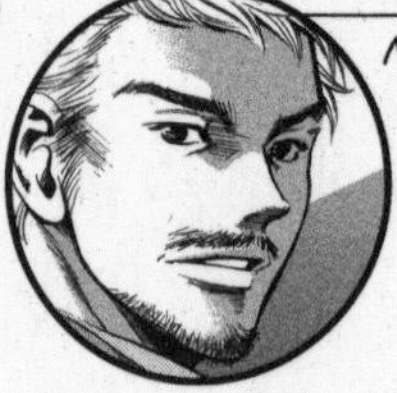

Manager of the main Woofles store and Teppei's boss. He is very passionate about the business and makes TV appearances from time to time.

Kentaro Osada

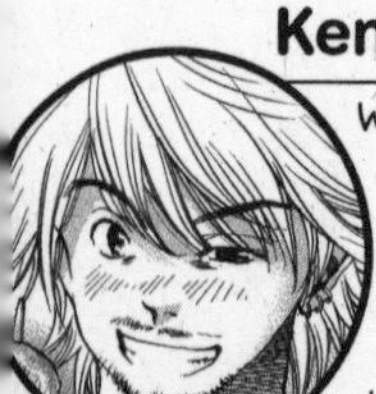

Wannabe musician and Teppei's buddy from their high school days. Teppei saved Kentaro when he was a down-and-out beggar. He's not a big fan of dogs.

Serina Ueda

A friend of Chizuru's from their school days. She decides to get a puppy to practice for raising a baby. She soon learns, however, that puppies aren't just cute, but tiring!

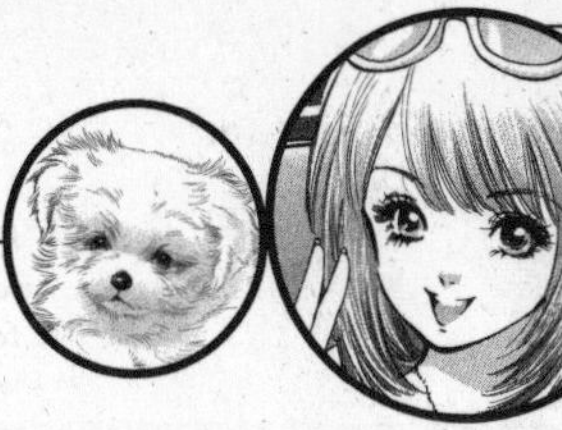

Milk

♂ Maltese

Woofles Regular Customers

Chizuru Sawamura

Adopted a Chihuahua, Melon, after her longtime pet golden retriever, Ricky, alerted her that Melon was ill. She works at a hostess bar to repay Melon's medical fees.

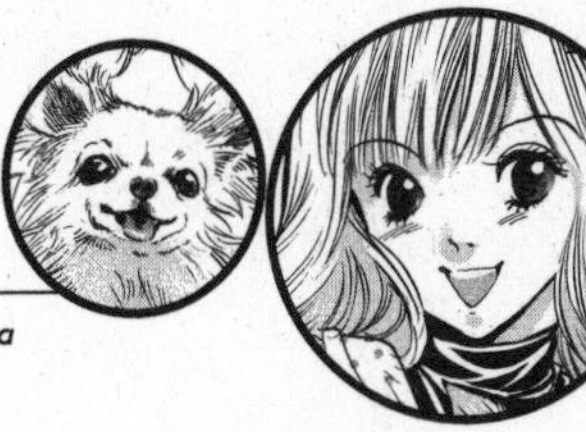

Melon

♂ Chihuahua

Hiroshi Akiba

Pop-idol otaku turned dog otaku. His dream is to publish a photo collection of his dog, Zidane. He is a government employee.

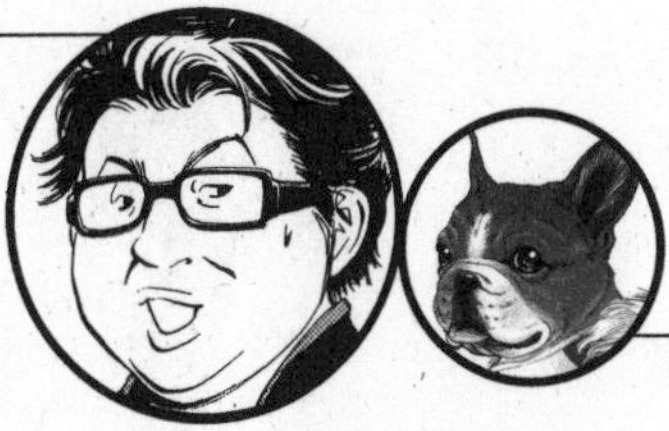

Zidane

♂ French bulldog

Fujita

Owner of Lupin's sister Amuro. He kidnapped Suguri when she was a child, and when he found out she was in Tokyo, he followed her to Woofles. He is obsessed with Suguri and persists in stalking her.

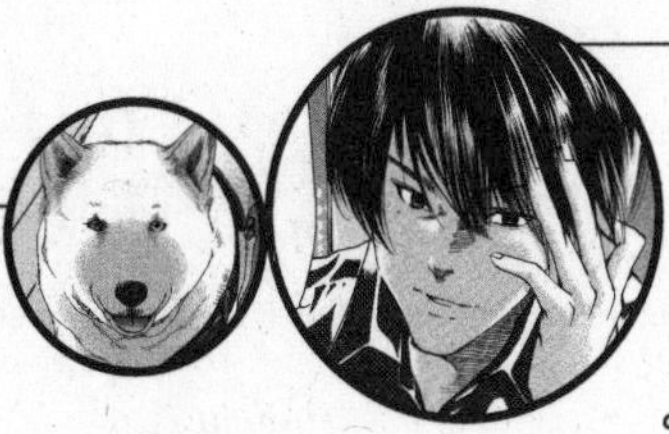

Amuro

♀ Mutt (mongrel)

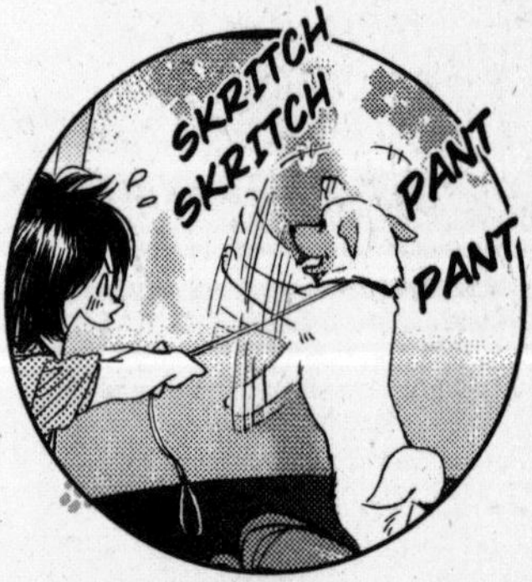
SKRITCH
SKRITCH
PANT
PANT

INUBAKA

CHAPTER 174: SERINA LOVES HERSELF

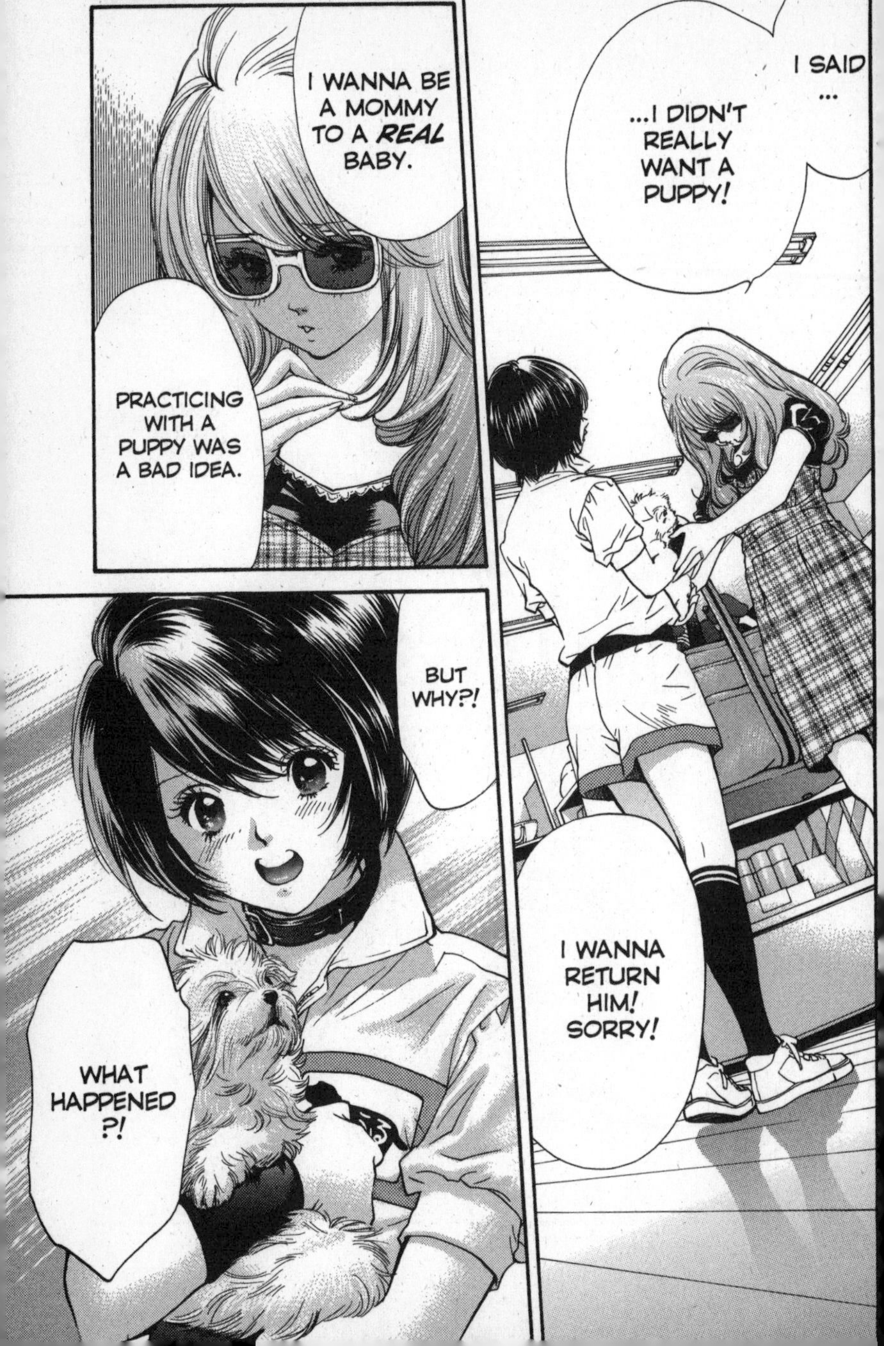
I SAID ...
...I DIDN'T REALLY WANT A PUPPY!
I WANNA RETURN HIM! SORRY!
I WANNA BE A MOMMY TO A *REAL* BABY.
PRACTICING WITH A PUPPY WAS A BAD IDEA.
BUT WHY?!
WHAT HAPPENED ?!

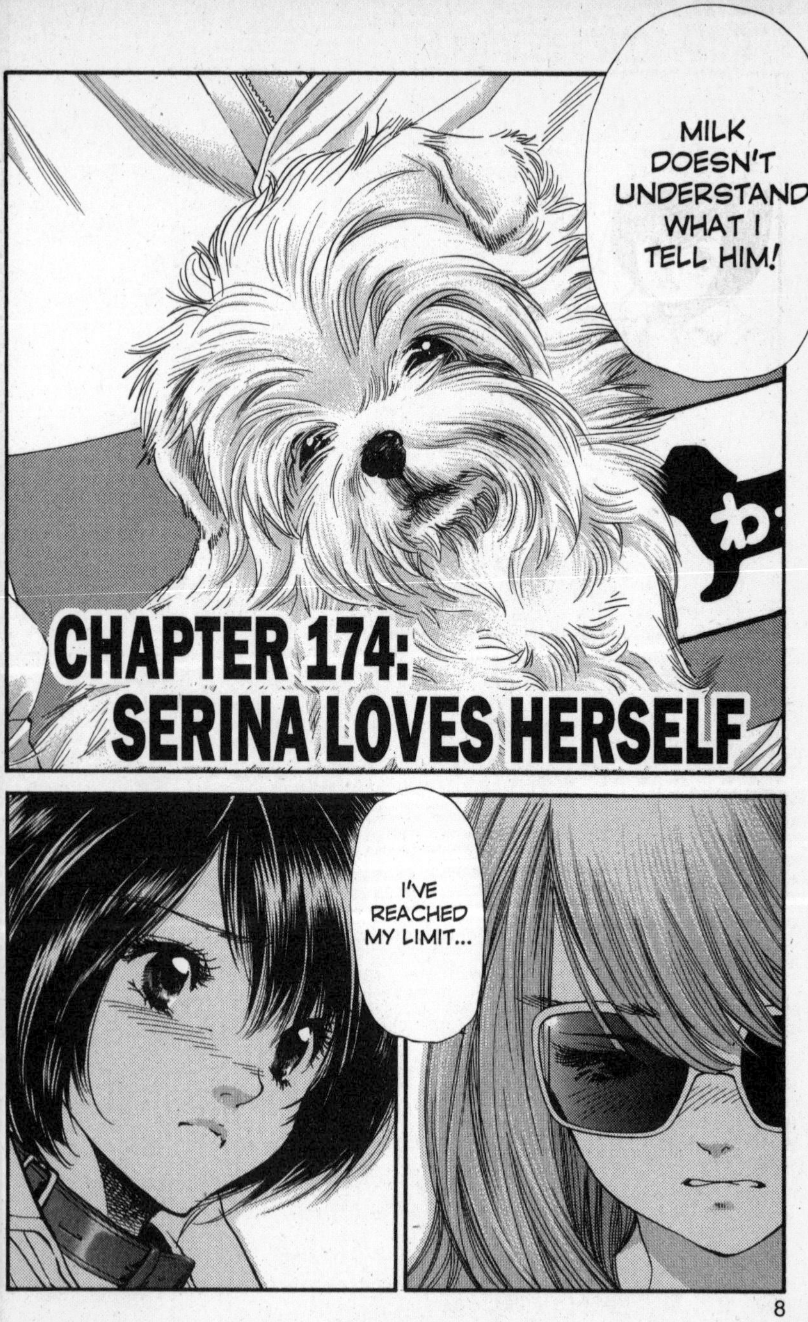
MILK DOESN'T UNDERSTAND WHAT I TELL HIM!
わ…
CHAPTER 174: SERINA LOVES HERSELF
I'VE REACHED MY LIMIT...

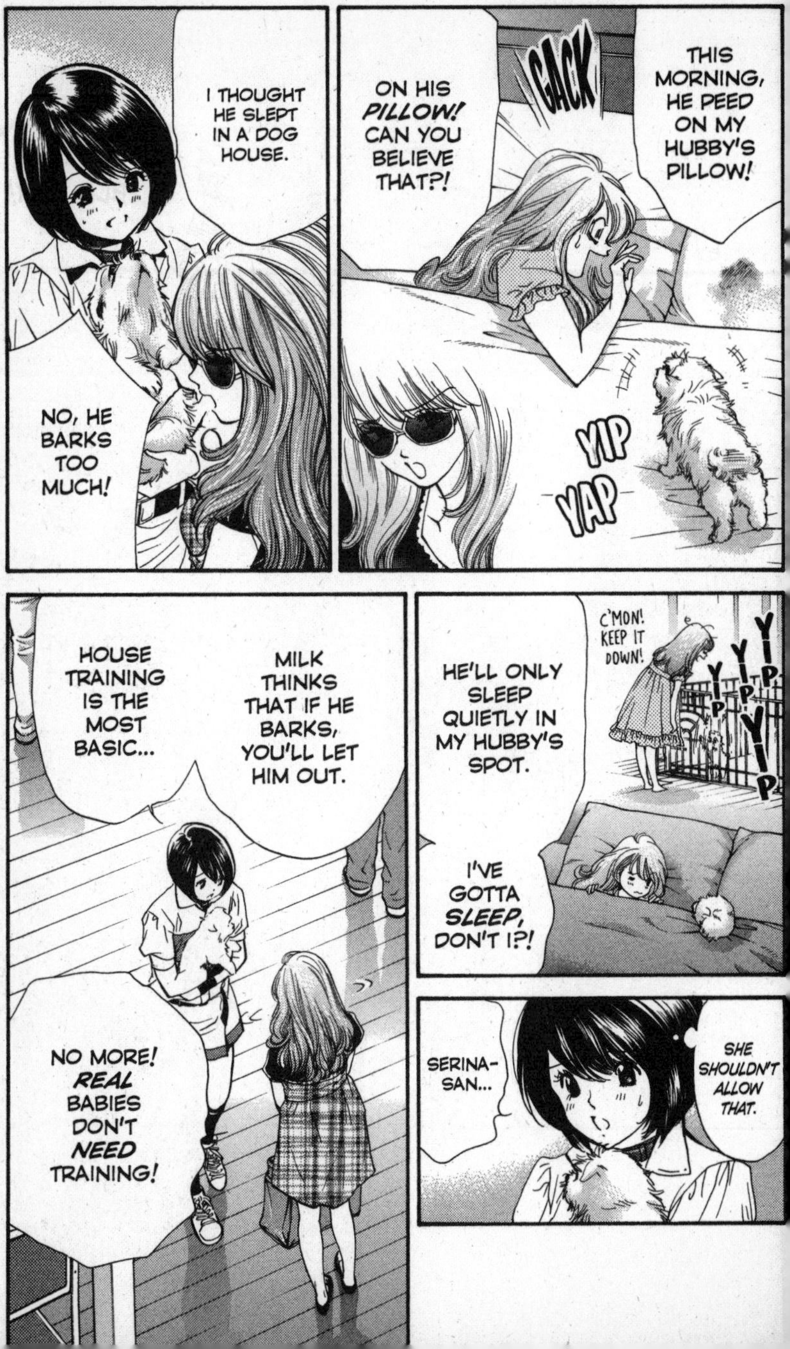
THIS MORNING, HE PEED ON MY HUBBY'S PILLOW!
GACK
ON HIS *PILLOW!* CAN YOU BELIEVE THAT?!
YIP
YAP
I THOUGHT HE SLEPT IN A DOG HOUSE.
NO, HE BARKS TOO MUCH!
C'MON! KEEP IT DOWN!
YIP YIP YIP YIP
HE'LL ONLY SLEEP QUIETLY IN MY HUBBY'S SPOT.
I'VE GOTTA *SLEEP,* DON'T I?!
SHE SHOULDN'T ALLOW THAT.
SERINA-SAN...
MILK THINKS THAT IF HE BARKS, YOU'LL LET HIM OUT.
HOUSE TRAINING IS THE MOST BASIC...
NO MORE! *REAL* BABIES DON'T *NEED* TRAINING!

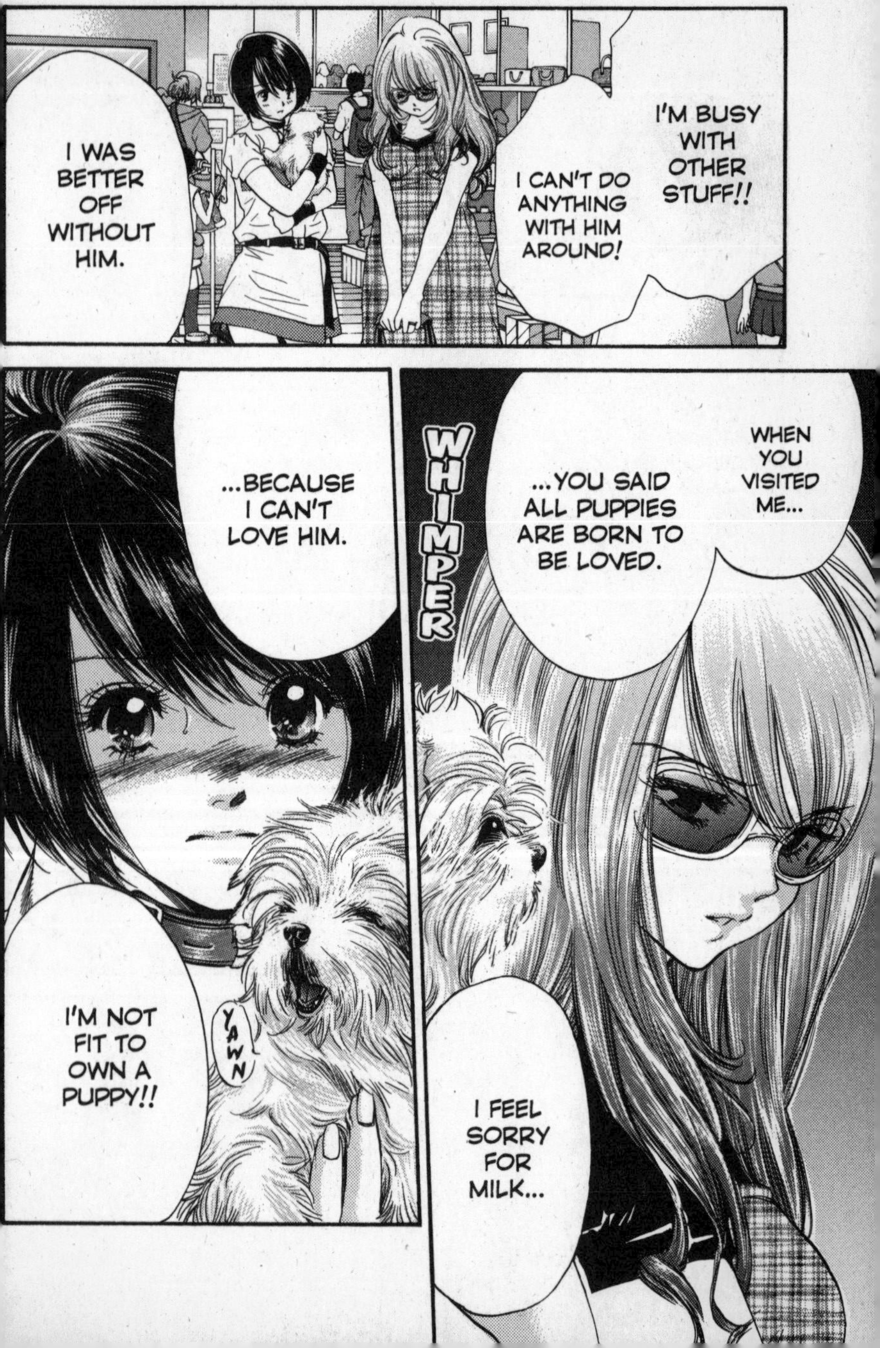
I'M BUSY WITH OTHER STUFF!!
I CAN'T DO ANYTHING WITH HIM AROUND!
I WAS BETTER OFF WITHOUT HIM.
WHEN YOU VISITED ME...
...YOU SAID ALL PUPPIES ARE BORN TO BE LOVED.
WHIMPER
I FEEL SORRY FOR MILK...
...BECAUSE I CAN'T LOVE HIM.
YAWN
I'M NOT FIT TO OWN A PUPPY!!

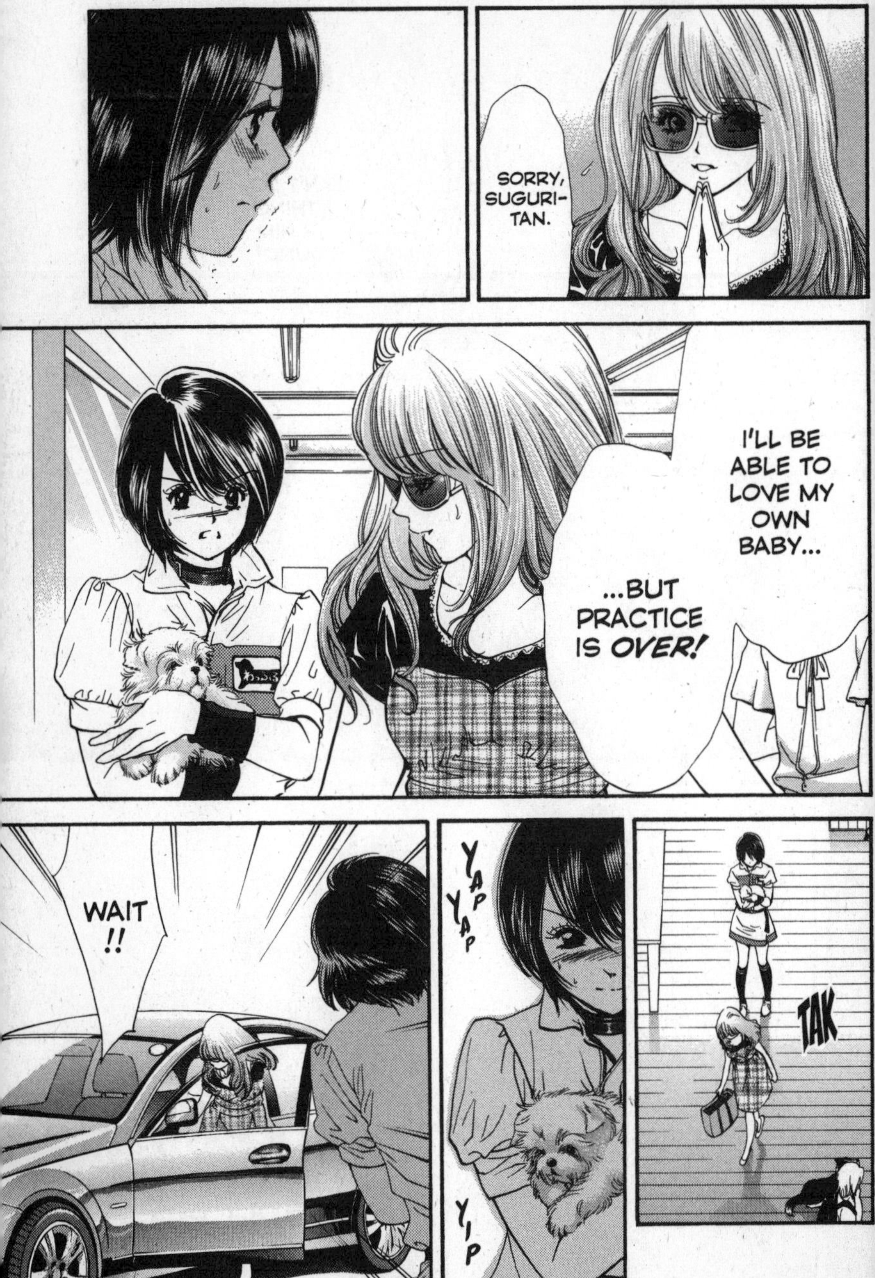
SORRY, SUGURI-TAN.
I'LL BE ABLE TO LOVE MY OWN BABY...
...BUT PRACTICE IS *OVER!*
TAK
YAP YAP
YIP
WAIT!!

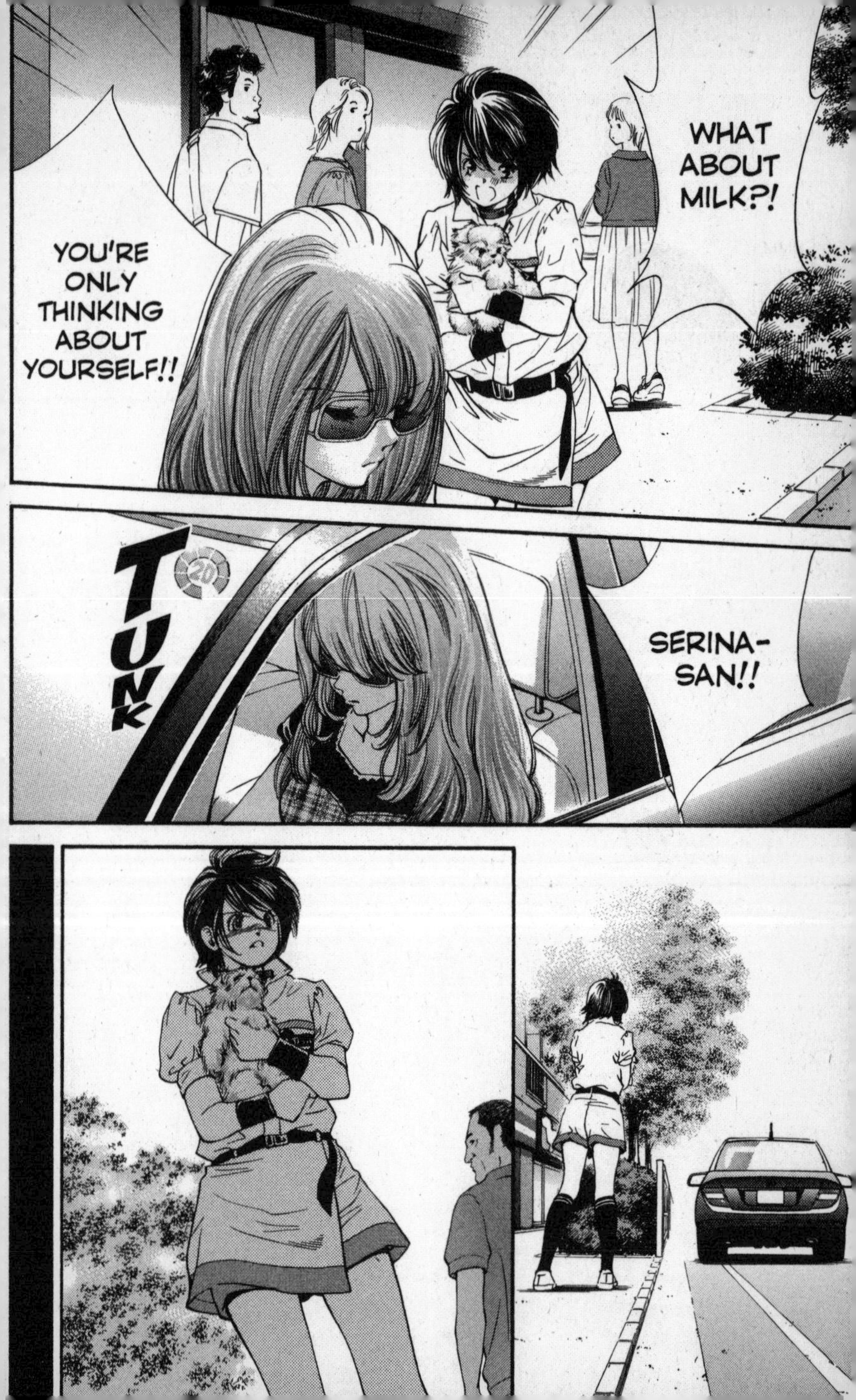
WHAT ABOUT MILK?!
YOU'RE ONLY THINKING ABOUT YOURSELF!!
SERINA-SAN!!
TUNK

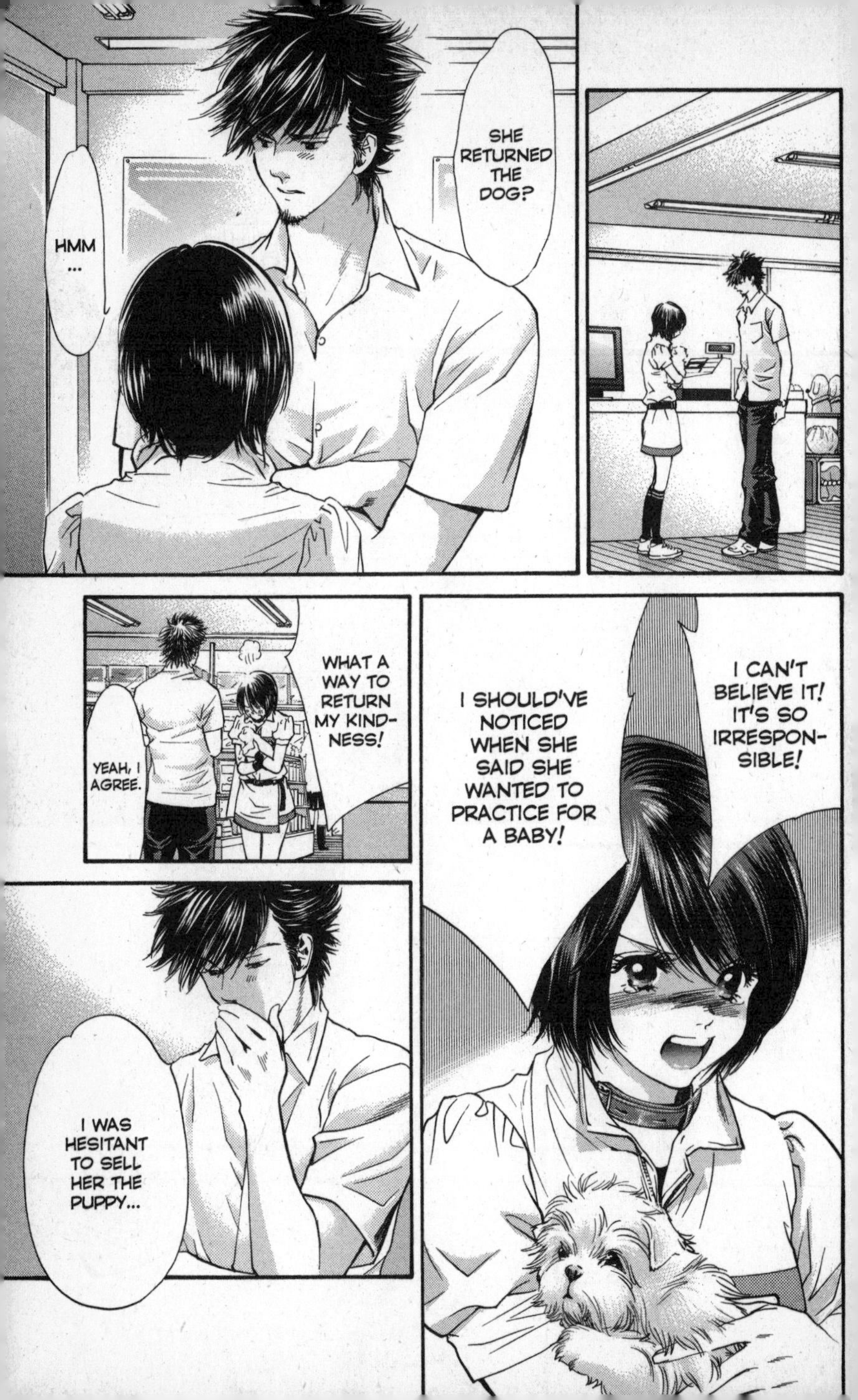
SHE RETURNED THE DOG?
HMM ...
I CAN'T BELIEVE IT! IT'S SO IRRESPON-SIBLE!
I SHOULD'VE NOTICED WHEN SHE SAID SHE WANTED TO PRACTICE FOR A BABY!
WHAT A WAY TO RETURN MY KIND-NESS!
YEAH, I AGREE.
I WAS HESITANT TO SELL HER THE PUPPY...

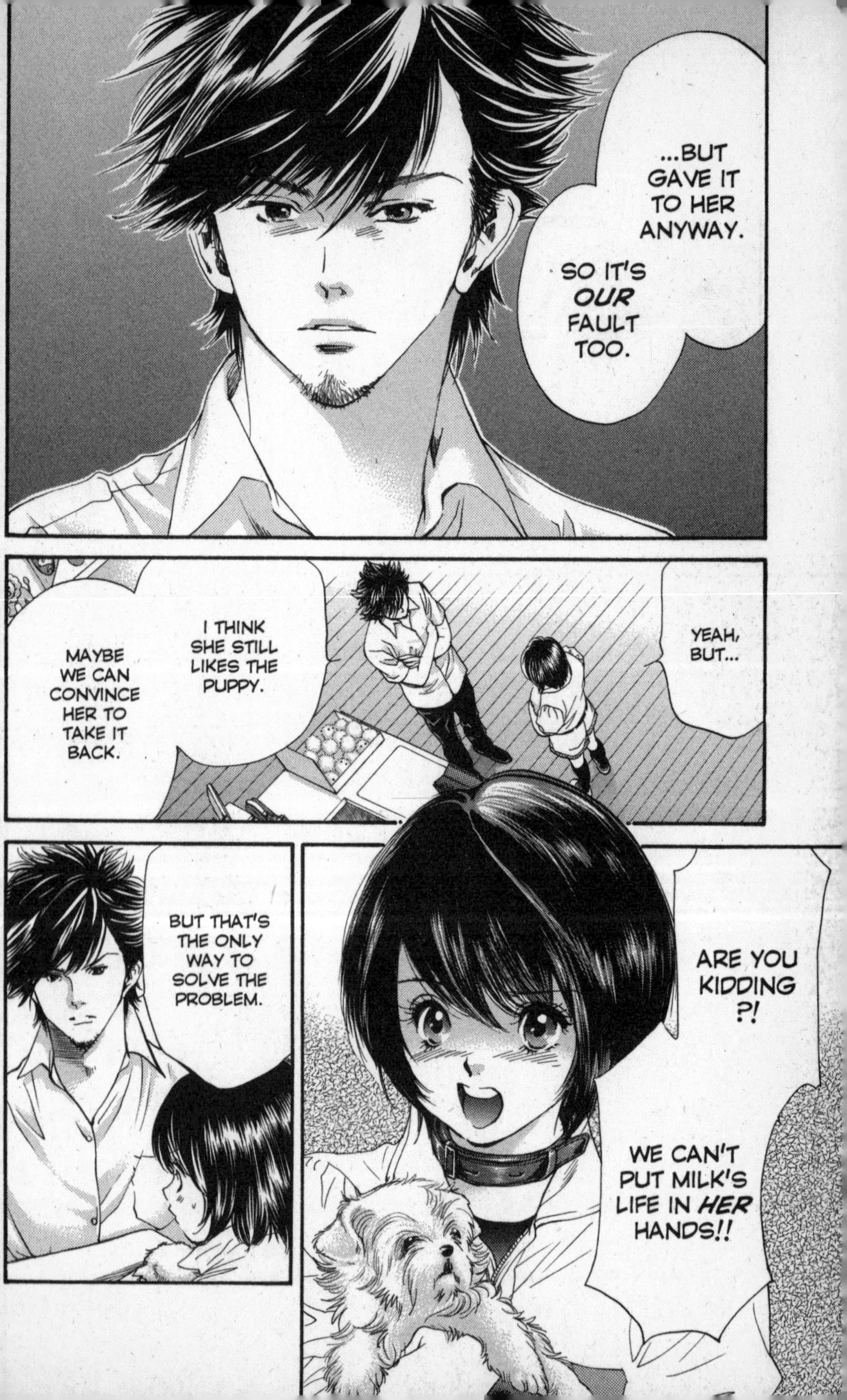
...BUT GAVE IT TO HER ANYWAY.
SO IT'S *OUR* FAULT TOO.
YEAH, BUT...
I THINK SHE STILL LIKES THE PUPPY.
MAYBE WE CAN CONVINCE HER TO TAKE IT BACK.
ARE YOU KIDDING?!
WE CAN'T PUT MILK'S LIFE IN *HER* HANDS!!
BUT THAT'S THE ONLY WAY TO SOLVE THE PROBLEM.

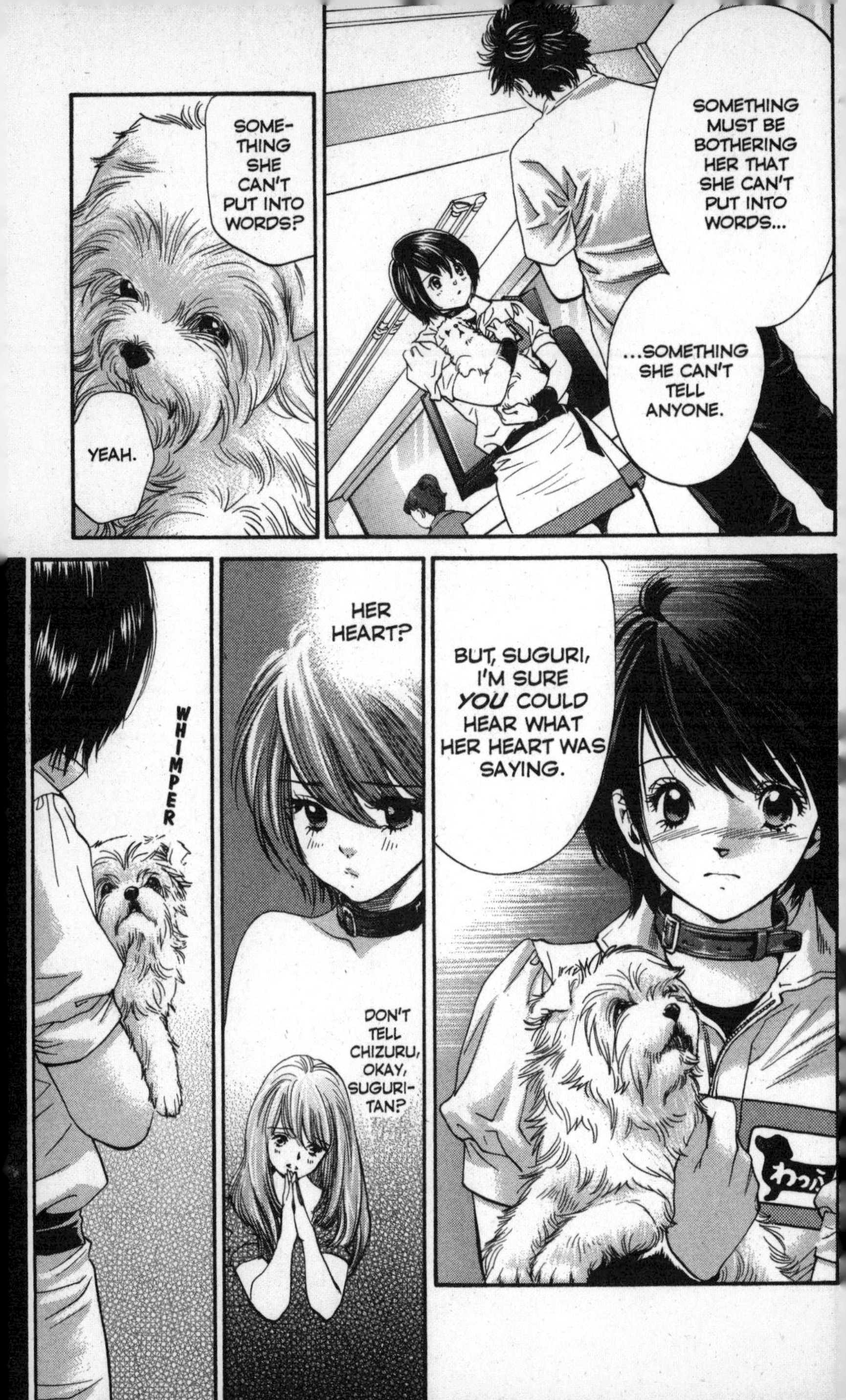
SOMETHING MUST BE BOTHERING HER THAT SHE CAN'T PUT INTO WORDS...
...SOMETHING SHE CAN'T TELL ANYONE.
SOME-THING SHE CAN'T PUT INTO WORDS?
YEAH.
BUT, SUGURI, I'M SURE *YOU* COULD HEAR WHAT HER HEART WAS SAYING.
HER HEART?
DON'T TELL CHIZURU, OKAY, SUGURI-TAN?
WHIMPER

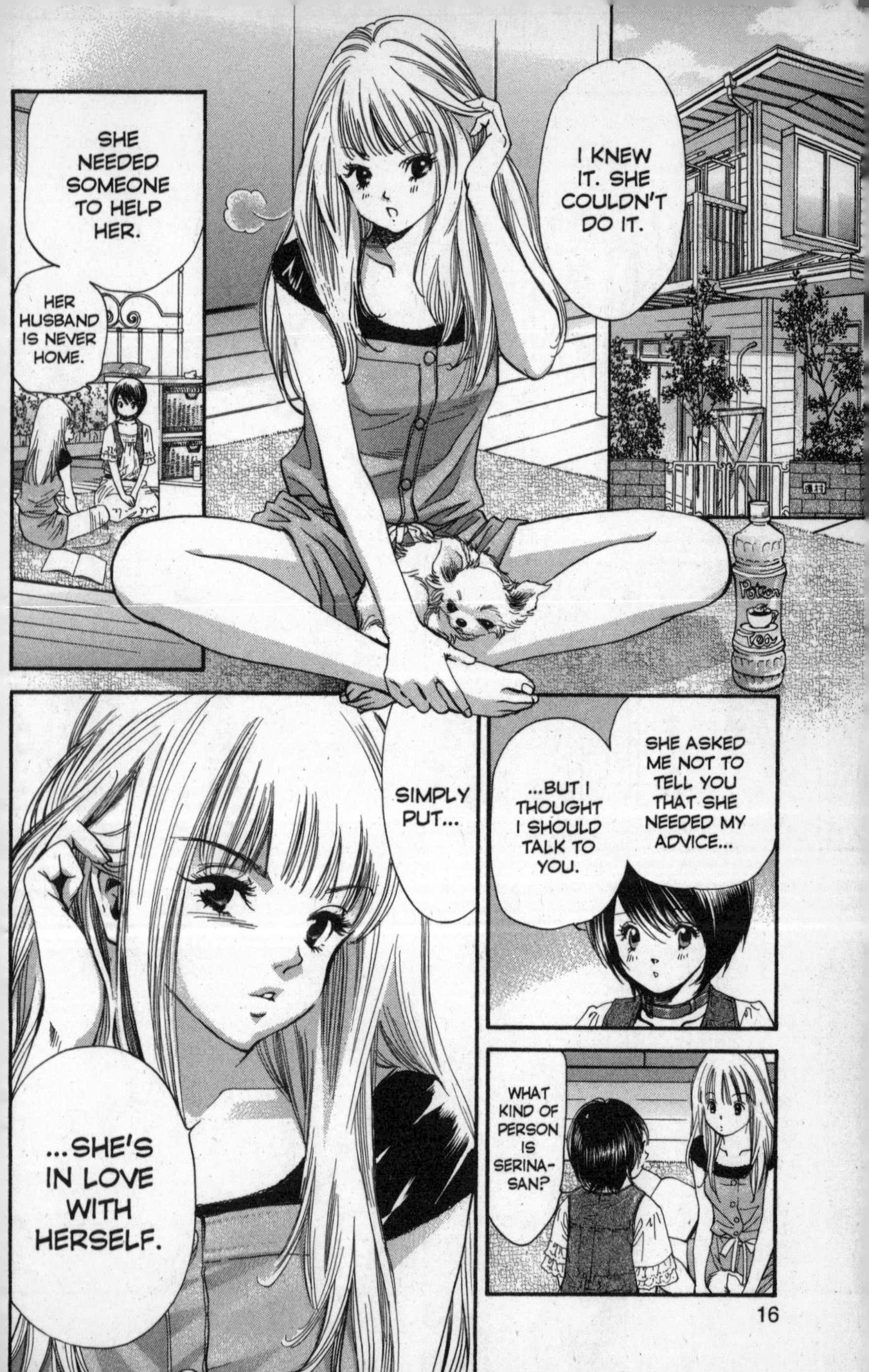
I KNEW IT. SHE COULDN'T DO IT.
SHE NEEDED SOMEONE TO HELP HER.
HER HUSBAND IS NEVER HOME.
SHE ASKED ME NOT TO TELL YOU THAT SHE NEEDED MY ADVICE...
...BUT I THOUGHT I SHOULD TALK TO YOU.
WHAT KIND OF PERSON IS SERINA-SAN?
SIMPLY PUT...
...SHE'S IN LOVE WITH HERSELF.

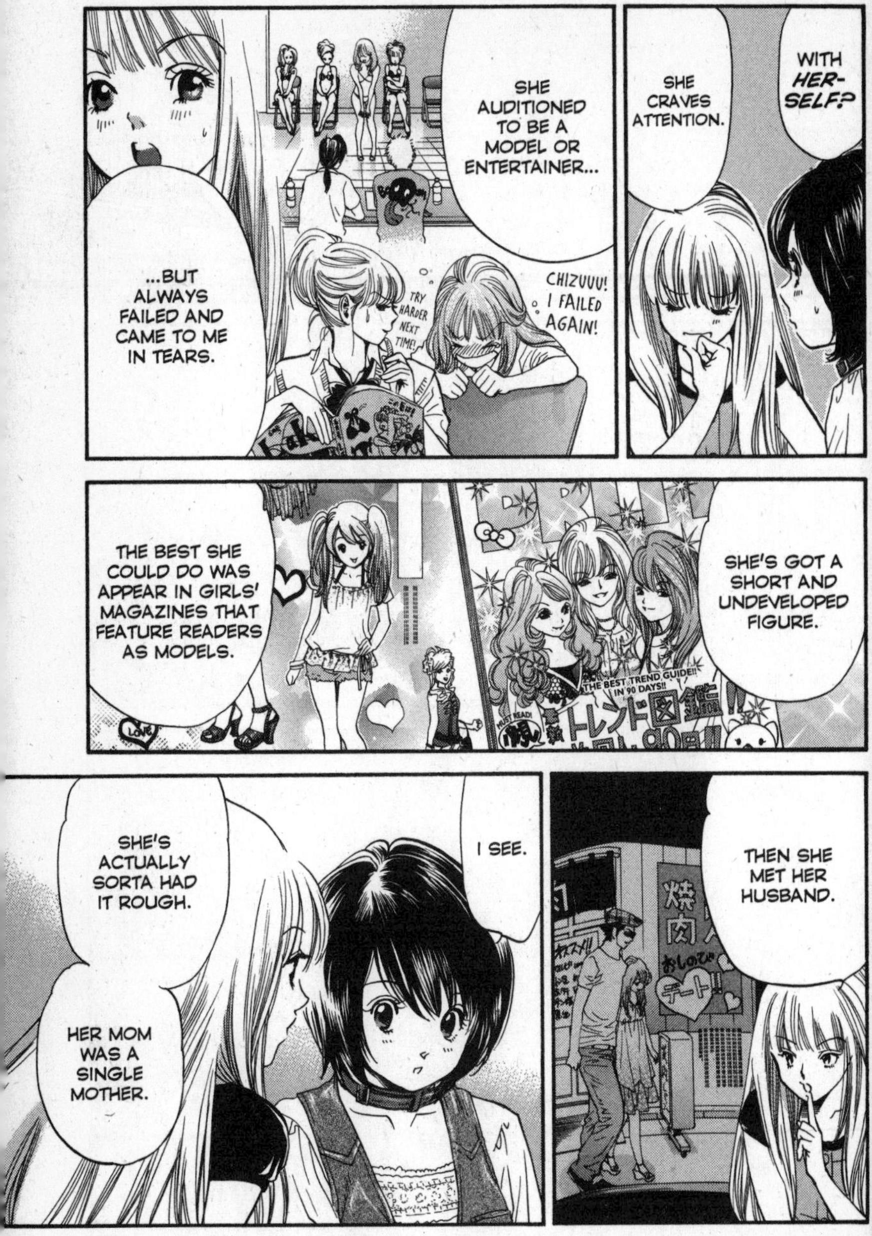
WITH HER-SELF?
SHE CRAVES ATTENTION.
SHE AUDITIONED TO BE A MODEL OR ENTERTAINER...
CHIZUUU! I FAILED AGAIN!
TRY HARDER NEXT TIME!
...BUT ALWAYS FAILED AND CAME TO ME IN TEARS.
SHE'S GOT A SHORT AND UNDEVELOPED FIGURE.
THE BEST TREND GUIDE!! IN 90 DAYS!!
MUST READ!
THE BEST SHE COULD DO WAS APPEAR IN GIRLS' MAGAZINES THAT FEATURE READERS AS MODELS.
LOVE
THEN SHE MET HER HUSBAND.
I SEE.
SHE'S ACTUALLY SORTA HAD IT ROUGH.
HER MOM WAS A SINGLE MOTHER.

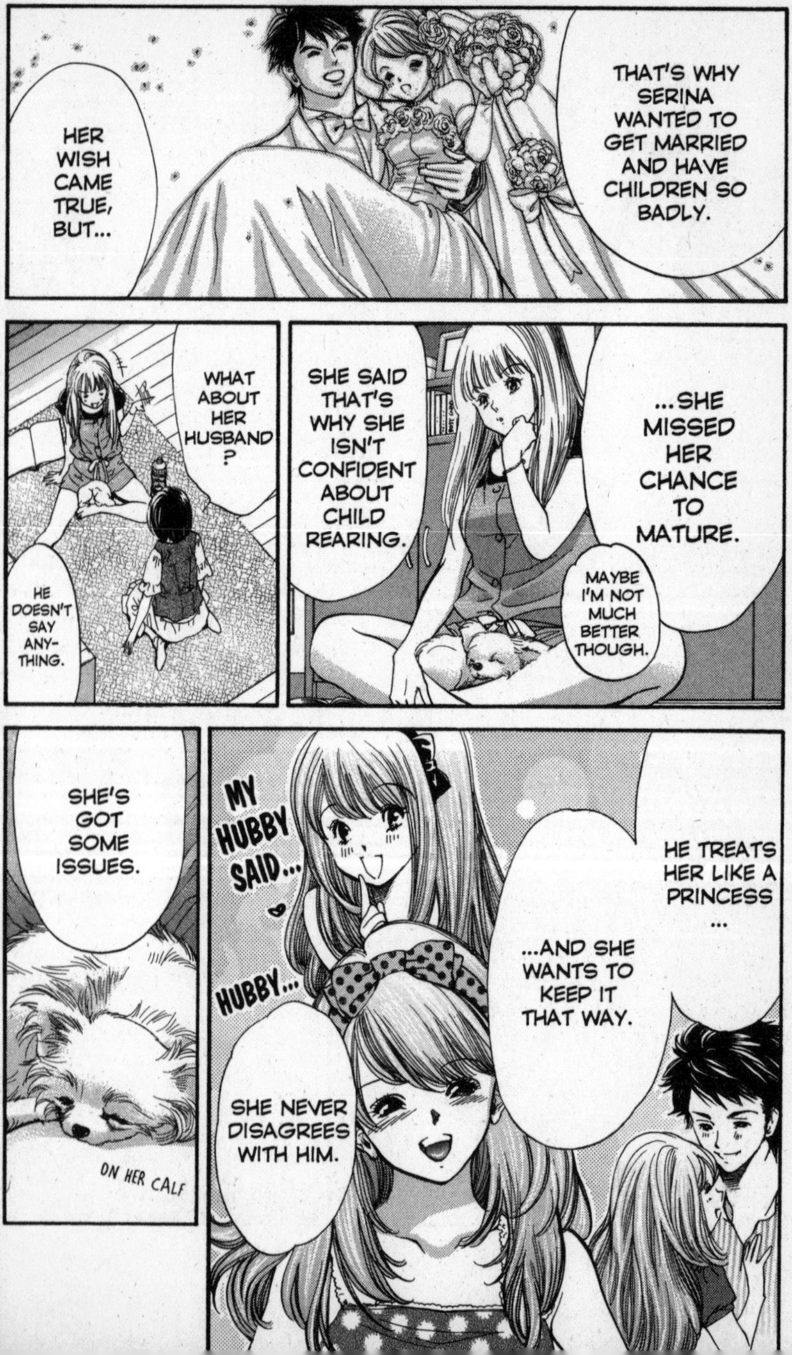
THAT'S WHY SERINA WANTED TO GET MARRIED AND HAVE CHILDREN SO BADLY.
HER WISH CAME TRUE, BUT...
...SHE MISSED HER CHANCE TO MATURE.
MAYBE I'M NOT MUCH BETTER THOUGH.
SHE SAID THAT'S WHY SHE ISN'T CONFIDENT ABOUT CHILD REARING.
WHAT ABOUT HER HUSBAND?
HE DOESN'T SAY ANY-THING.
HE TREATS HER LIKE A PRINCESS...
...AND SHE WANTS TO KEEP IT THAT WAY.
MY HUBBY SAID...
HUBBY...
SHE NEVER DISAGREES WITH HIM.
SHE'S GOT SOME ISSUES.
ON HER CALF

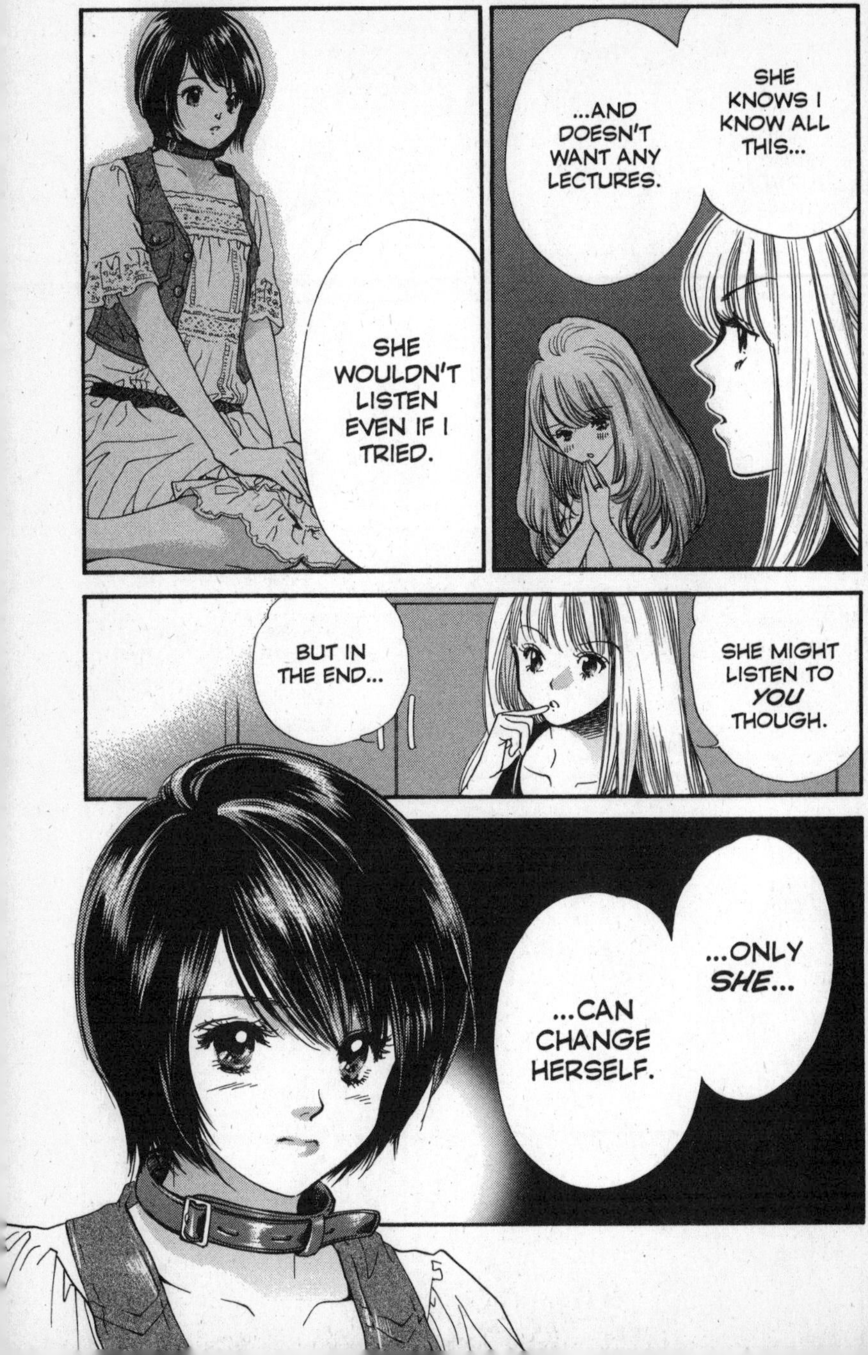
SHE KNOWS I KNOW ALL THIS...
...AND DOESN'T WANT ANY LECTURES.
SHE WOULDN'T LISTEN EVEN IF I TRIED.
SHE MIGHT LISTEN TO *YOU* THOUGH.
BUT IN THE END...
...ONLY *SHE*...
...CAN CHANGE HERSELF.

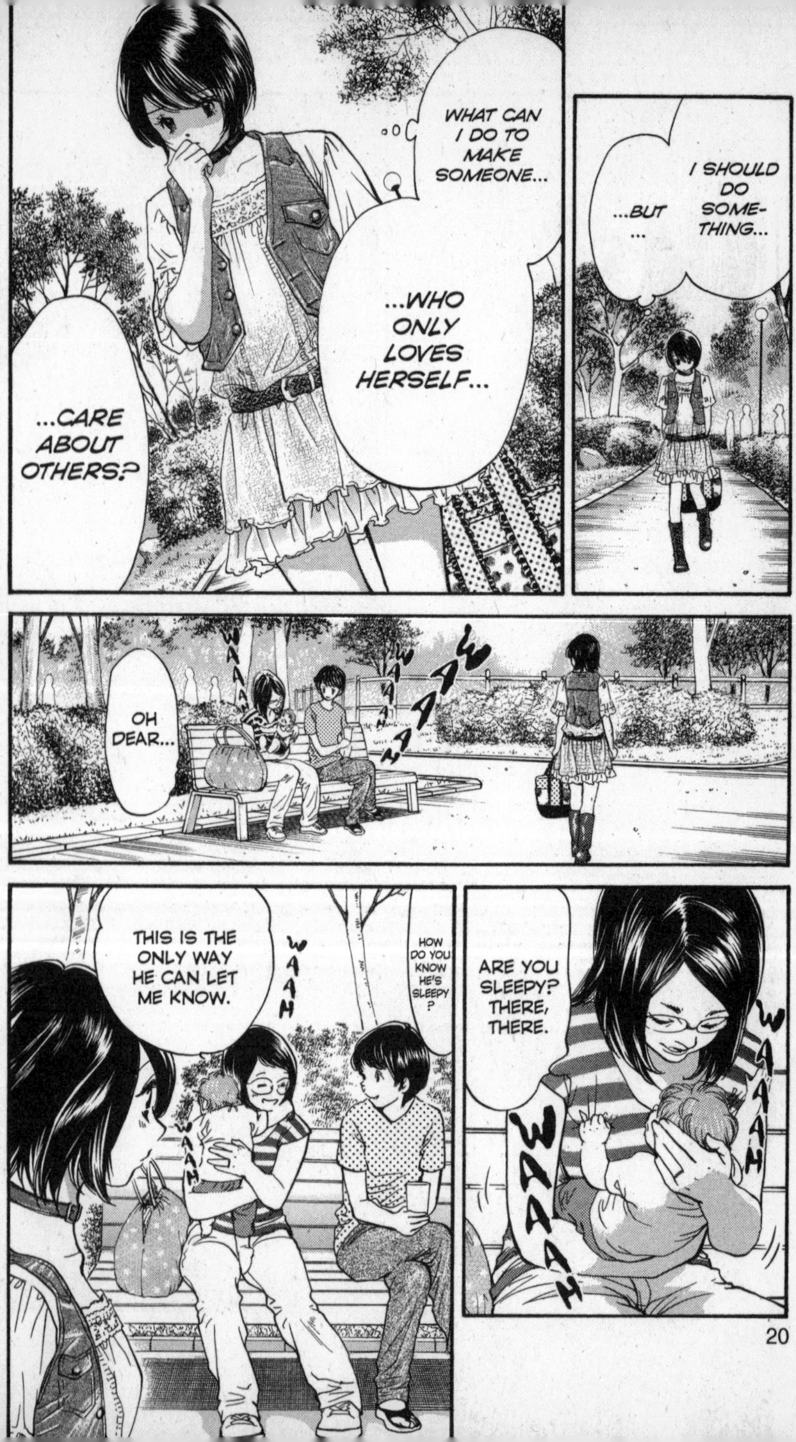
I SHOULD DO SOMETHING...
...BUT ...
WHAT CAN I DO TO MAKE SOMEONE...
...WHO ONLY LOVES HERSELF...
...CARE ABOUT OTHERS?
WAAAAH
WAAAAAH
WAAAAH
OH DEAR...
WAAAAH
ARE YOU SLEEPY? THERE, THERE.
WAAAAH
HOW DO YOU KNOW HE'S SLEEPY?
WAAH
THIS IS THE ONLY WAY HE CAN LET ME KNOW.
WAAH

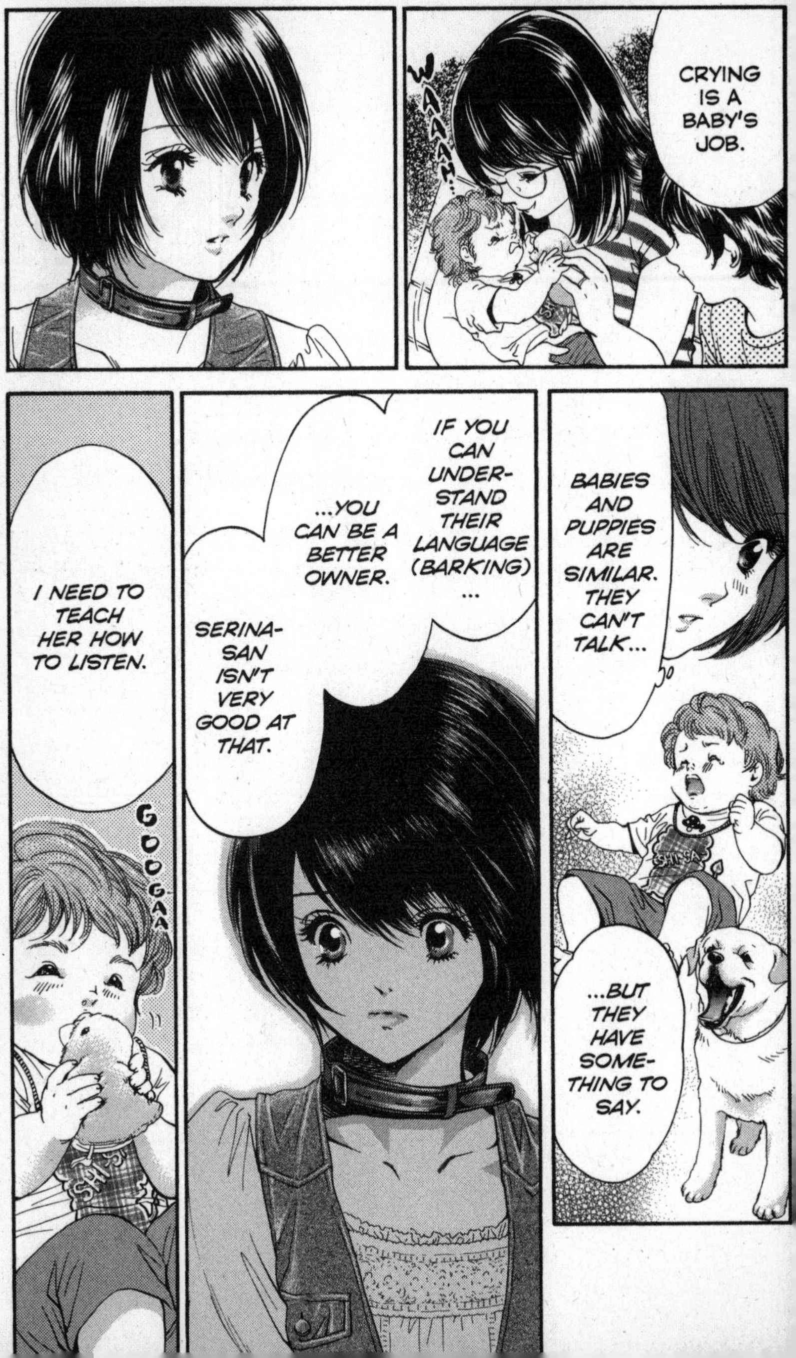
WAAAAH...
CRYING IS A BABY'S JOB.
BABIES AND PUPPIES ARE SIMILAR. THEY CAN'T TALK...
...BUT THEY HAVE SOMETHING TO SAY.
IF YOU CAN UNDERSTAND THEIR LANGUAGE (BARKING)...
...YOU CAN BE A BETTER OWNER.
SERINA-SAN ISN'T VERY GOOD AT THAT.
I NEED TO TEACH HER HOW TO LISTEN.
GOOGAA

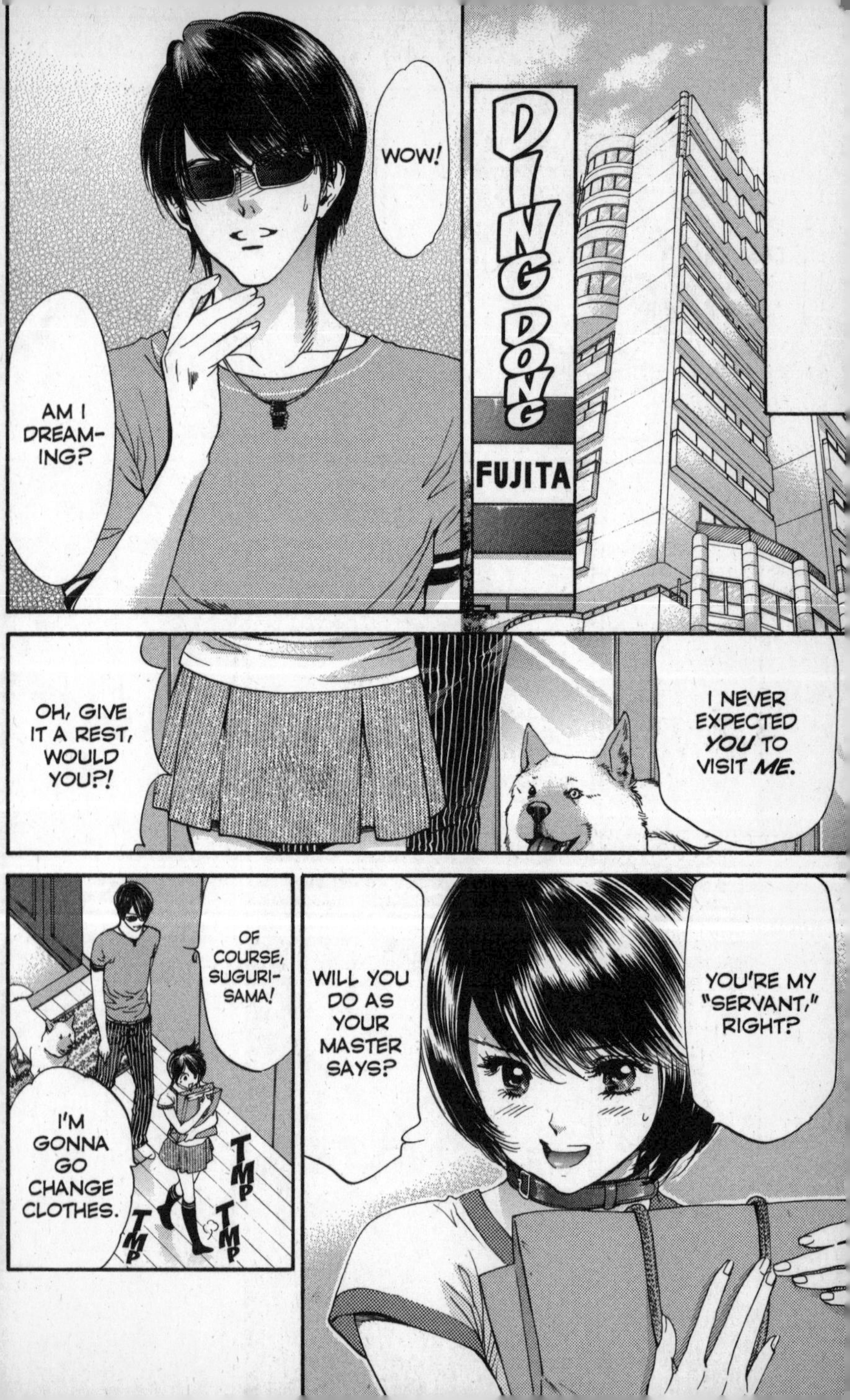
DING DONG
FUJITA
WOW!
AM I DREAMING?
I NEVER EXPECTED *YOU* TO VISIT *ME*.
OH, GIVE IT A REST, WOULD YOU?!
YOU'RE MY "SERVANT," RIGHT?
WILL YOU DO AS YOUR MASTER SAYS?
OF COURSE, SUGURI-SAMA!
I'M GONNA GO CHANGE CLOTHES.
TMP TMP TMP TMP

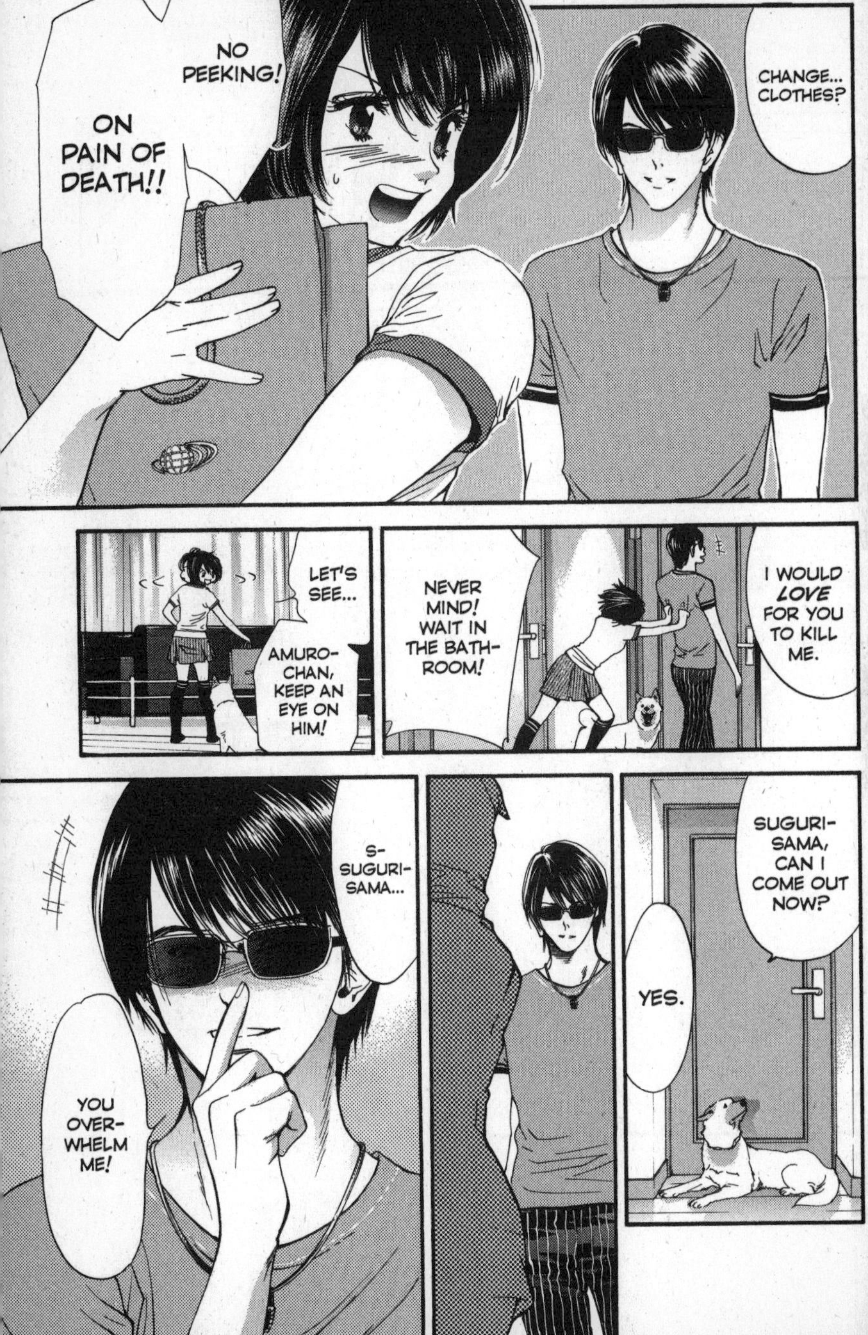
CHANGE... CLOTHES?
NO PEEKING!
ON PAIN OF DEATH!!
I WOULD *LOVE* FOR YOU TO KILL ME.
NEVER MIND! WAIT IN THE BATH-ROOM!
LET'S SEE...
AMURO-CHAN, KEEP AN EYE ON HIM!
SUGURI-SAMA, CAN I COME OUT NOW?
YES.
S-SUGURI-SAMA...
YOU OVER-WHELM ME!

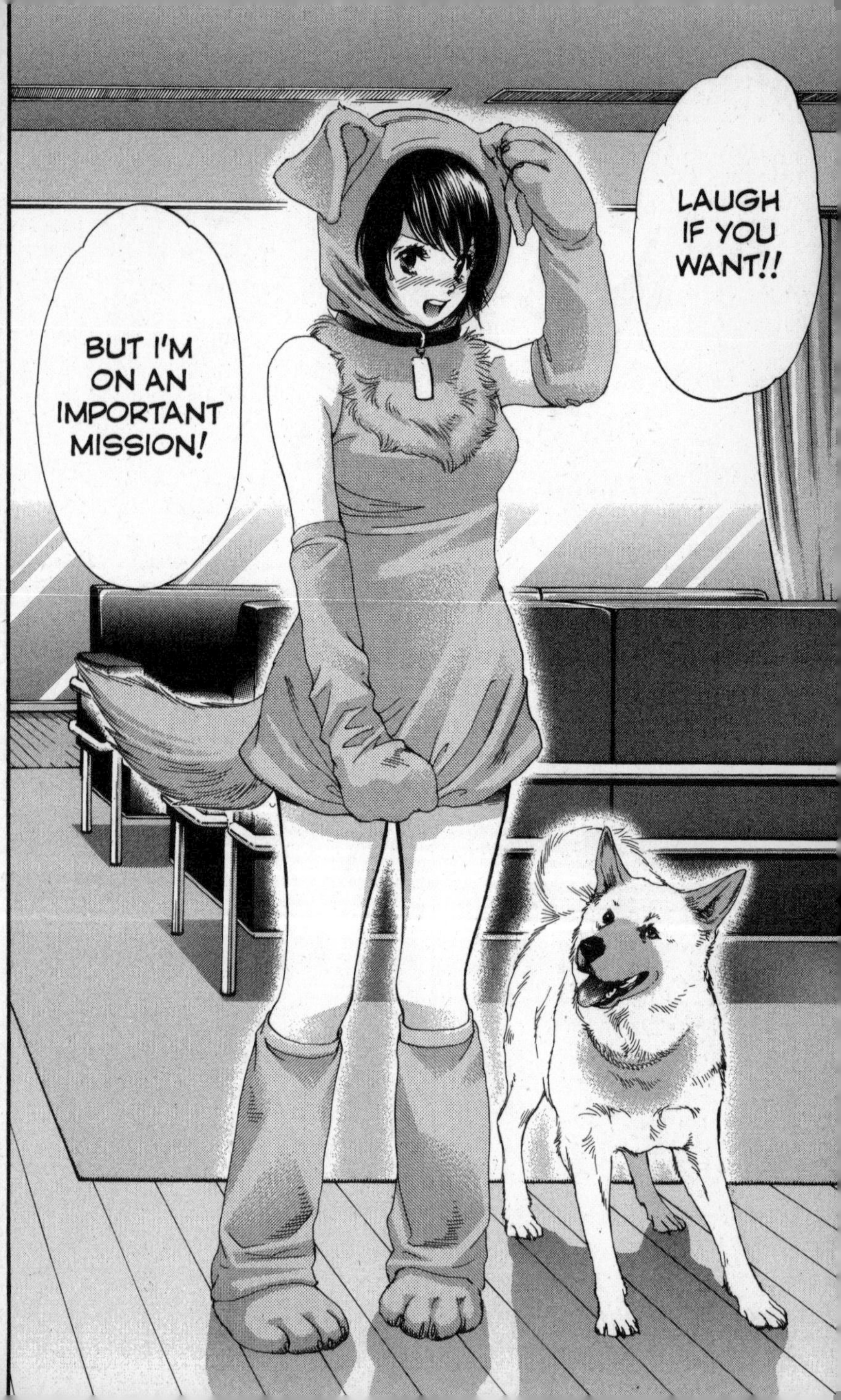
LAUGH IF YOU WANT!!
BUT I'M ON AN IMPORTANT MISSION!

CHAPTER 175: AN UNUSUAL TACTIC

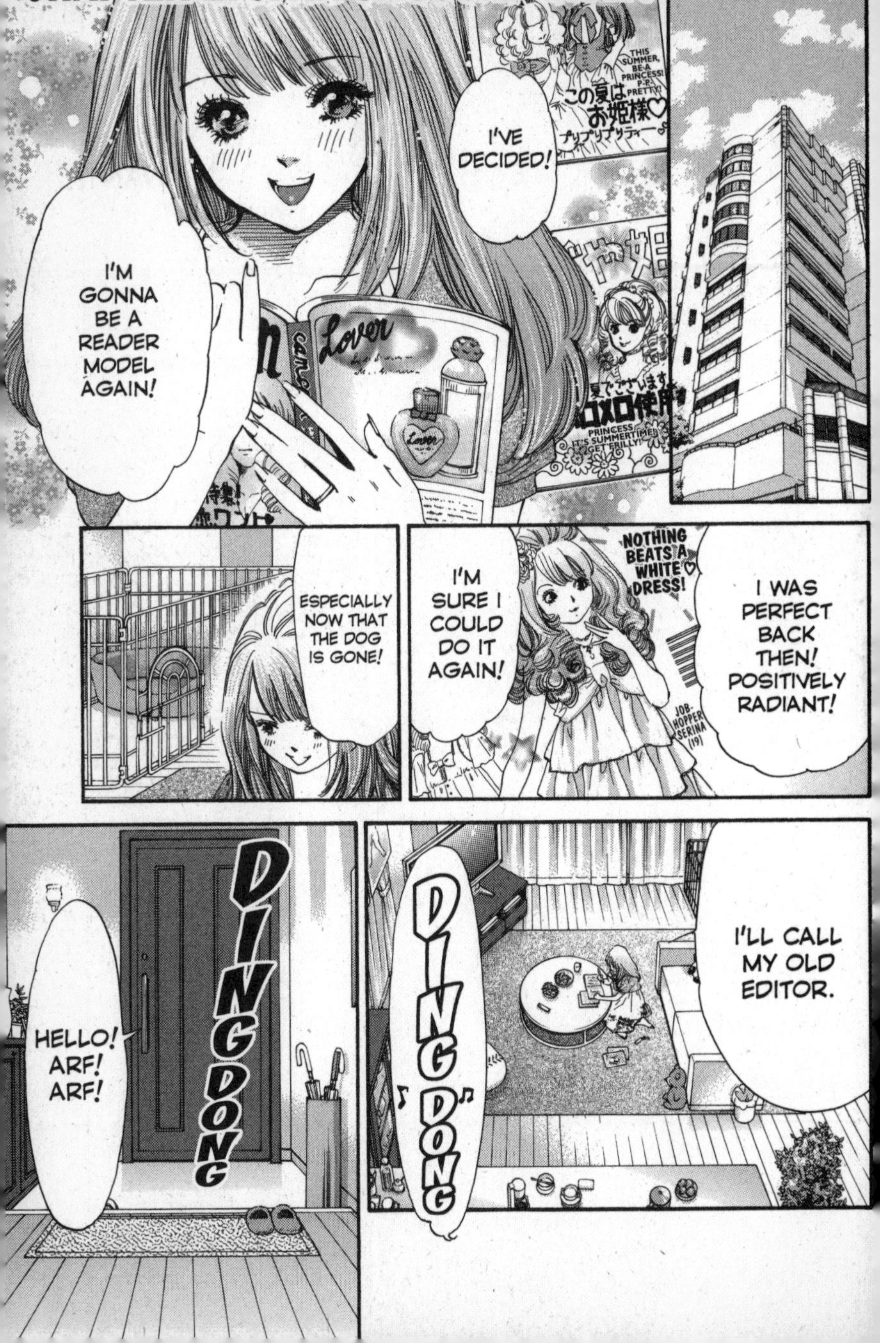
THIS SUMMER, BE A PRINCESS! P.P. PRETTY!
この夏はお姫様♡
I'VE DECIDED!
I'M GONNA BE A READER MODEL AGAIN!
PRINCESS IT'S SUMMERTIME! GET FRILLY!
I WAS PERFECT BACK THEN! POSITIVELY RADIANT!
NOTHING BEATS A WHITE♡ DRESS!
JOB-HOPPER SERINA (19)
I'M SURE I COULD DO IT AGAIN!
ESPECIALLY NOW THAT THE DOG IS GONE!
I'LL CALL MY OLD EDITOR.
DING DONG
DING DONG
HELLO! ARF! ARF!

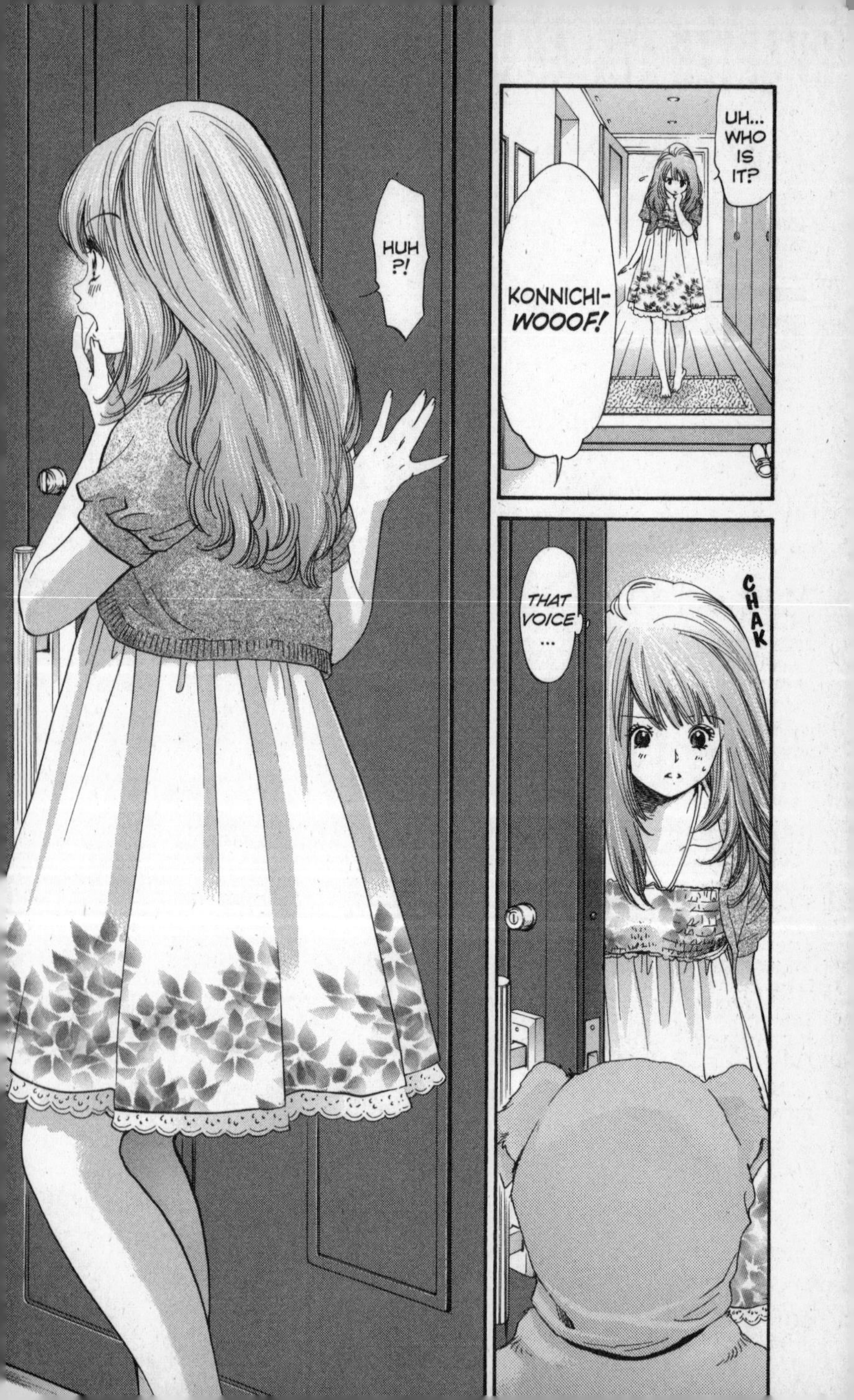
UH... WHO IS IT?
KONNICHI-WOOOF!
CHAK
THAT VOICE...
HUH ?!

CHAPTER 175: AN UNUSUAL TACTIC

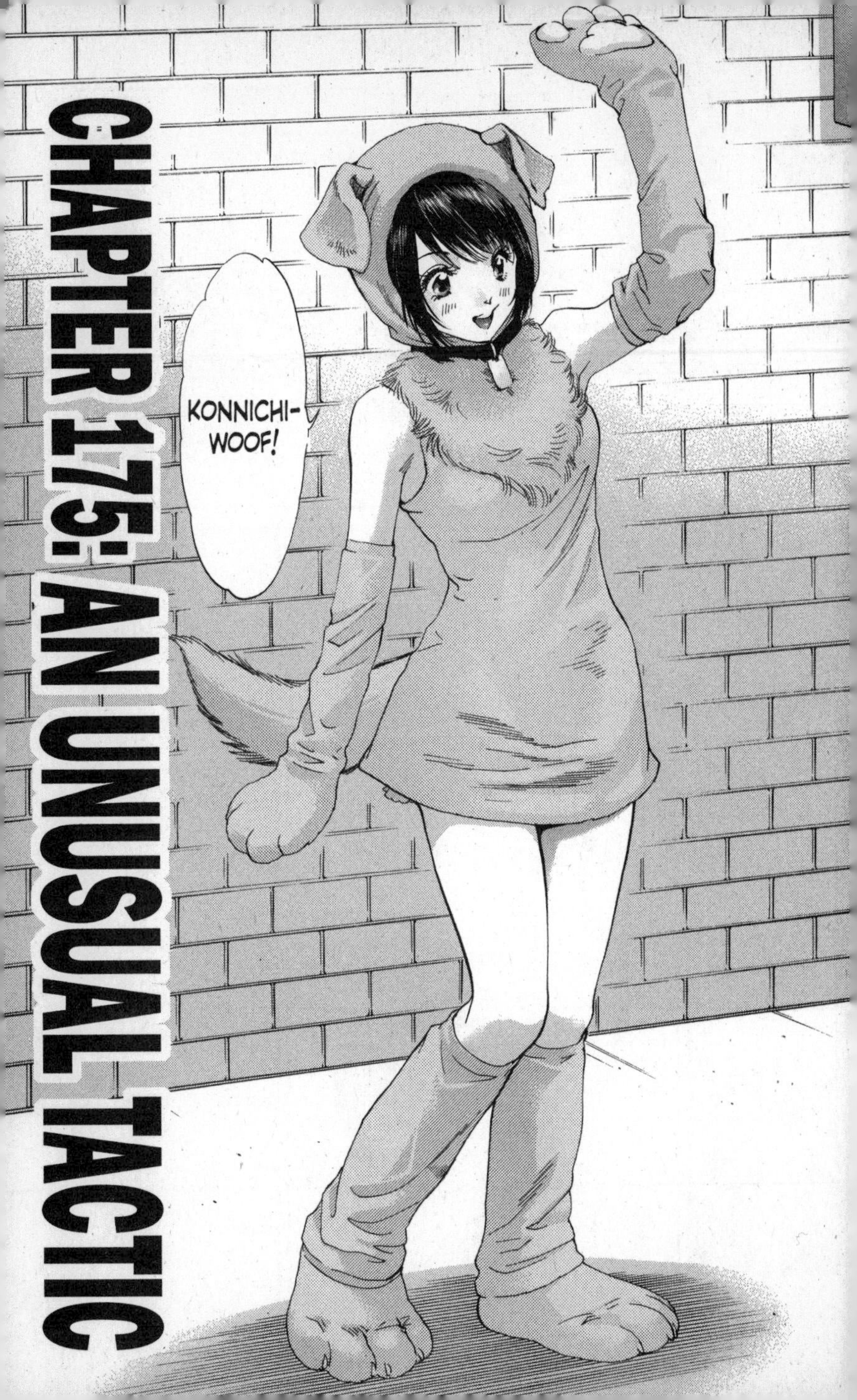
KONNICHI-WOOF!

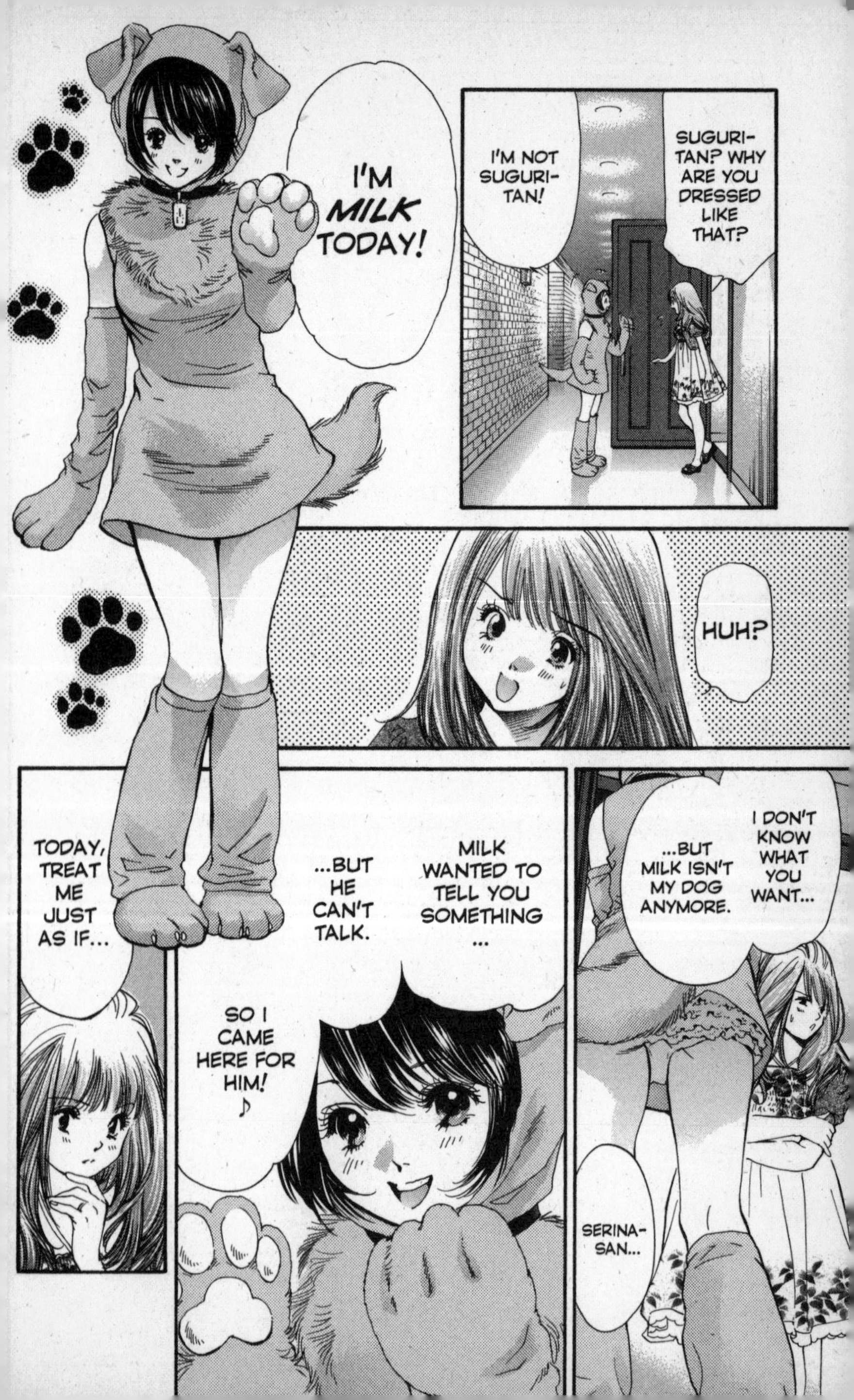
SUGURI-TAN? WHY ARE YOU DRESSED LIKE THAT?
I'M NOT SUGURI-TAN!
HUH?
I'M *MILK* TODAY!
I DON'T KNOW WHAT YOU WANT...
...BUT MILK ISN'T MY DOG ANYMORE.
SERINA-SAN...
MILK WANTED TO TELL YOU SOMETHING...
...BUT HE CAN'T TALK.
SO I CAME HERE FOR HIM! ♪
TODAY, TREAT ME JUST AS IF...

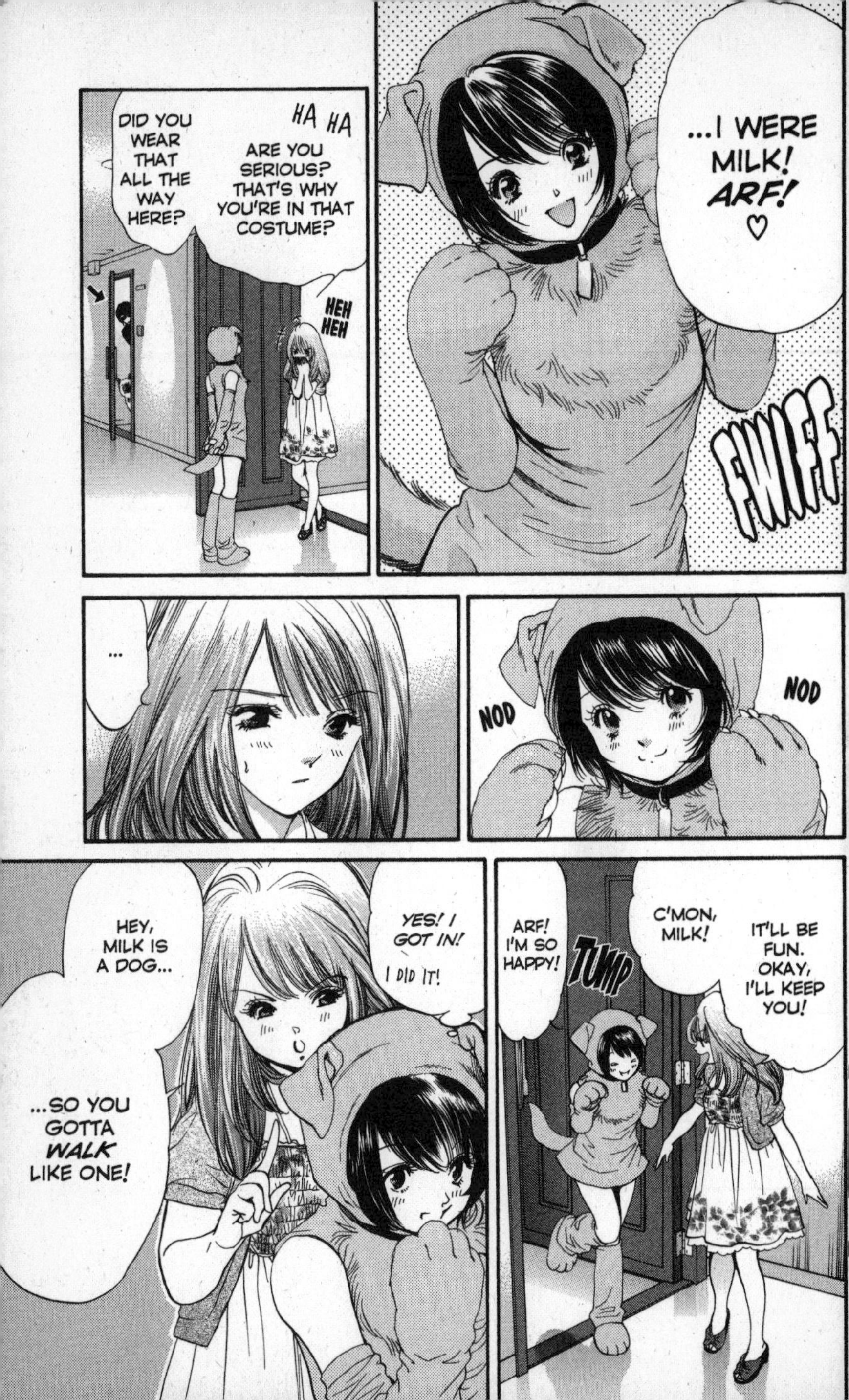
...I WERE MILK! ARF! ♡
FWIFF
HA HA
ARE YOU SERIOUS? THAT'S WHY YOU'RE IN THAT COSTUME?
DID YOU WEAR THAT ALL THE WAY HERE?
HEH HEH
NOD
NOD
...
IT'LL BE FUN. OKAY, I'LL KEEP YOU!
C'MON, MILK!
TUMP
ARF! I'M SO HAPPY!
YES! I GOT IN!
I DID IT!
HEY, MILK IS A DOG...
...SO YOU GOTTA WALK LIKE ONE!

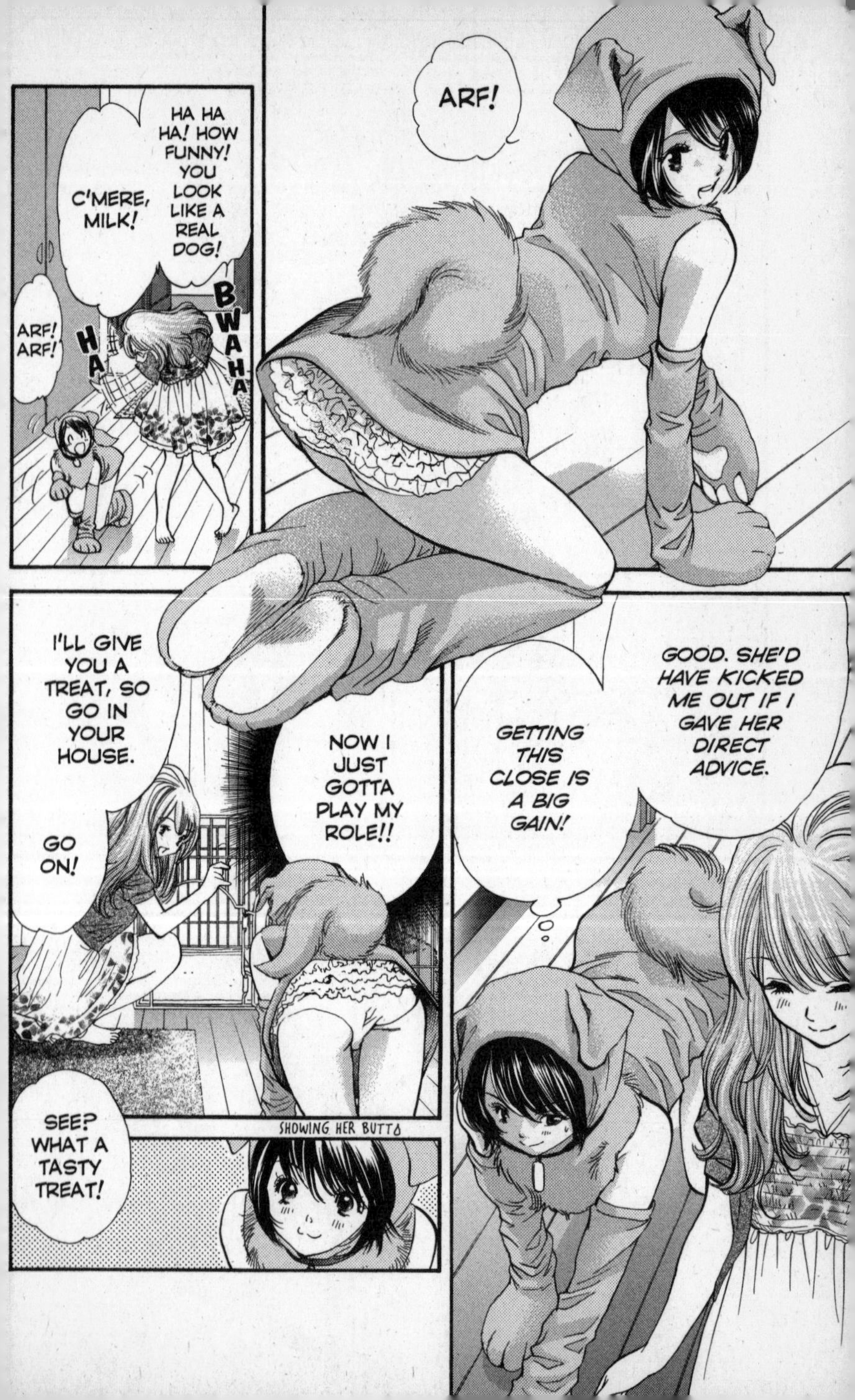
ARF!
HA HA HA! HOW FUNNY! YOU LOOK LIKE A REAL DOG!
C'MERE, MILK!
BWAHAHA
ARF! ARF!
HA
GOOD. SHE'D HAVE KICKED ME OUT IF I GAVE HER DIRECT ADVICE.
GETTING THIS CLOSE IS A BIG GAIN!
NOW I JUST GOTTA PLAY MY ROLE!!
I'LL GIVE YOU A TREAT, SO GO IN YOUR HOUSE.
GO ON!
SHOWING HER BUTT
SEE? WHAT A TASTY TREAT!

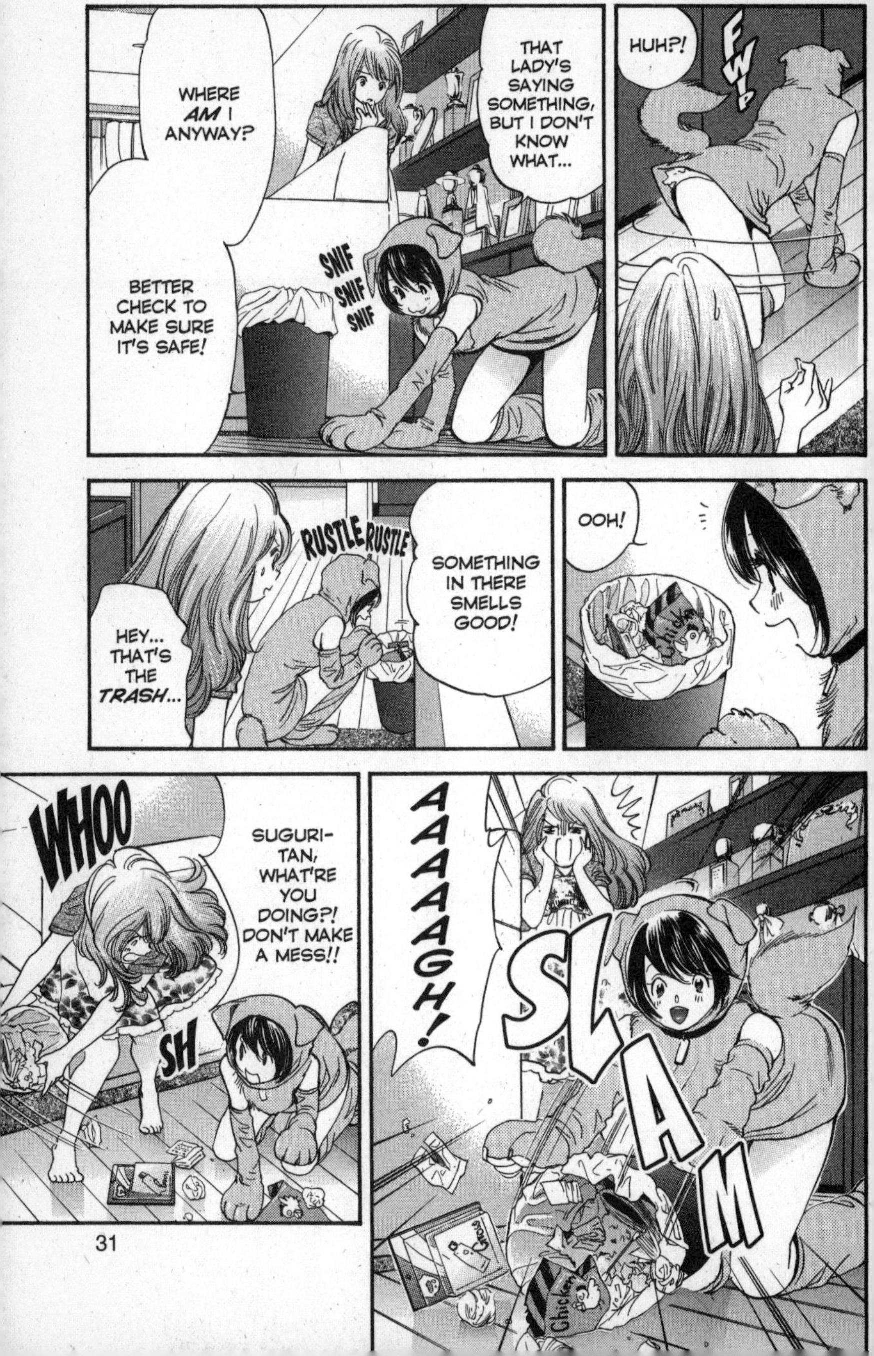
HUH?!
FWIP
THAT LADY'S SAYING SOMETHING, BUT I DON'T KNOW WHAT...
WHERE *AM* I ANYWAY?
SNIF SNIF SNIF
BETTER CHECK TO MAKE SURE IT'S SAFE!
OOH!
RUSTLE RUSTLE
SOMETHING IN THERE SMELLS GOOD!
HEY... THAT'S THE *TRASH*...
AAAAAAGH!
SLAM
SUGURI-TAN, WHAT'RE YOU DOING?! DON'T MAKE A MESS!!
WHOOSH

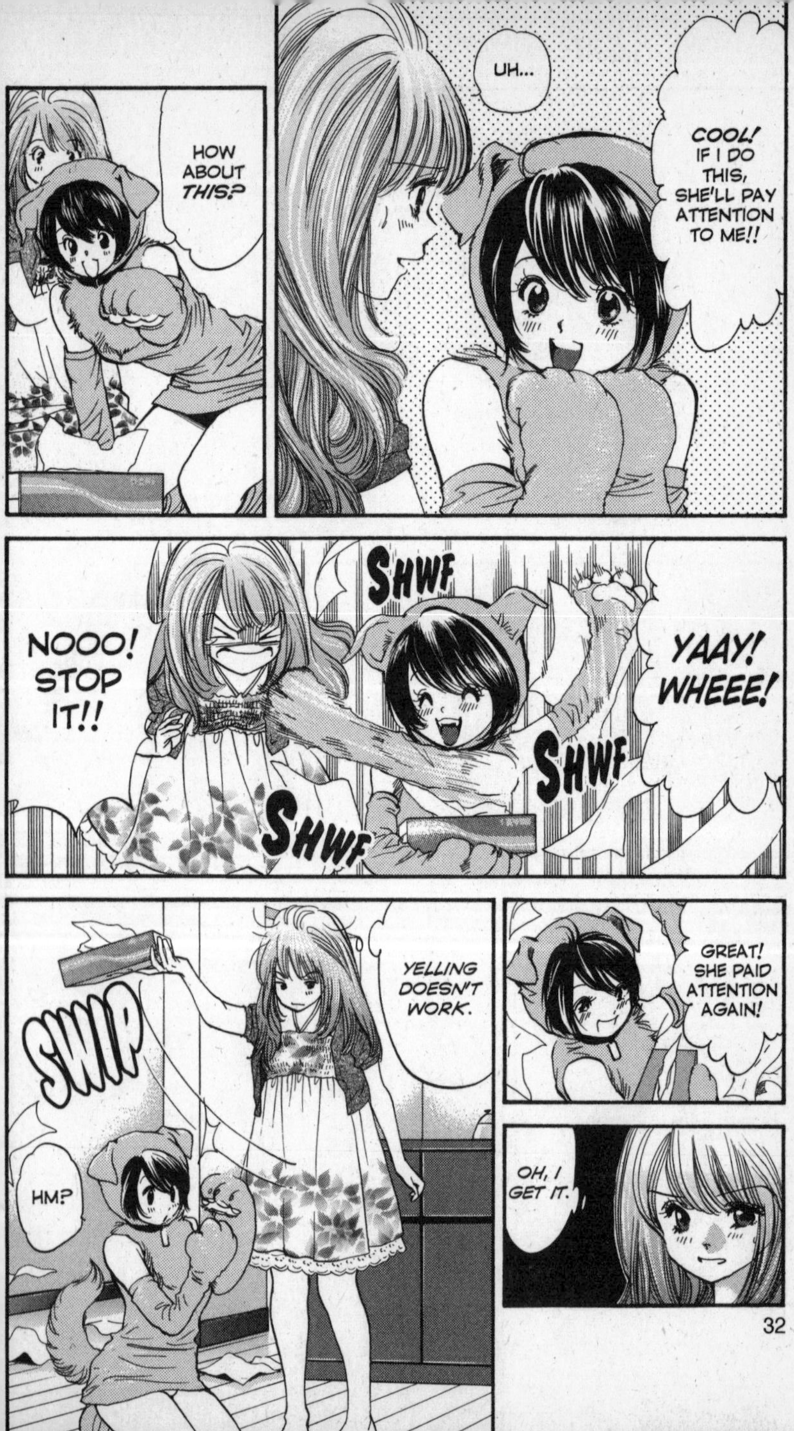
UH...
COOL! IF I DO THIS, SHE'LL PAY ATTENTION TO ME!!
HOW ABOUT THIS?
YAAY! WHEEE!
SHWF
NOOO! STOP IT!!
SHWF
SHWF
GREAT! SHE PAID ATTENTION AGAIN!
OH, I GET IT.
YELLING DOESN'T WORK.
SWIP
HM?

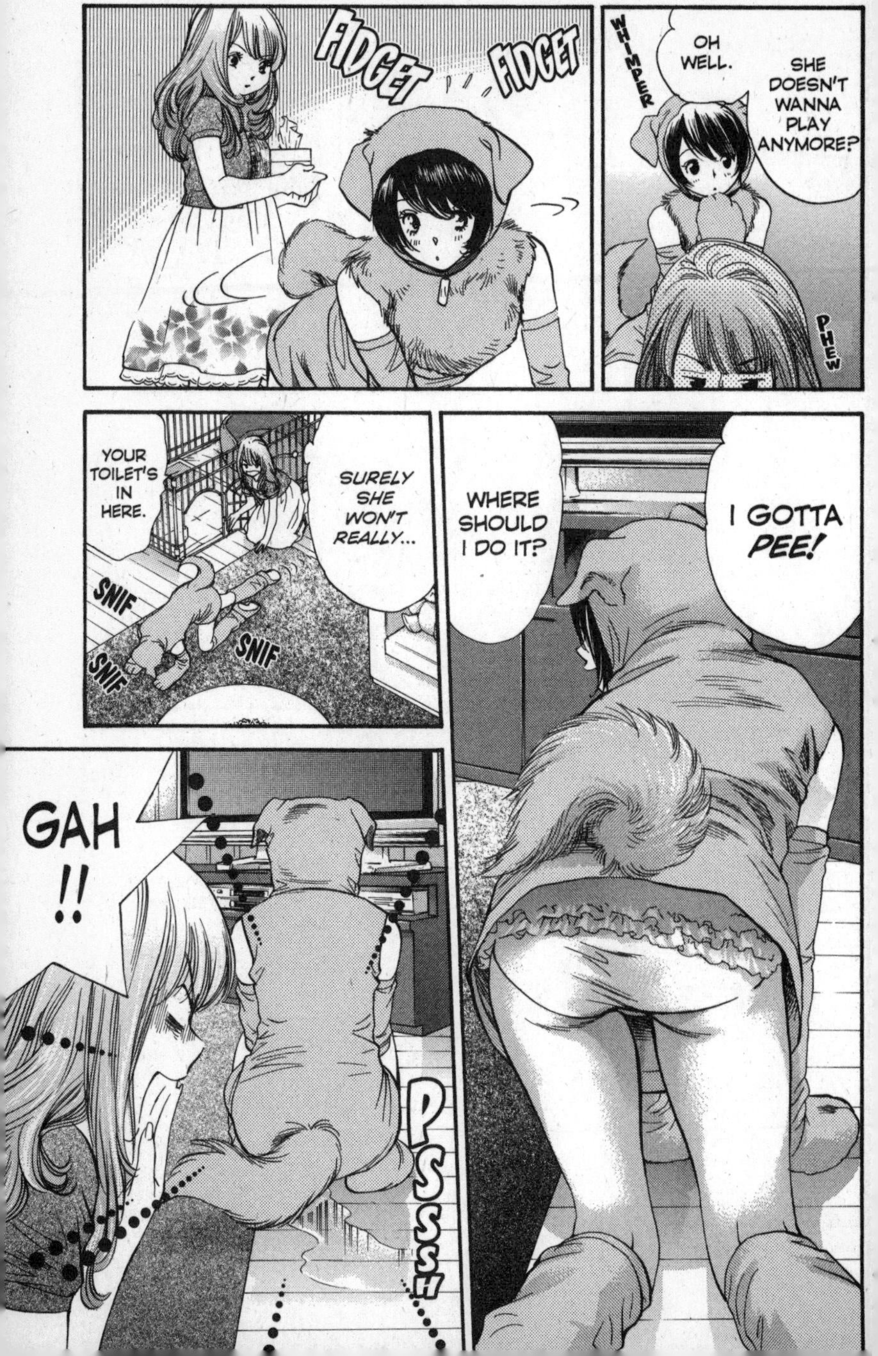
WHIMPER
OH WELL.
SHE DOESN'T WANNA PLAY ANYMORE?
PHEW
FIDGET
FIDGET
I GOTTA PEE!
WHERE SHOULD I DO IT?
SURELY SHE WON'T REALLY...
YOUR TOILET'S IN HERE.
SNIF
SNIF
SNIF
GAH !!
PSSSH

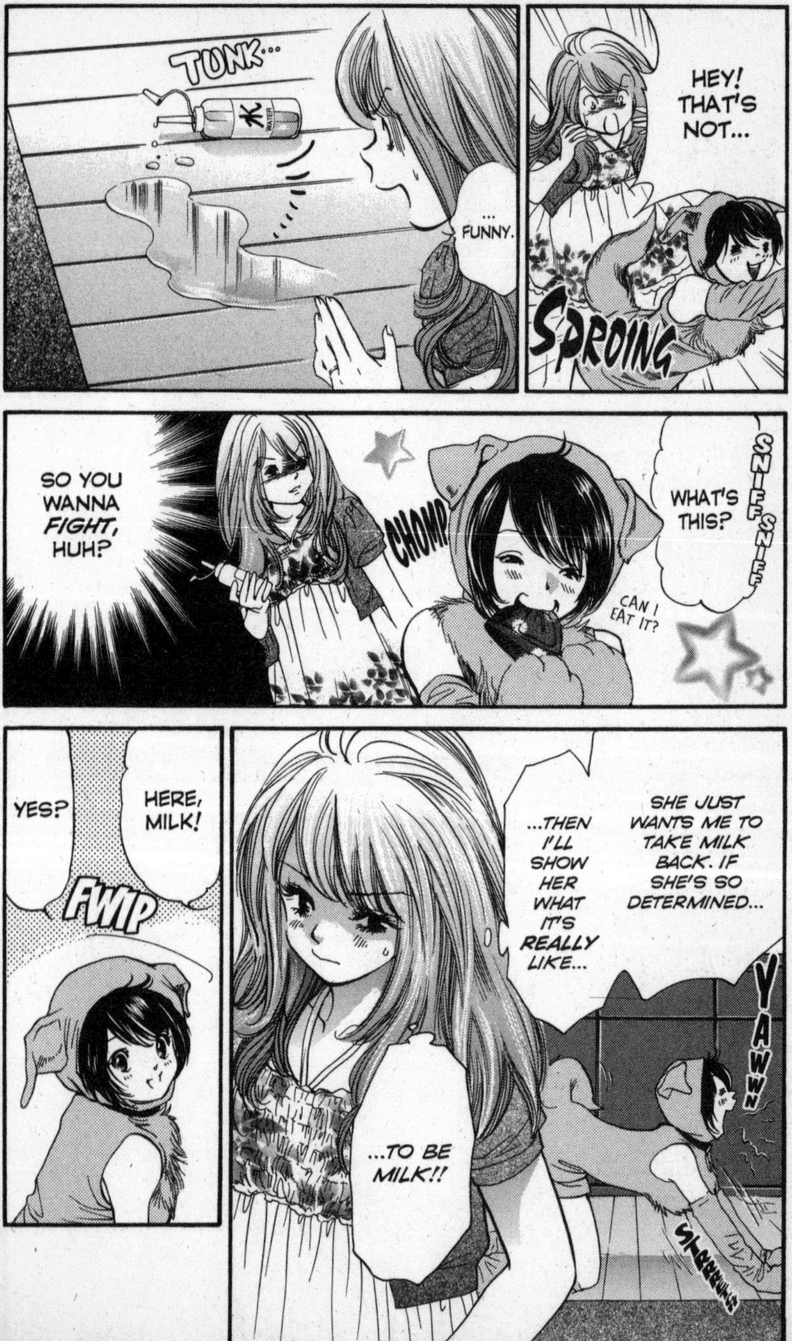
HEY! THAT'S NOT...
SPROING
TUNK...
...FUNNY.
SNIFF SNIFF
WHAT'S THIS?
CAN I EAT IT?
CHOMP
SO YOU WANNA *FIGHT*, HUH?
SHE JUST WANTS ME TO TAKE MILK BACK. IF SHE'S SO DETERMINED...
...THEN I'LL SHOW HER WHAT IT'S *REALLY* LIKE...
YAWWN
...TO BE MILK!!
HERE, MILK!
YES?
FWIP

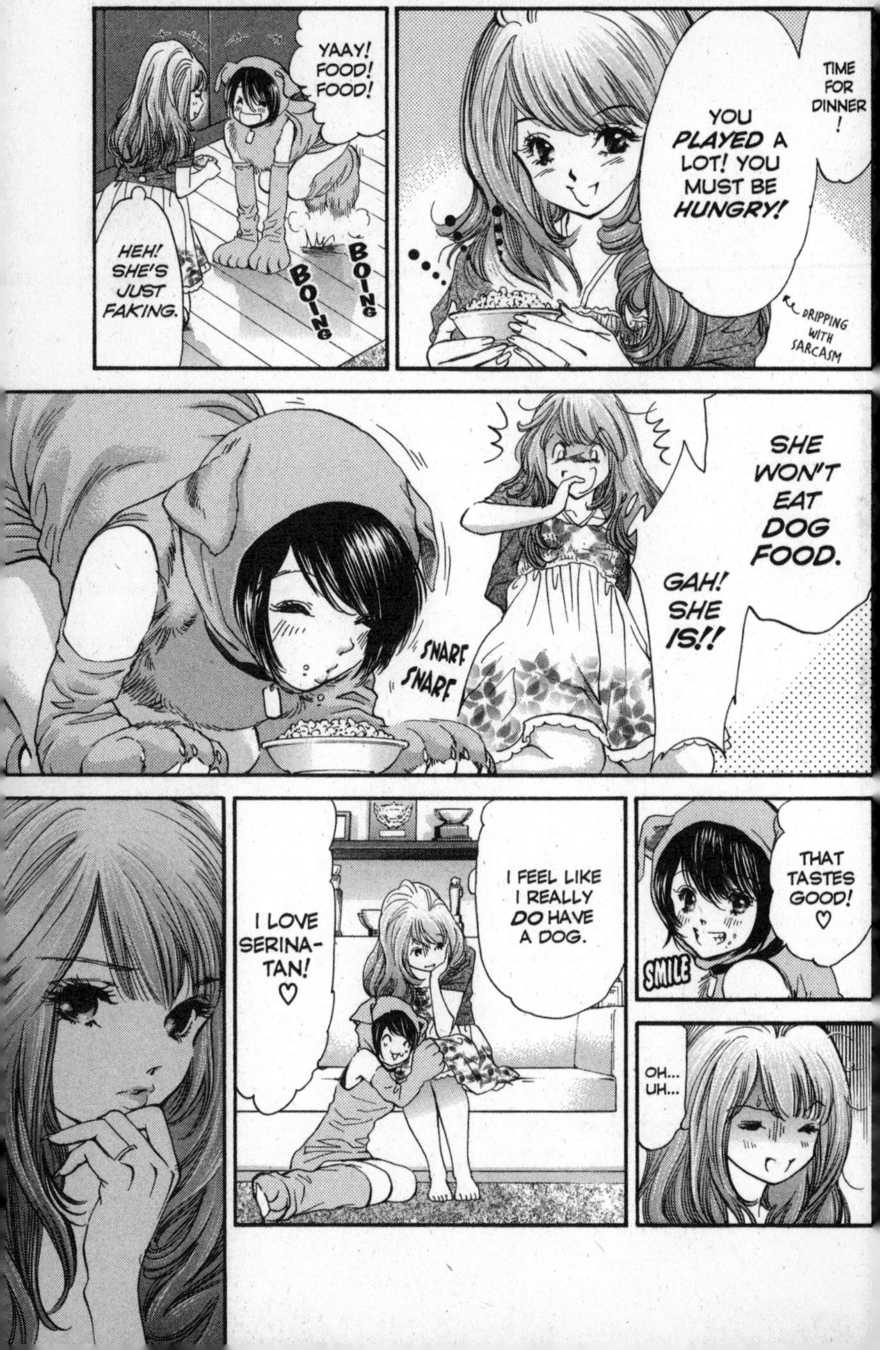
TIME FOR DINNER!
YOU PLAYED A LOT! YOU MUST BE HUNGRY!
DRIPPING WITH SARCASM
...
YAAY! FOOD! FOOD!
BOING
BOING
HEH! SHE'S JUST FAKING.
SHE WON'T EAT DOG FOOD.
GAH! SHE IS!!
SNARF SNARF
THAT TASTES GOOD! ♡
SMILE
OH... UH...
I FEEL LIKE I REALLY DO HAVE A DOG.
I LOVE SERINA-TAN! ♡

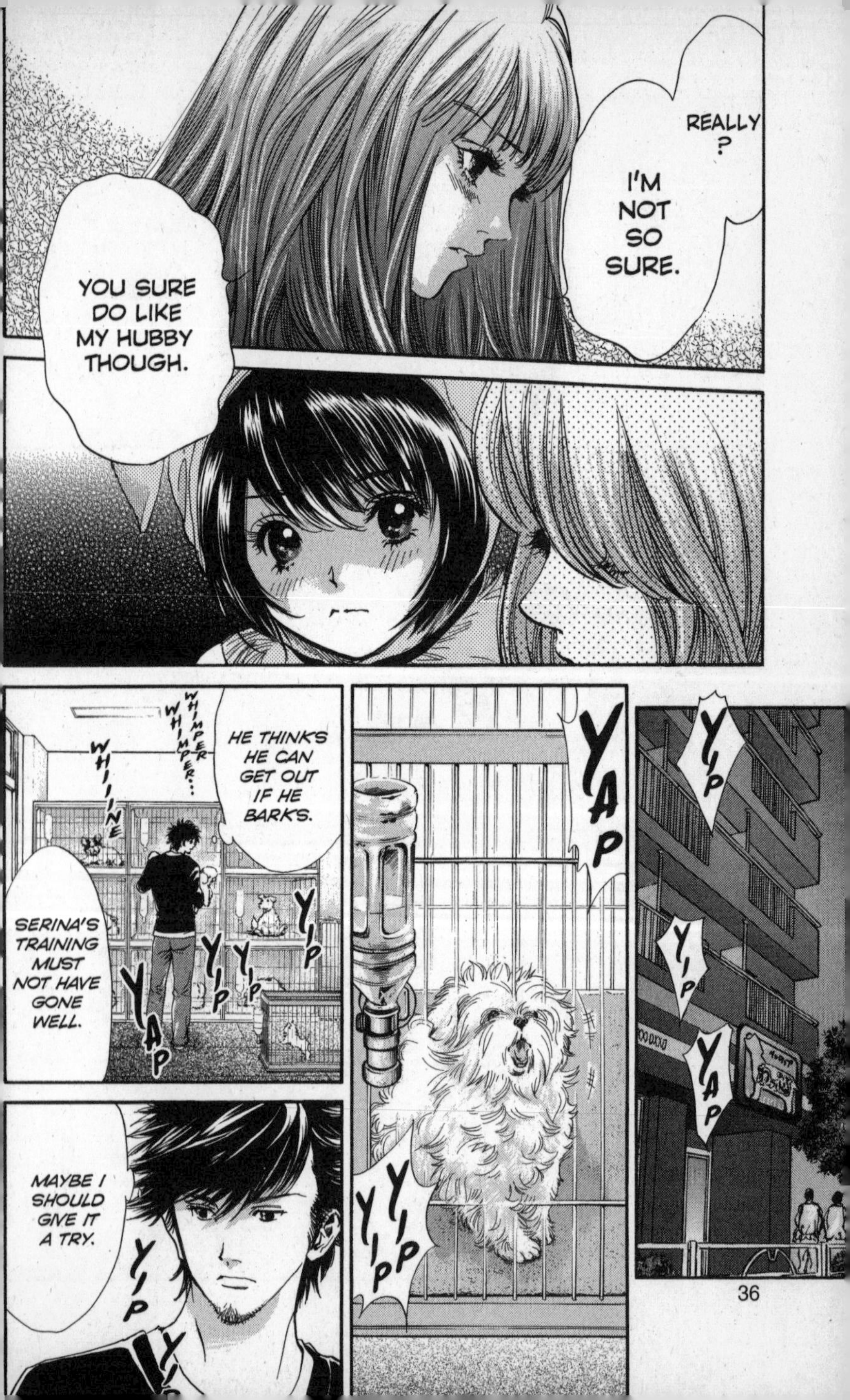
REALLY?
I'M NOT SO SURE.
YOU SURE DO LIKE MY HUBBY THOUGH.
YIP
YIP
YAP
YAP
YIP YIP
HE THINKS HE CAN GET OUT IF HE BARKS.
WHIMPER WHIMPER...
WHIIINE
YIP
SERINA'S TRAINING MUST NOT HAVE GONE WELL.
YIP YIP
YAP
MAYBE I SHOULD GIVE IT A TRY.
YIP

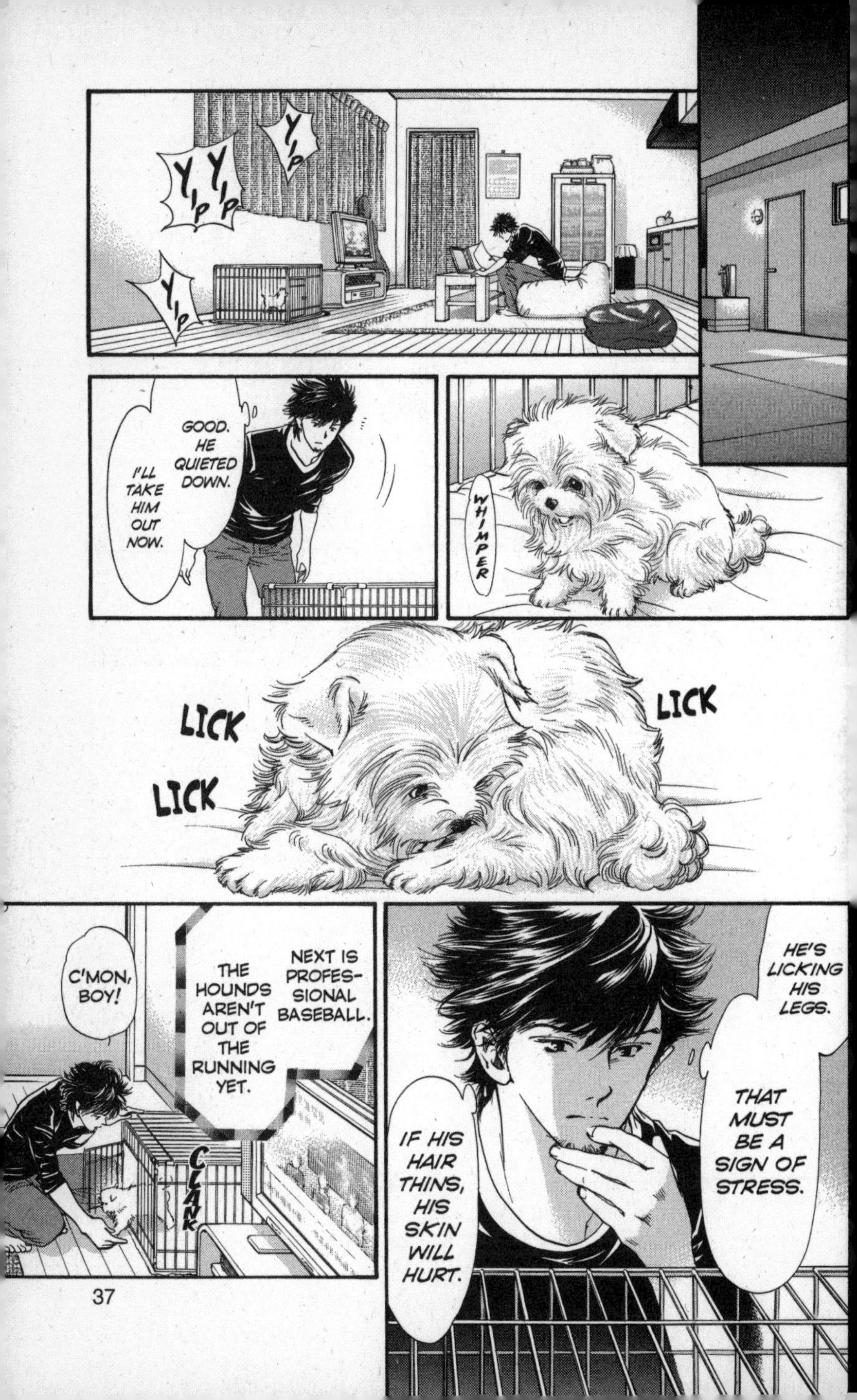
YIP
YIP YIP
YIP
WHIMPER
GOOD. HE QUIETED DOWN.
I'LL TAKE HIM OUT NOW.
LICK
LICK
LICK
HE'S LICKING HIS LEGS.
THAT MUST BE A SIGN OF STRESS.
IF HIS HAIR THINS, HIS SKIN WILL HURT.
NEXT IS PROFES-SIONAL BASEBALL.
THE HOUNDS AREN'T OUT OF THE RUNNING YET.
CLANK
C'MON, BOY!

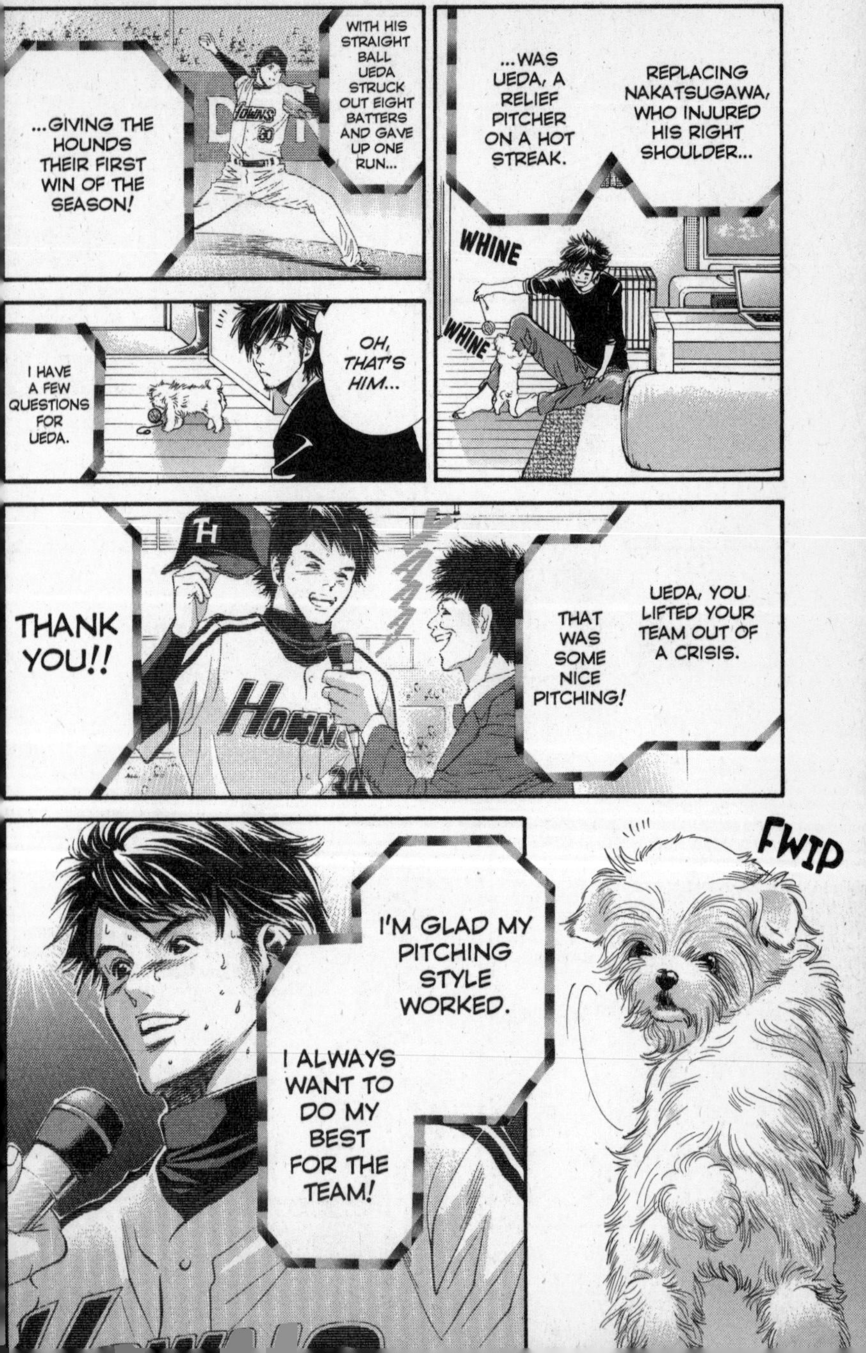
REPLACING NAKATSUGAWA, WHO INJURED HIS RIGHT SHOULDER...
...WAS UEDA, A RELIEF PITCHER ON A HOT STREAK.
WHINE
WHINE
WITH HIS STRAIGHT BALL UEDA STRUCK OUT EIGHT BATTERS AND GAVE UP ONE RUN...
...GIVING THE HOUNDS THEIR FIRST WIN OF THE SEASON!
OH, THAT'S HIM...
I HAVE A FEW QUESTIONS FOR UEDA.
UEDA, YOU LIFTED YOUR TEAM OUT OF A CRISIS.
THAT WAS SOME NICE PITCHING!
THANK YOU!!
FWIP
I'M GLAD MY PITCHING STYLE WORKED.
I ALWAYS WANT TO DO MY BEST FOR THE TEAM!

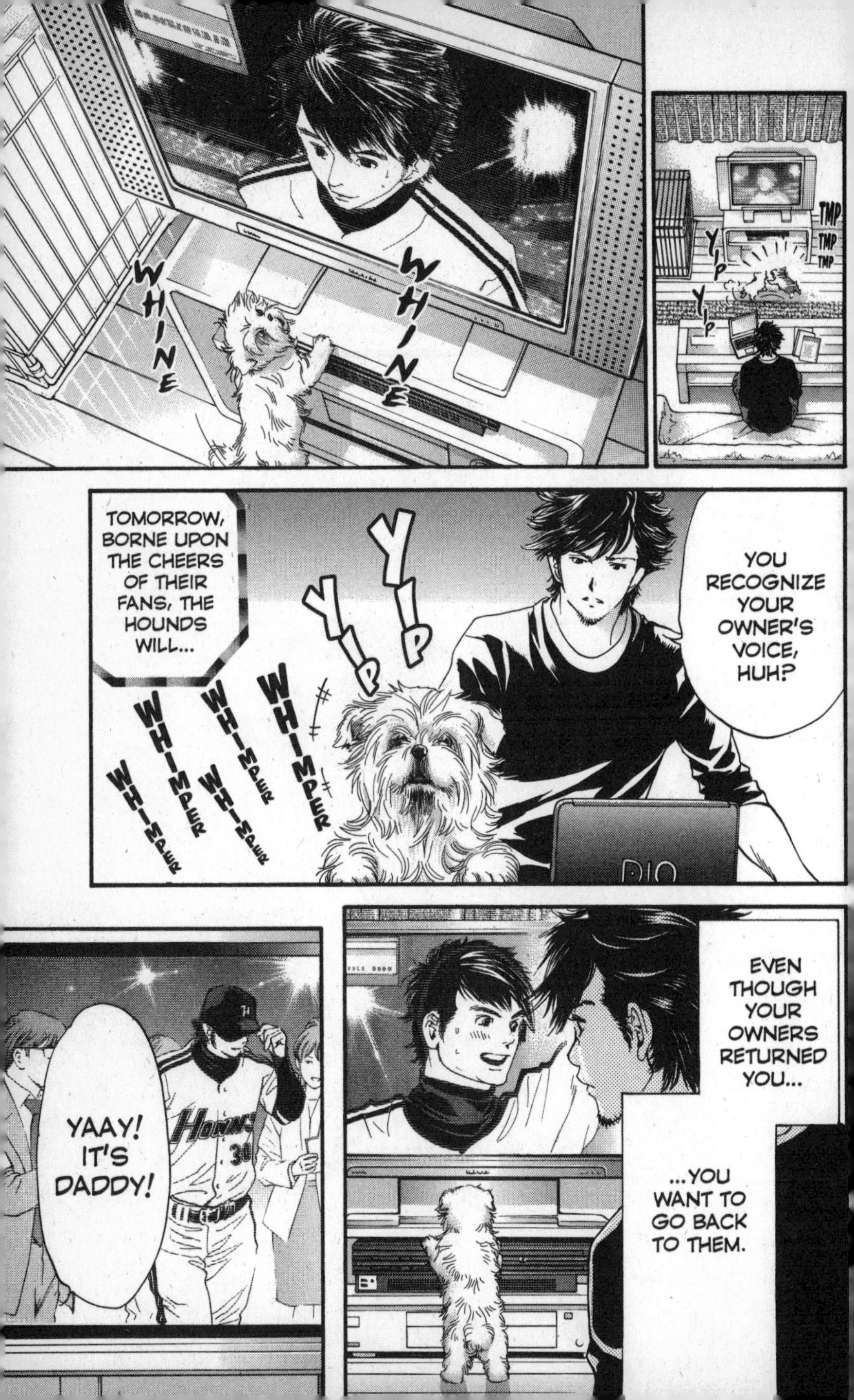
TMP TMP TMP
YIP YIP
WHINE
WHINE
YOU RECOGNIZE YOUR OWNER'S VOICE, HUH?
YIP YIP
TOMORROW, BORNE UPON THE CHEERS OF THEIR FANS, THE HOUNDS WILL...
WHIMPER WHIMPER WHIMPER WHIMPER
EVEN THOUGH YOUR OWNERS RETURNED YOU...
...YOU WANT TO GO BACK TO THEM.
YAAY! IT'S DADDY!

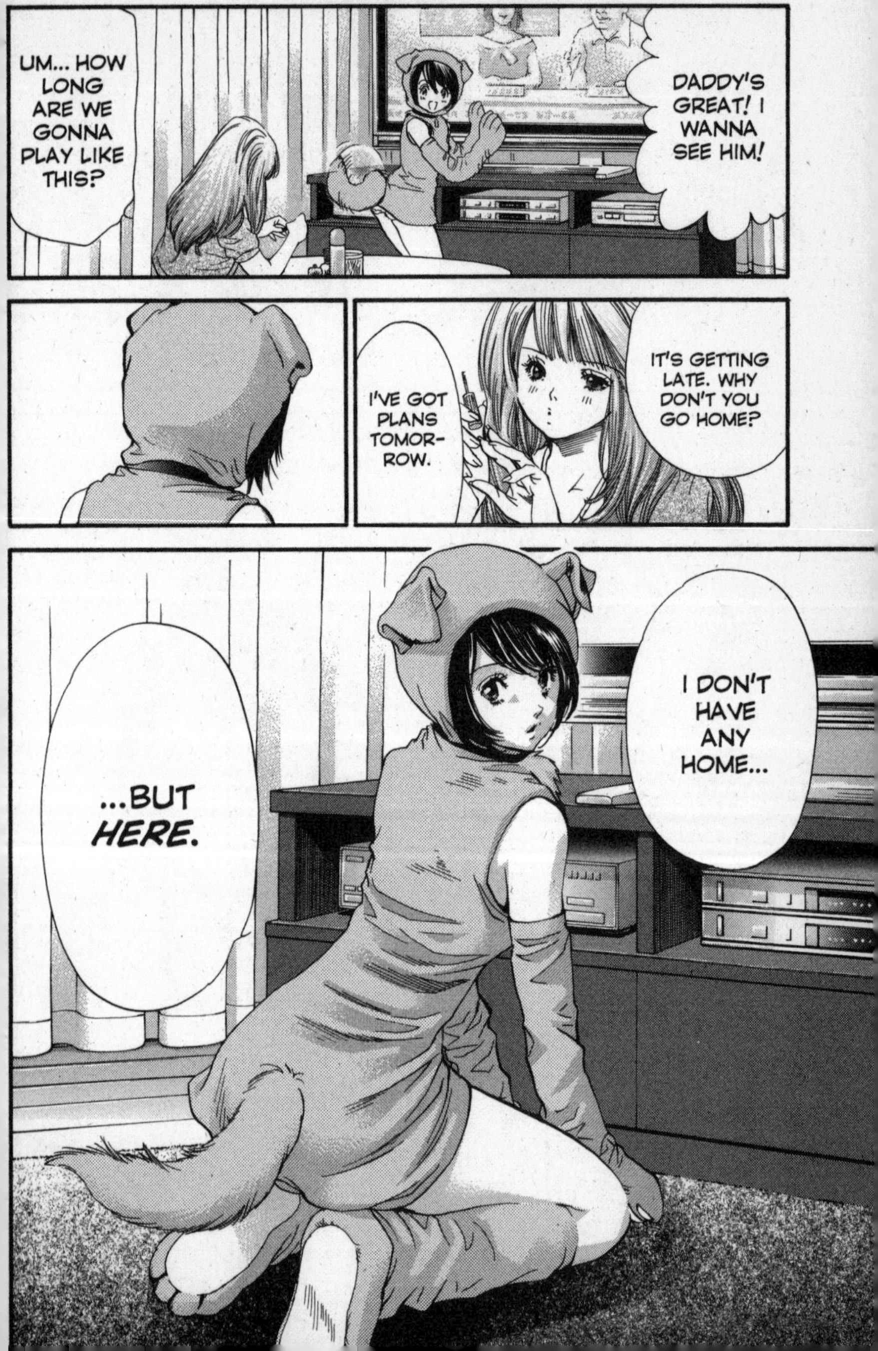
DADDY'S GREAT! I WANNA SEE HIM!
UM... HOW LONG ARE WE GONNA PLAY LIKE THIS?
IT'S GETTING LATE. WHY DON'T YOU GO HOME?
I'VE GOT PLANS TOMORROW.
I DON'T HAVE ANY HOME...
...BUT *HERE.*

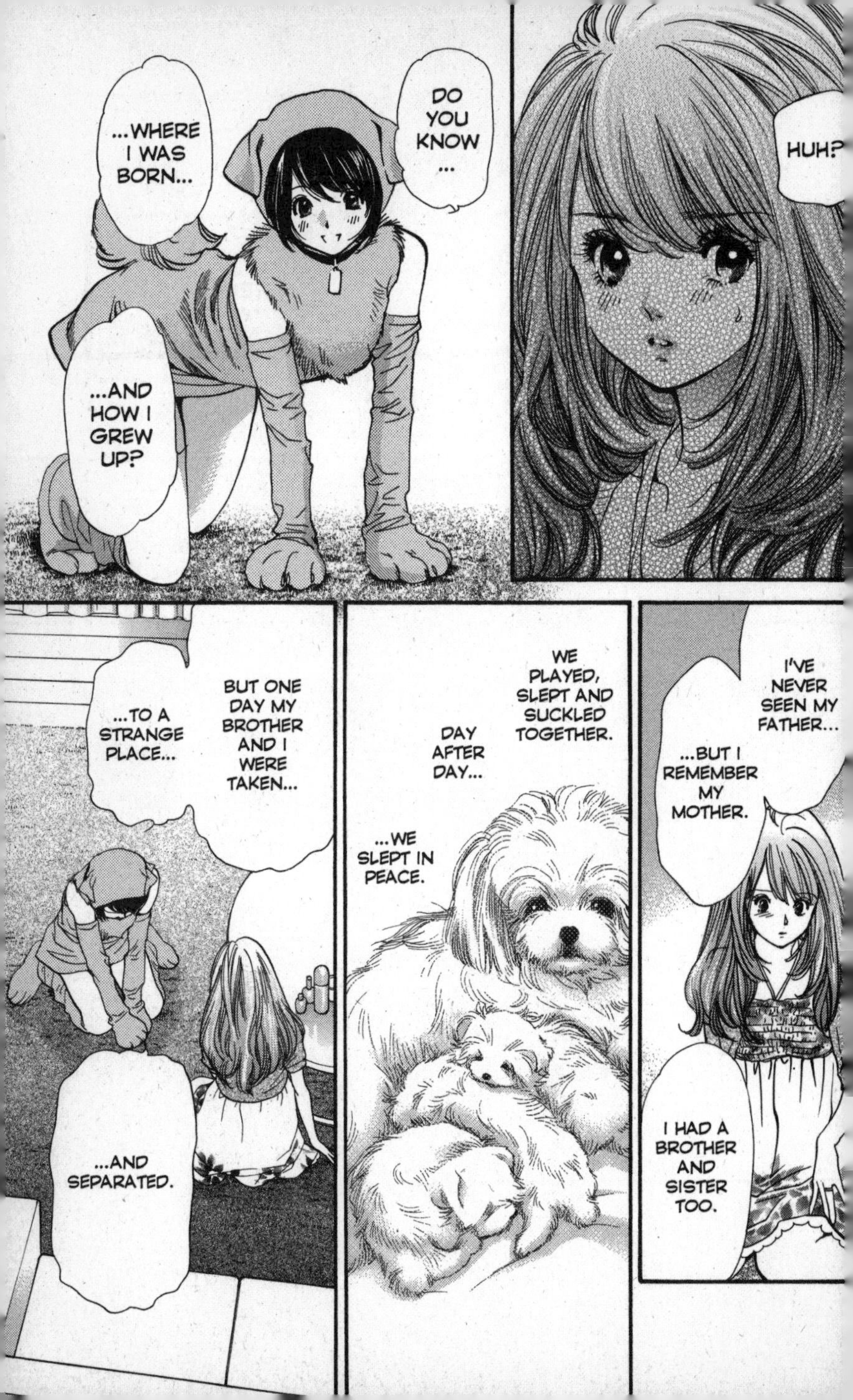
HUH?
DO YOU KNOW...
...WHERE I WAS BORN...
...AND HOW I GREW UP?
I'VE NEVER SEEN MY FATHER...
...BUT I REMEMBER MY MOTHER.
I HAD A BROTHER AND SISTER TOO.
WE PLAYED, SLEPT AND SUCKLED TOGETHER.
DAY AFTER DAY...
...WE SLEPT IN PEACE.
BUT ONE DAY MY BROTHER AND I WERE TAKEN...
...TO A STRANGE PLACE...
...AND SEPARATED.

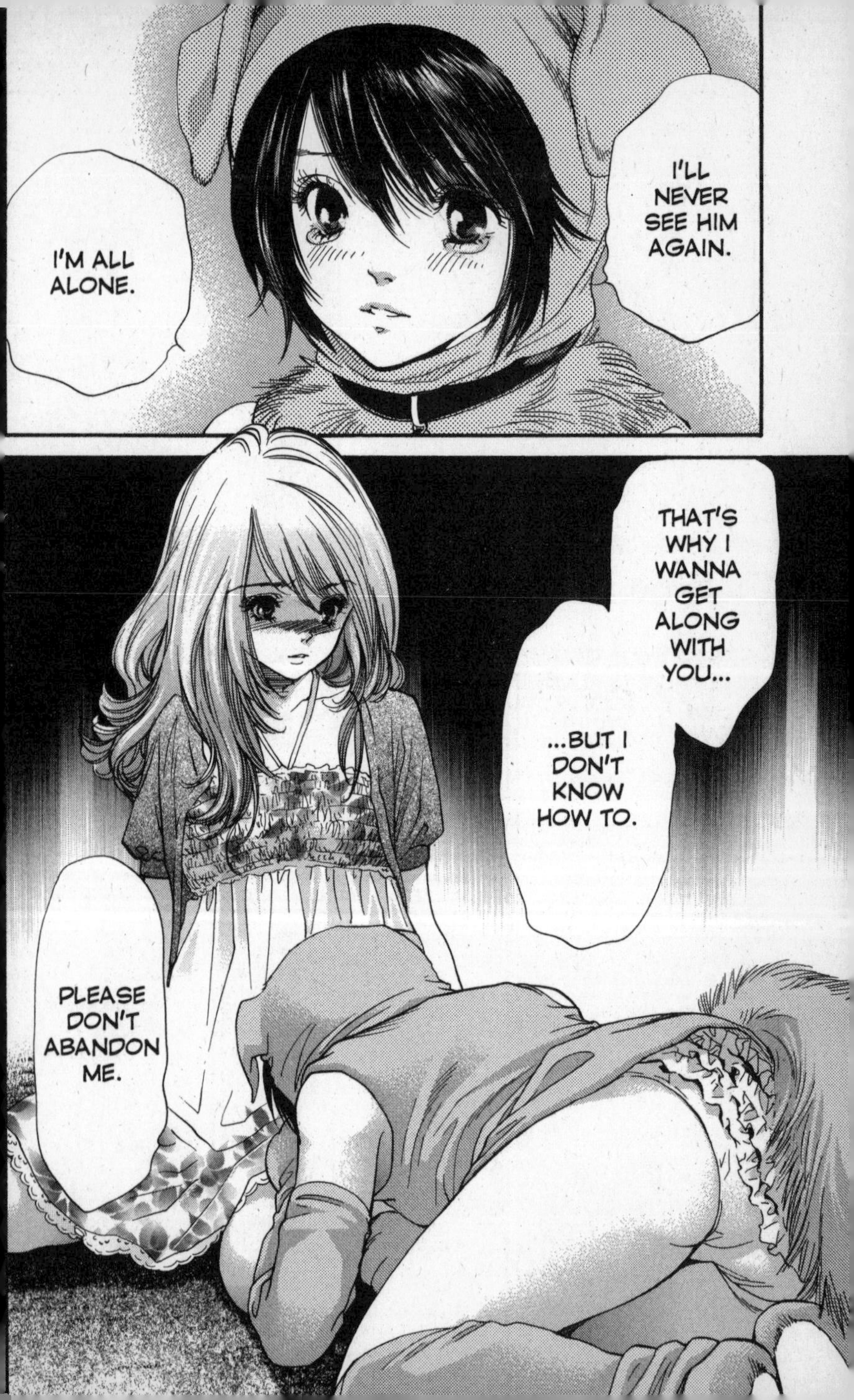
I'LL NEVER SEE HIM AGAIN.
I'M ALL ALONE.
THAT'S WHY I WANNA GET ALONG WITH YOU...
...BUT I DON'T KNOW HOW TO.
PLEASE DON'T ABANDON ME.

CHAPTER 176:

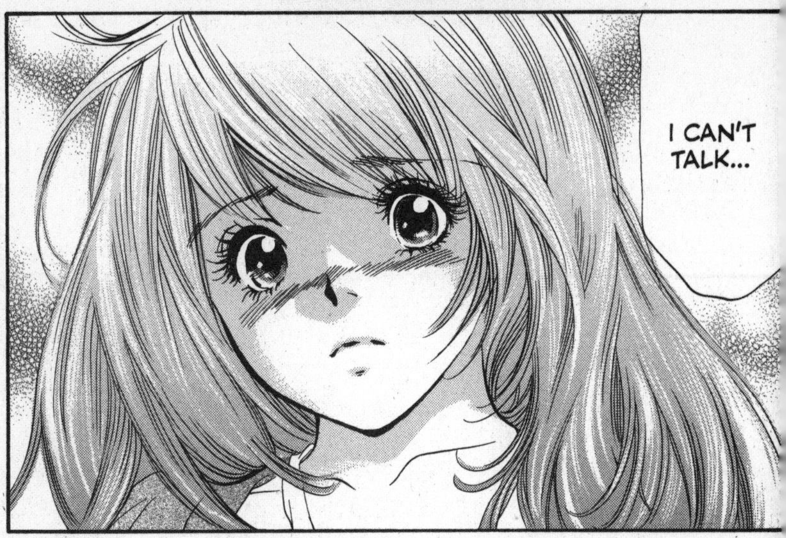
I CAN'T TALK...

WHAT SERINA DID TO MILK

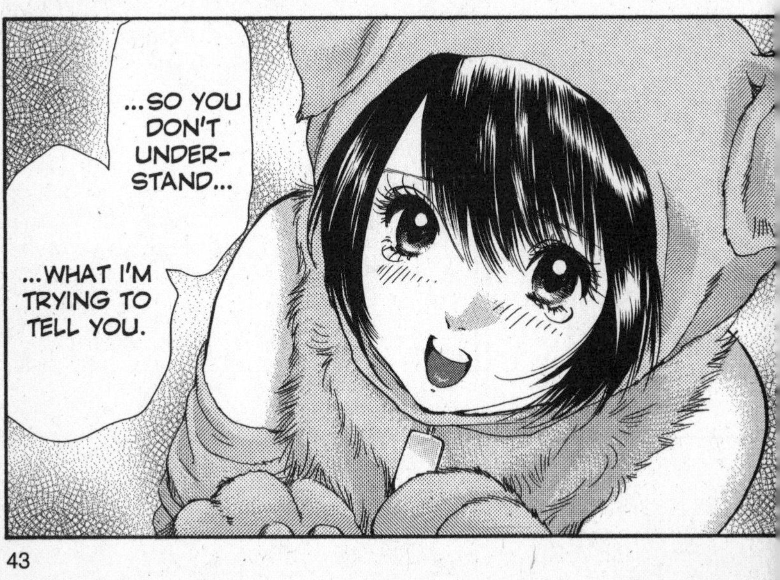
...SO YOU DON'T UNDER-STAND...
...WHAT I'M TRYING TO TELL YOU.

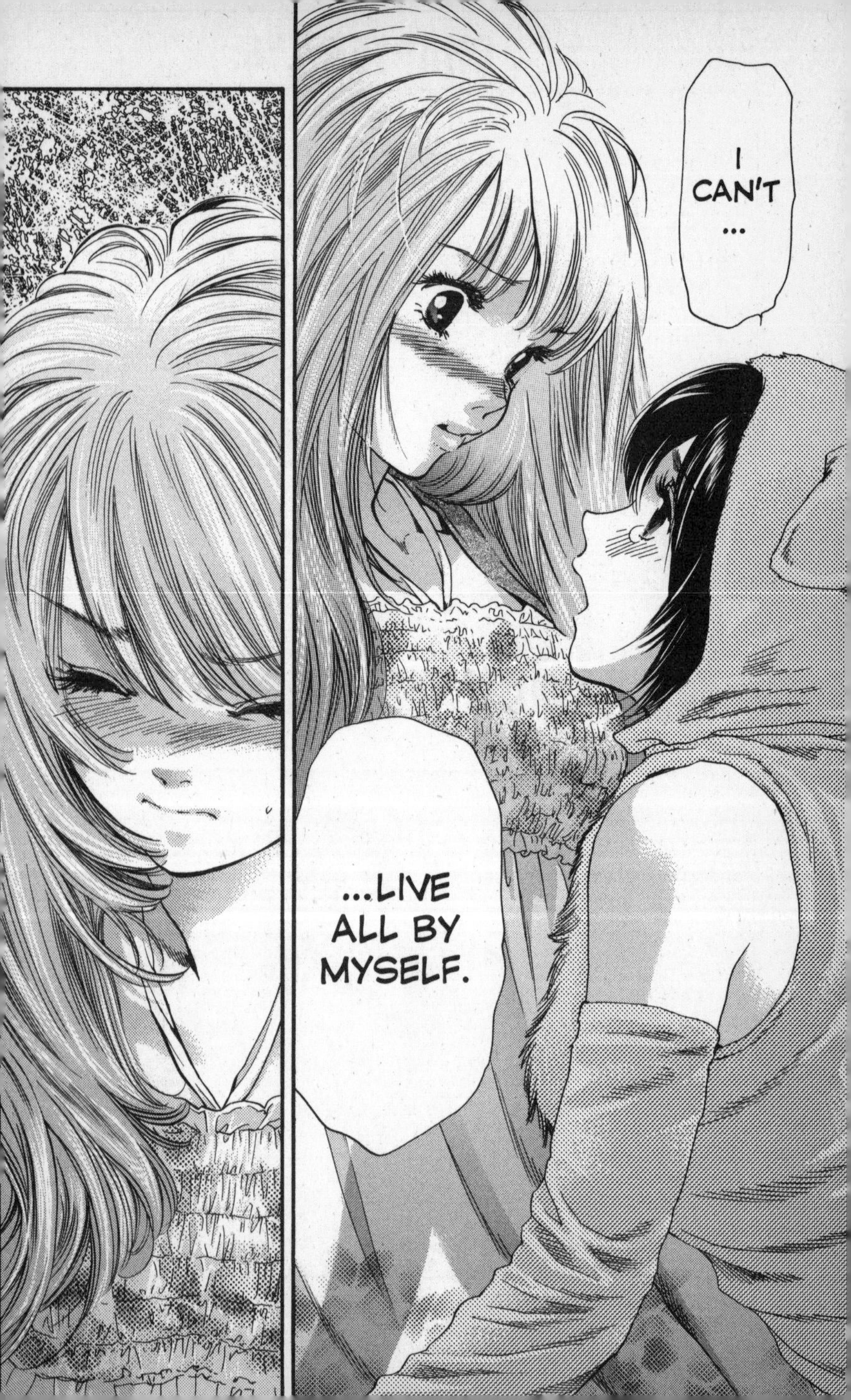
I CAN'T ...
...LIVE ALL BY MYSELF.

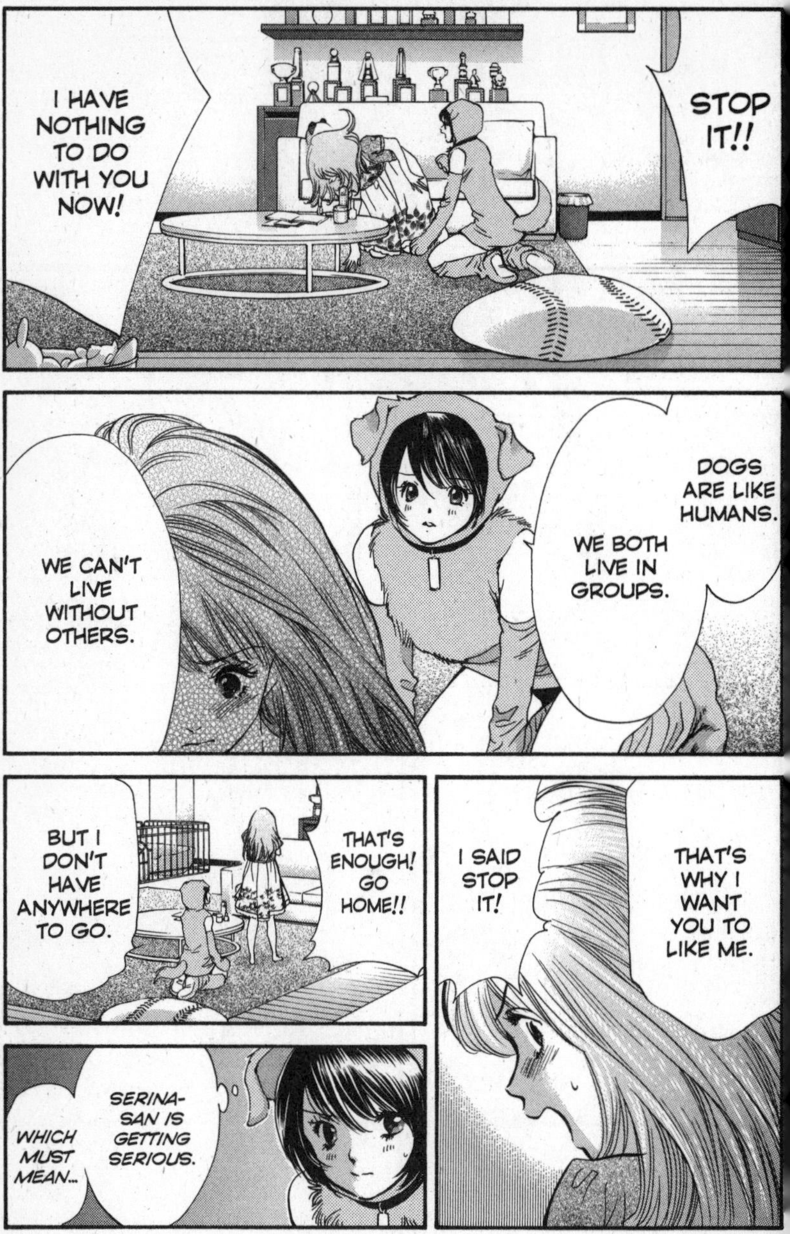
STOP IT!!
I HAVE NOTHING TO DO WITH YOU NOW!
DOGS ARE LIKE HUMANS.
WE BOTH LIVE IN GROUPS.
WE CAN'T LIVE WITHOUT OTHERS.
THAT'S WHY I WANT YOU TO LIKE ME.
I SAID STOP IT!
THAT'S ENOUGH! GO HOME!!
BUT I DON'T HAVE ANYWHERE TO GO.
SERINA-SAN IS GETTING SERIOUS.
WHICH MUST MEAN...

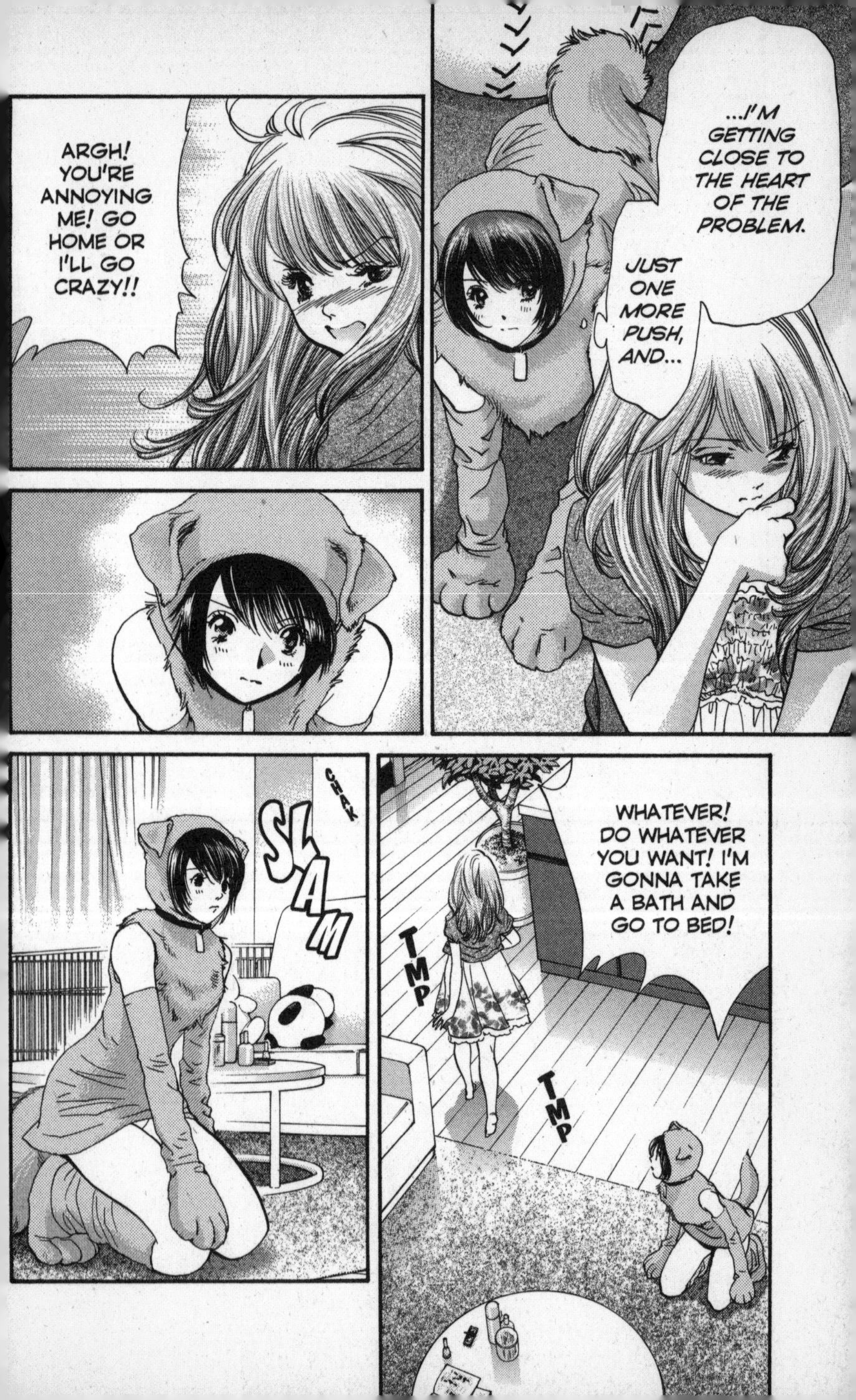
...I'M GETTING CLOSE TO THE HEART OF THE PROBLEM.
JUST ONE MORE PUSH, AND...
ARGH! YOU'RE ANNOYING ME! GO HOME OR I'LL GO CRAZY!!
WHATEVER! DO WHATEVER YOU WANT! I'M GONNA TAKE A BATH AND GO TO BED!
TMP
TMP
CHAK
SLAM

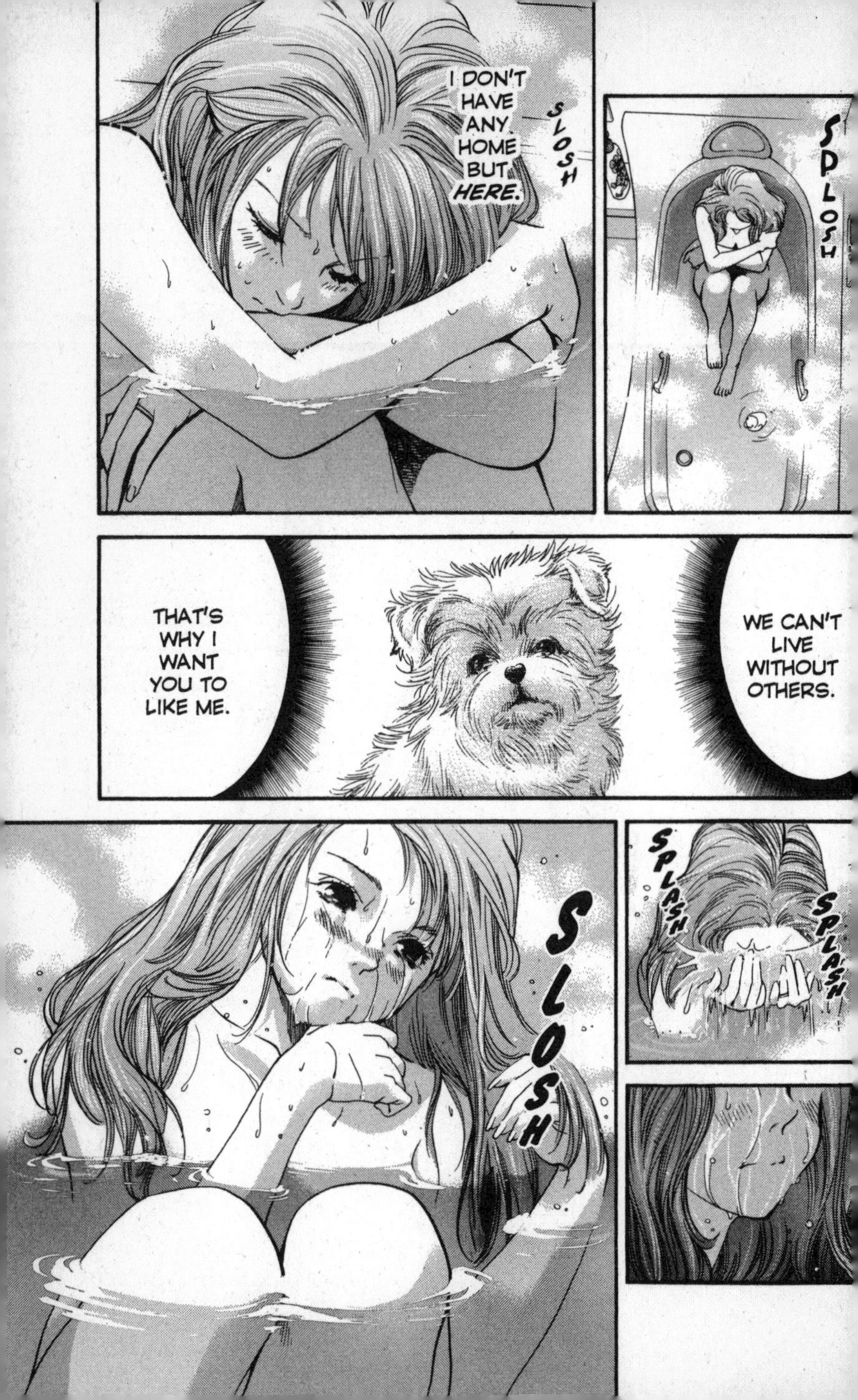
SPLOSH
I DON'T HAVE ANY HOME BUT HERE.
SLOSH
WE CAN'T LIVE WITHOUT OTHERS.
THAT'S WHY I WANT YOU TO LIKE ME.
SPLASH
SPLASH
SLOSH

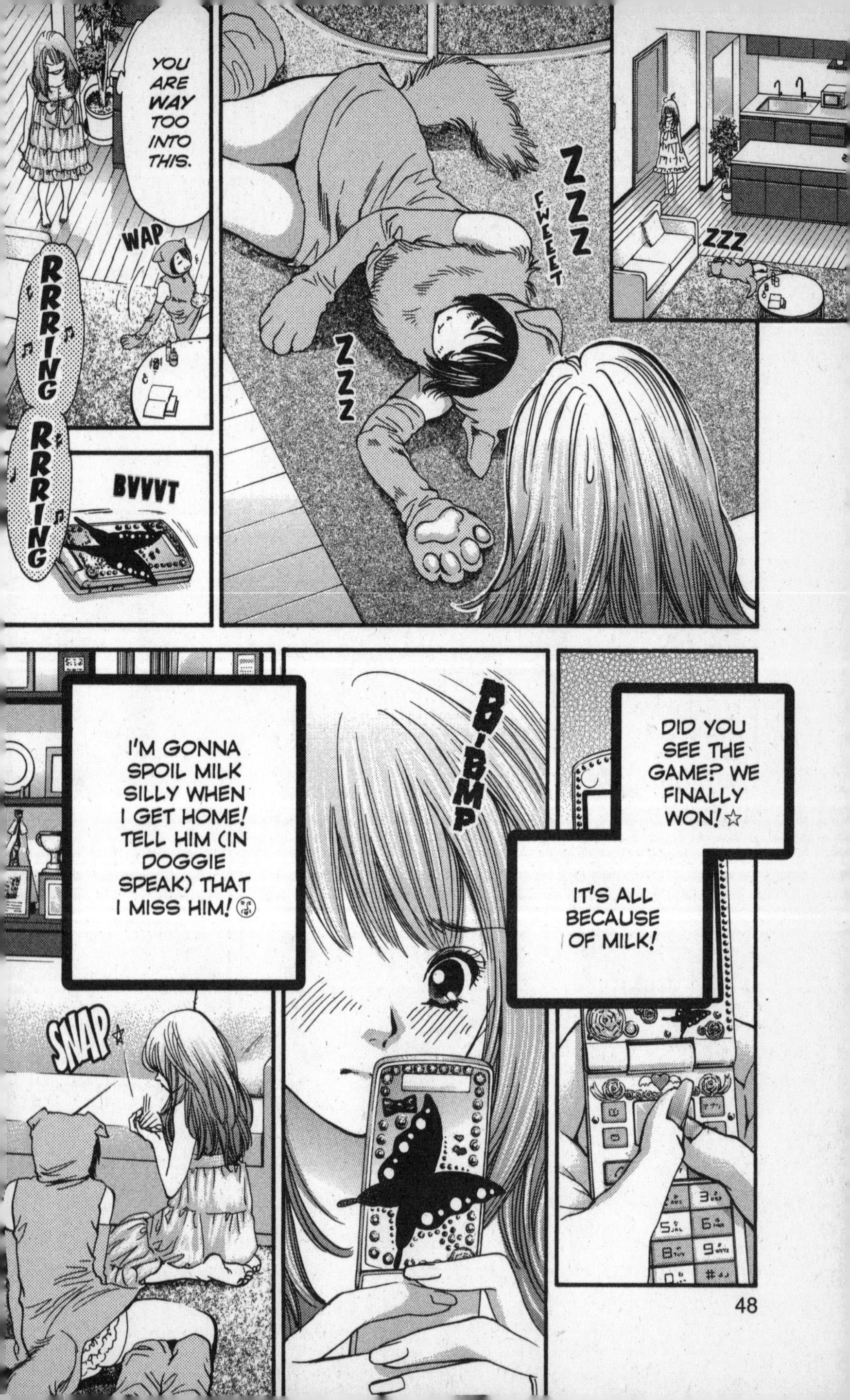
ZZZ
ZZZ
FWEEEET
ZZZ
YOU ARE WAY TOO INTO THIS.
WAP
RRRING
BVVVT
RRRING
DID YOU SEE THE GAME? WE FINALLY WON!☆
IT'S ALL BECAUSE OF MILK!
BIBMP
I'M GONNA SPOIL MILK SILLY WHEN I GET HOME! TELL HIM (IN DOGGIE SPEAK) THAT I MISS HIM!
SNAP☆

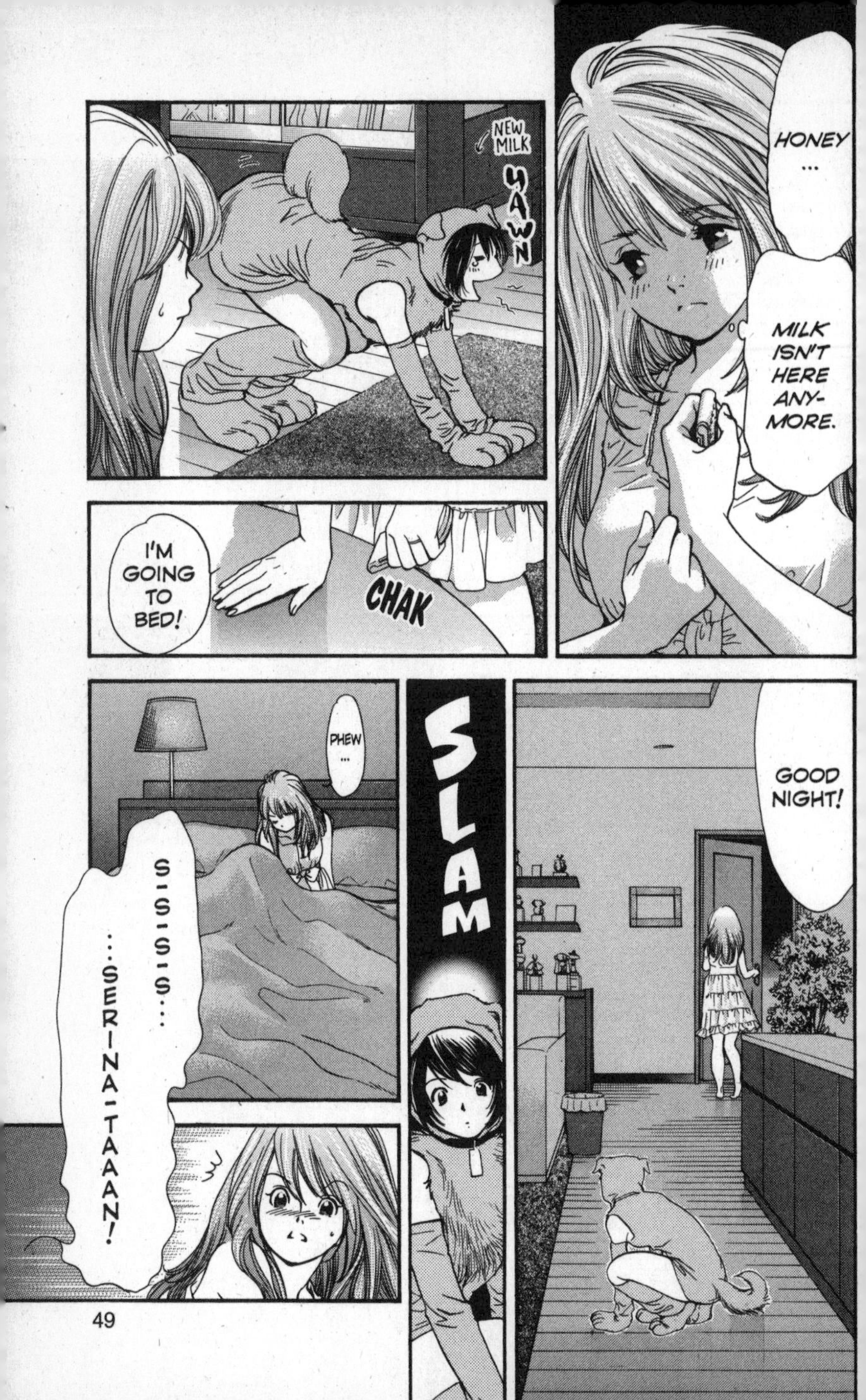
HONEY ...
MILK ISN'T HERE ANY-MORE.
NEW MILK
YAWN
I'M GOING TO BED!
CHAK
GOOD NIGHT!
SLAM
PHEW ...
S-S-S-S... ...SERINA-TAAAN!

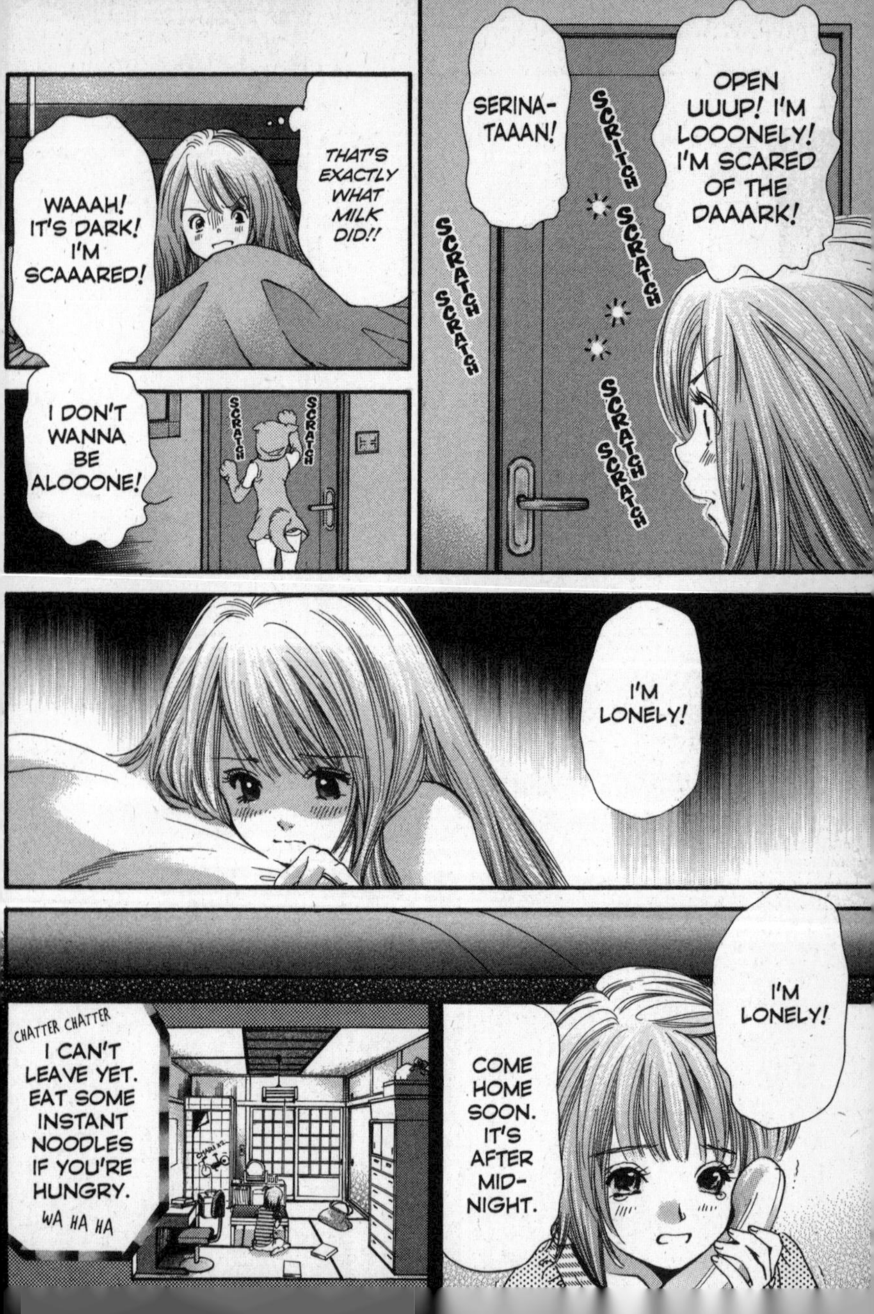
OPEN UUUP! I'M LOOONELY! I'M SCARED OF THE DAAARK!
SERINA-TAAAN!
SCRITCH SCRATCH
SCRATCH SCRATCH
SCRATCH SCRATCH
SCRATCH SCRATCH
THAT'S EXACTLY WHAT MILK DID!!
WAAAH! IT'S DARK! I'M SCAAARED!
I DON'T WANNA BE ALOOONE!
SCRATCH SCRATCH
I'M LONELY!
I'M LONELY!
COME HOME SOON. IT'S AFTER MID-NIGHT.
CHATTER CHATTER
I CAN'T LEAVE YET. EAT SOME INSTANT NOODLES IF YOU'RE HUNGRY.
WA HA HA

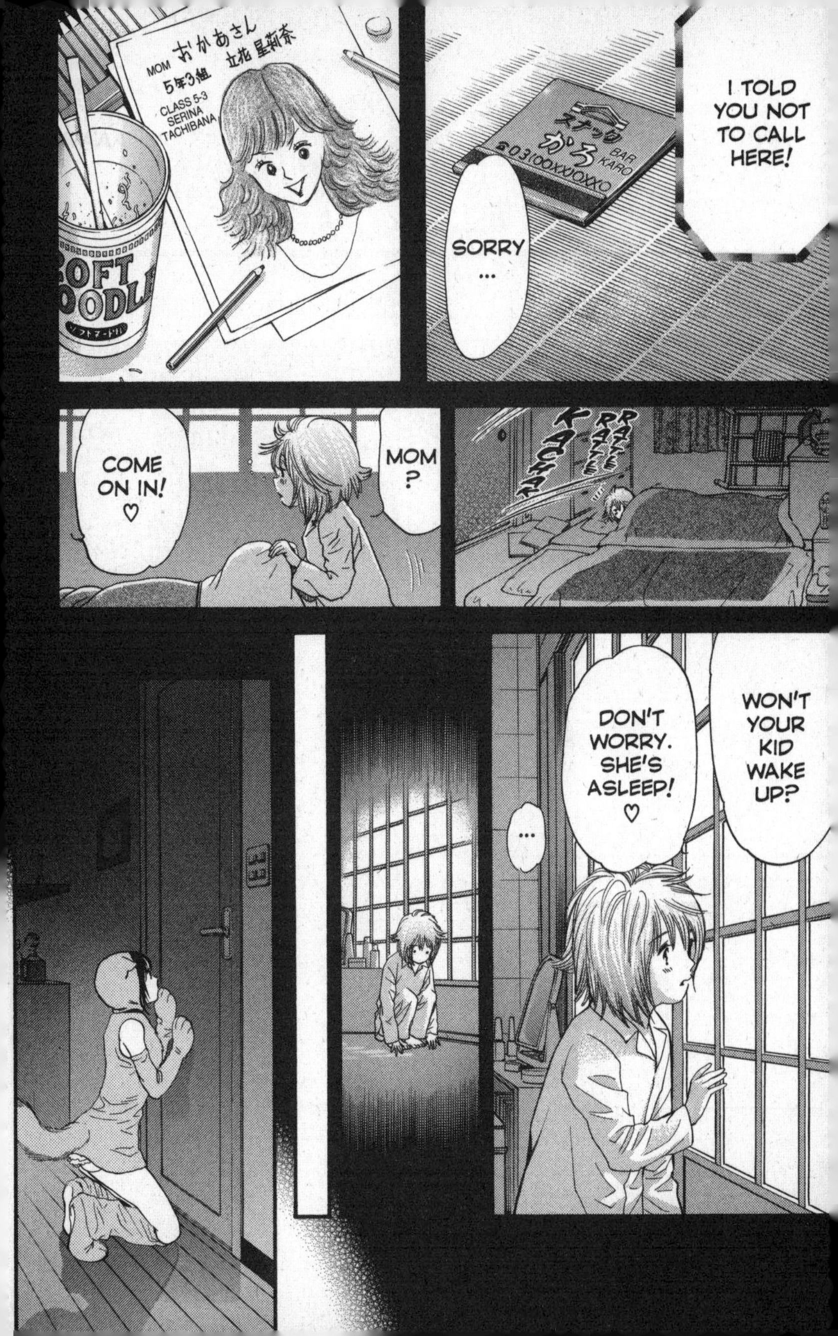
I TOLD YOU NOT TO CALL HERE!
スナック がろ
BAR KARO
☎03(00XX)OXXO
SORRY ...
MOM おかあさん
5年3組 立花 星莉奈
CLASS 5-3 SERINA TACHIBANA
RATTLE RATTLE
KACHAK
MOM ?
COME ON IN! ♡
WON'T YOUR KID WAKE UP?
DON'T WORRY. SHE'S ASLEEP! ♡
...

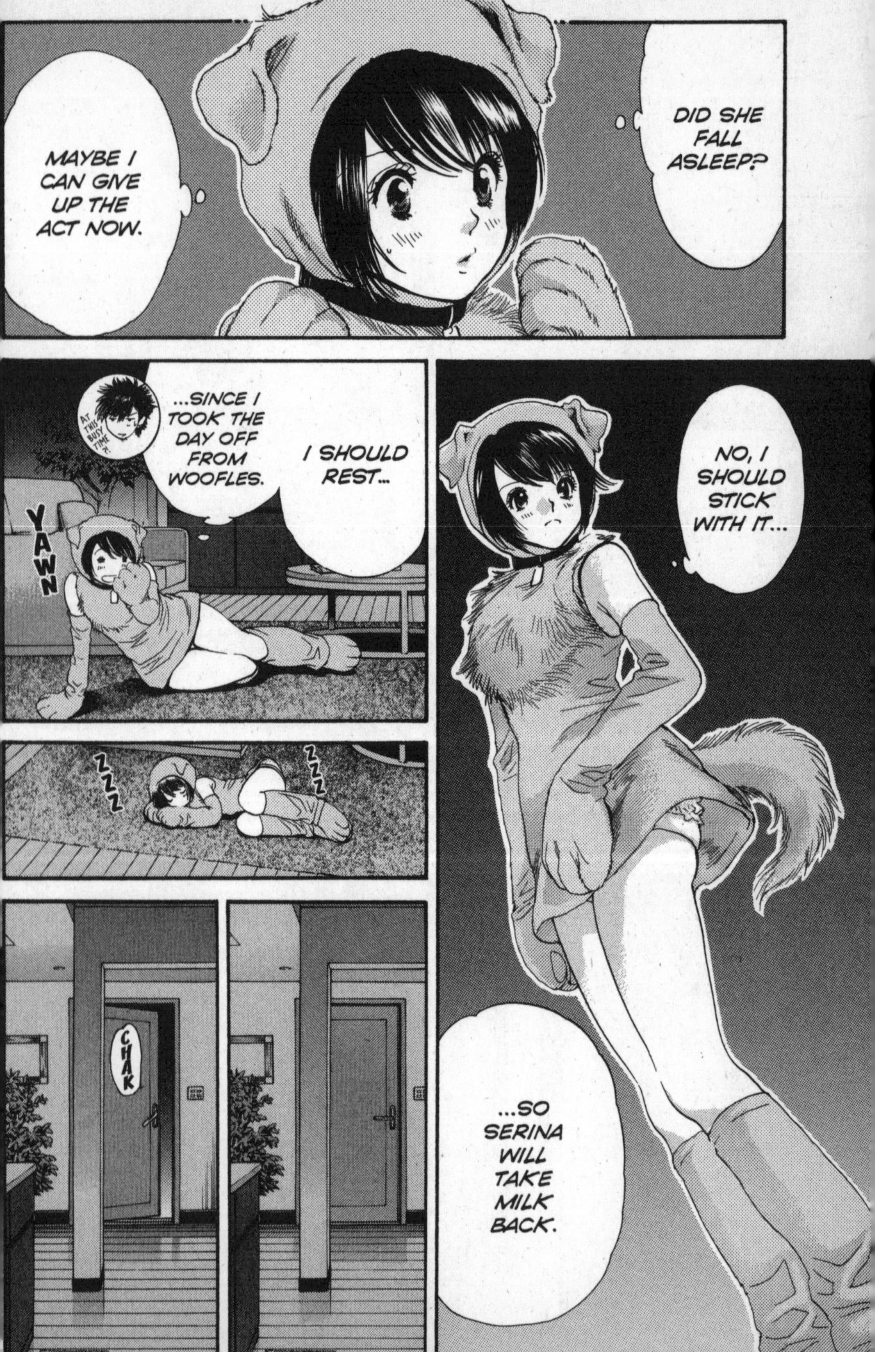
DID SHE FALL ASLEEP?
MAYBE I CAN GIVE UP THE ACT NOW.
NO, I SHOULD STICK WITH IT...
...SO SERINA WILL TAKE MILK BACK.
I SHOULD REST...
...SINCE I TOOK THE DAY OFF FROM WOOFLES.
AT THIS BUSY TIME ?!
YAWN
ZZZ
ZZZ
CHAK

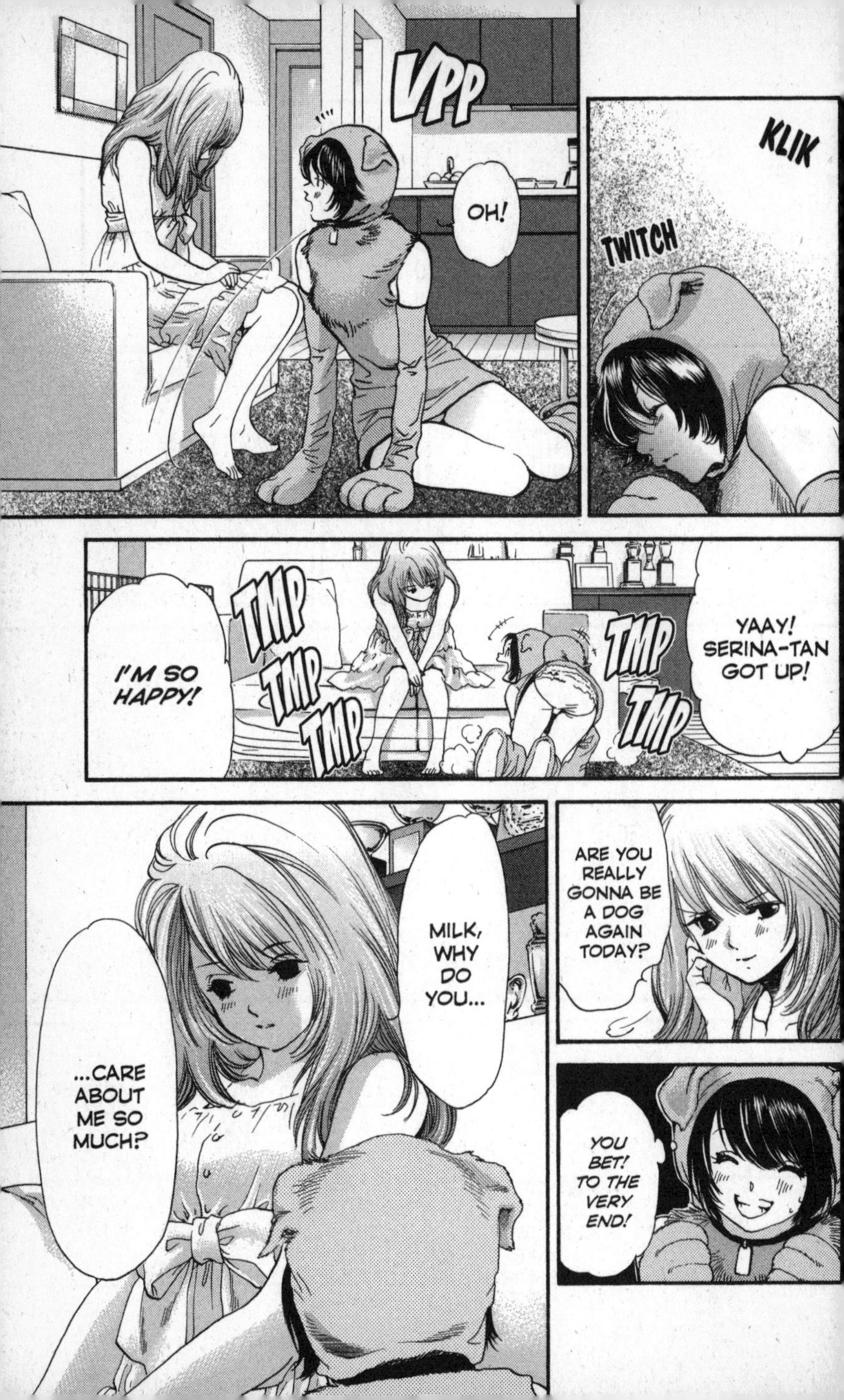
KLIK
TWITCH
VPP
OH!
YAAY! SERINA-TAN GOT UP!
TMP TMP
TMP TMP TMP
I'M SO HAPPY!
ARE YOU REALLY GONNA BE A DOG AGAIN TODAY?
YOU BET! TO THE VERY END!
MILK, WHY DO YOU...
...CARE ABOUT ME SO MUCH?

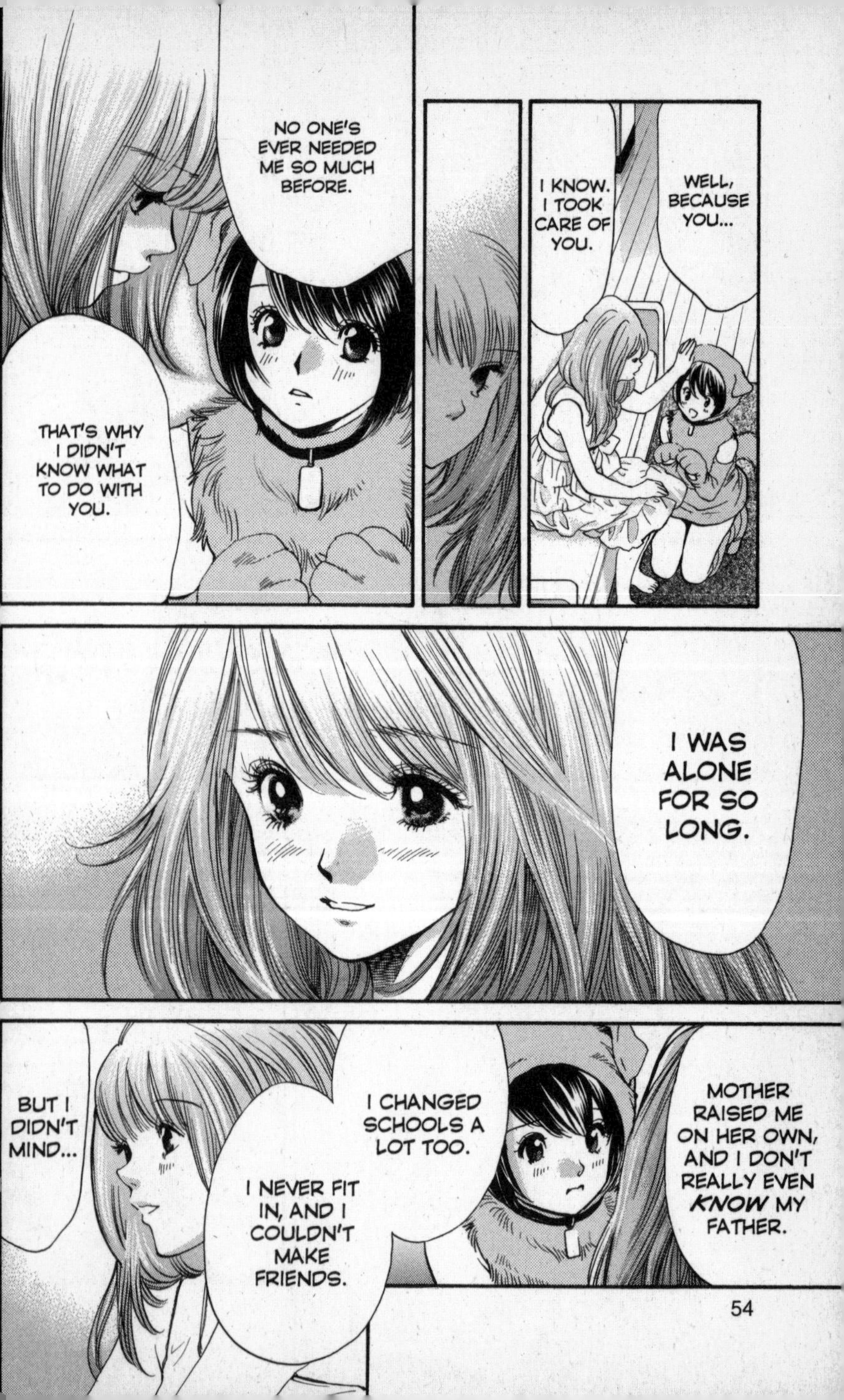
WELL, BECAUSE YOU...
I KNOW. I TOOK CARE OF YOU.
NO ONE'S EVER NEEDED ME SO MUCH BEFORE.
THAT'S WHY I DIDN'T KNOW WHAT TO DO WITH YOU.
I WAS ALONE FOR SO LONG.
MOTHER RAISED ME ON HER OWN, AND I DON'T REALLY EVEN *KNOW* MY FATHER.
I CHANGED SCHOOLS A LOT TOO.
I NEVER FIT IN, AND I COULDN'T MAKE FRIENDS.
BUT I DIDN'T MIND...

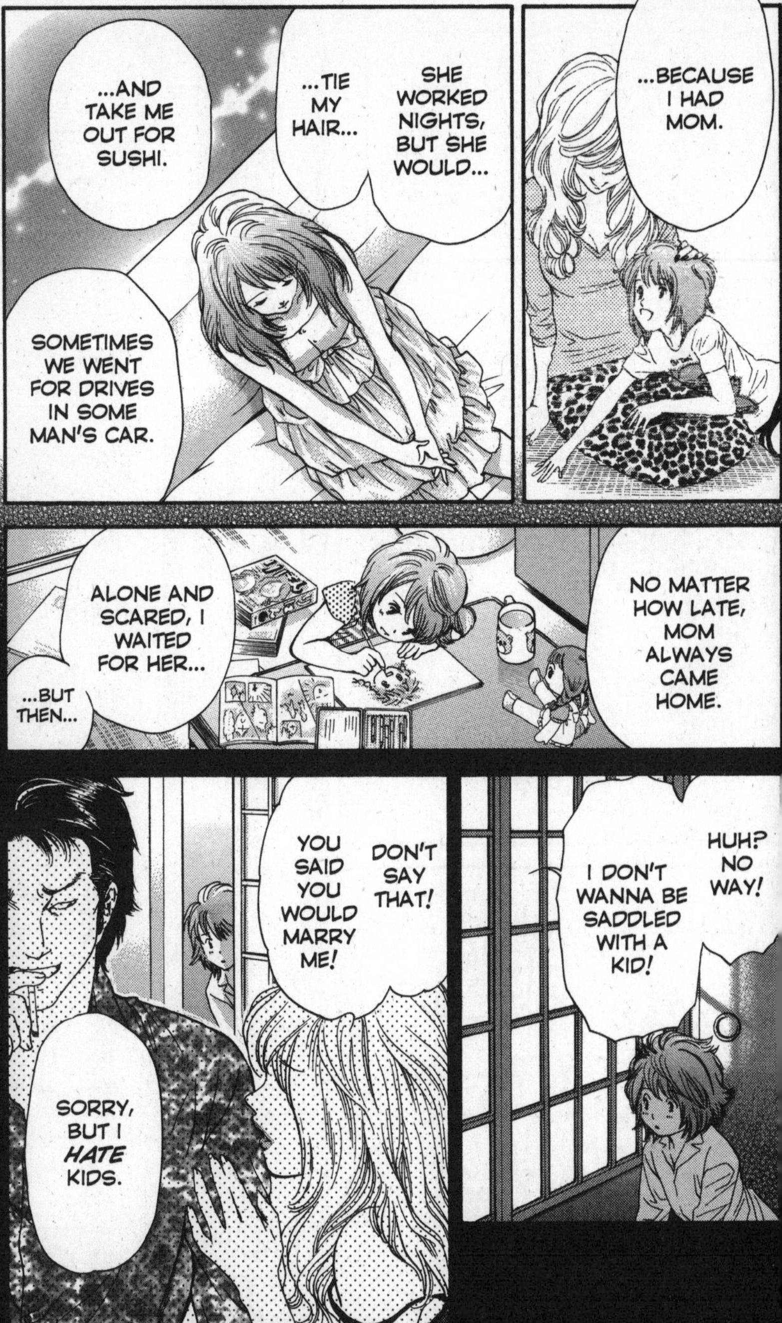
...BECAUSE I HAD MOM.
SHE WORKED NIGHTS, BUT SHE WOULD...
...TIE MY HAIR...
...AND TAKE ME OUT FOR SUSHI.
SOMETIMES WE WENT FOR DRIVES IN SOME MAN'S CAR.
NO MATTER HOW LATE, MOM ALWAYS CAME HOME.
ALONE AND SCARED, I WAITED FOR HER...
...BUT THEN...
HUH? NO WAY!
I DON'T WANNA BE SADDLED WITH A KID!
DON'T SAY THAT!
YOU SAID YOU WOULD MARRY ME!
SORRY, BUT I *HATE* KIDS.

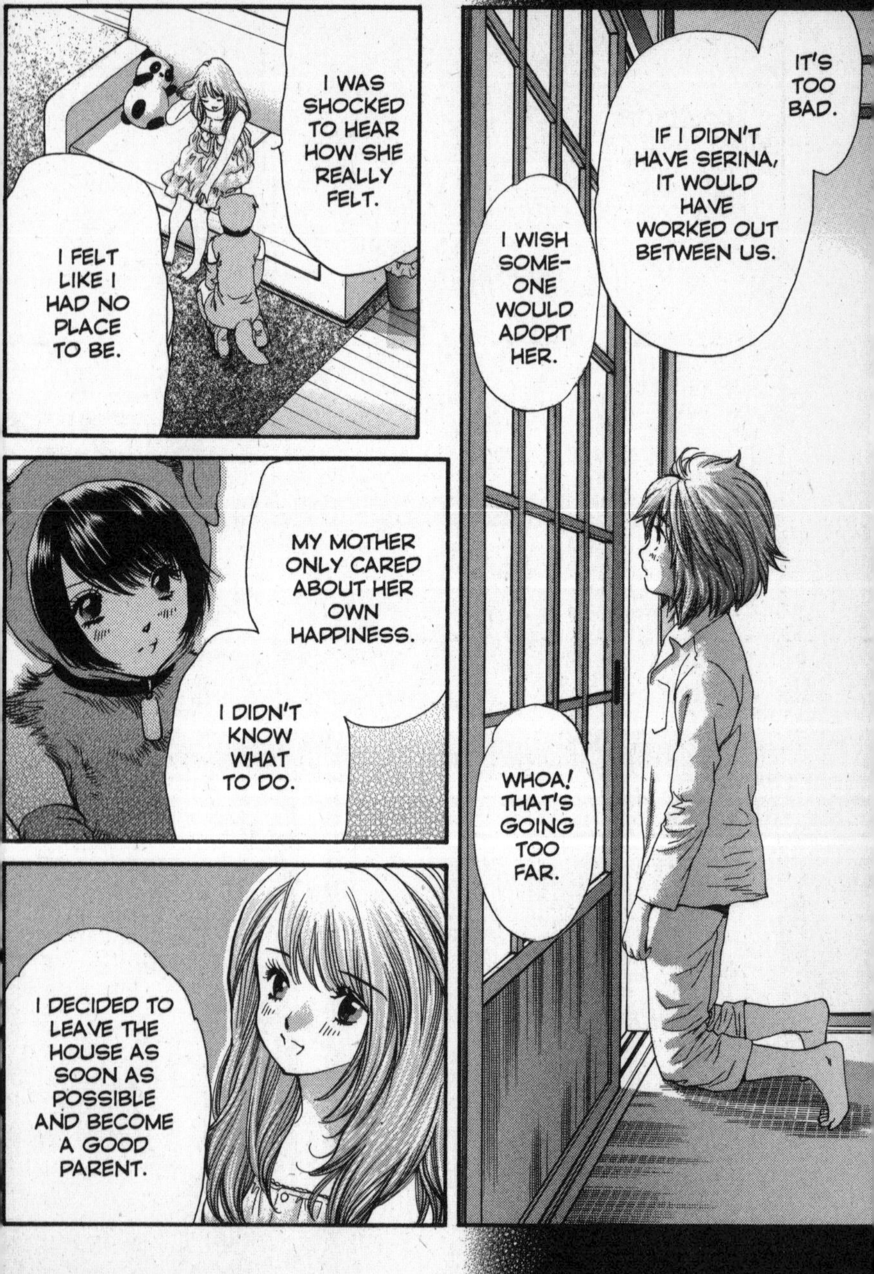
IT'S TOO BAD.
IF I DIDN'T HAVE SERINA, IT WOULD HAVE WORKED OUT BETWEEN US.
I WISH SOME-ONE WOULD ADOPT HER.
WHOA! THAT'S GOING TOO FAR.
I WAS SHOCKED TO HEAR HOW SHE REALLY FELT.
I FELT LIKE I HAD NO PLACE TO BE.
MY MOTHER ONLY CARED ABOUT HER OWN HAPPINESS.
I DIDN'T KNOW WHAT TO DO.
I DECIDED TO LEAVE THE HOUSE AS SOON AS POSSIBLE AND BECOME A GOOD PARENT.

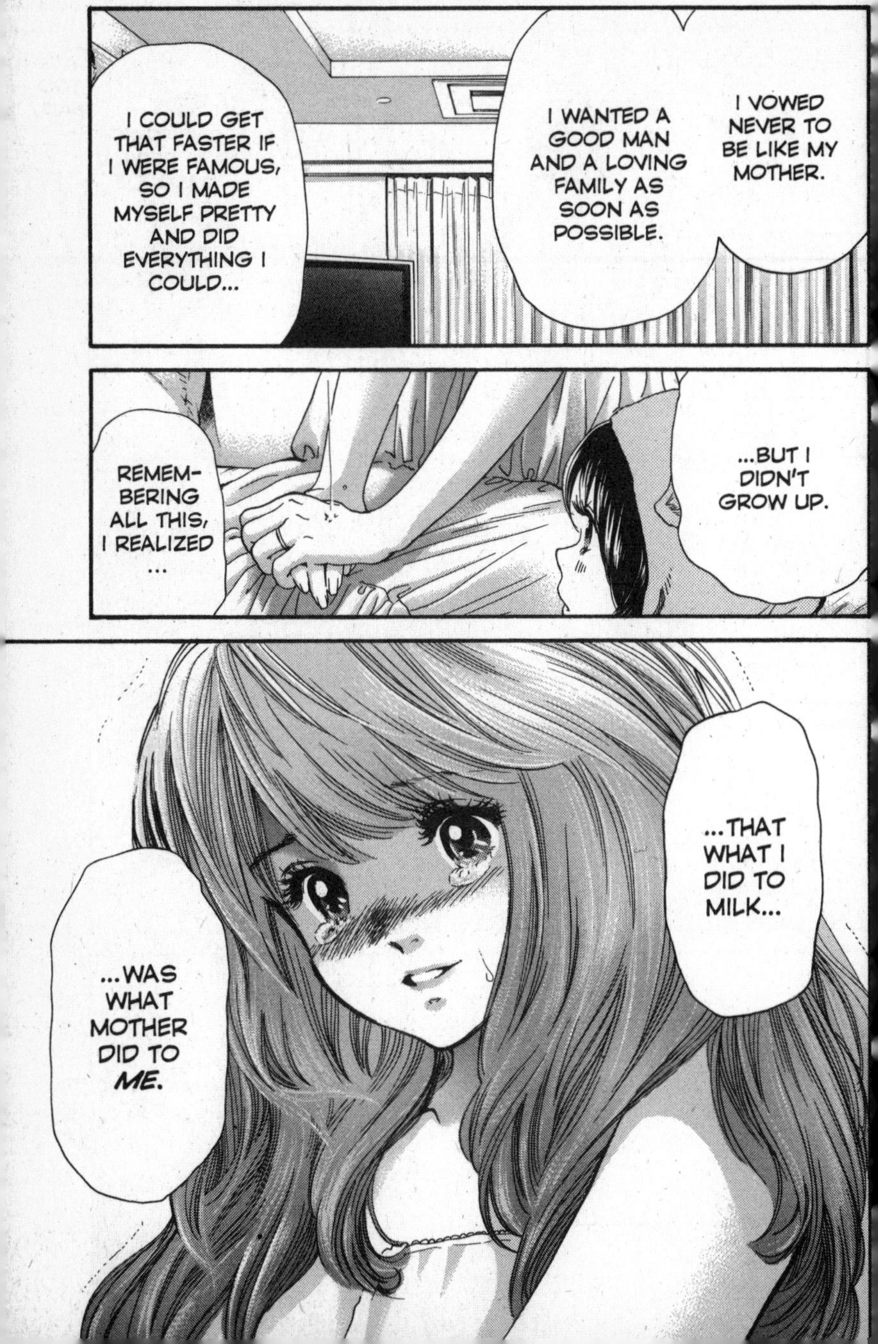
I VOWED NEVER TO BE LIKE MY MOTHER.
I WANTED A GOOD MAN AND A LOVING FAMILY AS SOON AS POSSIBLE.
I COULD GET THAT FASTER IF I WERE FAMOUS, SO I MADE MYSELF PRETTY AND DID EVERYTHING I COULD...
...BUT I DIDN'T GROW UP.
REMEM-BERING ALL THIS, I REALIZED ...
...THAT WHAT I DID TO MILK...
...WAS WHAT MOTHER DID TO *ME*.

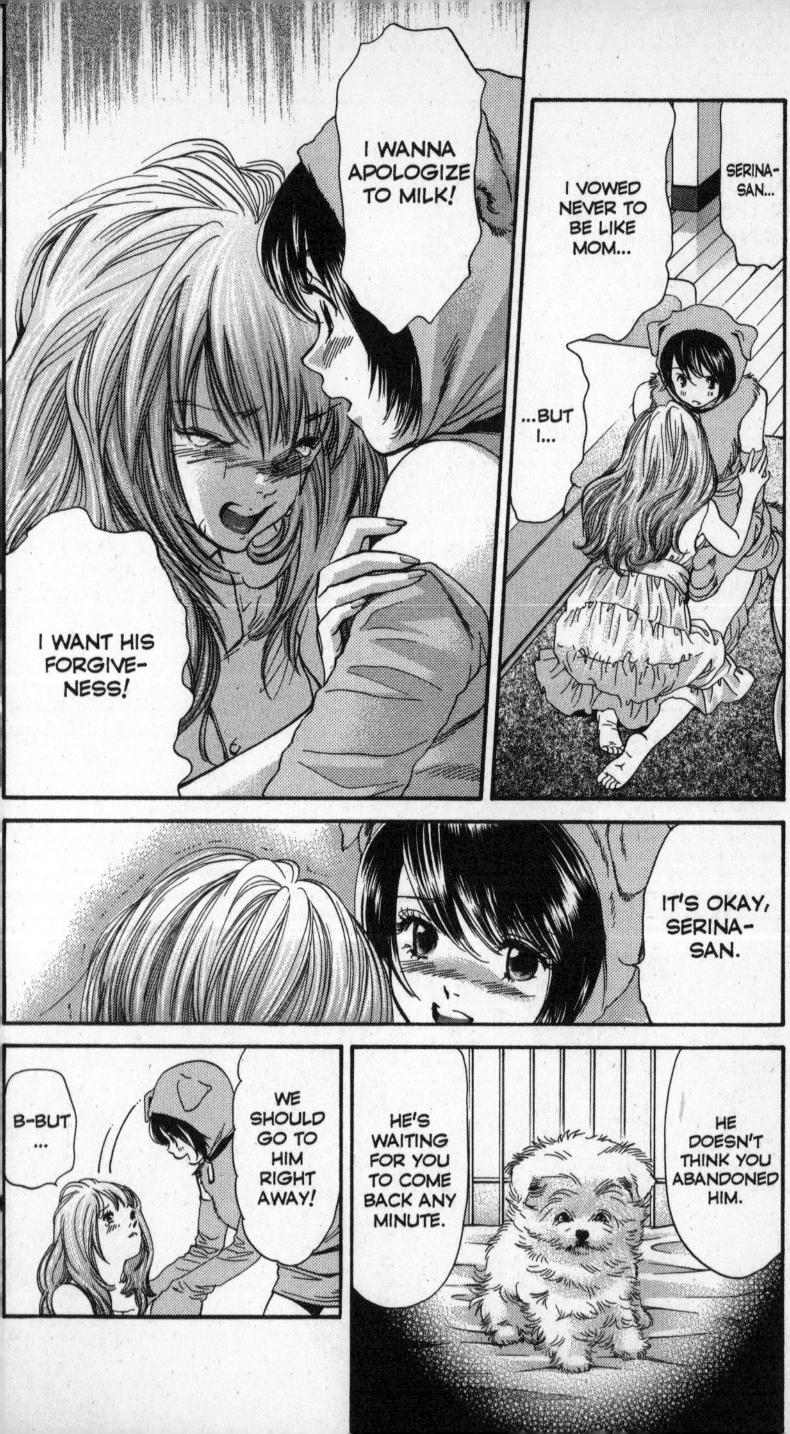
SERINA-SAN...
I VOWED NEVER TO BE LIKE MOM...
...BUT I...
I WANNA APOLOGIZE TO MILK!
I WANT HIS FORGIVENESS!
IT'S OKAY, SERINA-SAN.
HE DOESN'T THINK YOU ABANDONED HIM.
HE'S WAITING FOR YOU TO COME BACK ANY MINUTE.
WE SHOULD GO TO HIM RIGHT AWAY!
B-BUT ...

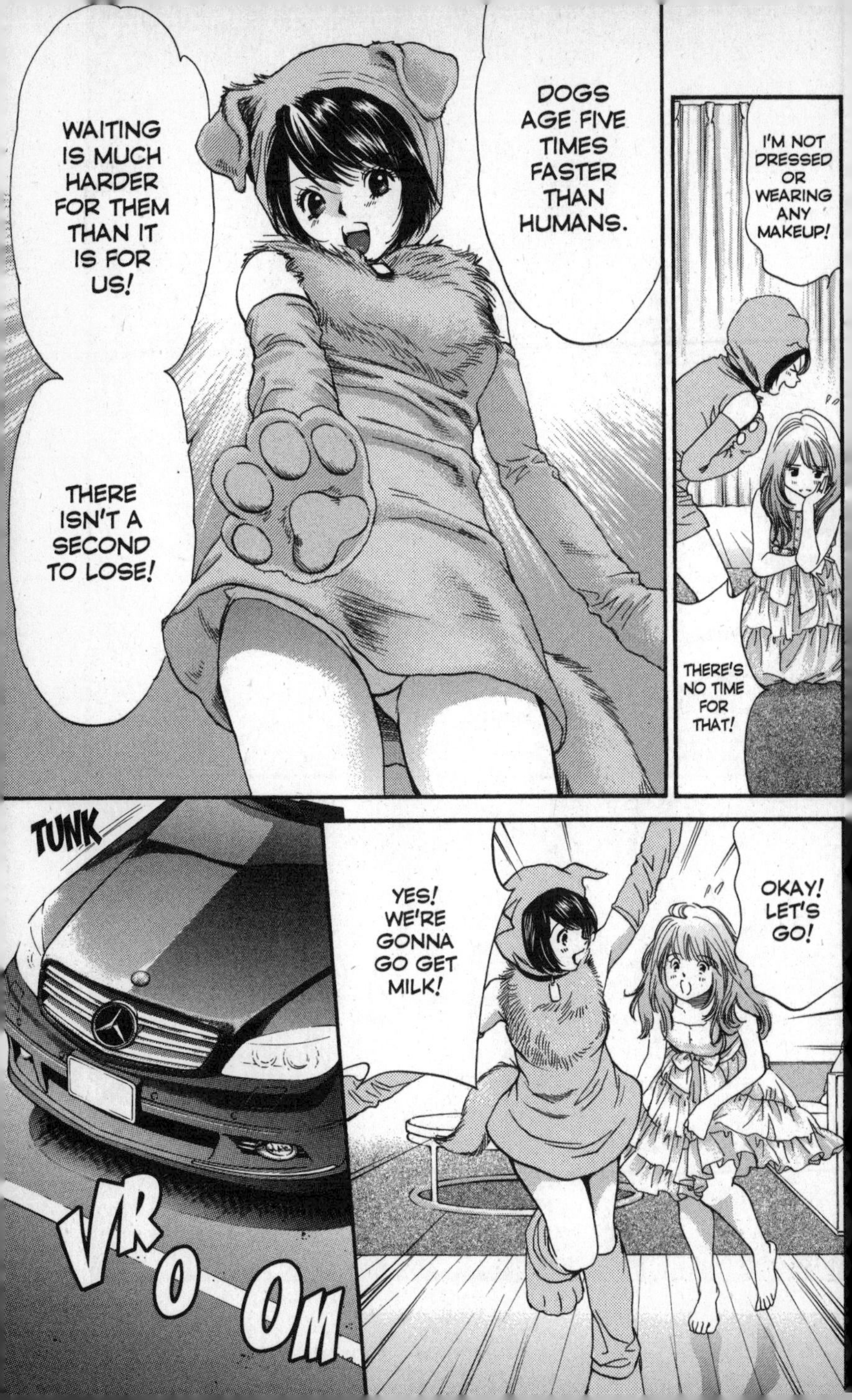
I'M NOT DRESSED OR WEARING ANY MAKEUP!
THERE'S NO TIME FOR THAT!
DOGS AGE FIVE TIMES FASTER THAN HUMANS.
WAITING IS MUCH HARDER FOR THEM THAN IT IS FOR US!
THERE ISN'T A SECOND TO LOSE!
OKAY! LET'S GO!
YES! WE'RE GONNA GO GET MILK!
TUNK
VROOM

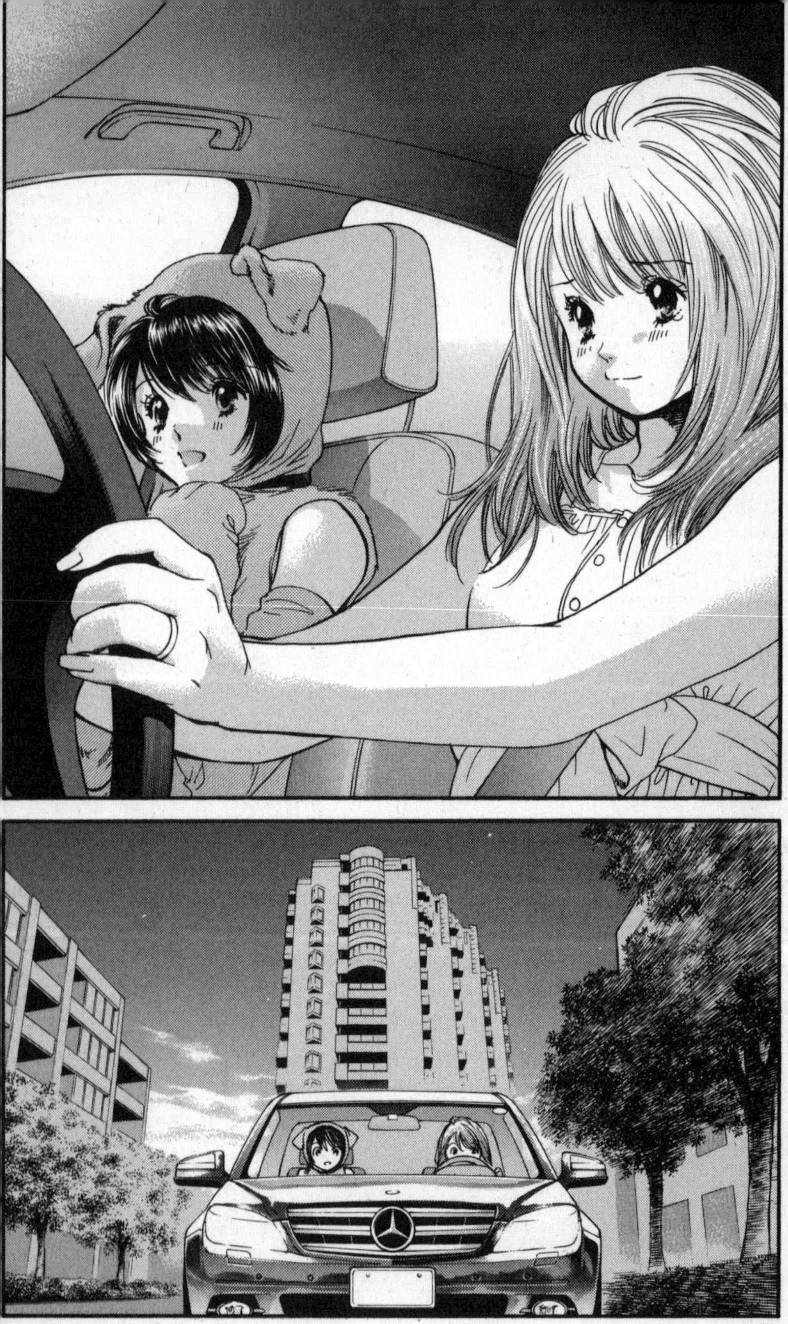

CHAPTER 177: LET'S GO HOME TOGETHER

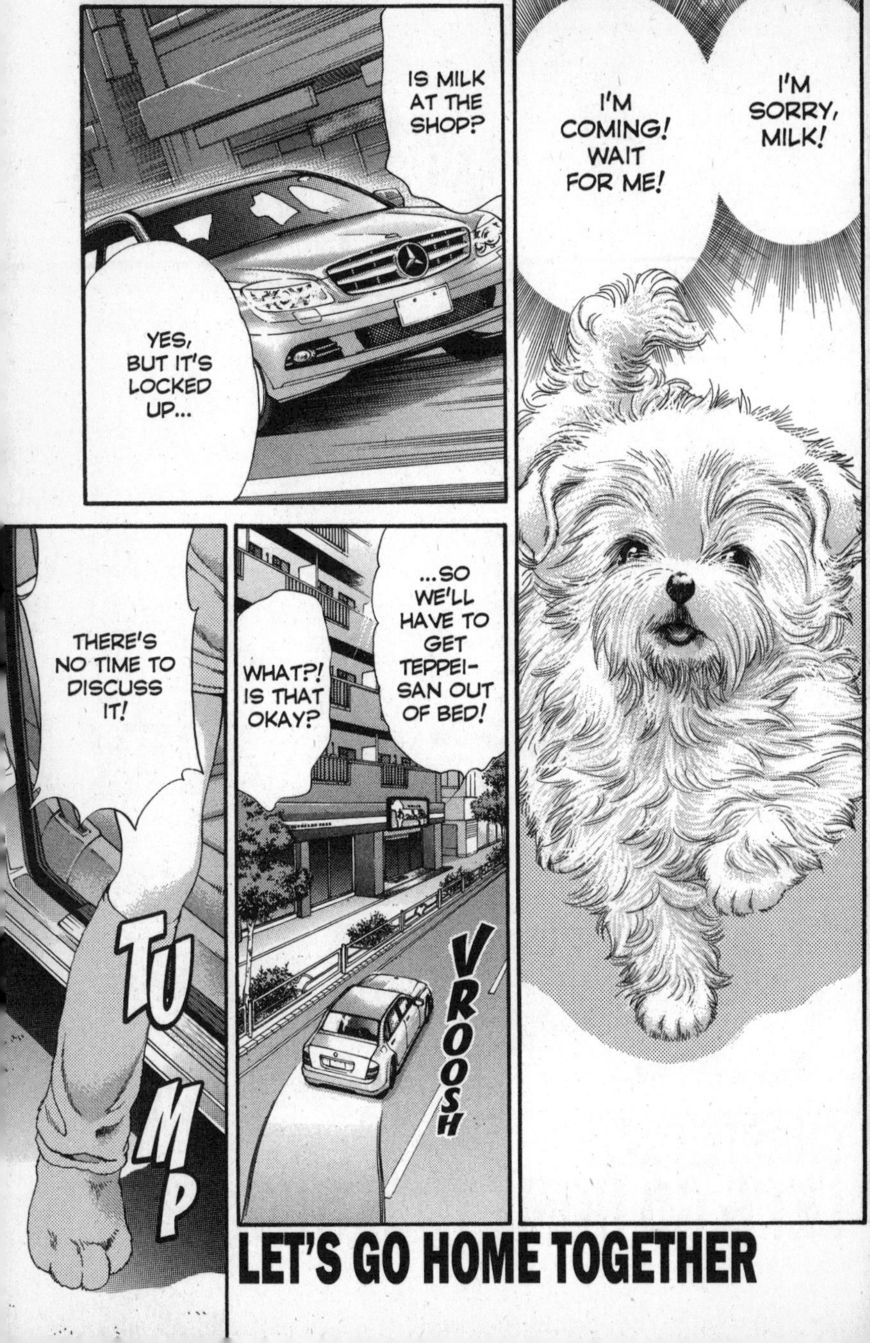
I'M SORRY, MILK!
I'M COMING! WAIT FOR ME!
IS MILK AT THE SHOP?
YES, BUT IT'S LOCKED UP...
...SO WE'LL HAVE TO GET TEPPEI-SAN OUT OF BED!
WHAT?! IS THAT OKAY?
VROOSH
THERE'S NO TIME TO DISCUSS IT!
TUMP

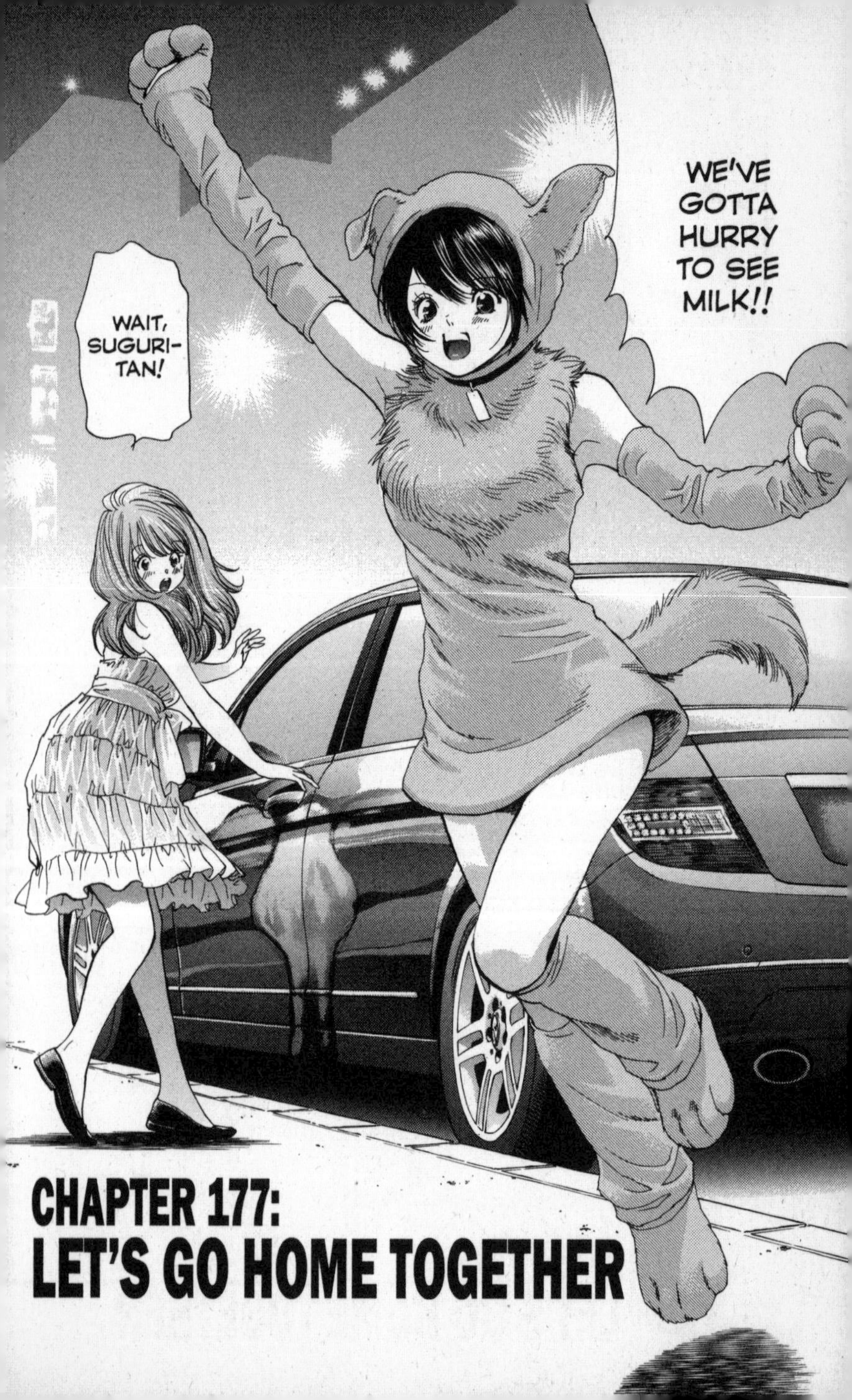
WE'VE GOTTA HURRY TO SEE MILK!!
WAIT, SUGURI-TAN!

CHAPTER 177: LET'S GO HOME TOGETHER

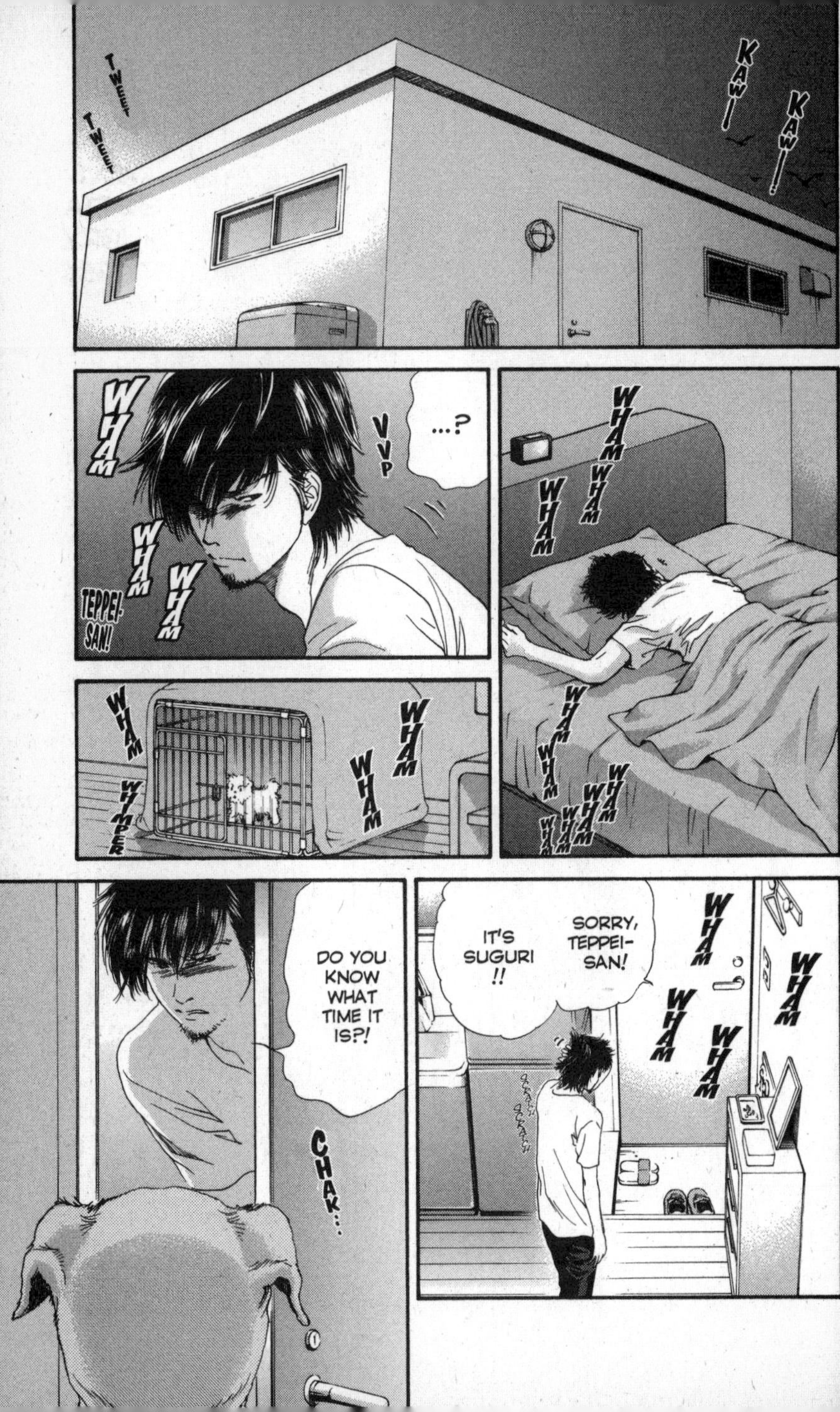
KAWI KAWI!
TWEET TWEET
WHAM WHAM
WHAM
WHAM WHAM WHAM WHAM
WHAM WHAM WHAM
...?
VVP
WHAM
WHAM WHAM
TEPPEI-SAN!
WHAM WHAM
WHAM
WHIMPER
WHAM WHAM
SORRY, TEPPEI-SAN!
IT'S SUGURI!!
WHAM WHAM WHAM WHAM
SCRATCH SCRATCH
DO YOU KNOW WHAT TIME IT IS?!
CHAK...

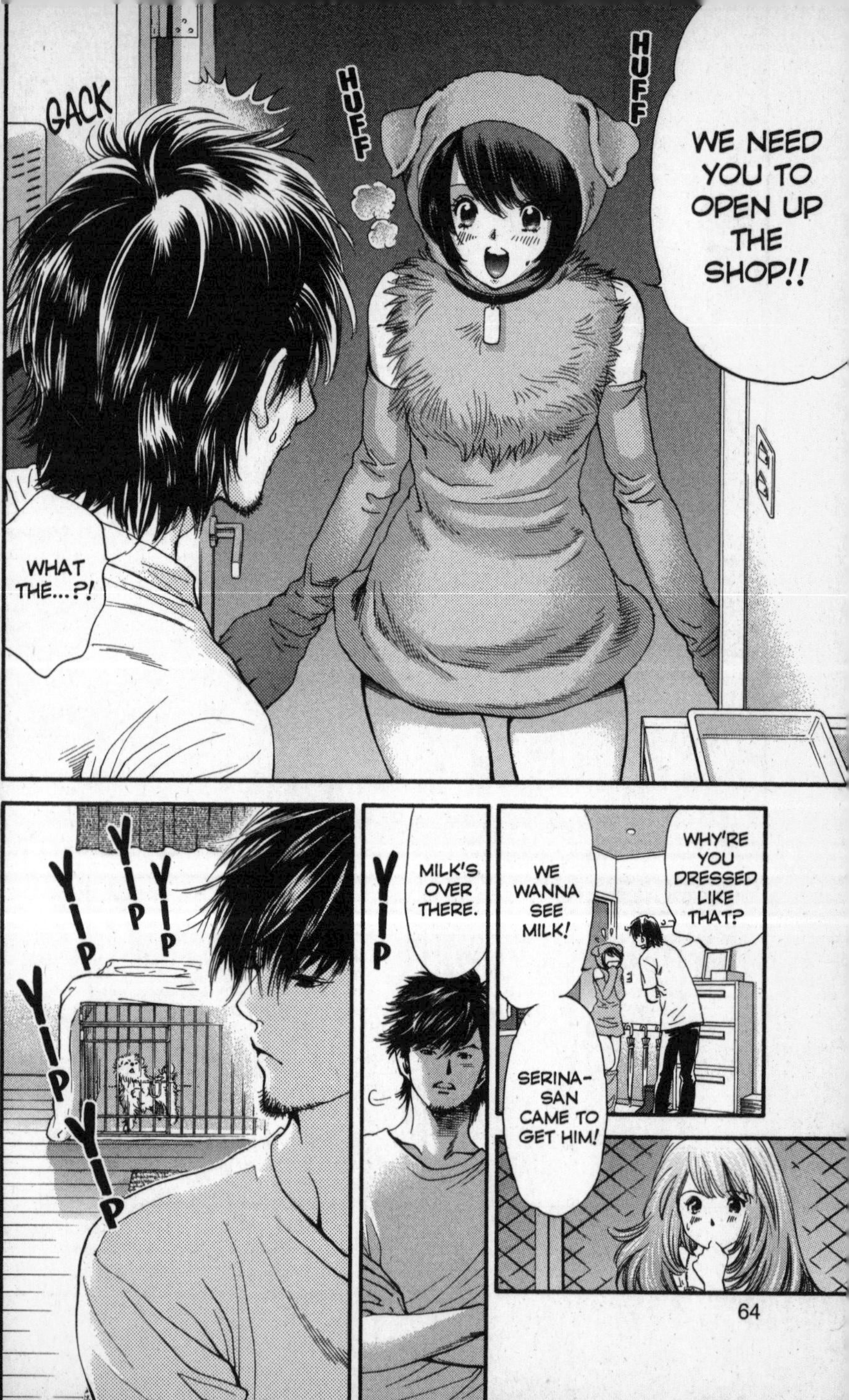
WE NEED YOU TO OPEN UP THE SHOP!!
HUFF
HUFF
GACK
WHAT THE...?!
WHY'RE YOU DRESSED LIKE THAT?
WE WANNA SEE MILK!
SERINA-SAN CAME TO GET HIM!
MILK'S OVER THERE.
YIP
YIP
YIP
YIP
YIP
YIP
YIP

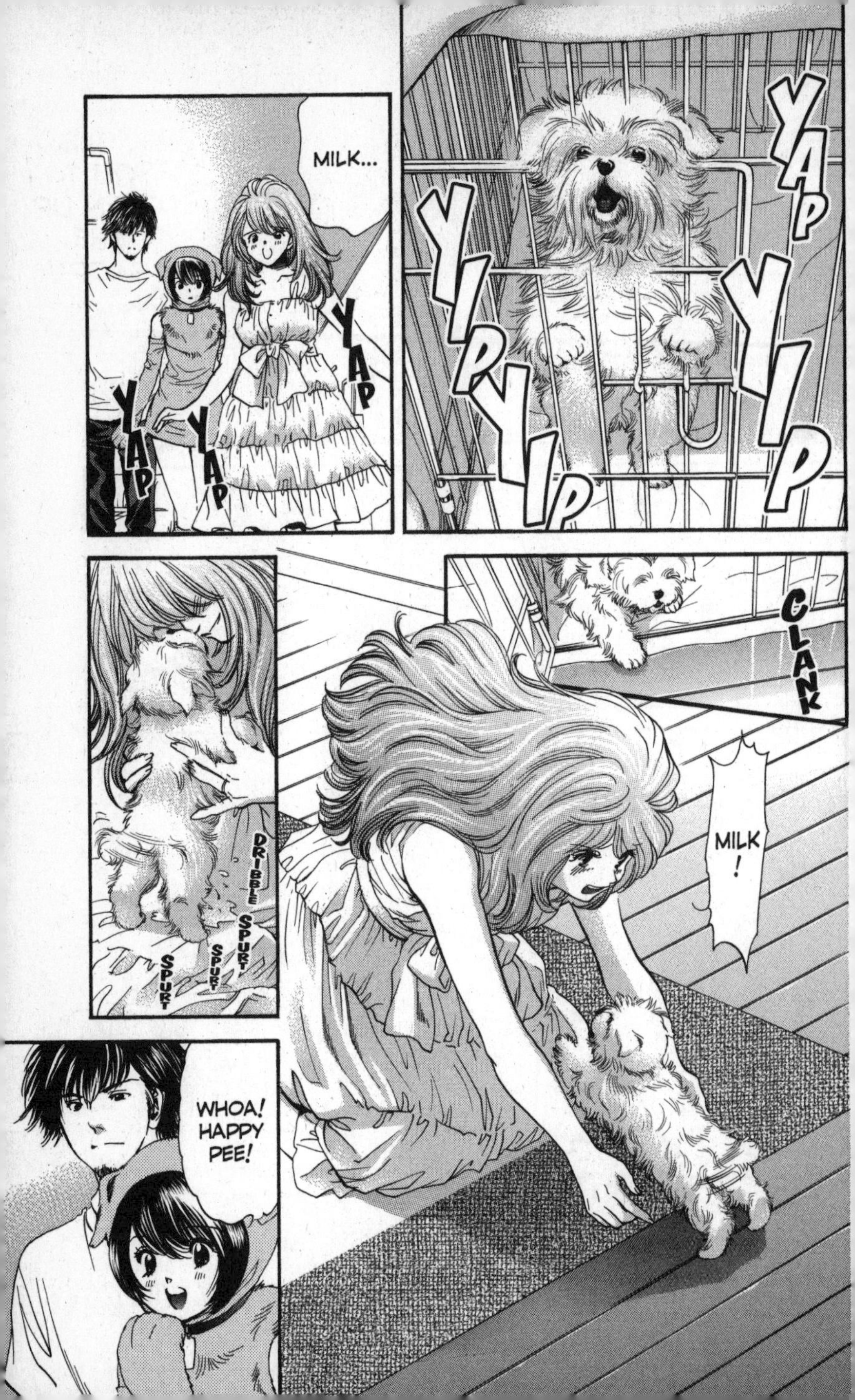
YAP
YIP
YIP
YIP
MILK...
YAP
YAP
YAP
CLANK
MILK!
DRIBBLE
SPURT
SPURT
SPURT
WHOA! HAPPY PEE!

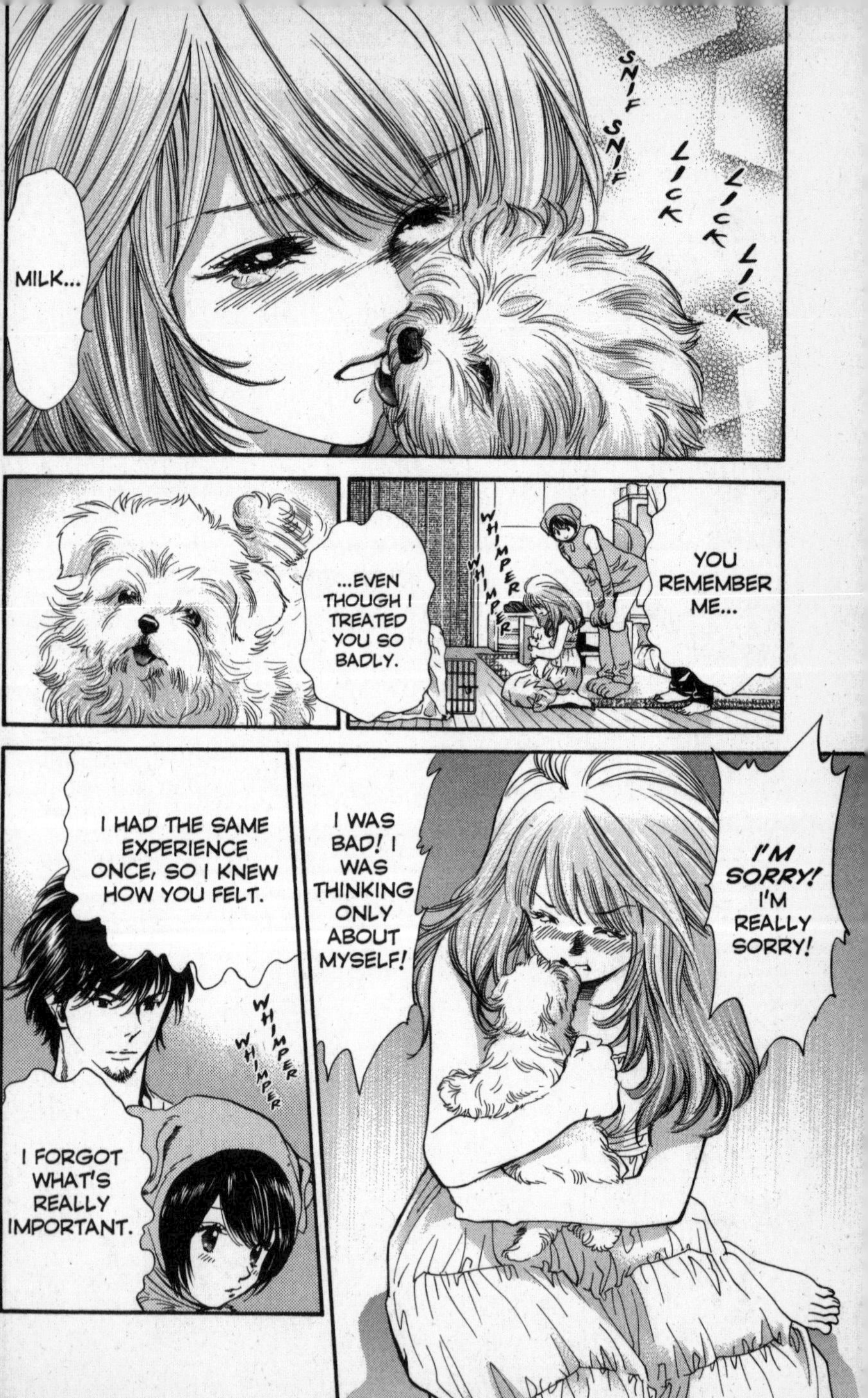
SNIF SNIF
LICK LICK LICK
MILK...
YOU REMEMBER ME...
WHIMPER WHIMPER
...EVEN THOUGH I TREATED YOU SO BADLY.
I'M SORRY! I'M REALLY SORRY!
I WAS BAD! I WAS THINKING ONLY ABOUT MYSELF!
I HAD THE SAME EXPERIENCE ONCE, SO I KNEW HOW YOU FELT.
WHIMPER WHIMPER
I FORGOT WHAT'S REALLY IMPORTANT.

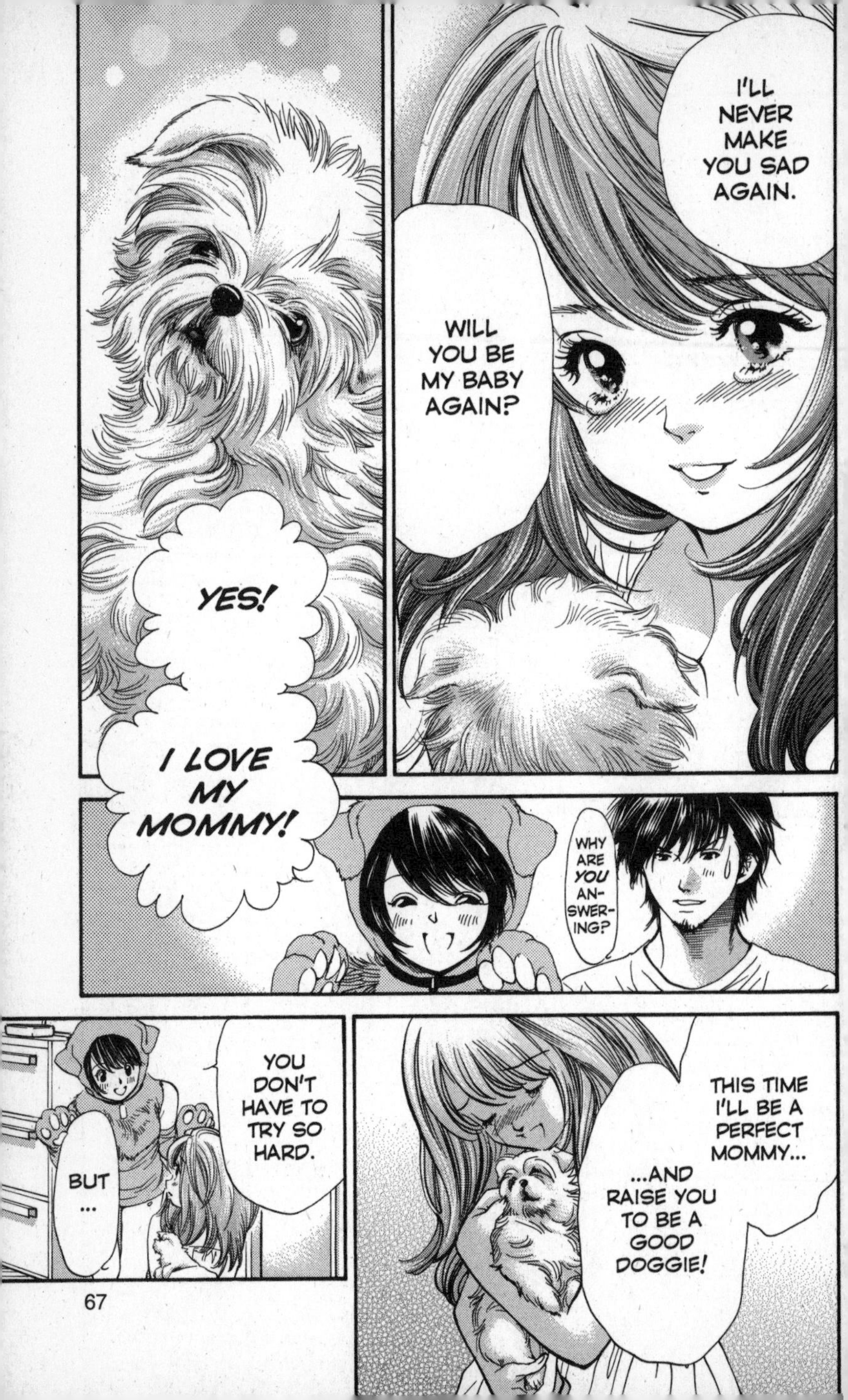
I'LL NEVER MAKE YOU SAD AGAIN.
WILL YOU BE MY BABY AGAIN?
YES!
I LOVE MY MOMMY!
WHY ARE *YOU* AN-SWER-ING?
THIS TIME I'LL BE A PERFECT MOMMY...
...AND RAISE YOU TO BE A GOOD DOGGIE!
YOU DON'T HAVE TO TRY SO HARD.
BUT ...

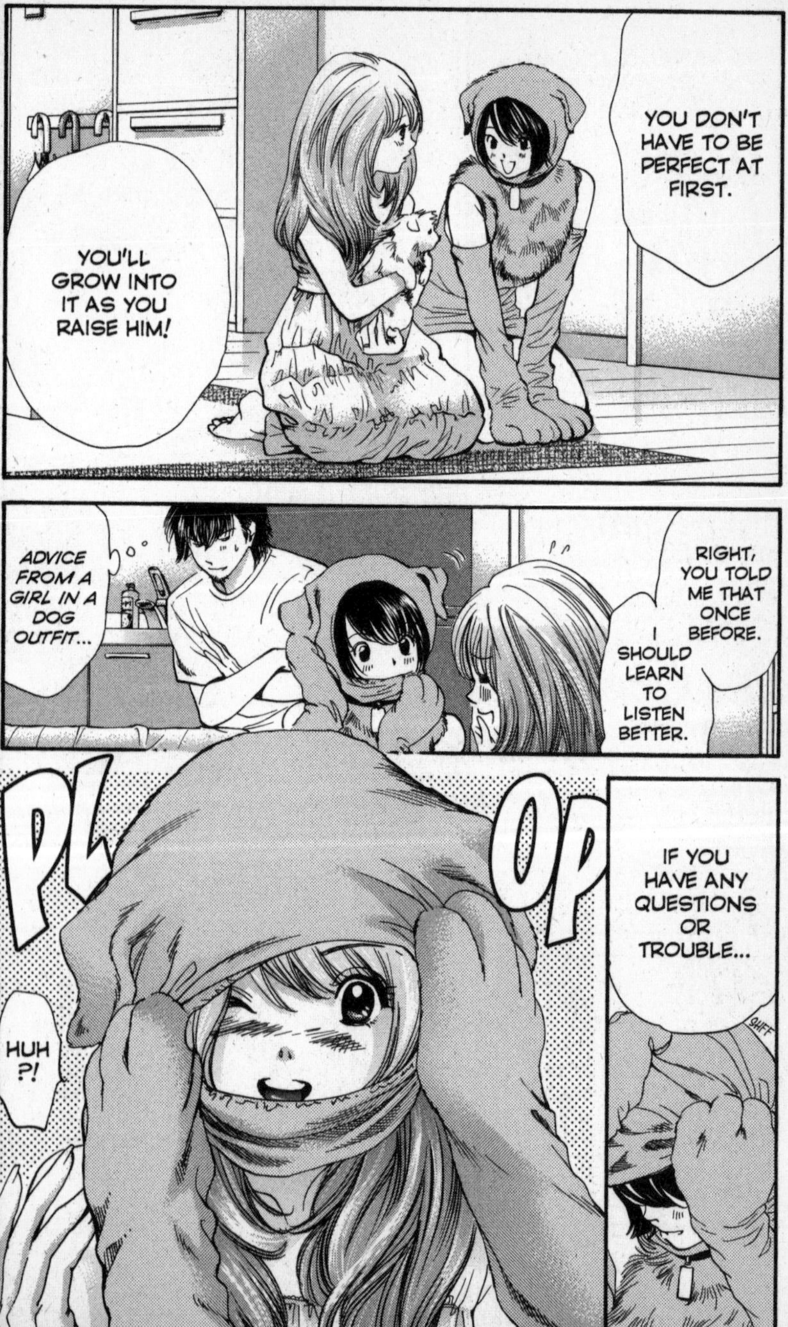
YOU DON'T HAVE TO BE PERFECT AT FIRST.
YOU'LL GROW INTO IT AS YOU RAISE HIM!
RIGHT, YOU TOLD ME THAT ONCE BEFORE.
I SHOULD LEARN TO LISTEN BETTER.
ADVICE FROM A GIRL IN A DOG OUTFIT...
IF YOU HAVE ANY QUESTIONS OR TROUBLE...
SHFF
PLOP
HUH?!

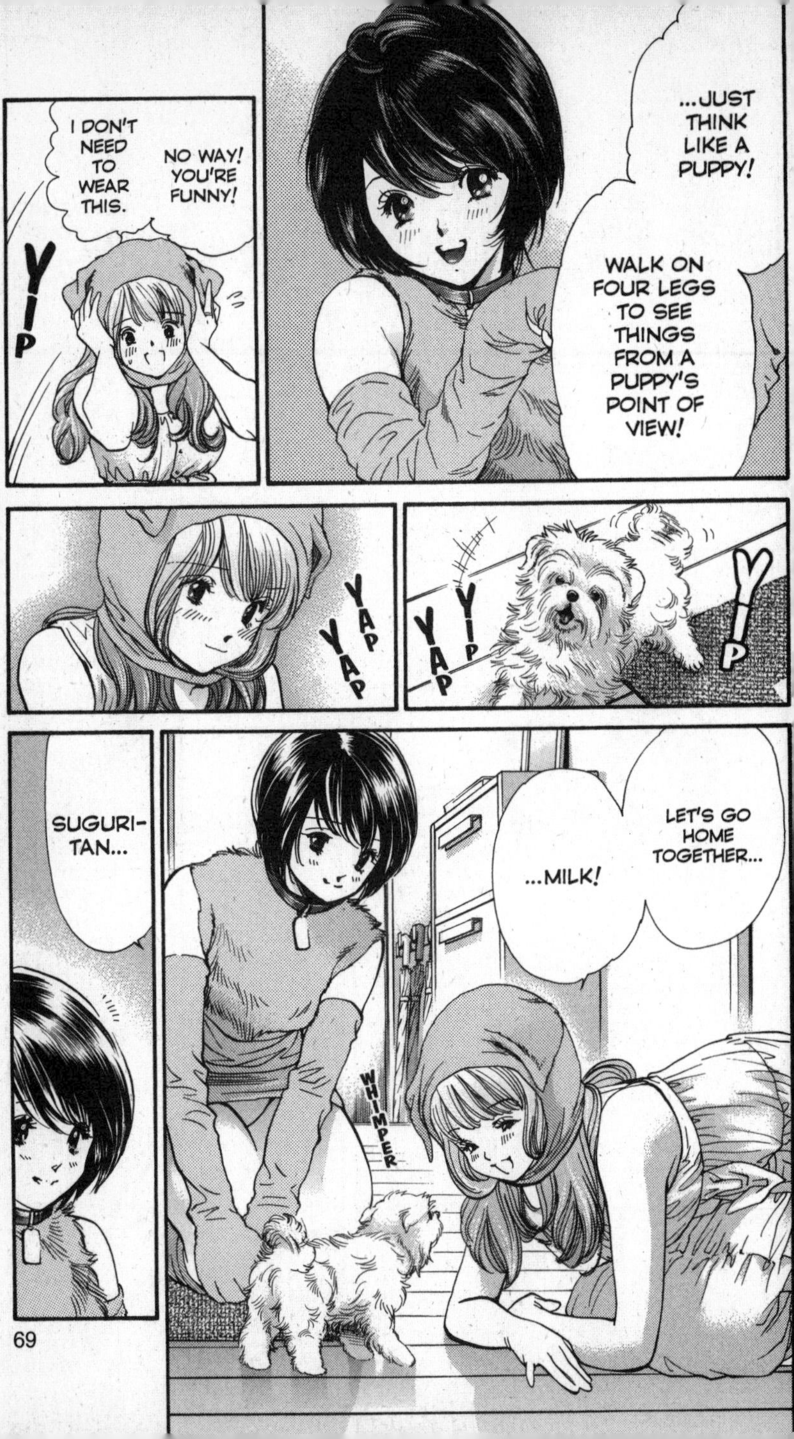
...JUST THINK LIKE A PUPPY!
WALK ON FOUR LEGS TO SEE THINGS FROM A PUPPY'S POINT OF VIEW!
NO WAY! YOU'RE FUNNY!
I DON'T NEED TO WEAR THIS.
YIP
YIP
YIP
YAP YAP
YAP YAP
LET'S GO HOME TOGETHER...
...MILK!
WHIMPER
SUGURI-TAN...

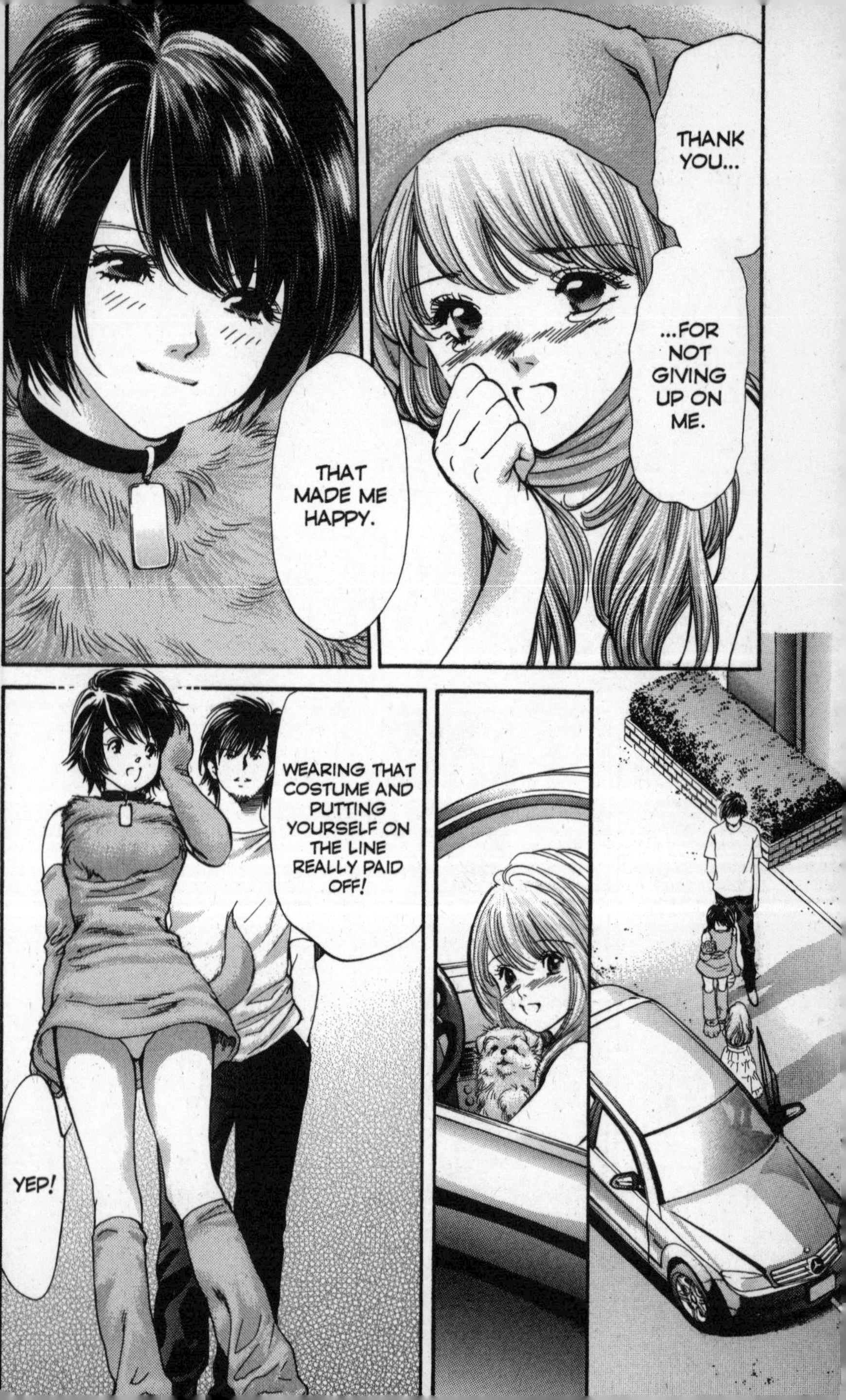
THANK YOU...
...FOR NOT GIVING UP ON ME.
THAT MADE ME HAPPY.
WEARING THAT COSTUME AND PUTTING YOURSELF ON THE LINE REALLY PAID OFF!
YEP!

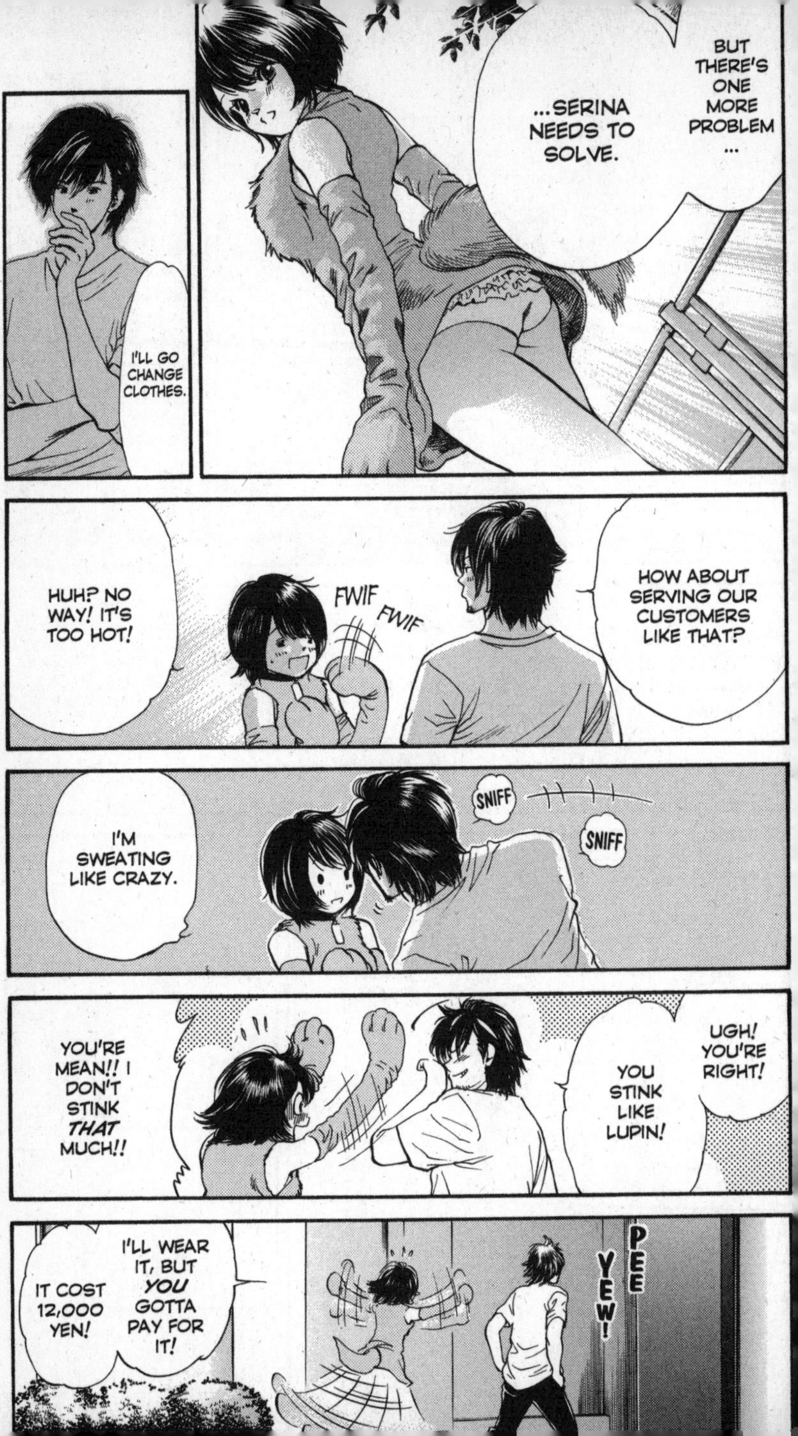
BUT THERE'S ONE MORE PROBLEM ...
...SERINA NEEDS TO SOLVE.
I'LL GO CHANGE CLOTHES.
HOW ABOUT SERVING OUR CUSTOMERS LIKE THAT?
FWIF FWIF
HUH? NO WAY! IT'S TOO HOT!
SNIFF
SNIFF
I'M SWEATING LIKE CRAZY.
UGH! YOU'RE RIGHT!
YOU STINK LIKE LUPIN!
YOU'RE MEAN!! I DON'T STINK *THAT* MUCH!!
PEE YEW!
I'LL WEAR IT, BUT *YOU* GOTTA PAY FOR IT!
IT COST 12,000 YEN!

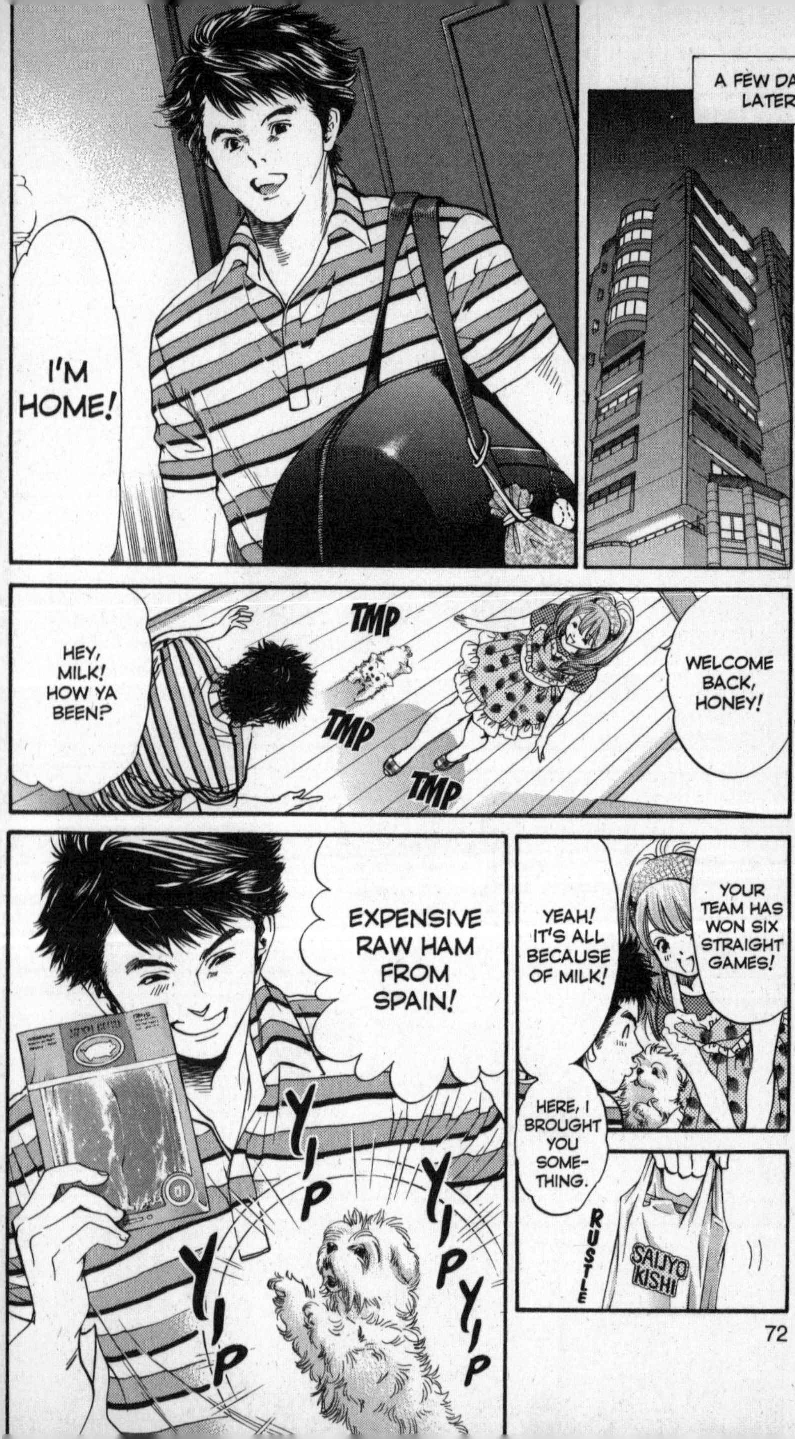
A FEW DAYS LATER
I'M HOME!
WELCOME BACK, HONEY!
TMP
TMP
TMP
HEY, MILK! HOW YA BEEN?
YOUR TEAM HAS WON SIX STRAIGHT GAMES!
YEAH! IT'S ALL BECAUSE OF MILK!
HERE, I BROUGHT YOU SOME-THING.
RUSTLE
SAIJYO KISHI
EXPENSIVE RAW HAM FROM SPAIN!
YIP
YIP
YIP
YIP
YIP

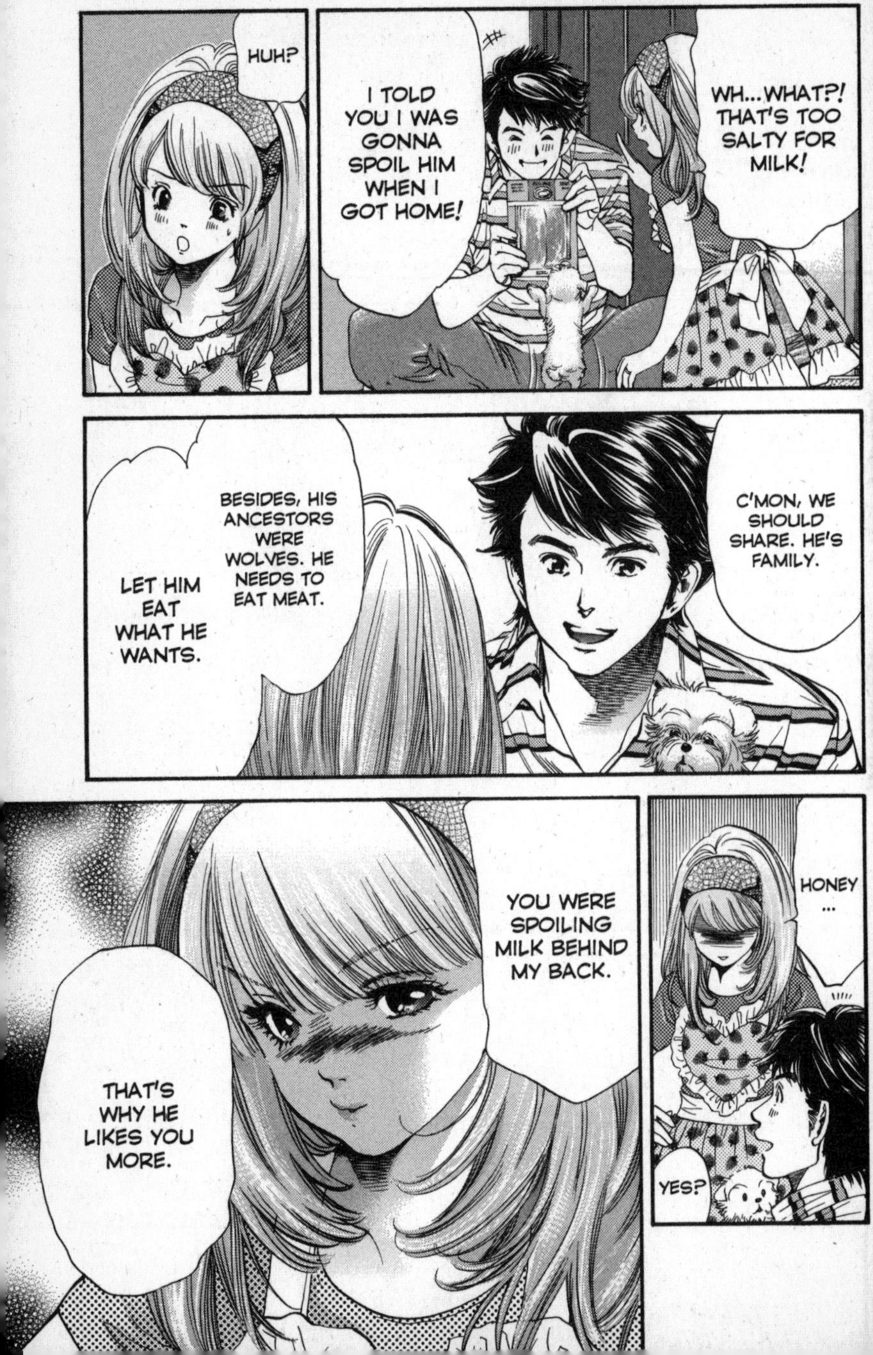
WH...WHAT?! THAT'S TOO SALTY FOR MILK!
I TOLD YOU I WAS GONNA SPOIL HIM WHEN I GOT HOME!
HUH?
C'MON, WE SHOULD SHARE. HE'S FAMILY.
BESIDES, HIS ANCESTORS WERE WOLVES. HE NEEDS TO EAT MEAT.
LET HIM EAT WHAT HE WANTS.
HONEY ...
YES?
YOU WERE SPOILING MILK BEHIND MY BACK.
THAT'S WHY HE LIKES YOU MORE.

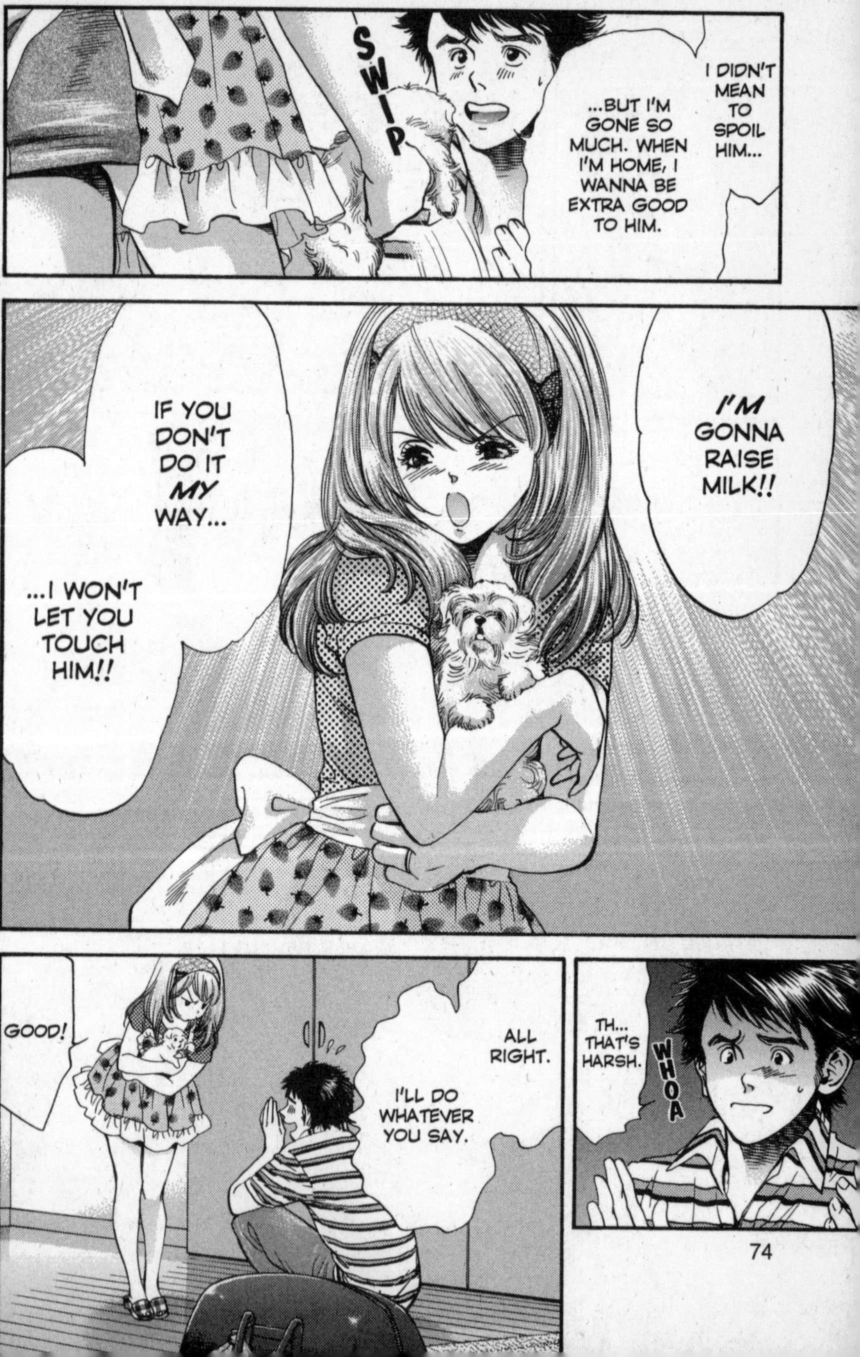
I DIDN'T MEAN TO SPOIL HIM...
...BUT I'M GONE SO MUCH. WHEN I'M HOME, I WANNA BE EXTRA GOOD TO HIM.
SWIP
I'M GONNA RAISE MILK!!
IF YOU DON'T DO IT *MY* WAY...
...I WON'T LET YOU TOUCH HIM!!
TH... THAT'S HARSH.
WHOA
ALL RIGHT.
I'LL DO WHATEVER YOU SAY.
GOOD!

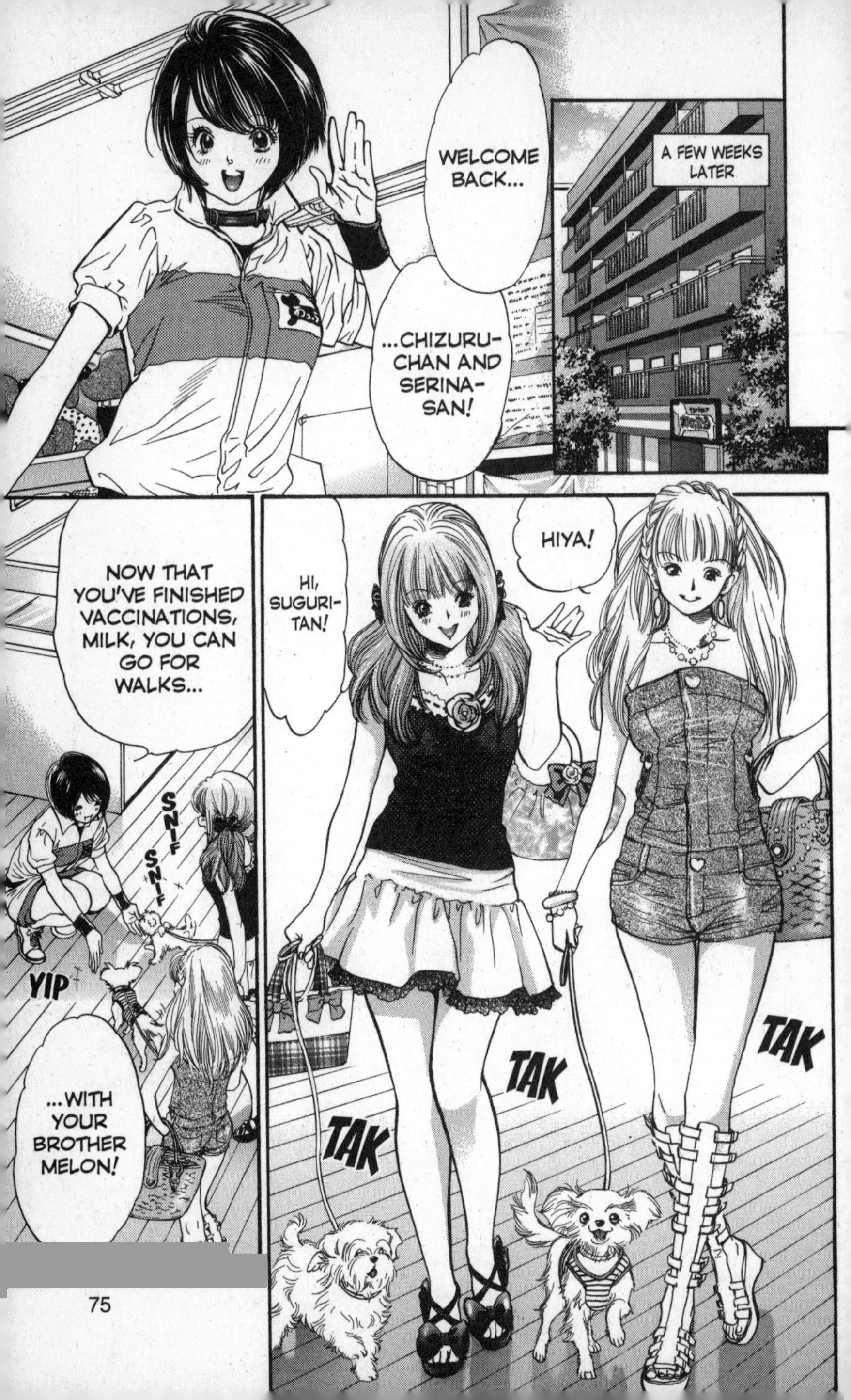
A FEW WEEKS LATER
WELCOME BACK...
...CHIZURU-CHAN AND SERINA-SAN!
HIYA!
HI, SUGURI-TAN!
TAK
TAK
TAK
NOW THAT YOU'VE FINISHED VACCINATIONS, MILK, YOU CAN GO FOR WALKS...
SNIF
SNIF
YIP
...WITH YOUR BROTHER MELON!

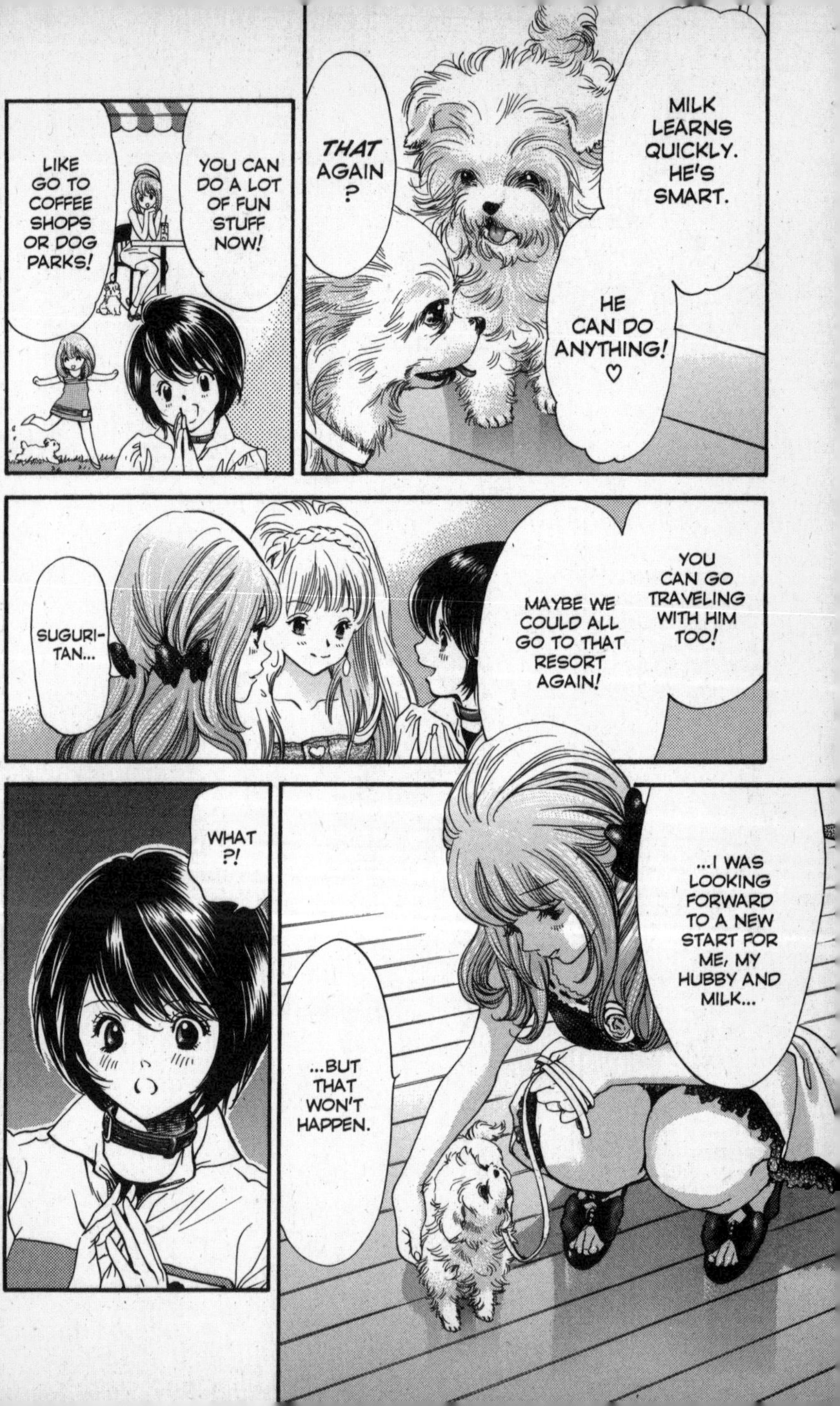
MILK LEARNS QUICKLY. HE'S SMART.
HE CAN DO ANYTHING! ♡
THAT AGAIN?
YOU CAN DO A LOT OF FUN STUFF NOW!
LIKE GO TO COFFEE SHOPS OR DOG PARKS!
YOU CAN GO TRAVELING WITH HIM TOO!
MAYBE WE COULD ALL GO TO THAT RESORT AGAIN!
SUGURI-TAN...
...I WAS LOOKING FORWARD TO A NEW START FOR ME, MY HUBBY AND MILK...
...BUT THAT WON'T HAPPEN.
WHAT?!

WHY NOT?!

I CAN'T DEVOTE ALL MY ATTENTION TO MILK.

WHIIIIINE

?

HMM?

HEE

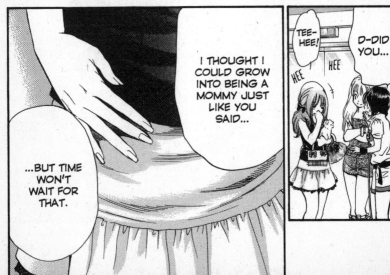

I THOUGHT I COULD GROW INTO BEING A MOMMY JUST LIKE YOU SAID...

...BUT TIME WON'T WAIT FOR THAT.

TEE-HEE!

HEE

HEE

D-DID YOU...

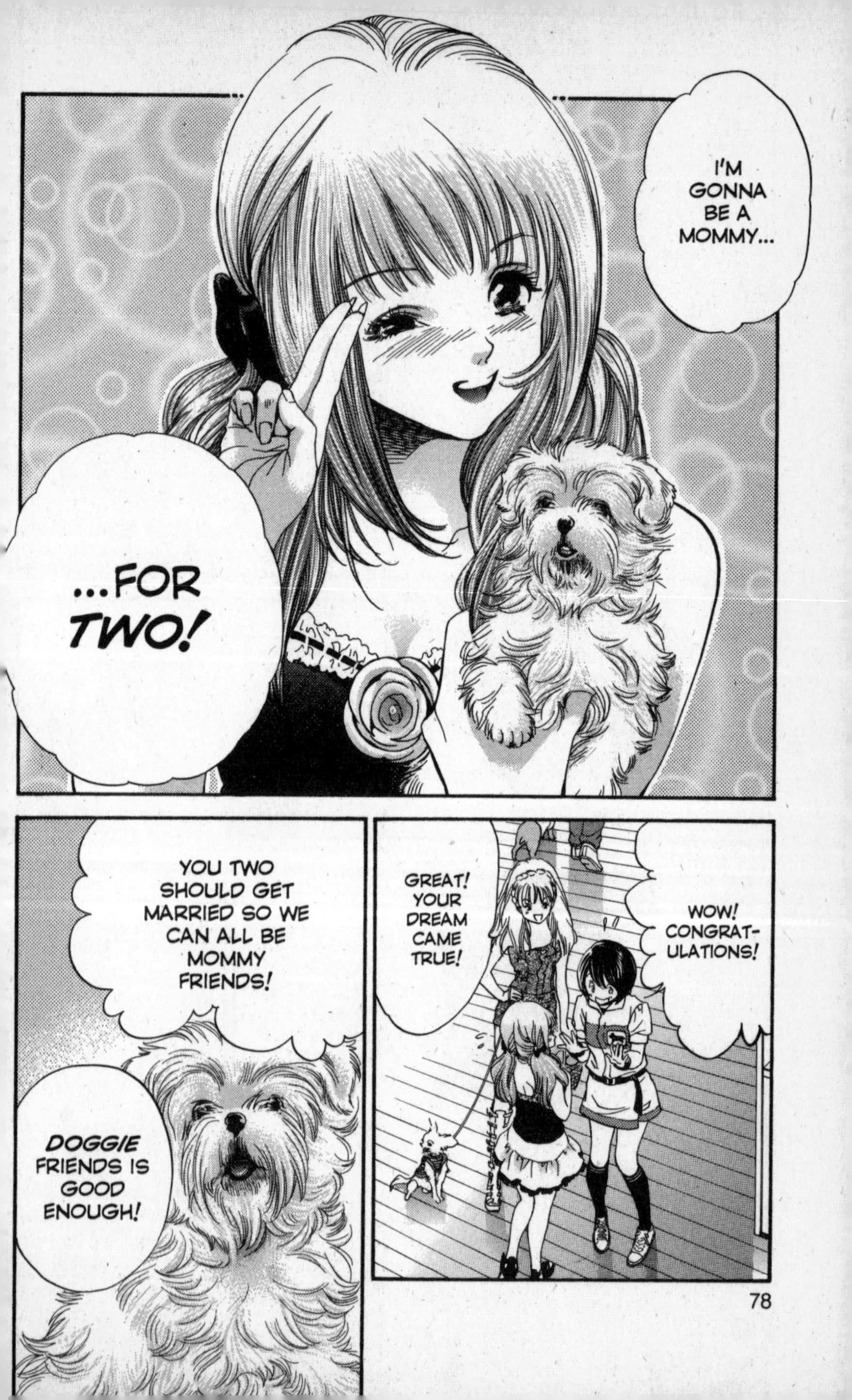
I'M GONNA BE A MOMMY...
...FOR *TWO!*
WOW! CONGRAT-ULATIONS!
GREAT! YOUR DREAM CAME TRUE!
YOU TWO SHOULD GET MARRIED SO WE CAN ALL BE MOMMY FRIENDS!
DOGGIE FRIENDS IS GOOD ENOUGH!

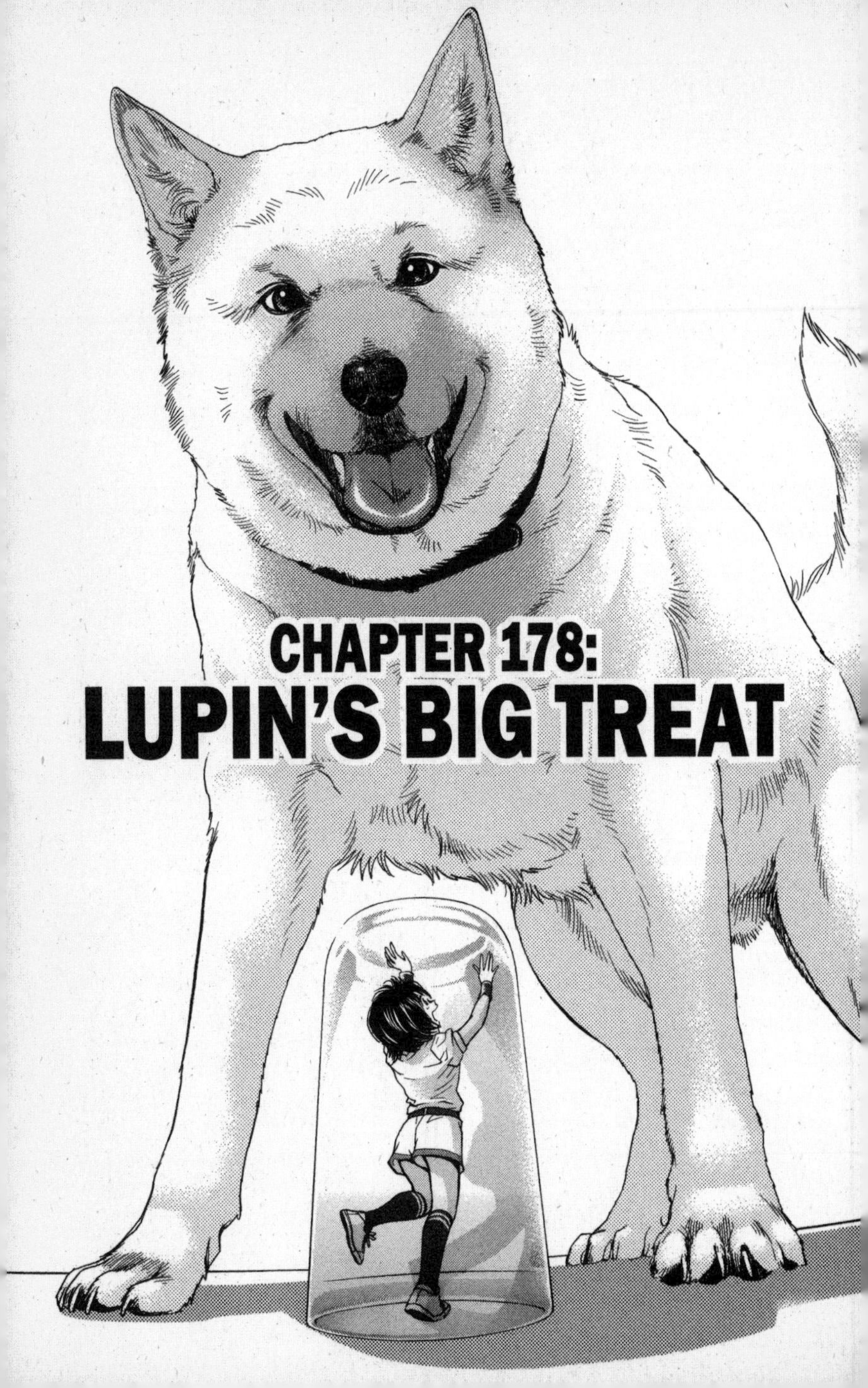
CHAPTER 178:
LUPIN'S BIG TREAT

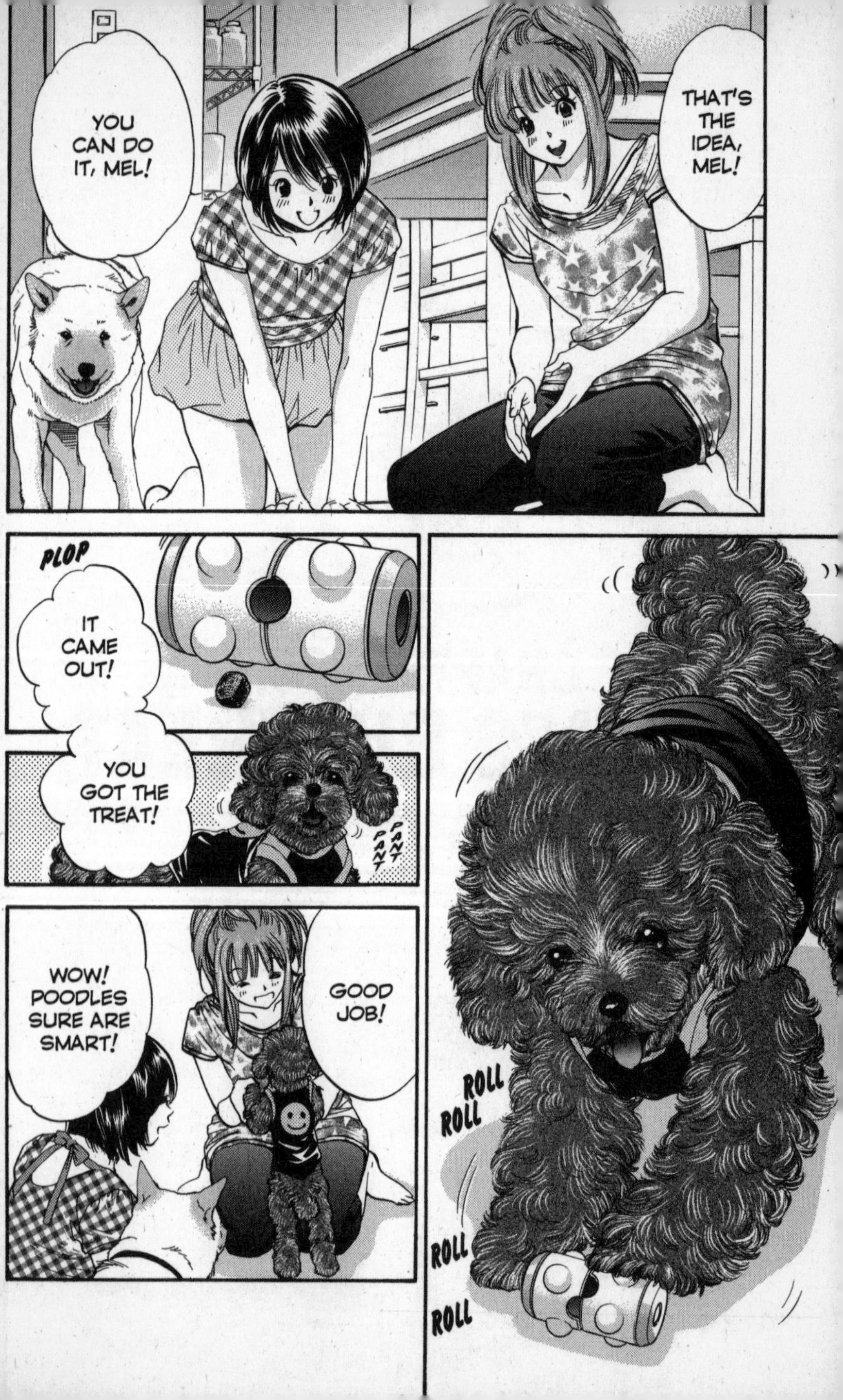
THAT'S THE IDEA, MEL!
YOU CAN DO IT, MEL!
ROLL ROLL
ROLL
ROLL
PLOP
IT CAME OUT!
YOU GOT THE TREAT!
PANT PANT
GOOD JOB!
WOW! POODLES SURE ARE SMART!

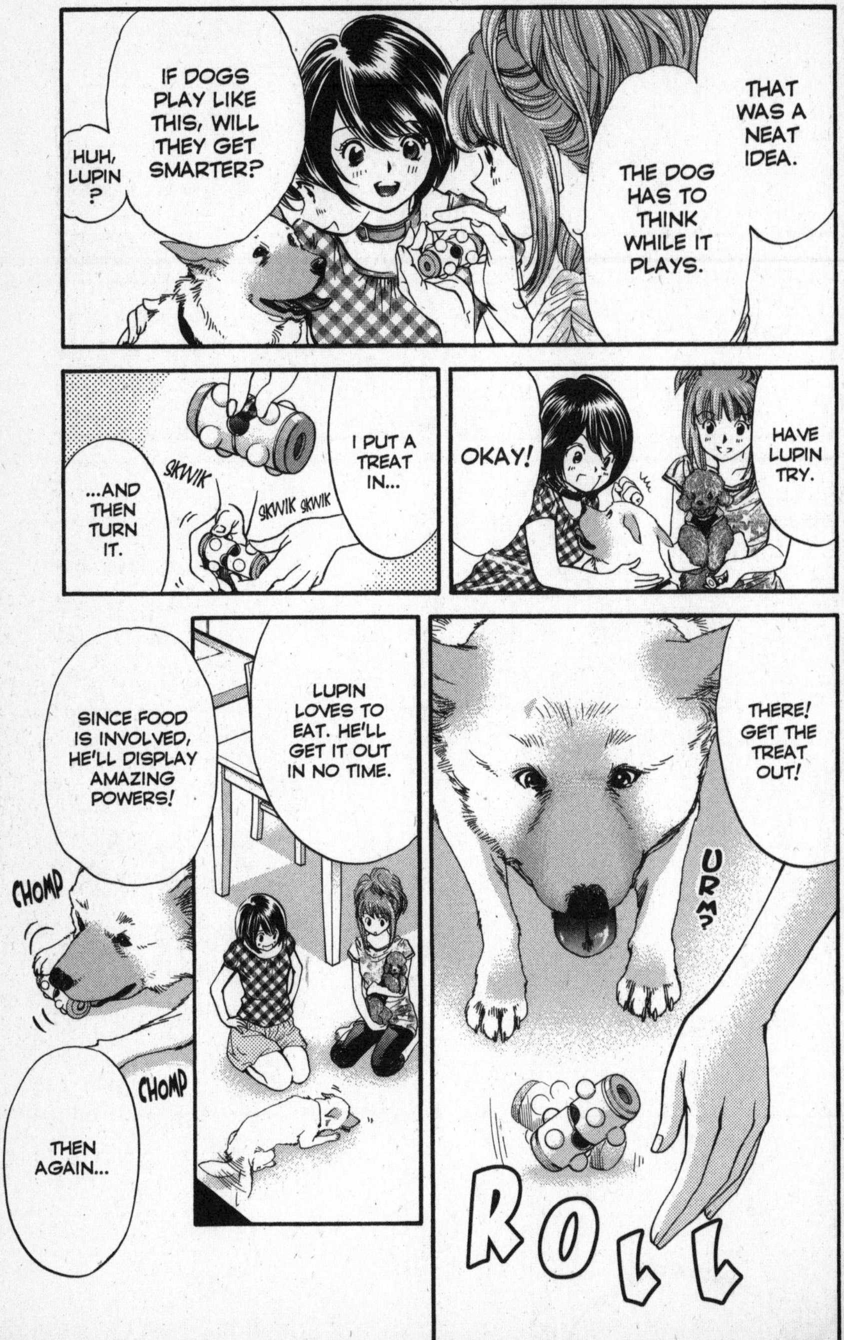
THAT WAS A NEAT IDEA.
THE DOG HAS TO THINK WHILE IT PLAYS.
IF DOGS PLAY LIKE THIS, WILL THEY GET SMARTER?
HUH, LUPIN?
HAVE LUPIN TRY.
OKAY!
I PUT A TREAT IN...
SKWIK
SKWIK SKWIK
...AND THEN TURN IT.
THERE! GET THE TREAT OUT!
URM?
ROLL
LUPIN LOVES TO EAT. HE'LL GET IT OUT IN NO TIME.
SINCE FOOD IS INVOLVED, HE'LL DISPLAY AMAZING POWERS!
CHOMP
CHOMP
THEN AGAIN...

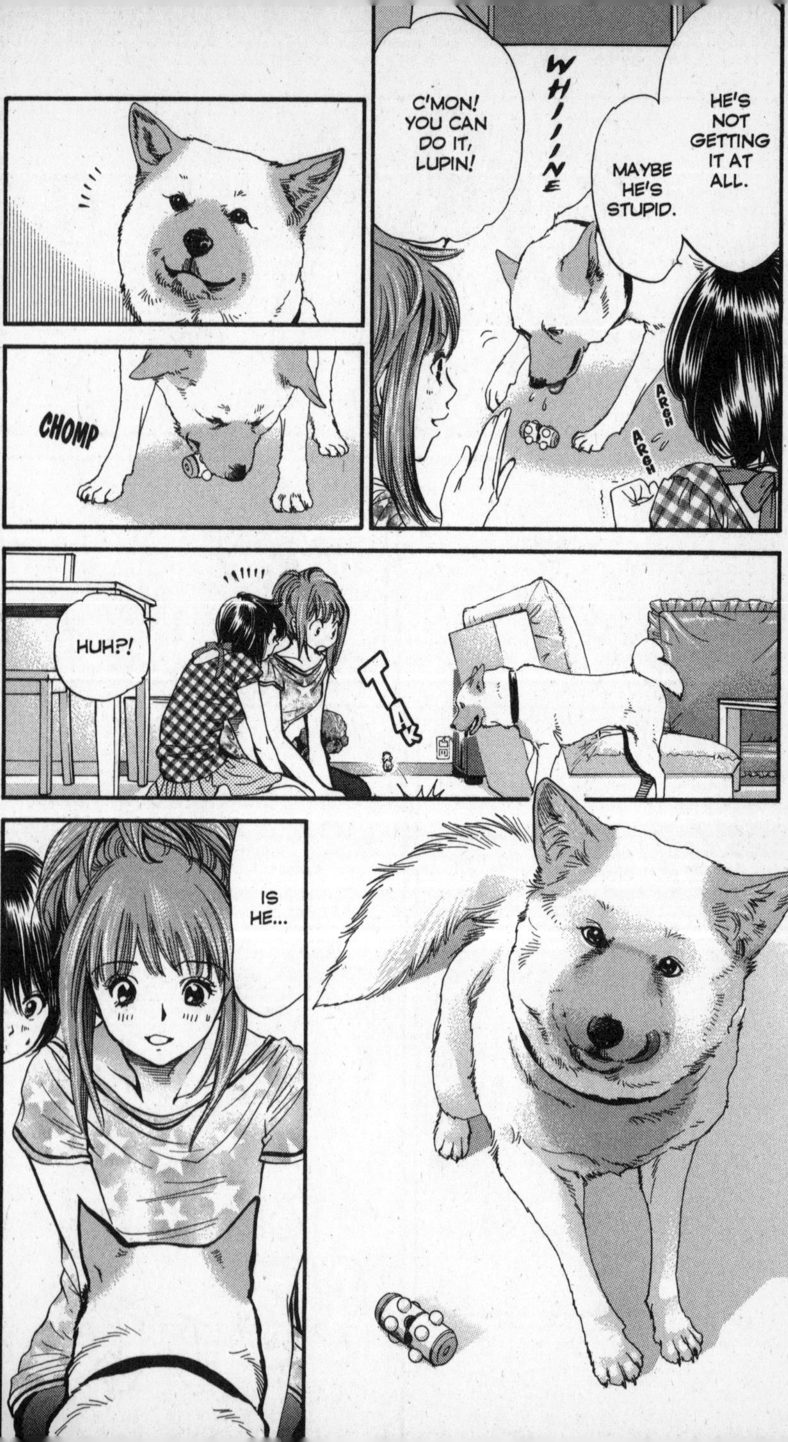
HE'S NOT GETTING IT AT ALL.
MAYBE HE'S STUPID.
WHIIIINE
C'MON! YOU CAN DO IT, LUPIN!
ARGH
ARGH
CHOMP
TAK
HUH?!
IS HE...

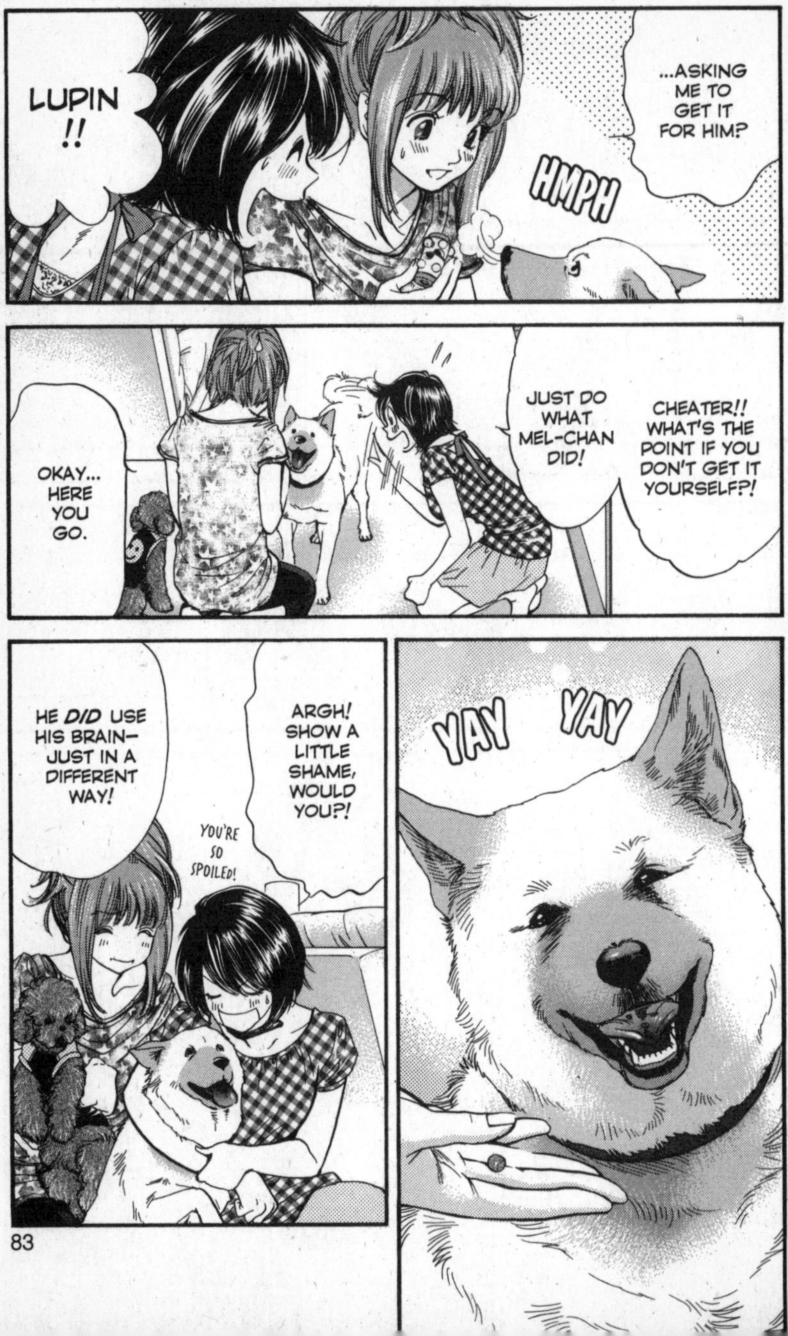
...ASKING ME TO GET IT FOR HIM?
HMPH
LUPIN!!
CHEATER!! WHAT'S THE POINT IF YOU DON'T GET IT YOURSELF?!
JUST DO WHAT MEL-CHAN DID!
OKAY... HERE YOU GO.
YAY YAY
ARGH! SHOW A LITTLE SHAME, WOULD YOU?!
HE *DID* USE HIS BRAIN–JUST IN A DIFFERENT WAY!
YOU'RE SO SPOILED!

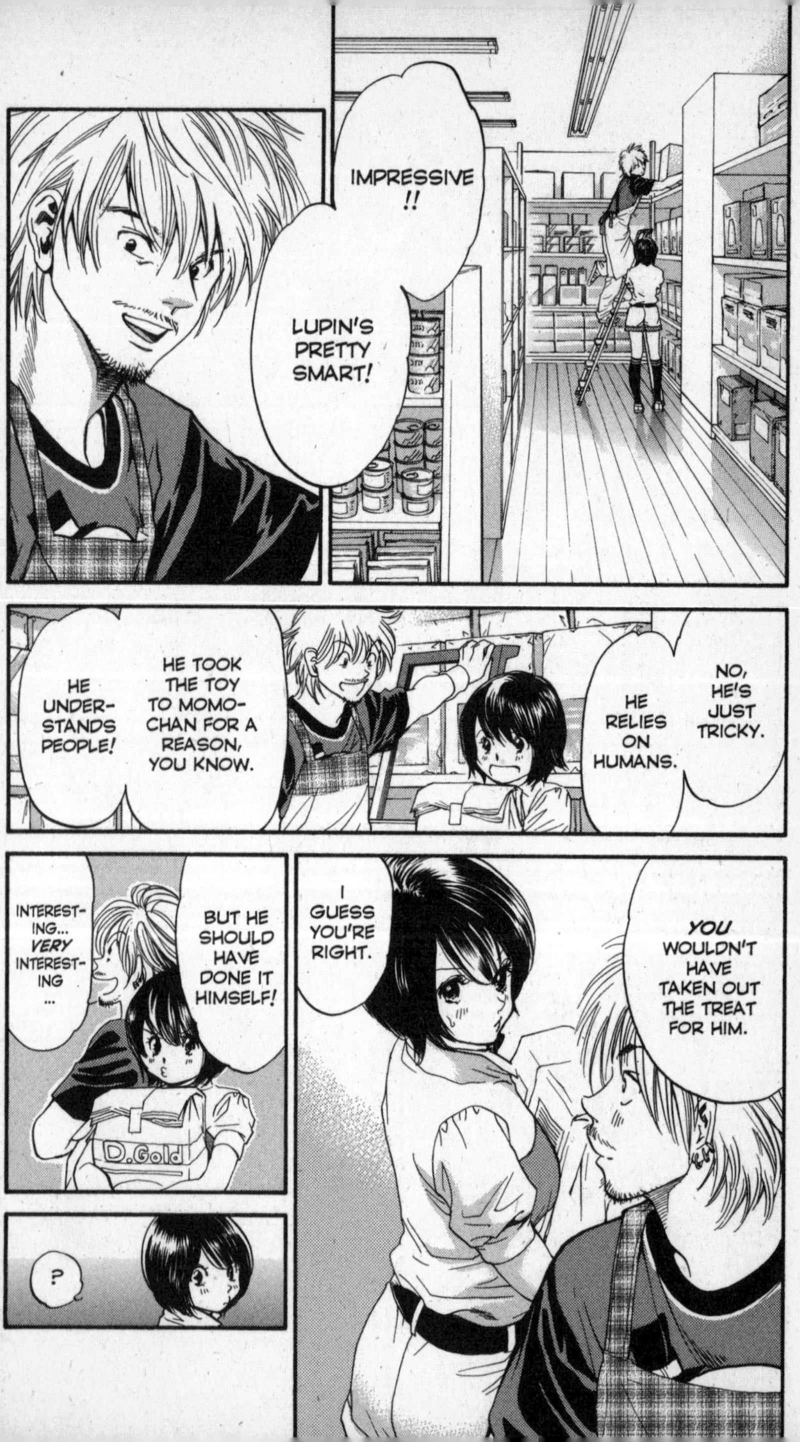
IMPRESSIVE!!
LUPIN'S PRETTY SMART!
NO, HE'S JUST TRICKY.
HE RELIES ON HUMANS.
HE TOOK THE TOY TO MOMO-CHAN FOR A REASON, YOU KNOW.
HE UNDER-STANDS PEOPLE!
YOU WOULDN'T HAVE TAKEN OUT THE TREAT FOR HIM.
I GUESS YOU'RE RIGHT.
BUT HE SHOULD HAVE DONE IT HIMSELF!
INTERESTING... *VERY* INTERESTING...
D.Gold
?

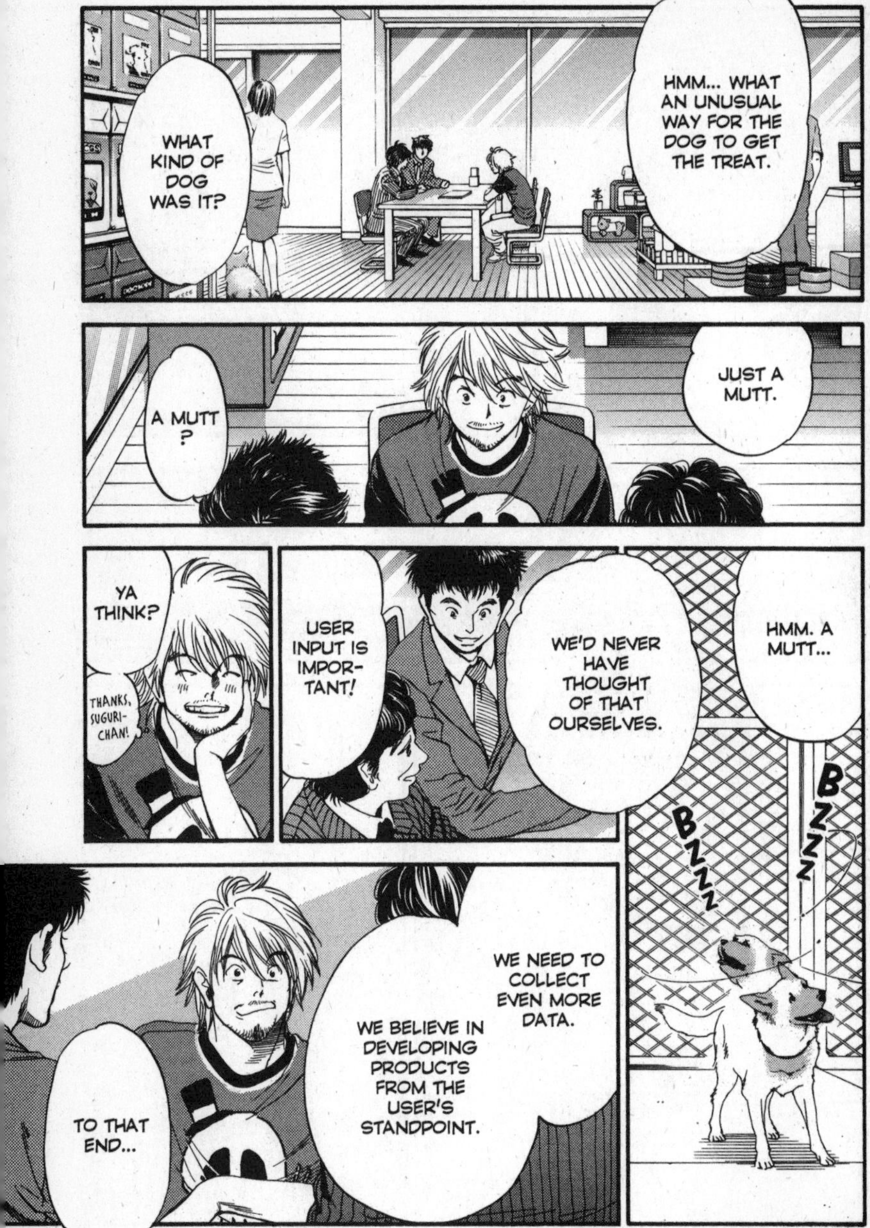
HMM... WHAT AN UNUSUAL WAY FOR THE DOG TO GET THE TREAT.
WHAT KIND OF DOG WAS IT?
JUST A MUTT.
A MUTT?
HMM. A MUTT...
BZZZ
BZZZ
WE'D NEVER HAVE THOUGHT OF THAT OURSELVES.
USER INPUT IS IMPOR-TANT!
YA THINK?
THANKS, SUGURI-CHAN!
WE NEED TO COLLECT EVEN MORE DATA.
WE BELIEVE IN DEVELOPING PRODUCTS FROM THE USER'S STANDPOINT.
TO THAT END...

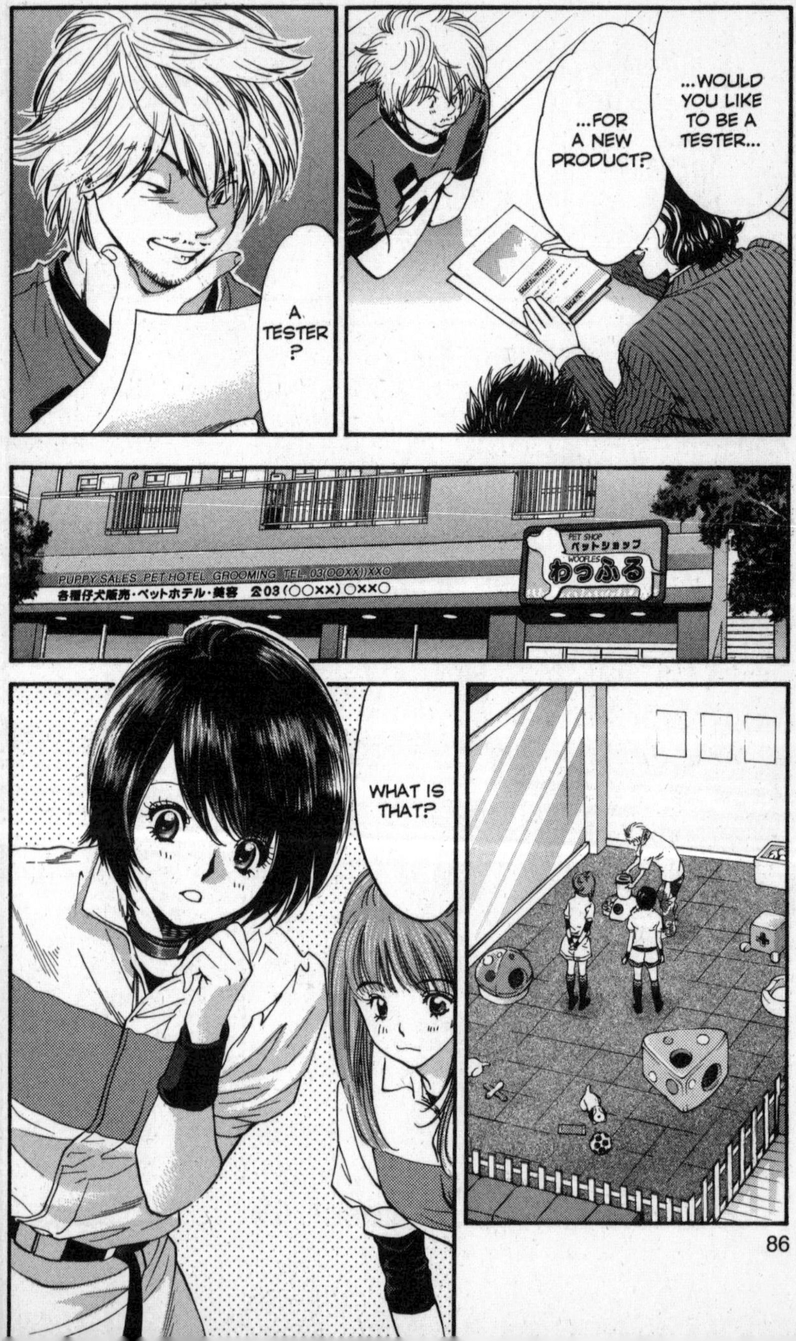
...WOULD YOU LIKE TO BE A TESTER...
...FOR A NEW PRODUCT?
A TESTER?
PET SHOP
ペットショップ
WOOFLES
わつふる
PUPPY SALES PET HOTEL GROOMING TEL. 03(OOXX)XXO
各種仔犬販売・ペットホテル・美容 ☎03(○○××)○××○
WHAT IS THAT?

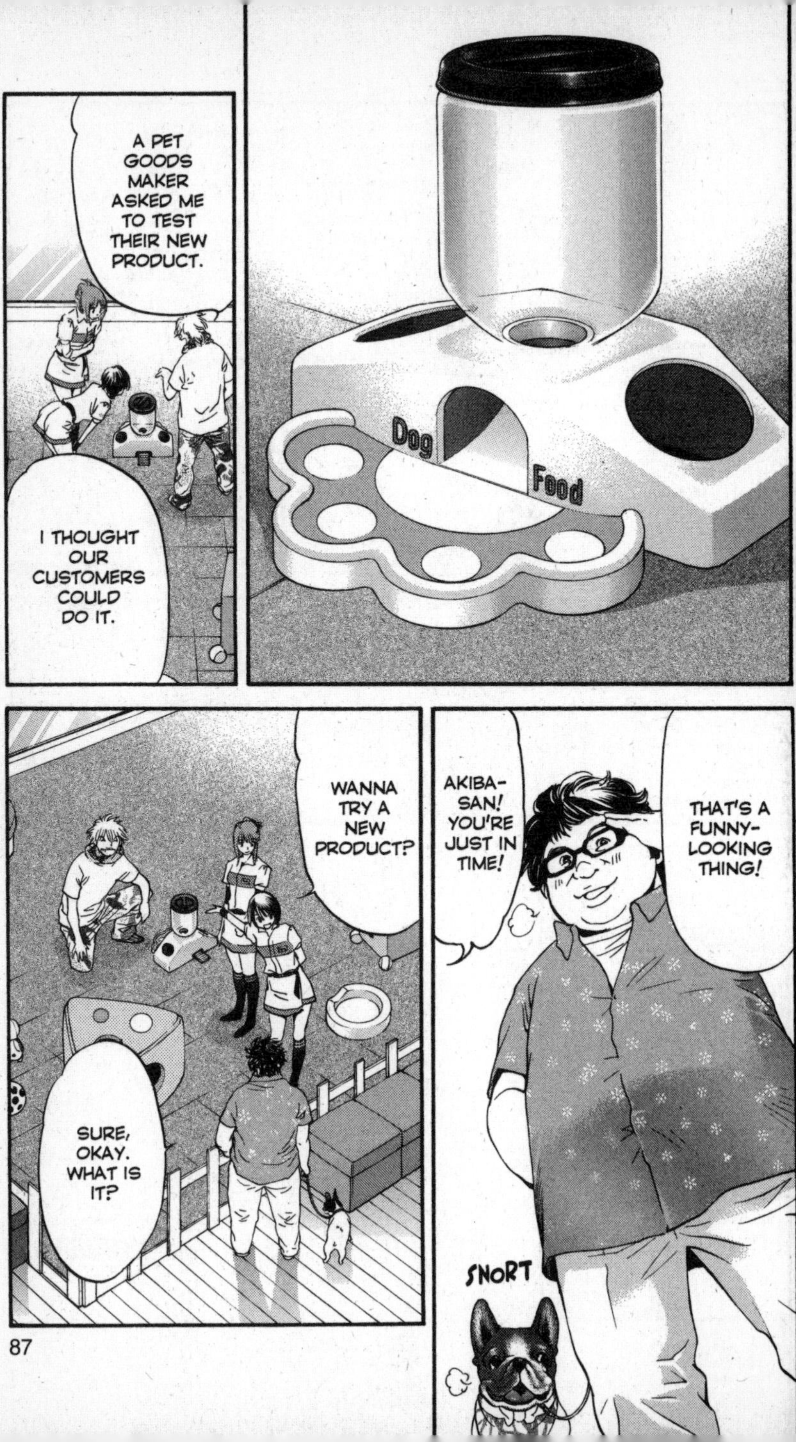
Dog
Food
A PET GOODS MAKER ASKED ME TO TEST THEIR NEW PRODUCT.
I THOUGHT OUR CUSTOMERS COULD DO IT.
THAT'S A FUNNY-LOOKING THING!
AKIBA-SAN! YOU'RE JUST IN TIME!
SNORT
WANNA TRY A NEW PRODUCT?
SURE, OKAY. WHAT IS IT?

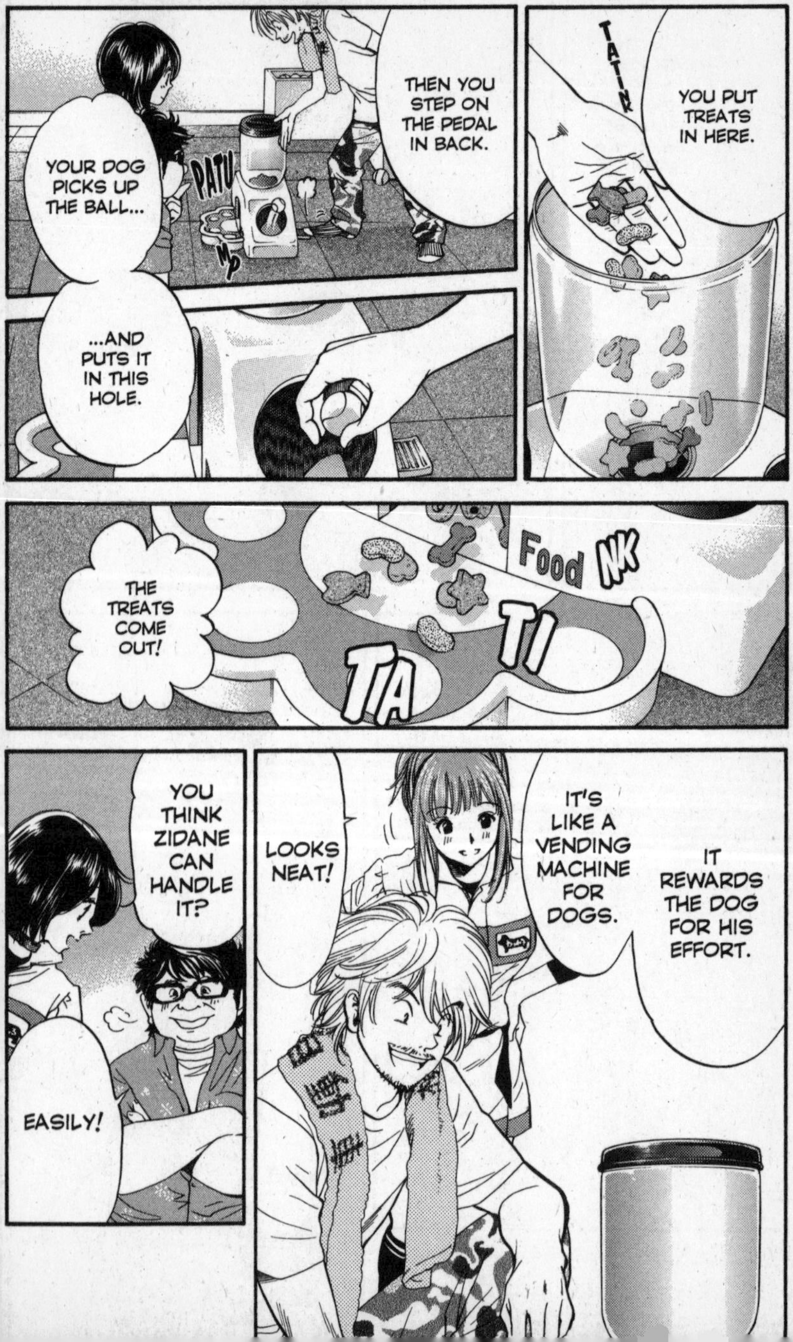
TATINK
YOU PUT TREATS IN HERE.
THEN YOU STEP ON THE PEDAL IN BACK.
YOUR DOG PICKS UP THE BALL...
PATU
MP
...AND PUTS IT IN THIS HOLE.
Food
NK
TI
TA
THE TREATS COME OUT!
IT REWARDS THE DOG FOR HIS EFFORT.
IT'S LIKE A VENDING MACHINE FOR DOGS.
LOOKS NEAT!
YOU THINK ZIDANE CAN HANDLE IT?
EASILY!

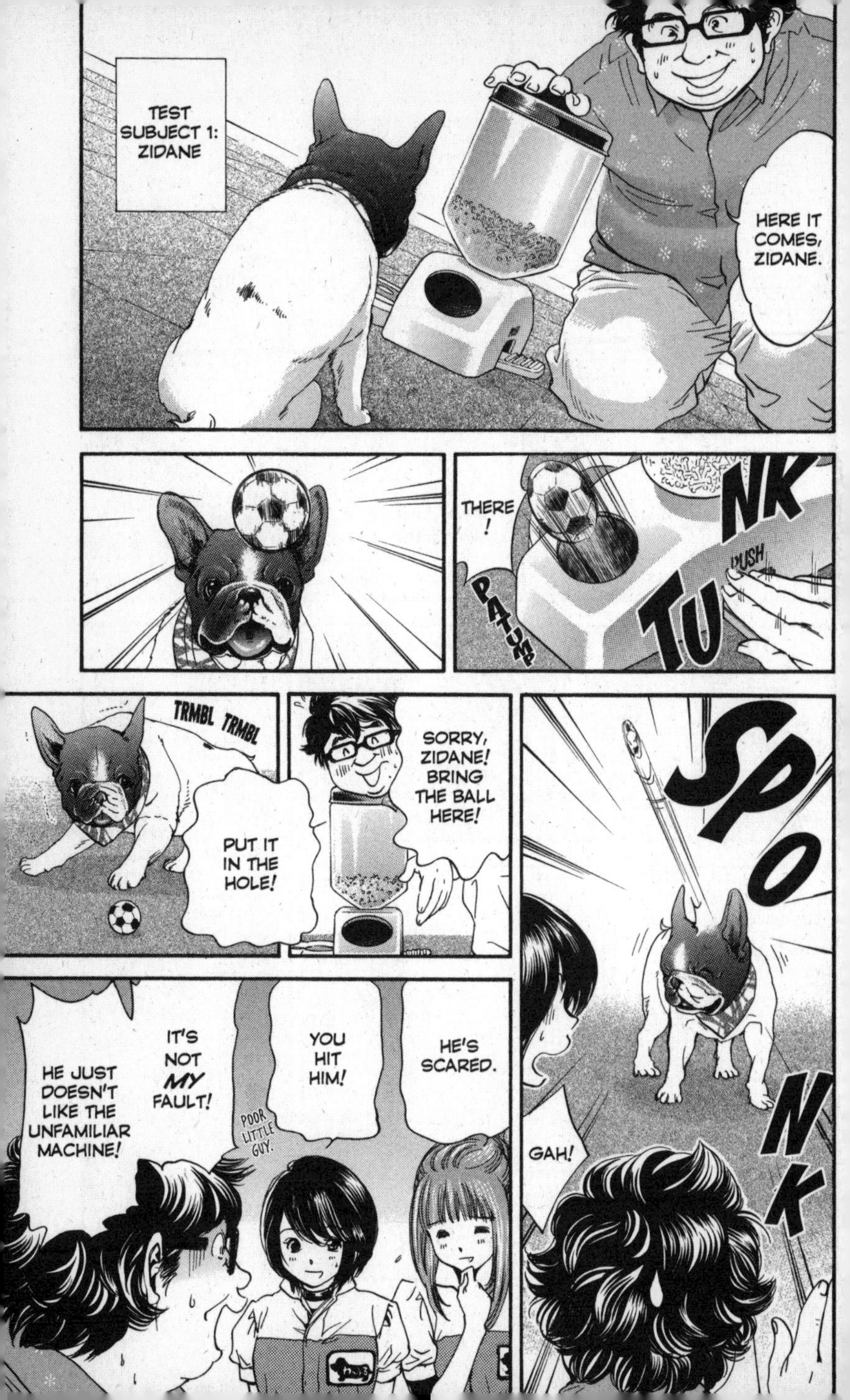
TEST SUBJECT 1: ZIDANE
HERE IT COMES, ZIDANE.
THERE!
PATUMP
TUNK
PUSH
SPONK
GAH!
SORRY, ZIDANE! BRING THE BALL HERE!
TRMBL TRMBL
PUT IT IN THE HOLE!
HE'S SCARED.
YOU HIT HIM!
IT'S NOT MY FAULT!
POOR LITTLE GUY.
HE JUST DOESN'T LIKE THE UNFAMILIAR MACHINE!

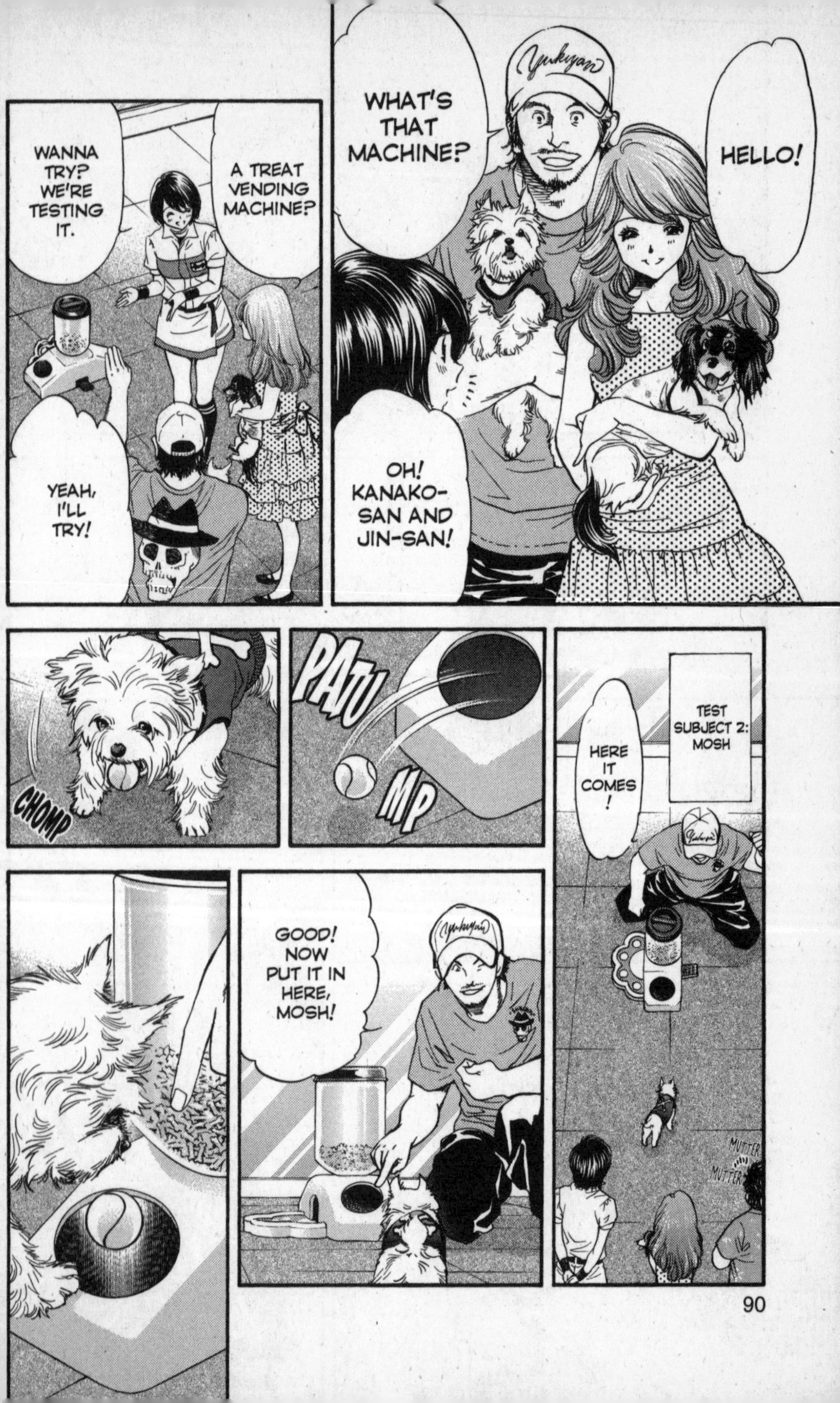
HELLO!
WHAT'S THAT MACHINE?
OH! KANAKO-SAN AND JIN-SAN!
A TREAT VENDING MACHINE?
WANNA TRY? WE'RE TESTING IT.
YEAH, I'LL TRY!
TEST SUBJECT 2: MOSH
HERE IT COMES!
MUTTER
MUTTER
PATUMP
CHOMP
GOOD! NOW PUT IT IN HERE, MOSH!

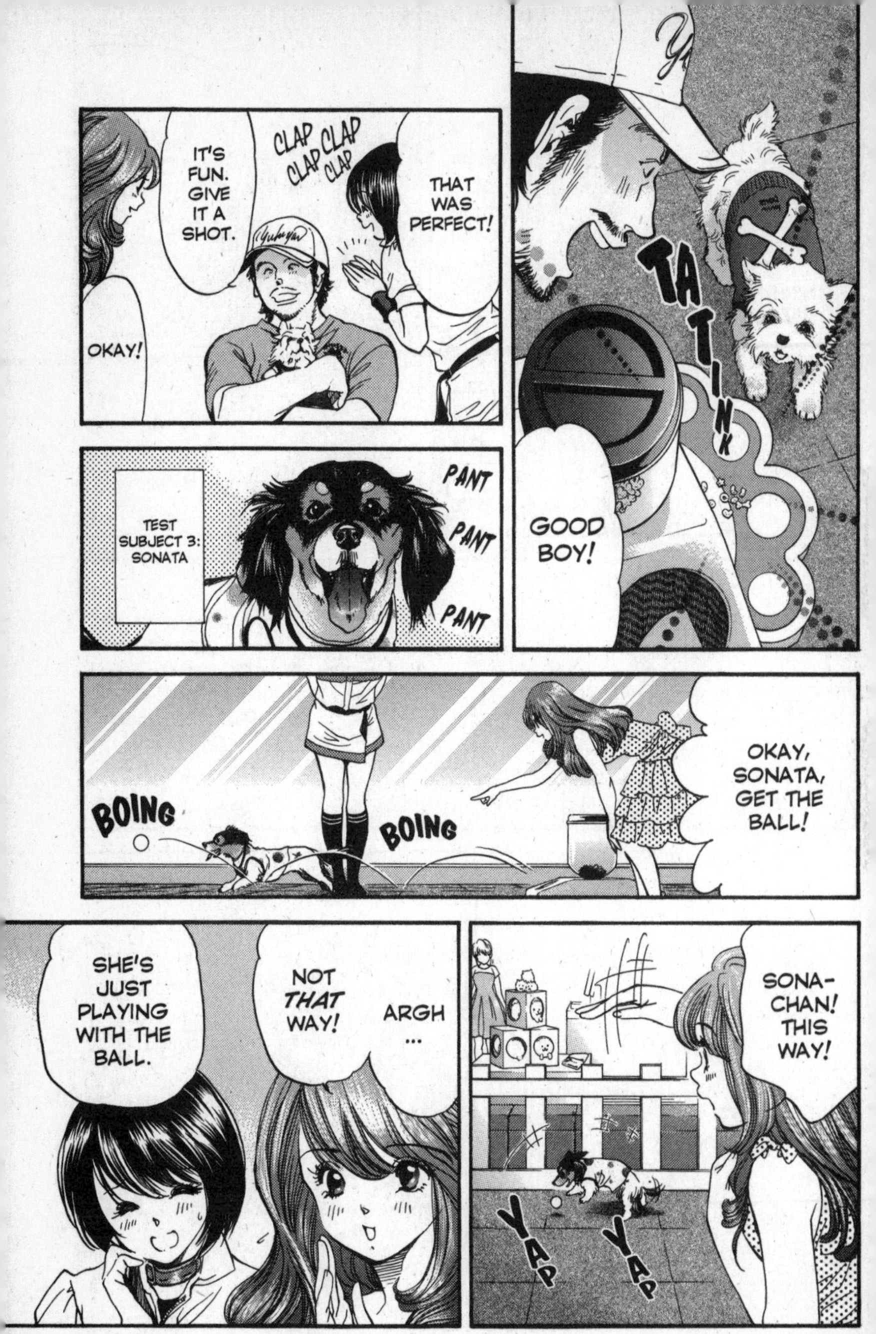
TATINK
GOOD BOY!
THAT WAS PERFECT!
CLAP CLAP CLAP CLAP
IT'S FUN. GIVE IT A SHOT.
OKAY!
PANT PANT PANT
TEST SUBJECT 3: SONATA
OKAY, SONATA, GET THE BALL!
BOING
BOING
SONA-CHAN! THIS WAY!
YAP
YAP
ARGH...
NOT *THAT* WAY!
SHE'S JUST PLAYING WITH THE BALL.

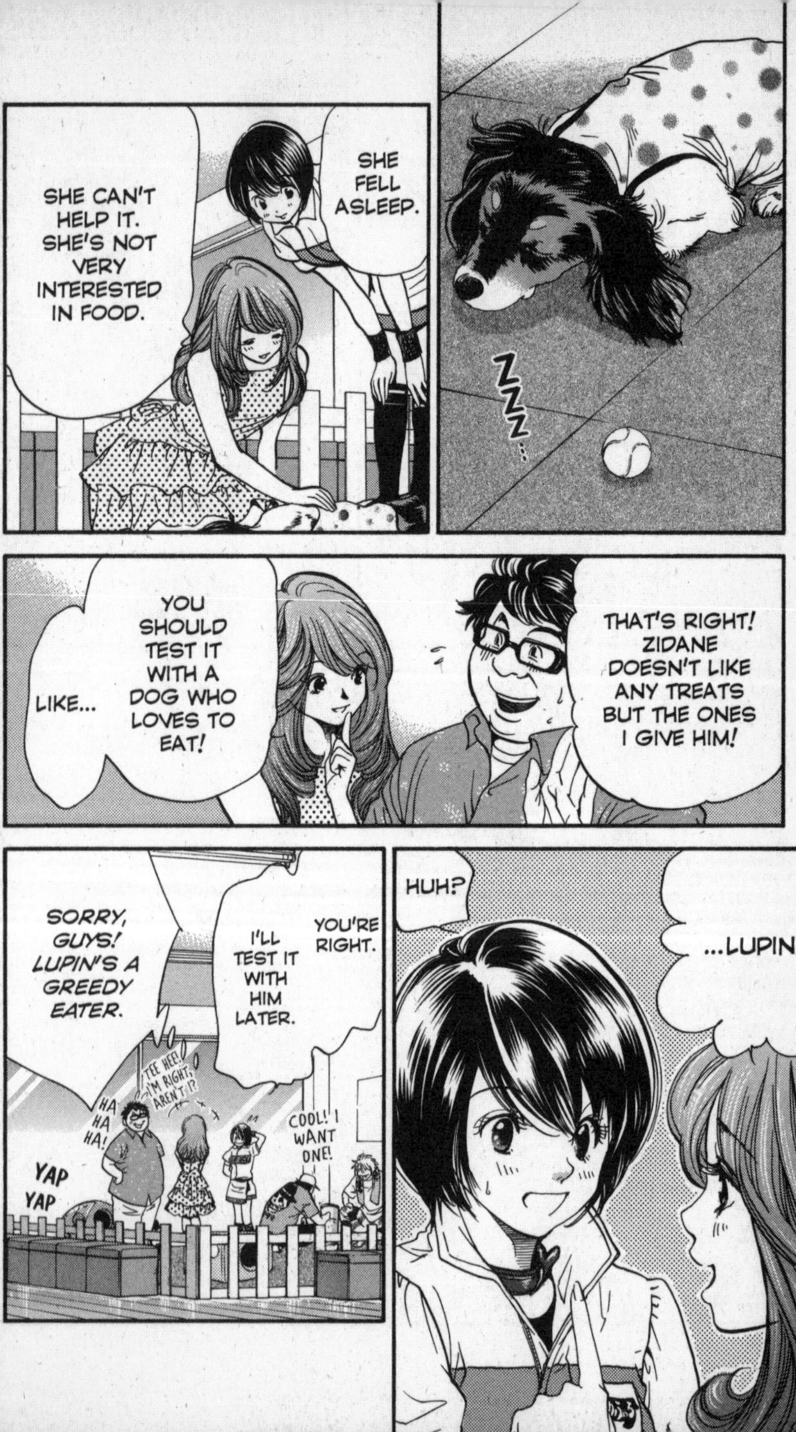
ZZZ...
SHE FELL ASLEEP.
SHE CAN'T HELP IT. SHE'S NOT VERY INTERESTED IN FOOD.
THAT'S RIGHT! ZIDANE DOESN'T LIKE ANY TREATS BUT THE ONES I GIVE HIM!
YOU SHOULD TEST IT WITH A DOG WHO LOVES TO EAT!
LIKE...
...LUPIN!
HUH?
YOU'RE RIGHT.
I'LL TEST IT WITH HIM LATER.
SORRY, GUYS! LUPIN'S A GREEDY EATER.
COOL! I WANT ONE!
TEE HEE! I'M RIGHT, AREN'T I!?
HA HA HA!
YAP YAP

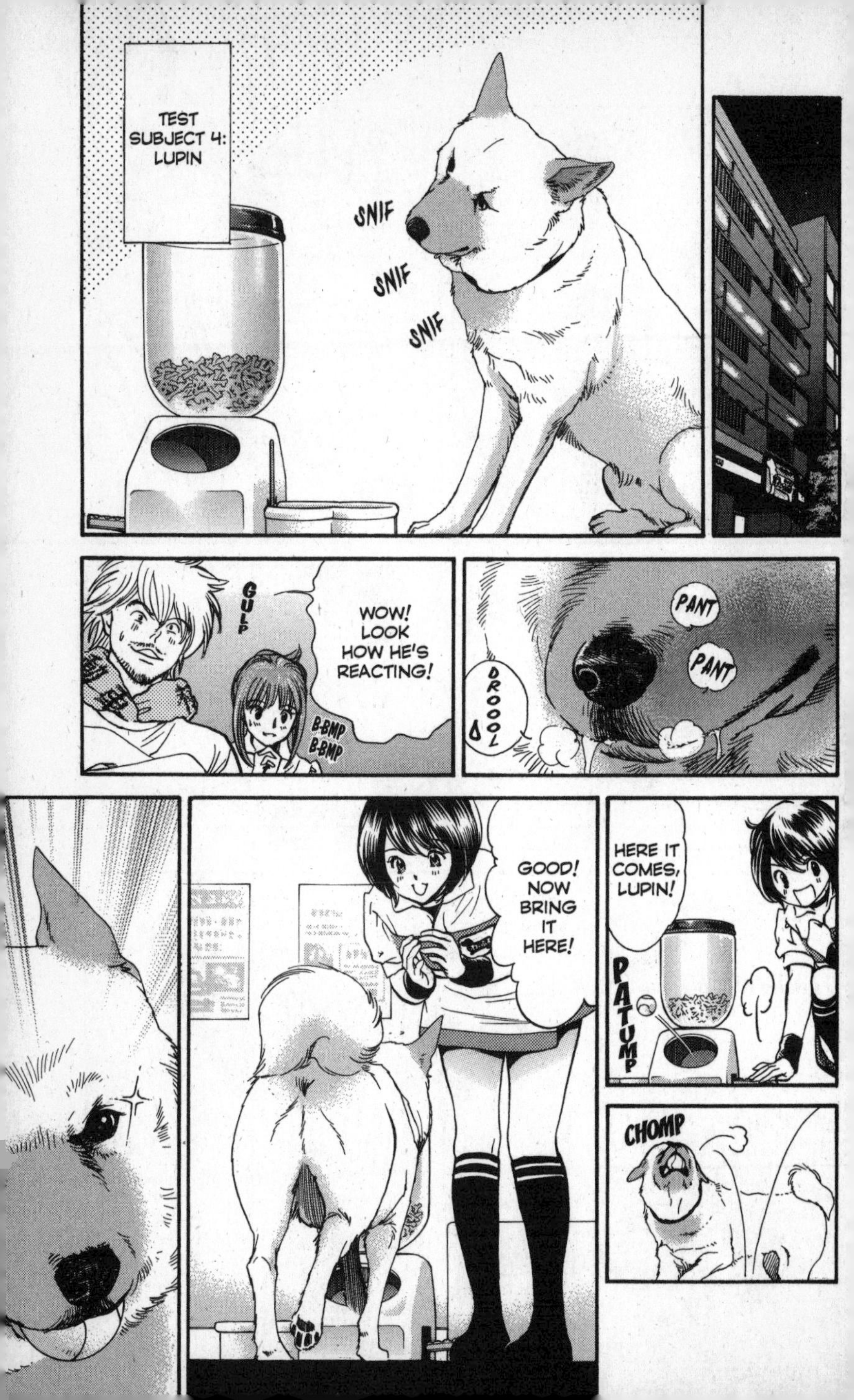
TEST SUBJECT 4: LUPIN
SNIF
SNIF
SNIF
PANT
PANT
DROOOL
WOW! LOOK HOW HE'S REACTING!
GULP
B-BMP B-BMP
HERE IT COMES, LUPIN!
PATUMP
CHOMP
GOOD! NOW BRING IT HERE!

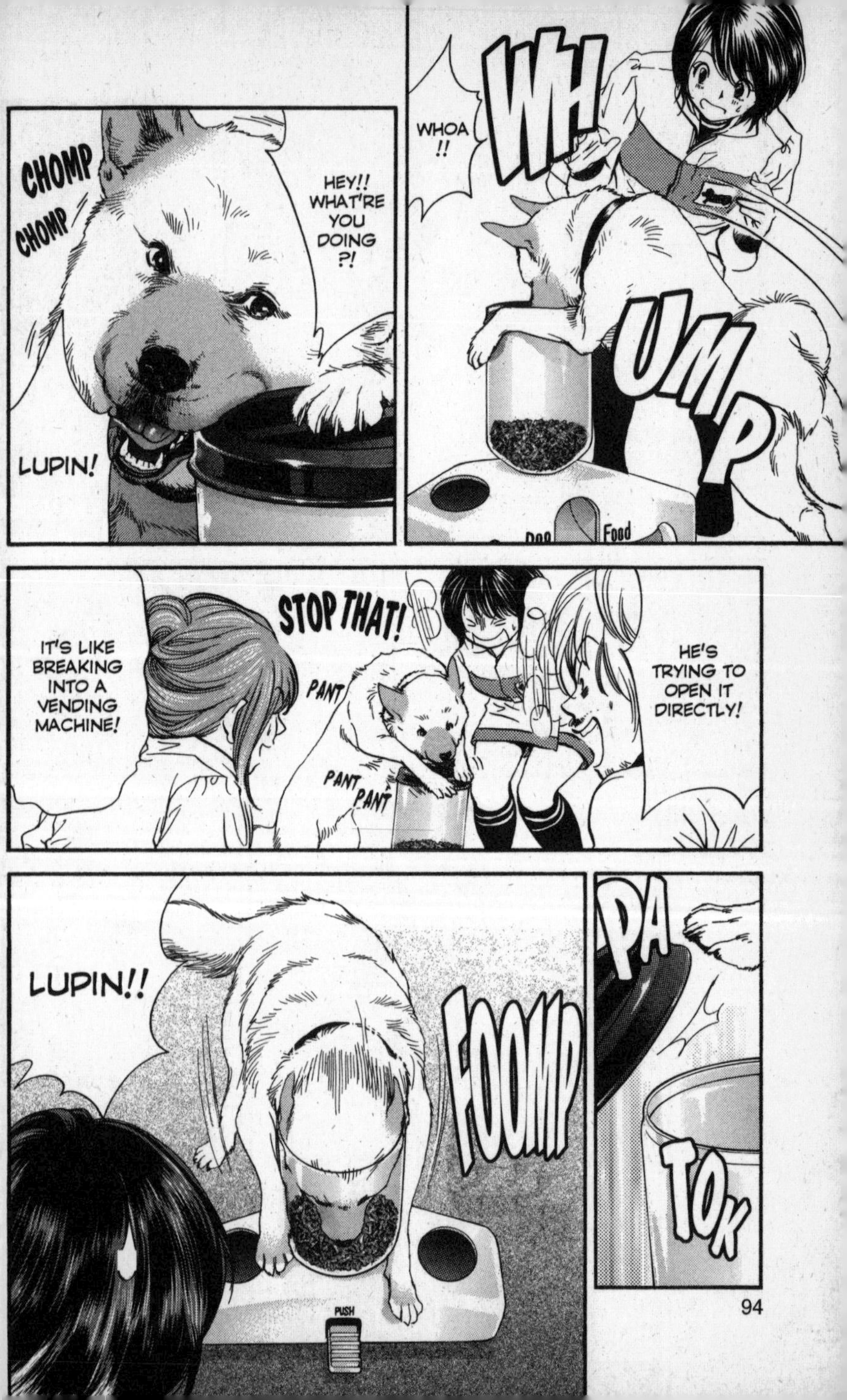
WHOA!!
WH
UMP
Food
CHOMP
CHOMP
HEY!! WHAT'RE YOU DOING?!
LUPIN!
STOP THAT!
HE'S TRYING TO OPEN IT DIRECTLY!
PANT
PANT PANT
IT'S LIKE BREAKING INTO A VENDING MACHINE!
PA
TOK
FOOMP
LUPIN!!
PUSH

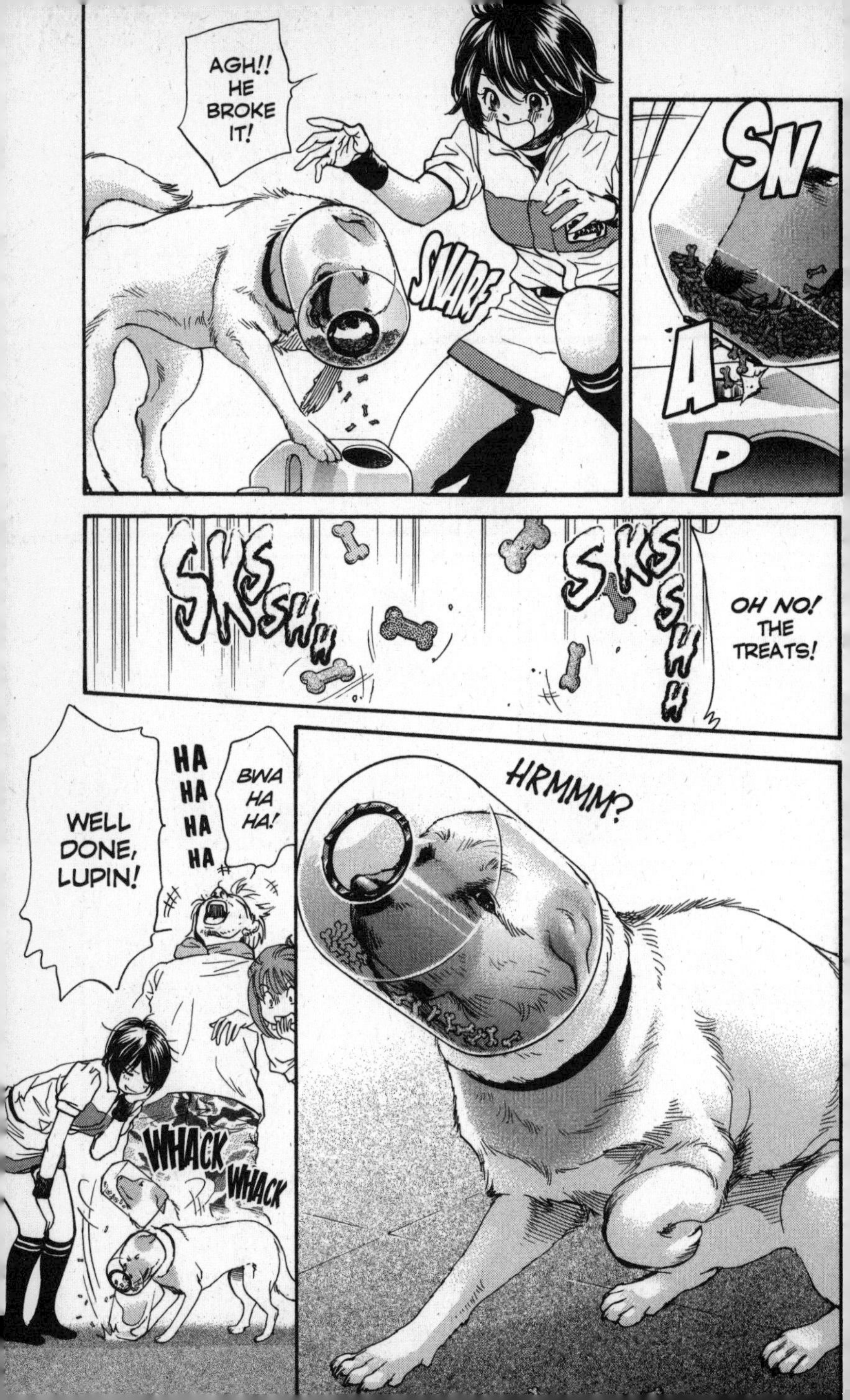
SNAP
AGH!! HE BROKE IT!
SNARF
OH NO! THE TREATS!
SKSSHH
SKSSHH
HRMMM?
BWA HA HA HA!
HA HA HA HA
WELL DONE, LUPIN!
WHACK
WHACK

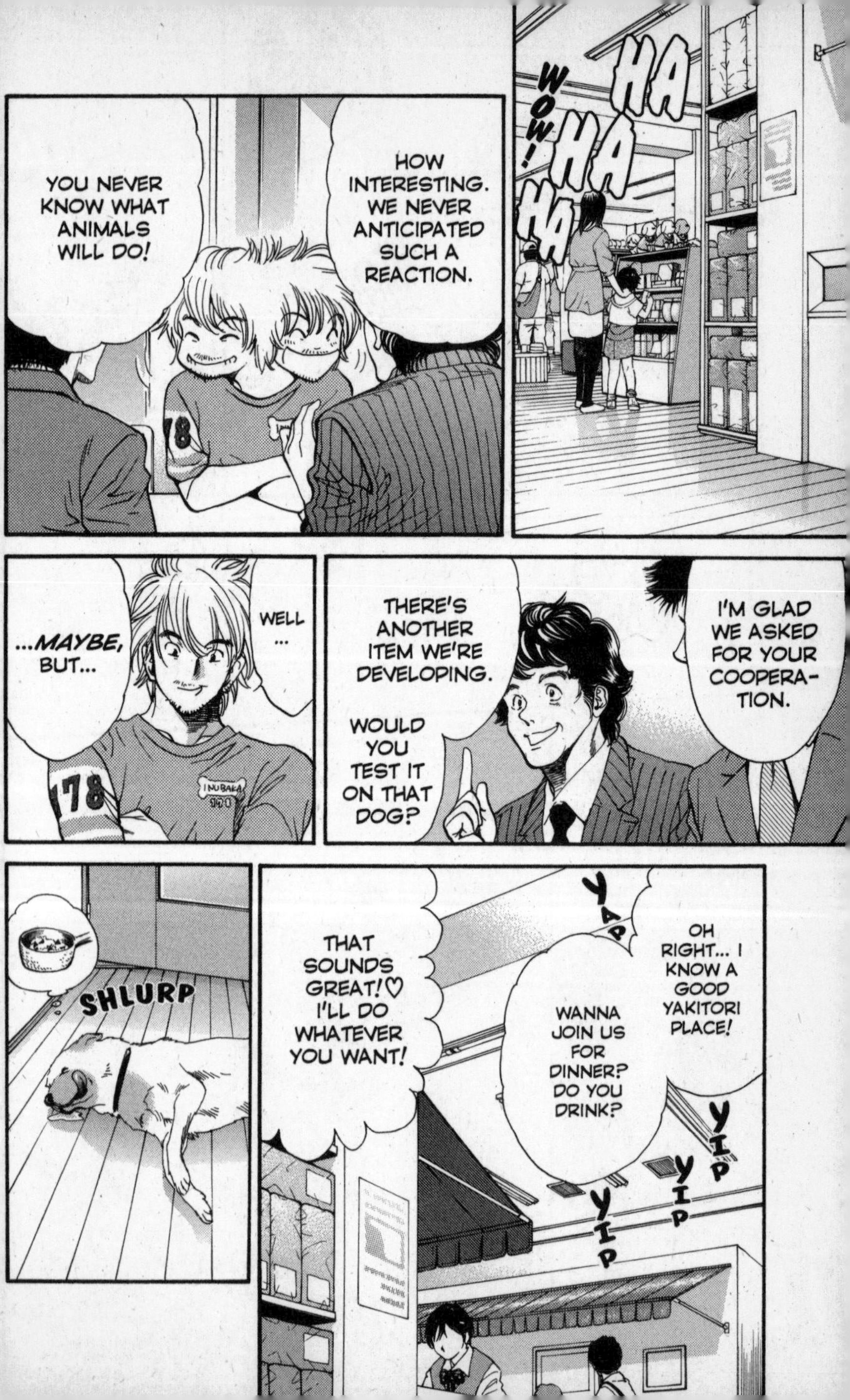
HA HA HA
WOW!
HOW INTERESTING. WE NEVER ANTICIPATED SUCH A REACTION.
YOU NEVER KNOW WHAT ANIMALS WILL DO!
I'M GLAD WE ASKED FOR YOUR COOPERA-TION.
THERE'S ANOTHER ITEM WE'RE DEVELOPING.
WOULD YOU TEST IT ON THAT DOG?
WELL ...
...MAYBE, BUT...
OH RIGHT... I KNOW A GOOD YAKITORI PLACE!
YAP
WANNA JOIN US FOR DINNER? DO YOU DRINK?
YIP YIP YIP
THAT SOUNDS GREAT!♡ I'LL DO WHATEVER YOU WANT!
SHLURP

CHAPTER 179: VIRTUAL WALKING MACHINE

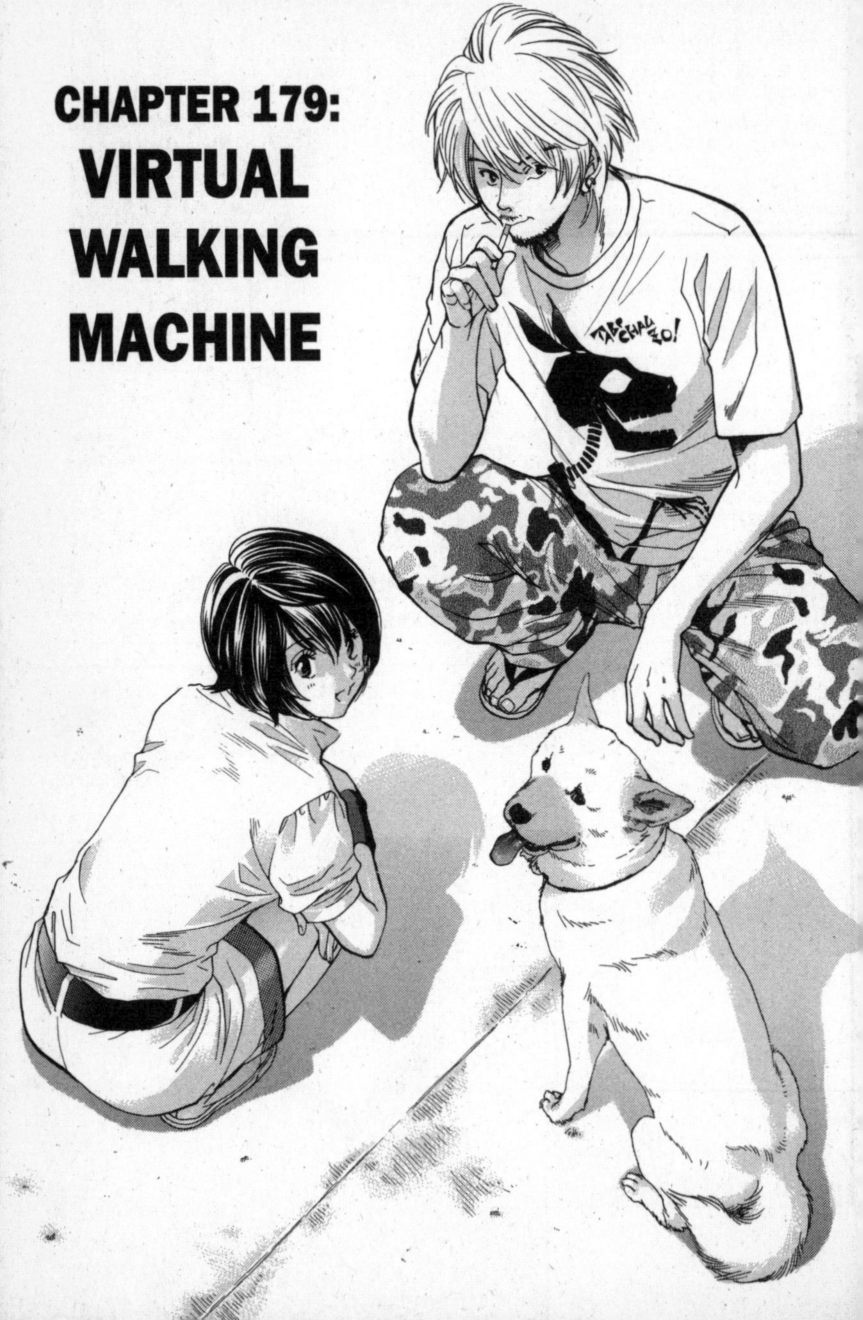
TABECHAU ZO!

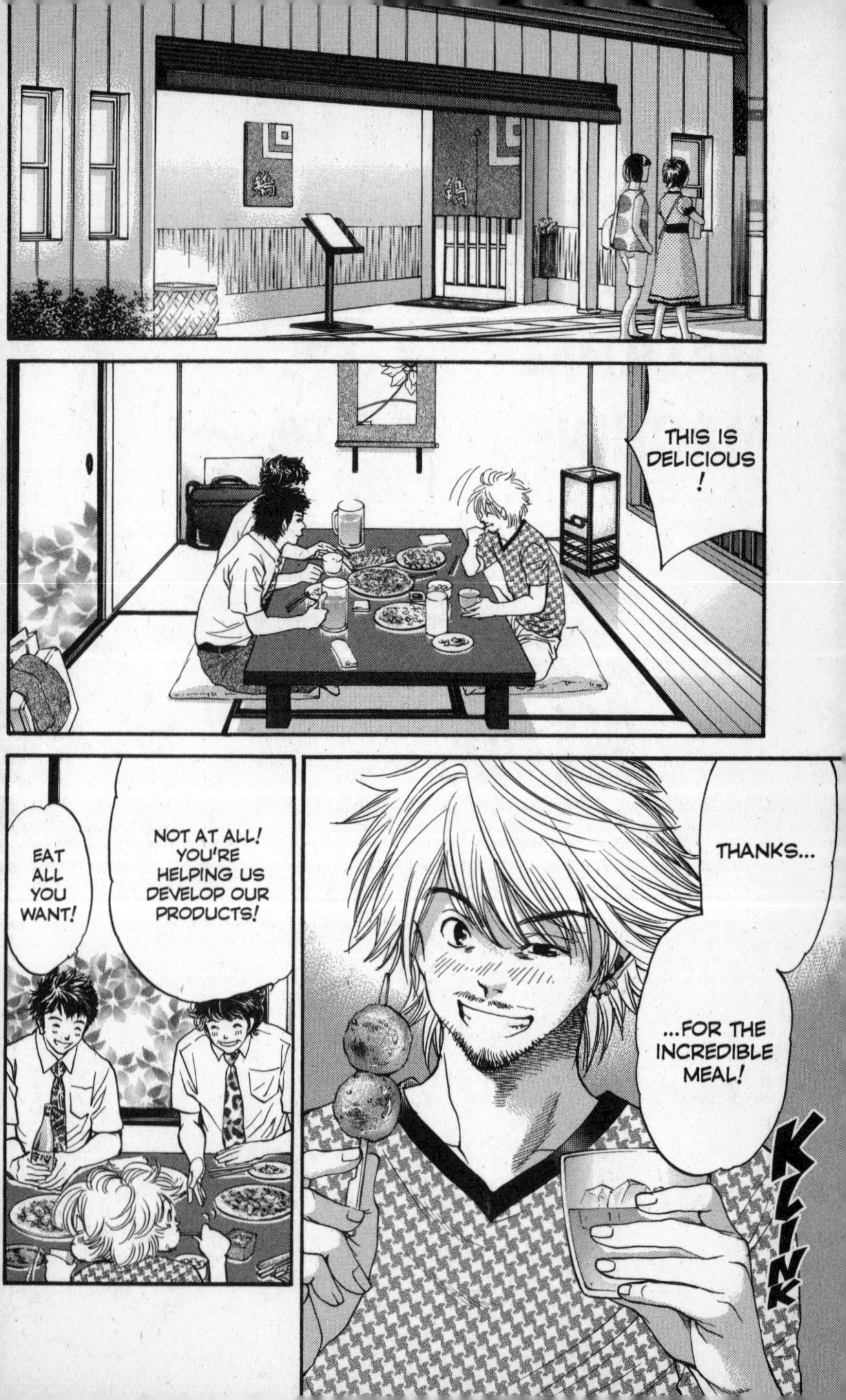
THIS IS DELICIOUS!
THANKS...
...FOR THE INCREDIBLE MEAL!
KLINK
NOT AT ALL! YOU'RE HELPING US DEVELOP OUR PRODUCTS!
EAT ALL YOU WANT!

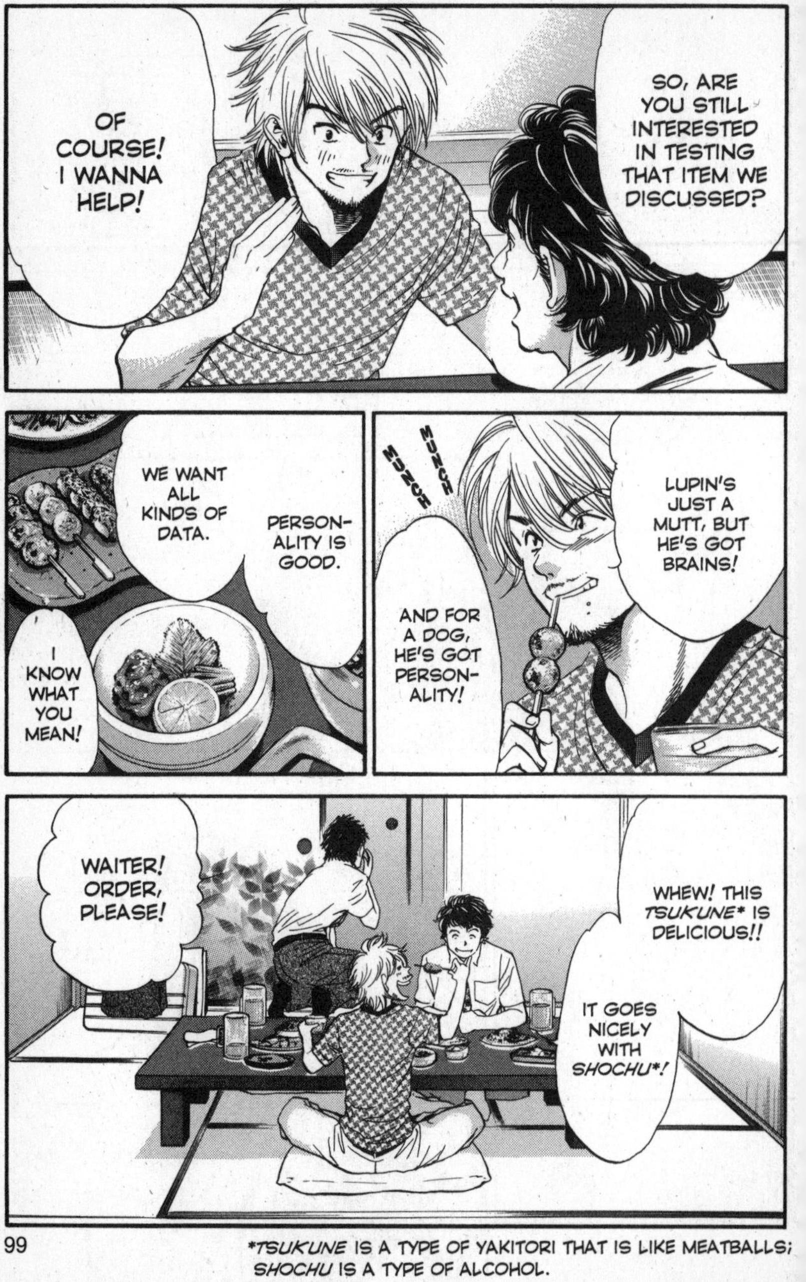
SO, ARE YOU STILL INTERESTED IN TESTING THAT ITEM WE DISCUSSED?
OF COURSE! I WANNA HELP!
MUNCH MUNCH
LUPIN'S JUST A MUTT, BUT HE'S GOT BRAINS!
AND FOR A DOG, HE'S GOT PERSON-ALITY!
PERSON-ALITY IS GOOD.
WE WANT ALL KINDS OF DATA.
I KNOW WHAT YOU MEAN!
WHEW! THIS *TSUKUNE** IS DELICIOUS!!
IT GOES NICELY WITH *SHOCHU**!
WAITER! ORDER, PLEASE!

**TSUKUNE* IS A TYPE OF YAKITORI THAT IS LIKE MEATBALLS; *SHOCHU* IS A TYPE OF ALCOHOL.

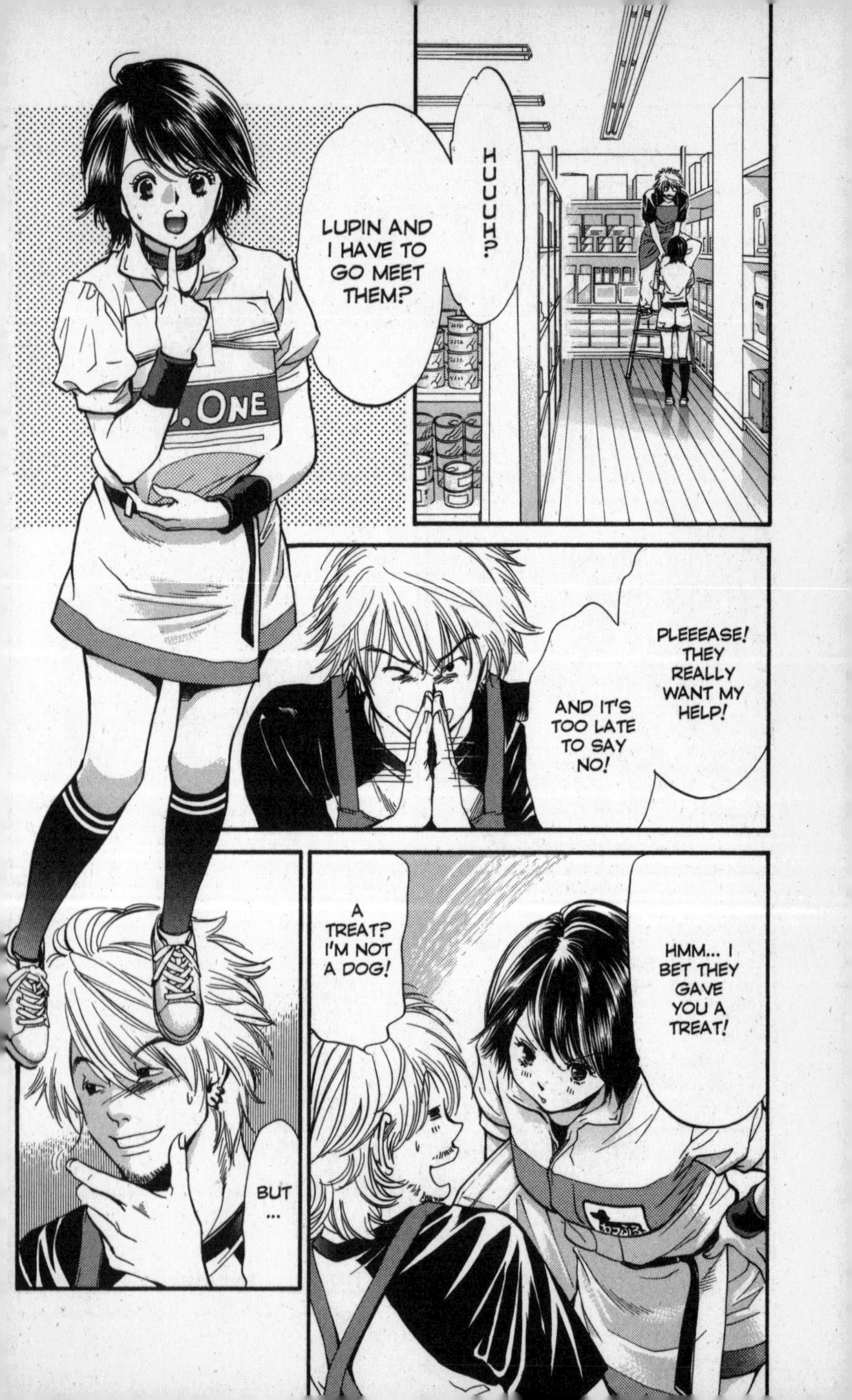
HUUUH?
LUPIN AND I HAVE TO GO MEET THEM?
PLEEEASE! THEY REALLY WANT MY HELP!
AND IT'S TOO LATE TO SAY NO!
HMM... I BET THEY GAVE YOU A TREAT!
A TREAT? I'M NOT A DOG!
BUT ...

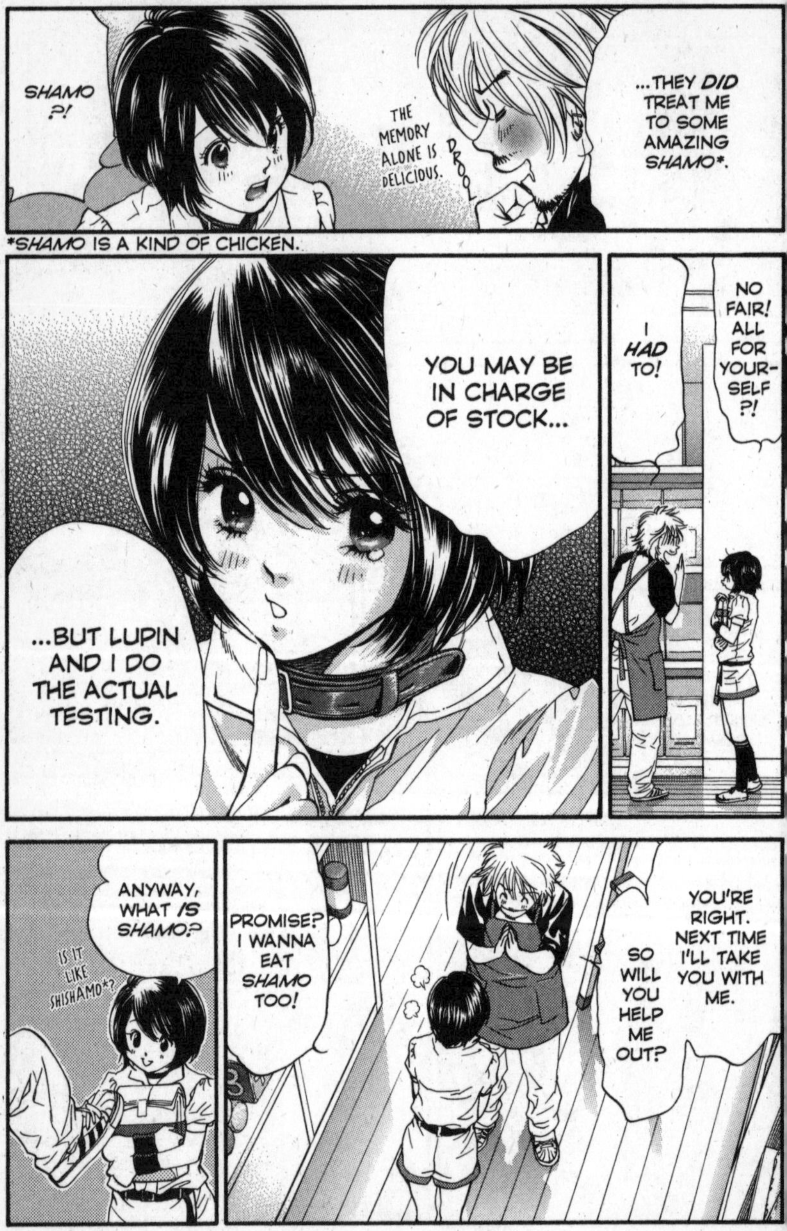
...THEY *DID* TREAT ME TO SOME AMAZING *SHAMO**.
THE MEMORY ALONE IS DELICIOUS.
DROOL
SHAMO ?!
NO FAIR! ALL FOR YOUR-SELF ?!
I *HAD* TO!
YOU MAY BE IN CHARGE OF STOCK...
...BUT LUPIN AND I DO THE ACTUAL TESTING.
YOU'RE RIGHT. NEXT TIME I'LL TAKE YOU WITH ME.
SO WILL YOU HELP ME OUT?
PROMISE? I WANNA EAT *SHAMO* TOO!
ANYWAY, WHAT *IS* *SHAMO*?
IS IT LIKE SHISHAMO*?

**SHAMO* IS A KIND OF CHICKEN.

**SHISHAMO* IS A TYPE OF FISH.

KRIK

PANT PANT
DO YOUR BEST, LUPIN!

GOOD LUCK!
I'LL PICK YOU UP WHEN YOU'RE DONE.
THANKS!
URF

I HOPE THIS GOES ALL RIGHT.

TAK
TAK
TAK
TAK
TAK
YOU MUST BE SUGURI MIYAUCHI AND LUPIN.

CAN LUPIN REALLY BE USEFUL TO SUCH A BIG COMPANY?

株式会社
ユキヤーン
YUKIYERN

1 F	LOBBY / RECEPTION
2 F	ACCOUNTING / SALES
3 F	HUMAN AFFAIRS / PROJECT DEVELOPMENT
4 F	MEETING ROOMS / PRESIDENT'S OFFICE
5 F	DINING

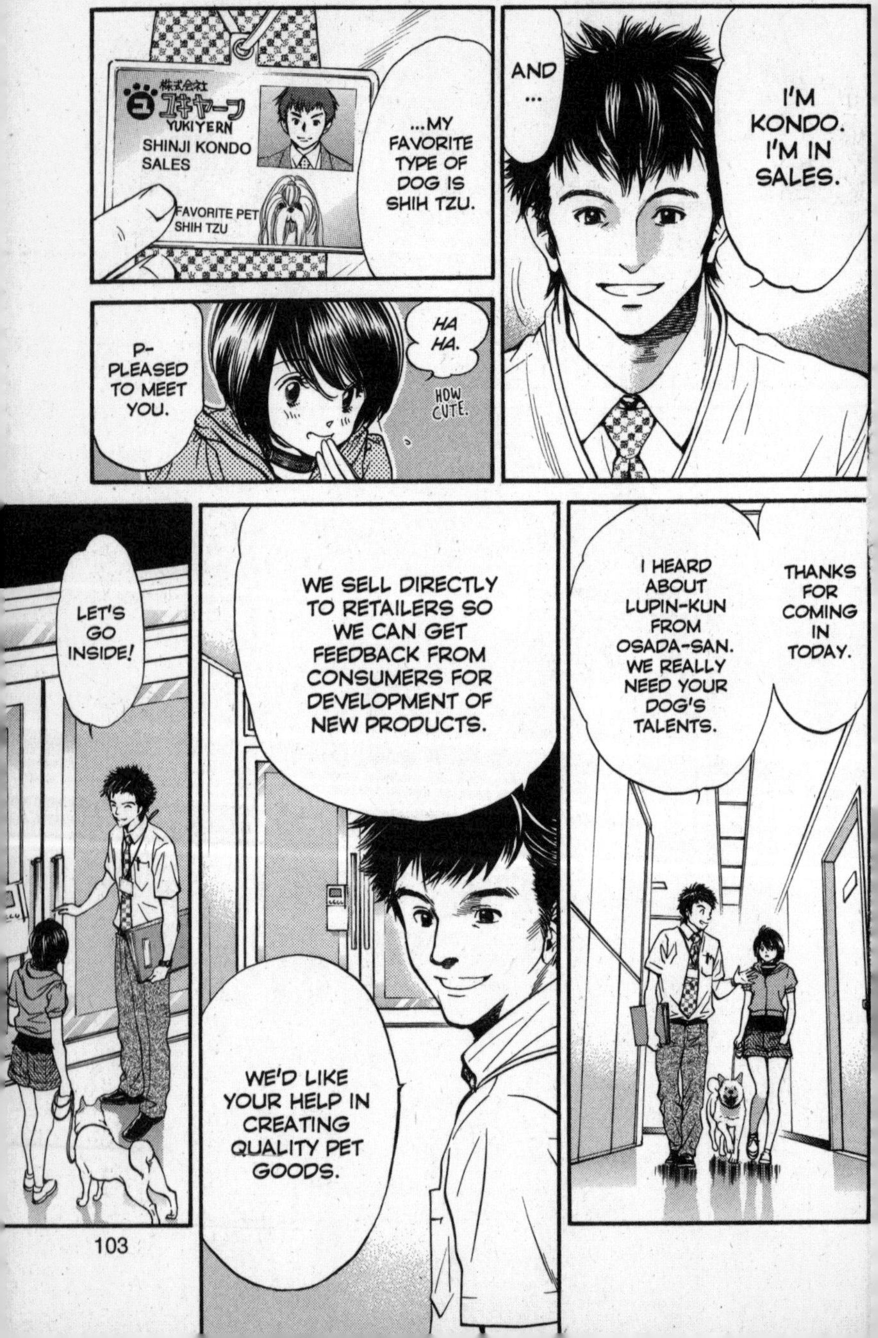
I'M KONDO. I'M IN SALES.
AND ...
株式会社
ユキヤーン
YUKIYERN
SHINJI KONDO
SALES
FAVORITE PET
SHIH TZU
...MY FAVORITE TYPE OF DOG IS SHIH TZU.
HA HA.
HOW CUTE.
P- PLEASED TO MEET YOU.
THANKS FOR COMING IN TODAY.
I HEARD ABOUT LUPIN-KUN FROM OSADA-SAN. WE REALLY NEED YOUR DOG'S TALENTS.
WE SELL DIRECTLY TO RETAILERS SO WE CAN GET FEEDBACK FROM CONSUMERS FOR DEVELOPMENT OF NEW PRODUCTS.
WE'D LIKE YOUR HELP IN CREATING QUALITY PET GOODS.
LET'S GO INSIDE!

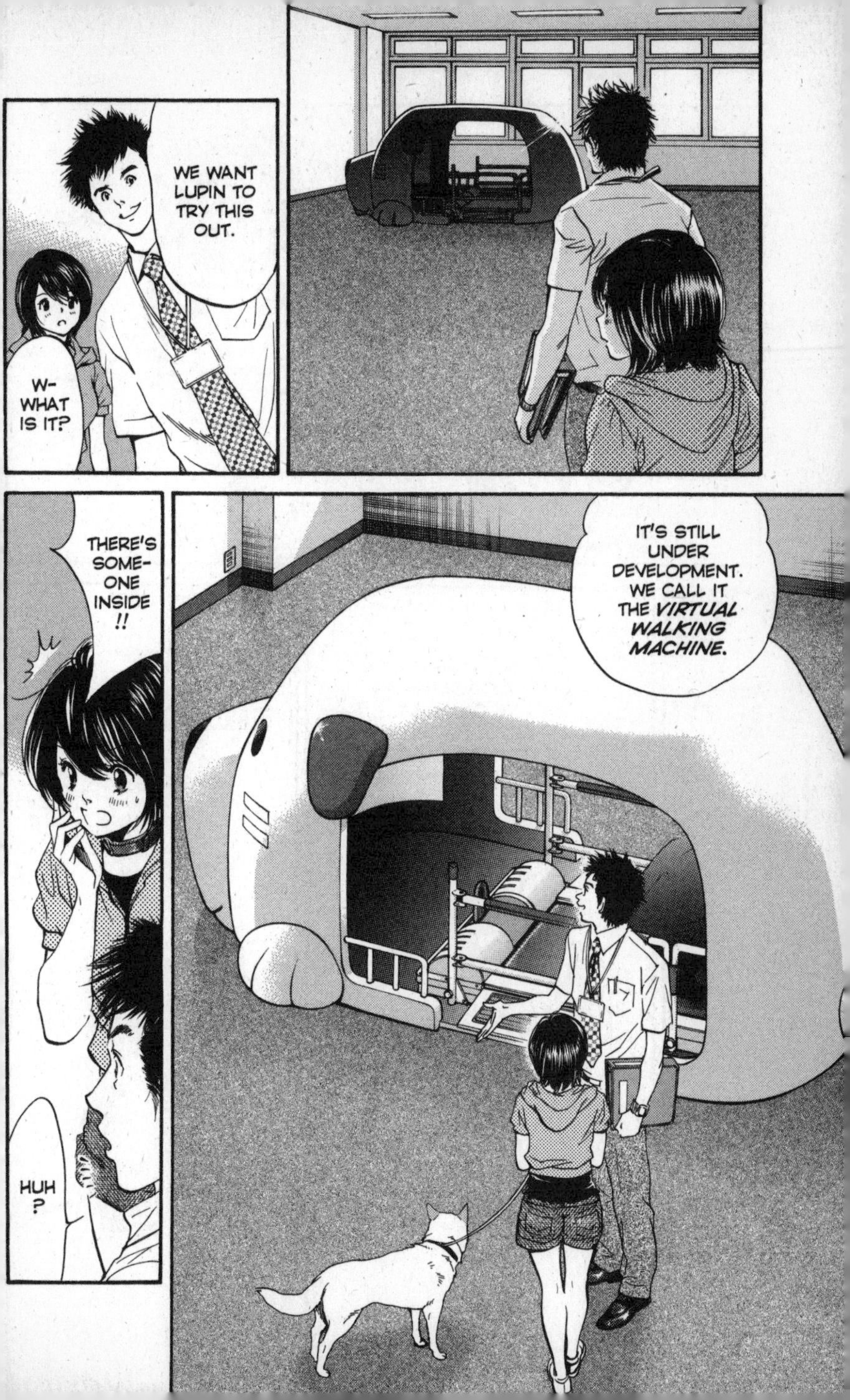
WE WANT LUPIN TO TRY THIS OUT.
W-WHAT IS IT?
IT'S STILL UNDER DEVELOPMENT. WE CALL IT THE *VIRTUAL WALKING MACHINE*.
THERE'S SOME-ONE INSIDE !!
HUH ?

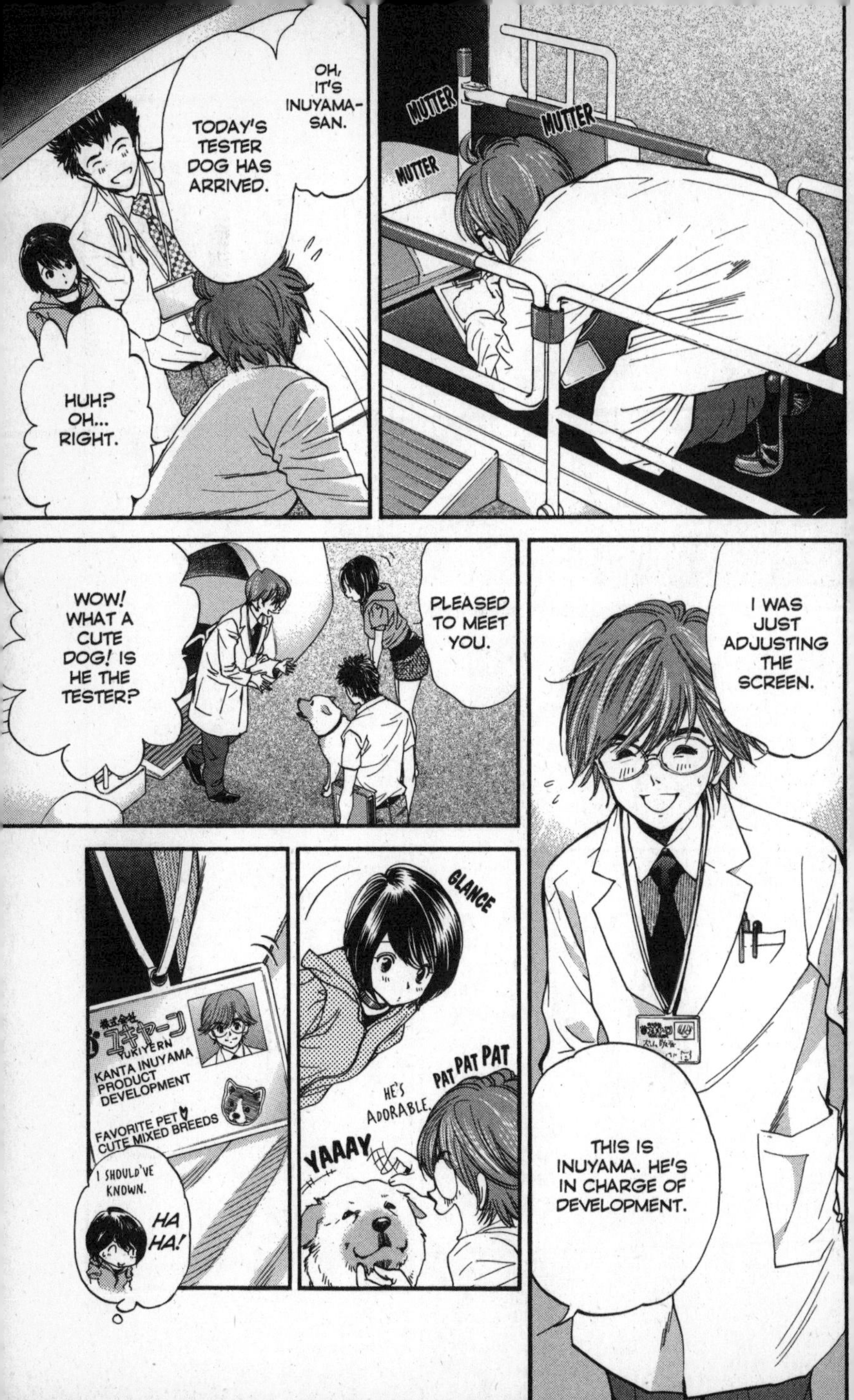
MUTTER
MUTTER
MUTTER
OH, IT'S INUYAMA-SAN.
TODAY'S TESTER DOG HAS ARRIVED.
HUH? OH... RIGHT.
I WAS JUST ADJUSTING THE SCREEN.
THIS IS INUYAMA. HE'S IN CHARGE OF DEVELOPMENT.
PLEASED TO MEET YOU.
WOW! WHAT A CUTE DOG! IS HE THE TESTER?
GLANCE
PAT PAT PAT
HE'S ADORABLE.
YAAAY
YUKIYERN
KANTA INUYAMA
PRODUCT DEVELOPMENT
FAVORITE PET
CUTE MIXED BREEDS
I SHOULD'VE KNOWN.
HA HA!

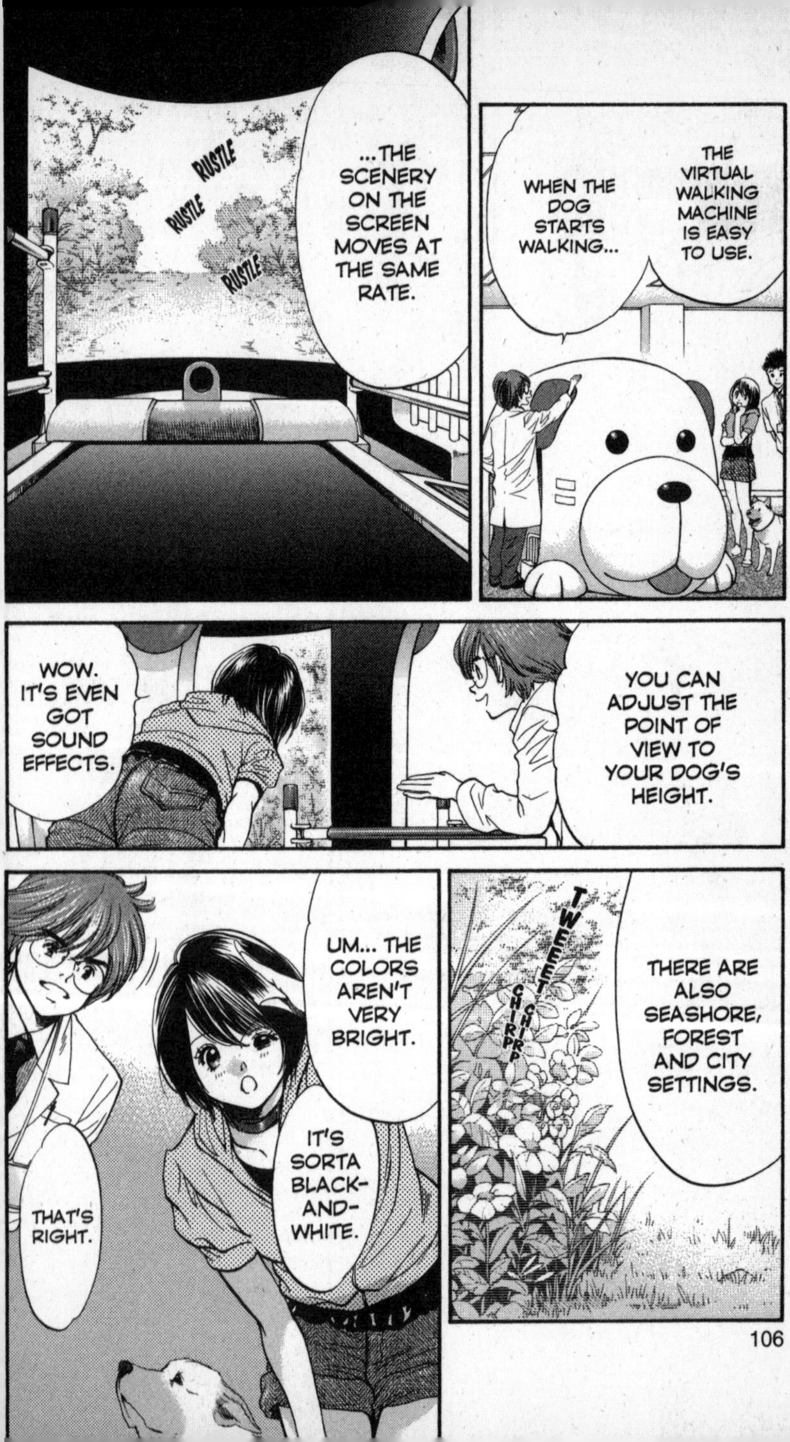
THE VIRTUAL WALKING MACHINE IS EASY TO USE.
WHEN THE DOG STARTS WALKING...
...THE SCENERY ON THE SCREEN MOVES AT THE SAME RATE.
RUSTLE
RUSTLE
RUSTLE
YOU CAN ADJUST THE POINT OF VIEW TO YOUR DOG'S HEIGHT.
WOW. IT'S EVEN GOT SOUND EFFECTS.
THERE ARE ALSO SEASHORE, FOREST AND CITY SETTINGS.
TWEEET
CHIRP
CHIRP
UM... THE COLORS AREN'T VERY BRIGHT.
IT'S SORTA BLACK-AND-WHITE.
THAT'S RIGHT.

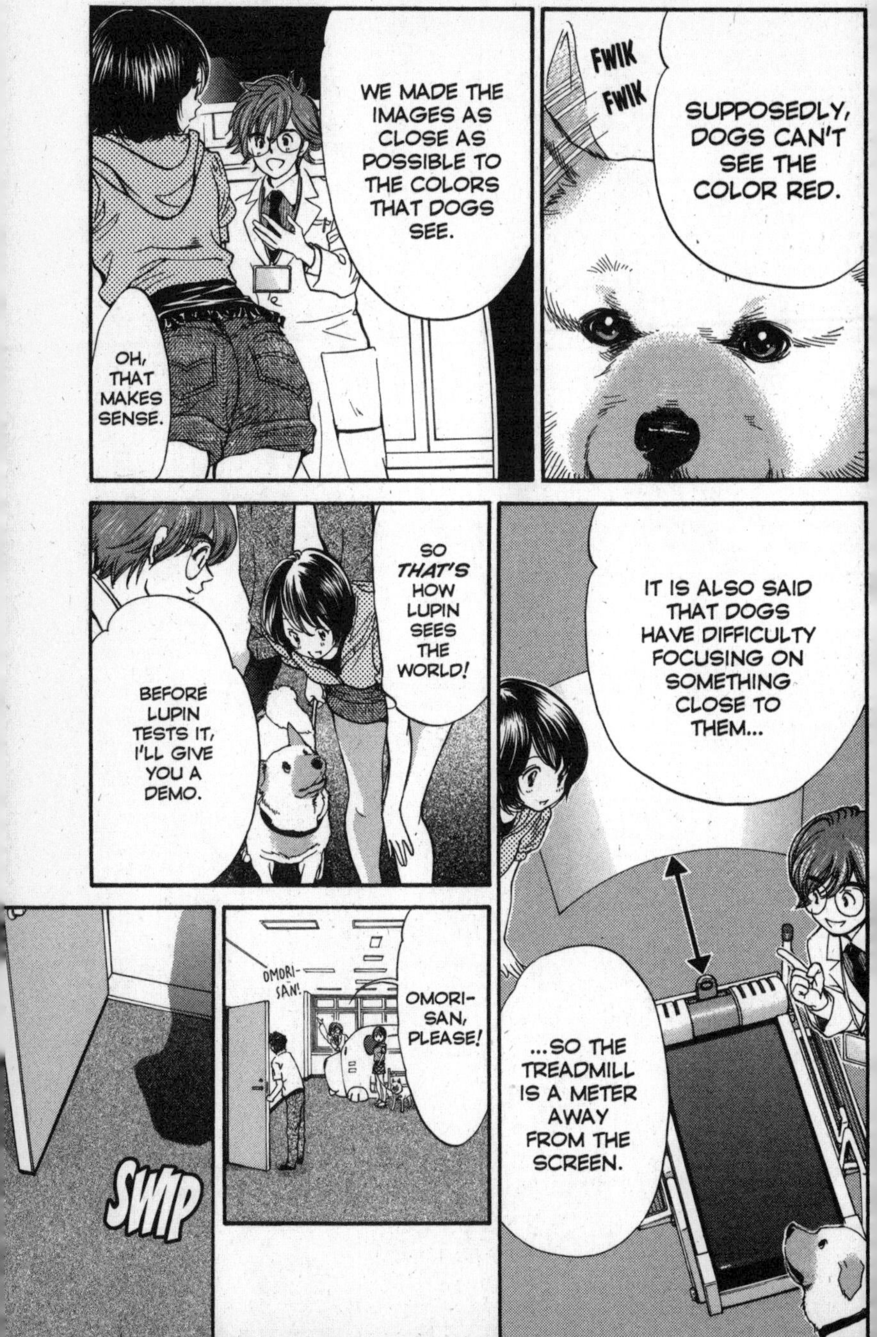
FWIK
FWIK
SUPPOSEDLY, DOGS CAN'T SEE THE COLOR RED.
WE MADE THE IMAGES AS CLOSE AS POSSIBLE TO THE COLORS THAT DOGS SEE.
OH, THAT MAKES SENSE.
IT IS ALSO SAID THAT DOGS HAVE DIFFICULTY FOCUSING ON SOMETHING CLOSE TO THEM...
...SO THE TREADMILL IS A METER AWAY FROM THE SCREEN.
SO *THAT'S* HOW LUPIN SEES THE WORLD!
BEFORE LUPIN TESTS IT, I'LL GIVE YOU A DEMO.
OMORI-SAN, PLEASE!
OMORI-SAN!
SWIP

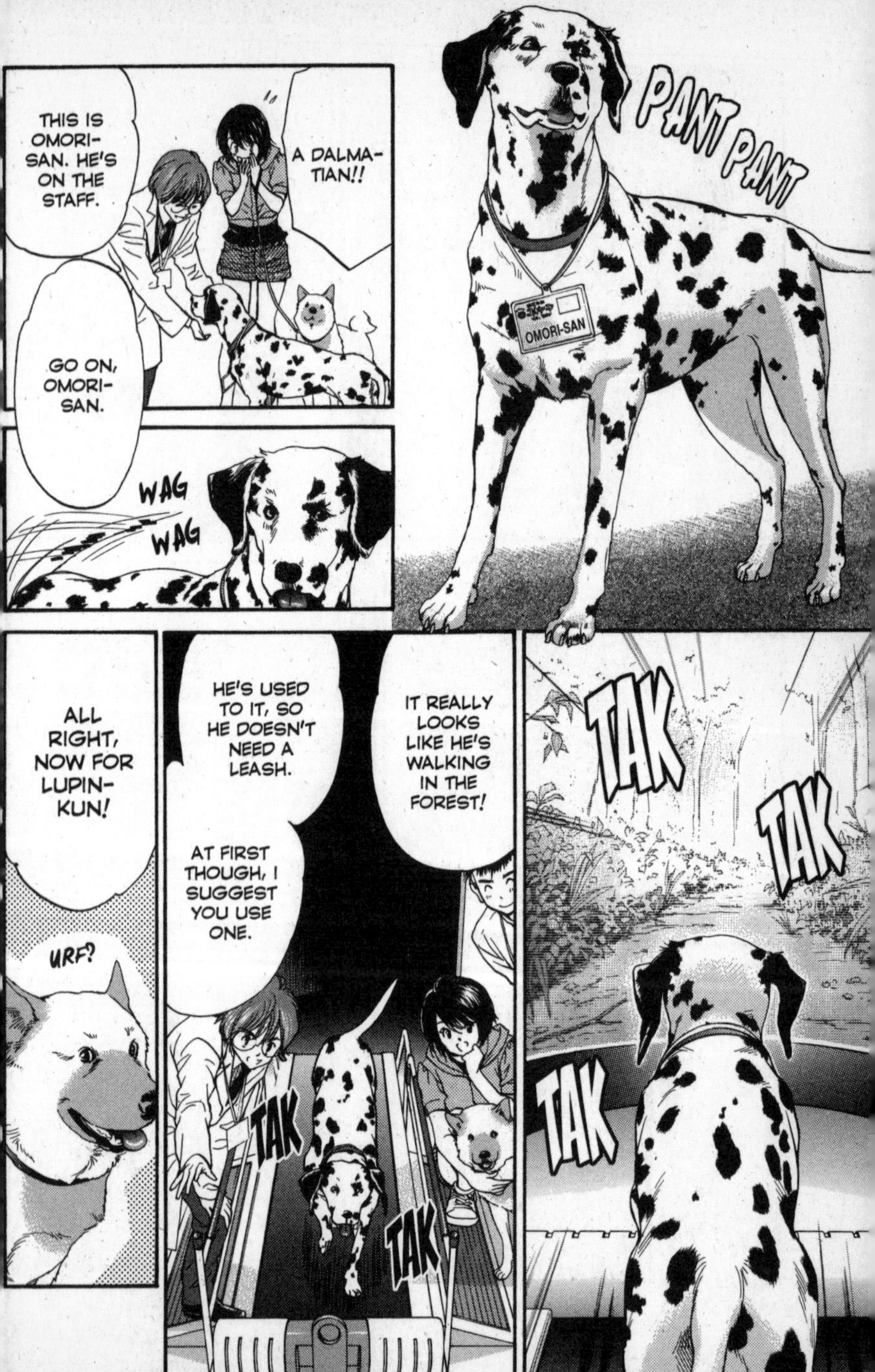
PANT PANT
OMORI-SAN
A DALMATIAN!!
THIS IS OMORI-SAN. HE'S ON THE STAFF.
GO ON, OMORI-SAN.
WAG WAG
TAK
TAK
TAK
IT REALLY LOOKS LIKE HE'S WALKING IN THE FOREST!
HE'S USED TO IT, SO HE DOESN'T NEED A LEASH.
AT FIRST THOUGH, I SUGGEST YOU USE ONE.
TAK
TAK
ALL RIGHT, NOW FOR LUPIN-KUN!
URF?

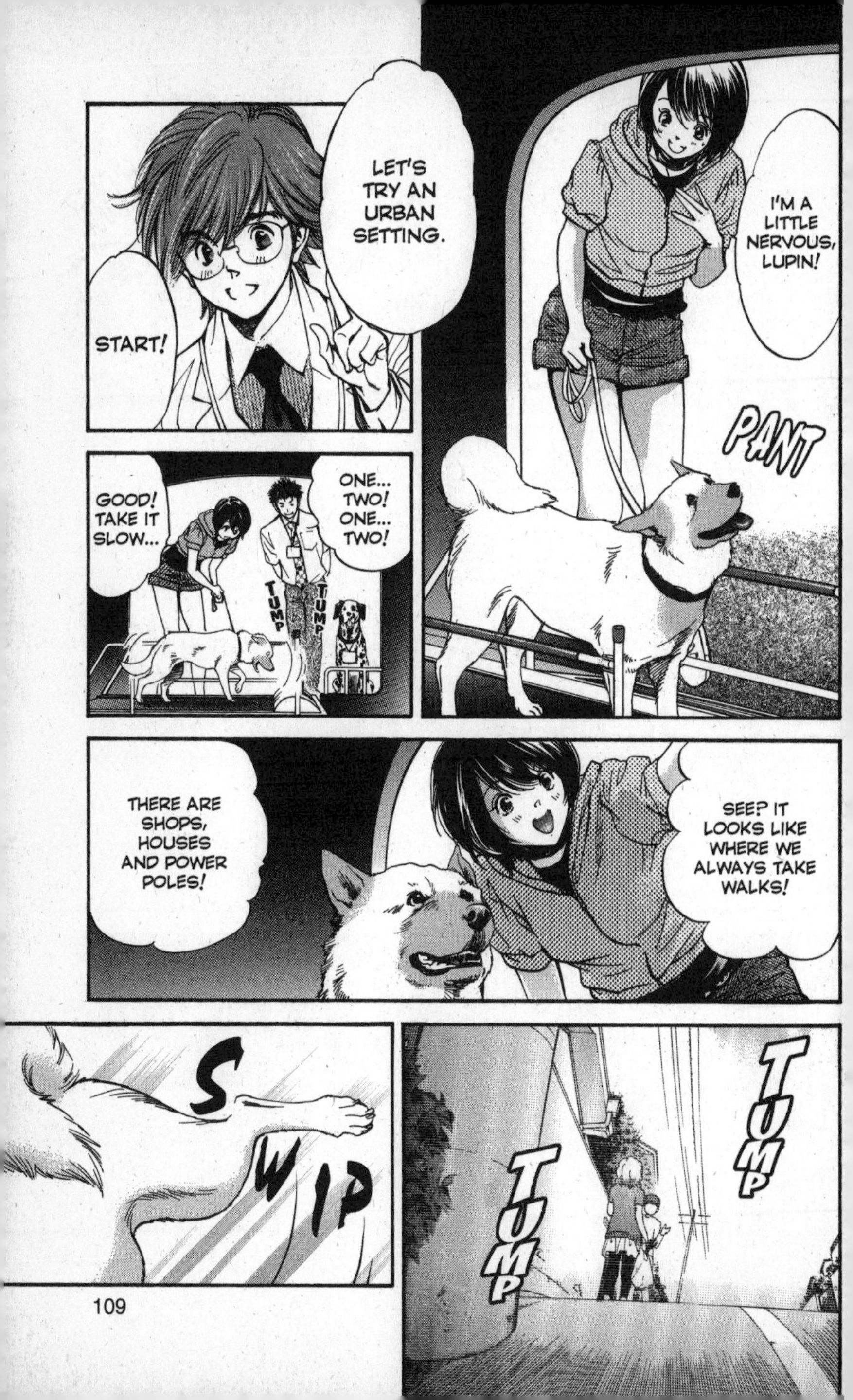
I'M A LITTLE NERVOUS, LUPIN!
PANT
LET'S TRY AN URBAN SETTING.
START!
ONE... TWO! ONE... TWO!
GOOD! TAKE IT SLOW...
TUMP
TUMP
SEE? IT LOOKS LIKE WHERE WE ALWAYS TAKE WALKS!
THERE ARE SHOPS, HOUSES AND POWER POLES!
TUMP
TUMP
S
SWIP

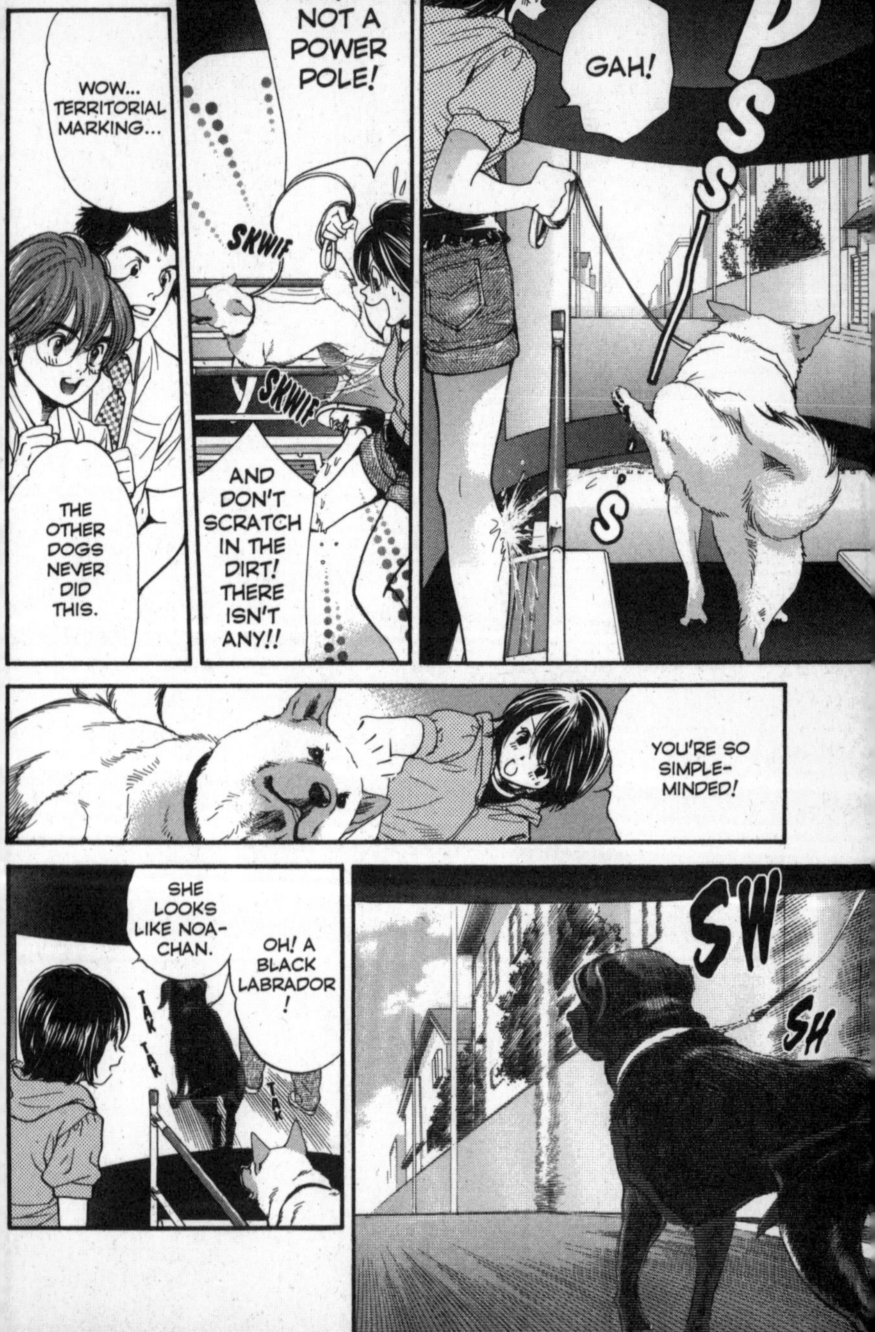
PSSS
GAH!
S
HEY! I'M NOT A POWER POLE!
SKWIF
SKWIF
AND DON'T SCRATCH IN THE DIRT! THERE ISN'T ANY!!
WOW... TERRITORIAL MARKING...
THE OTHER DOGS NEVER DID THIS.
YOU'RE SO SIMPLE-MINDED!
SW
SH
OH! A BLACK LABRADOR!
SHE LOOKS LIKE NOA-CHAN.
TAK TAK
TAK

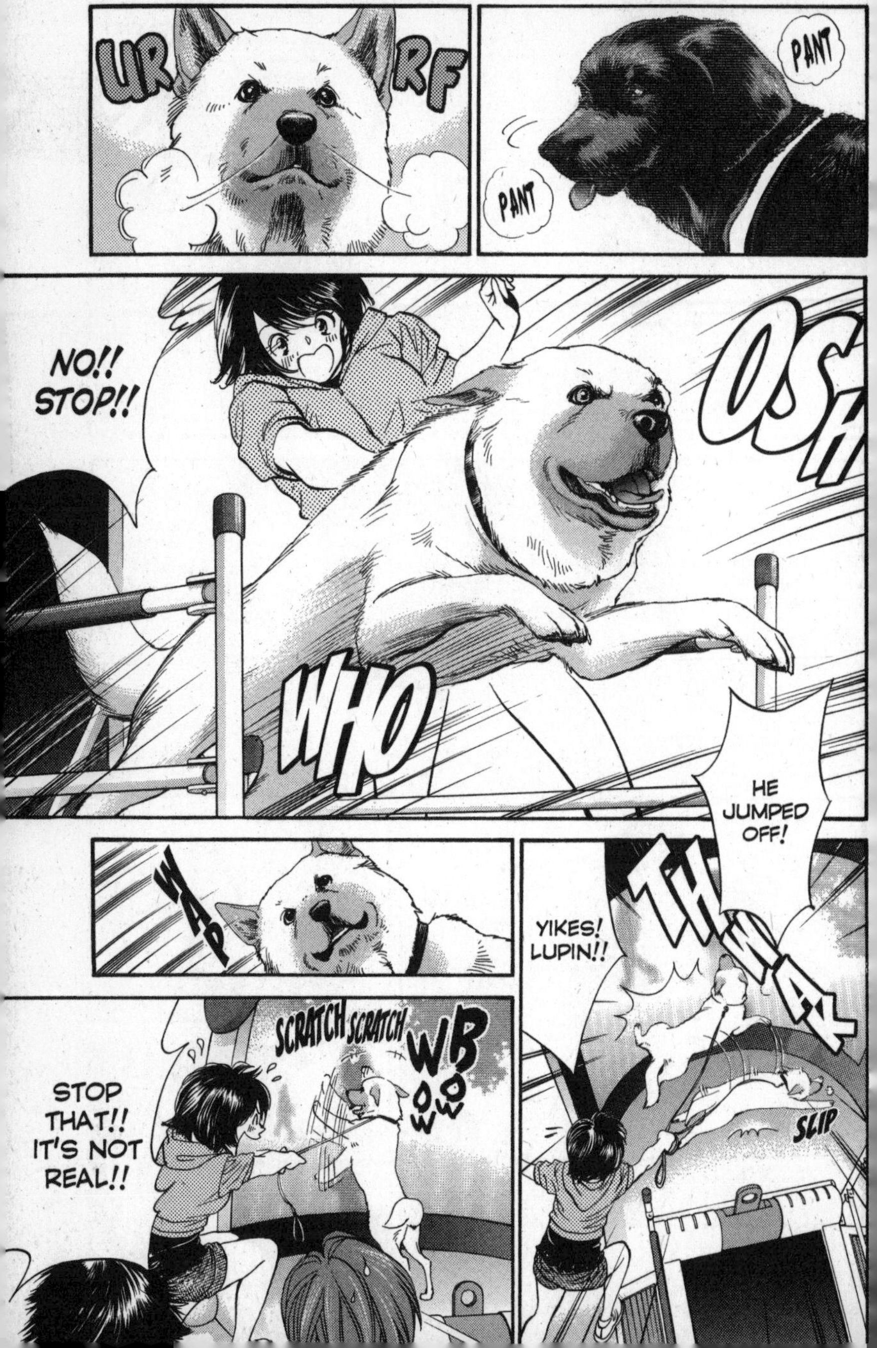
PANT
PANT
UR
RF
OSH
NO!! STOP!!
WHO
HE JUMPED OFF!
TH
YIKES! LUPIN!!
SLIP
WAP
SCRATCH SCRATCH
BOW WOW
STOP THAT!! IT'S NOT REAL!!

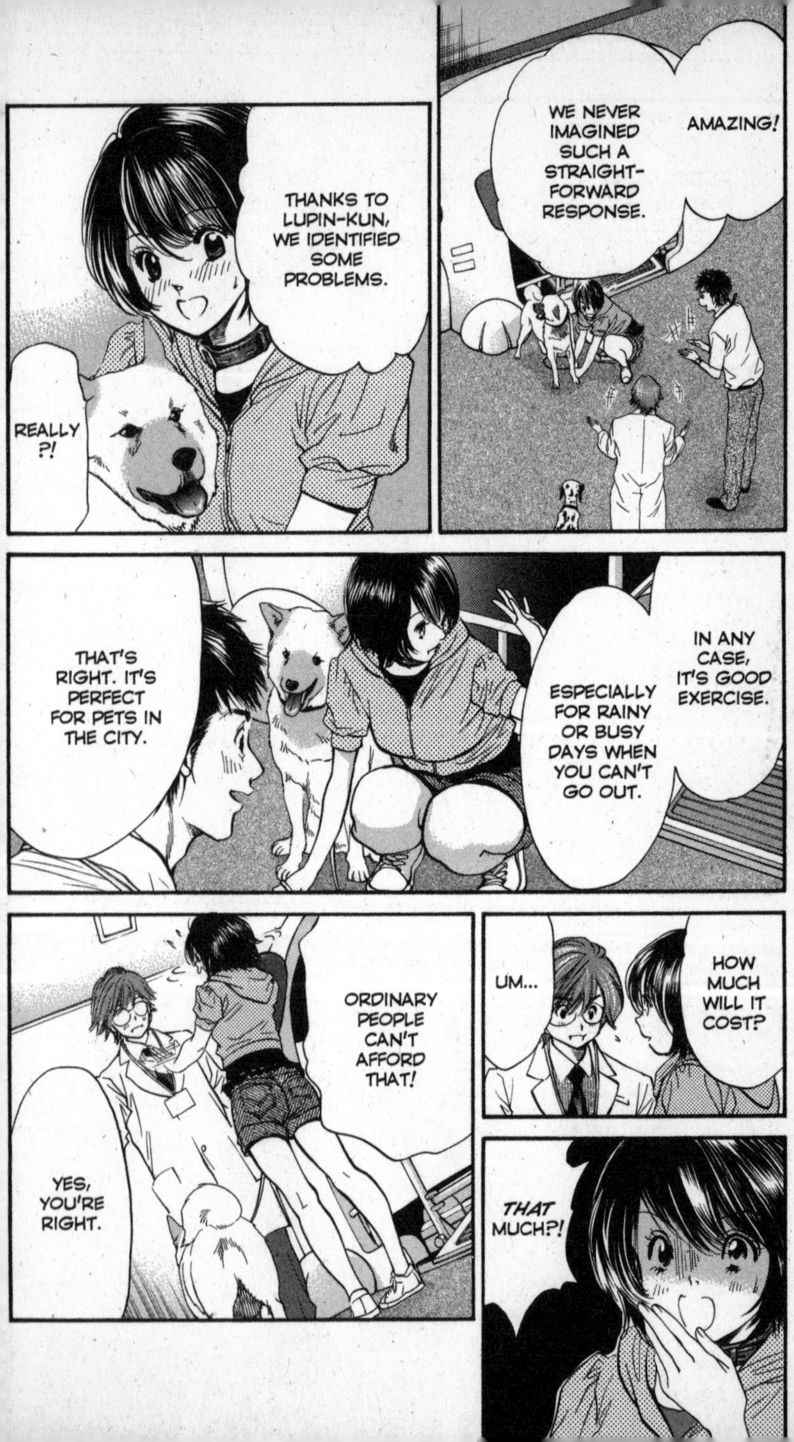
AMAZING!
WE NEVER IMAGINED SUCH A STRAIGHT-FORWARD RESPONSE.
THANKS TO LUPIN-KUN, WE IDENTIFIED SOME PROBLEMS.
REALLY?!
IN ANY CASE, IT'S GOOD EXERCISE.
ESPECIALLY FOR RAINY OR BUSY DAYS WHEN YOU CAN'T GO OUT.
THAT'S RIGHT. IT'S PERFECT FOR PETS IN THE CITY.
HOW MUCH WILL IT COST?
UM...
THAT MUCH?!
ORDINARY PEOPLE CAN'T AFFORD THAT!
YES, YOU'RE RIGHT.

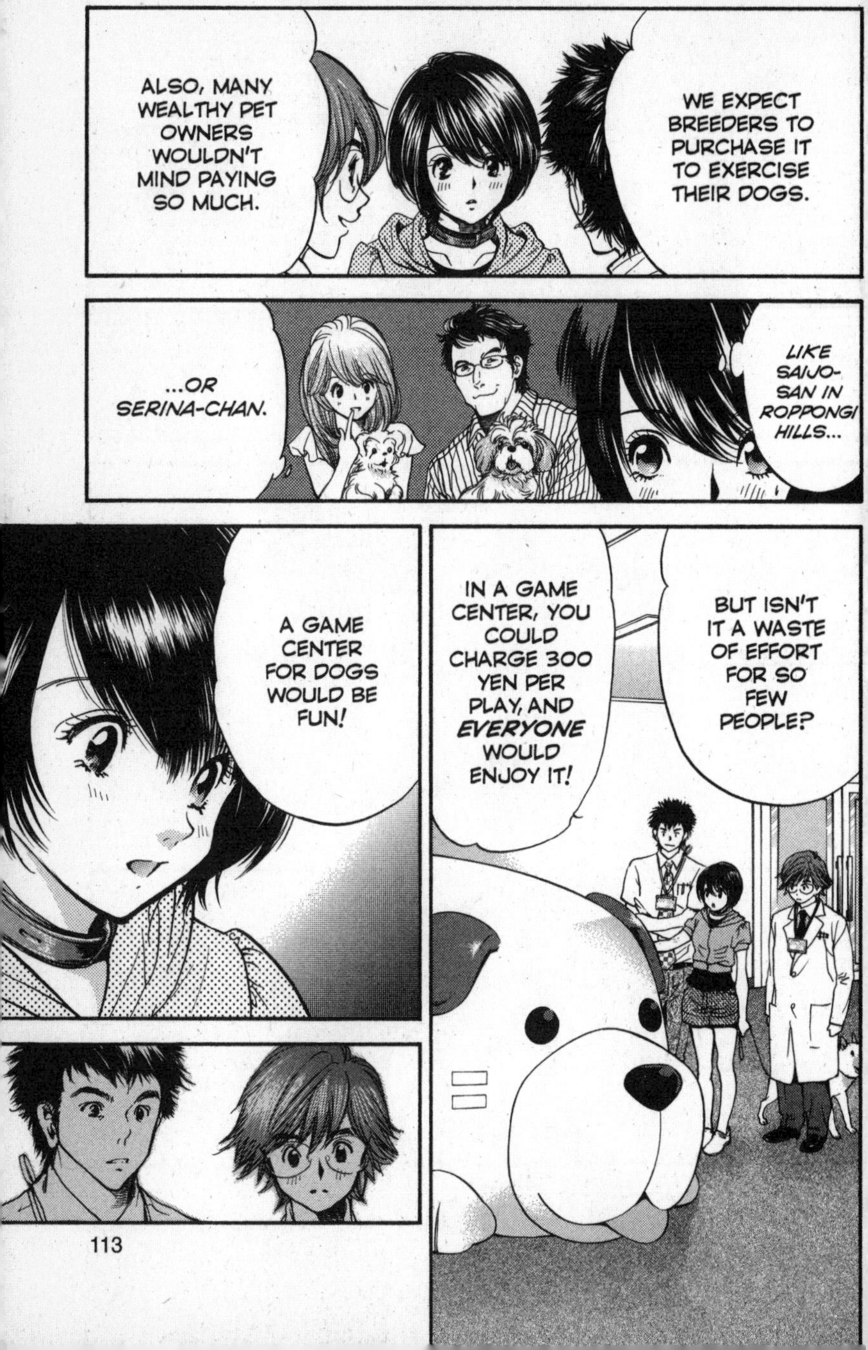
WE EXPECT BREEDERS TO PURCHASE IT TO EXERCISE THEIR DOGS.
ALSO, MANY WEALTHY PET OWNERS WOULDN'T MIND PAYING SO MUCH.
LIKE SAIJO-SAN IN ROPPONGI HILLS...
...OR SERINA-CHAN.
BUT ISN'T IT A WASTE OF EFFORT FOR SO FEW PEOPLE?
IN A GAME CENTER, YOU COULD CHARGE 300 YEN PER PLAY, AND *EVERYONE* WOULD ENJOY IT!
A GAME CENTER FOR DOGS WOULD BE FUN!

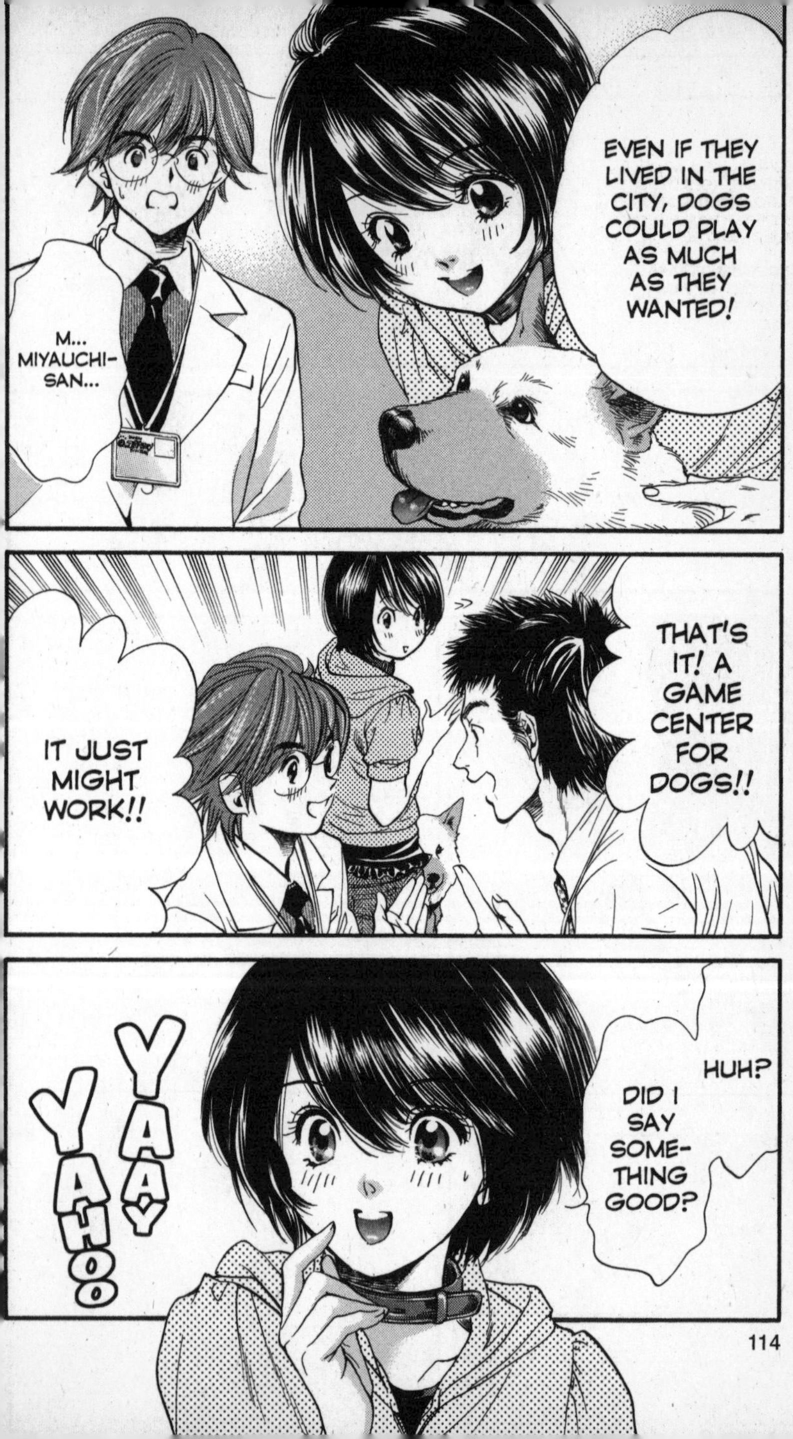
EVEN IF THEY LIVED IN THE CITY, DOGS COULD PLAY AS MUCH AS THEY WANTED!
M... MIYAUCHI-SAN...
THAT'S IT! A GAME CENTER FOR DOGS!!
IT JUST MIGHT WORK!!
HUH? DID I SAY SOME-THING GOOD?
YAAAY
YAHOO

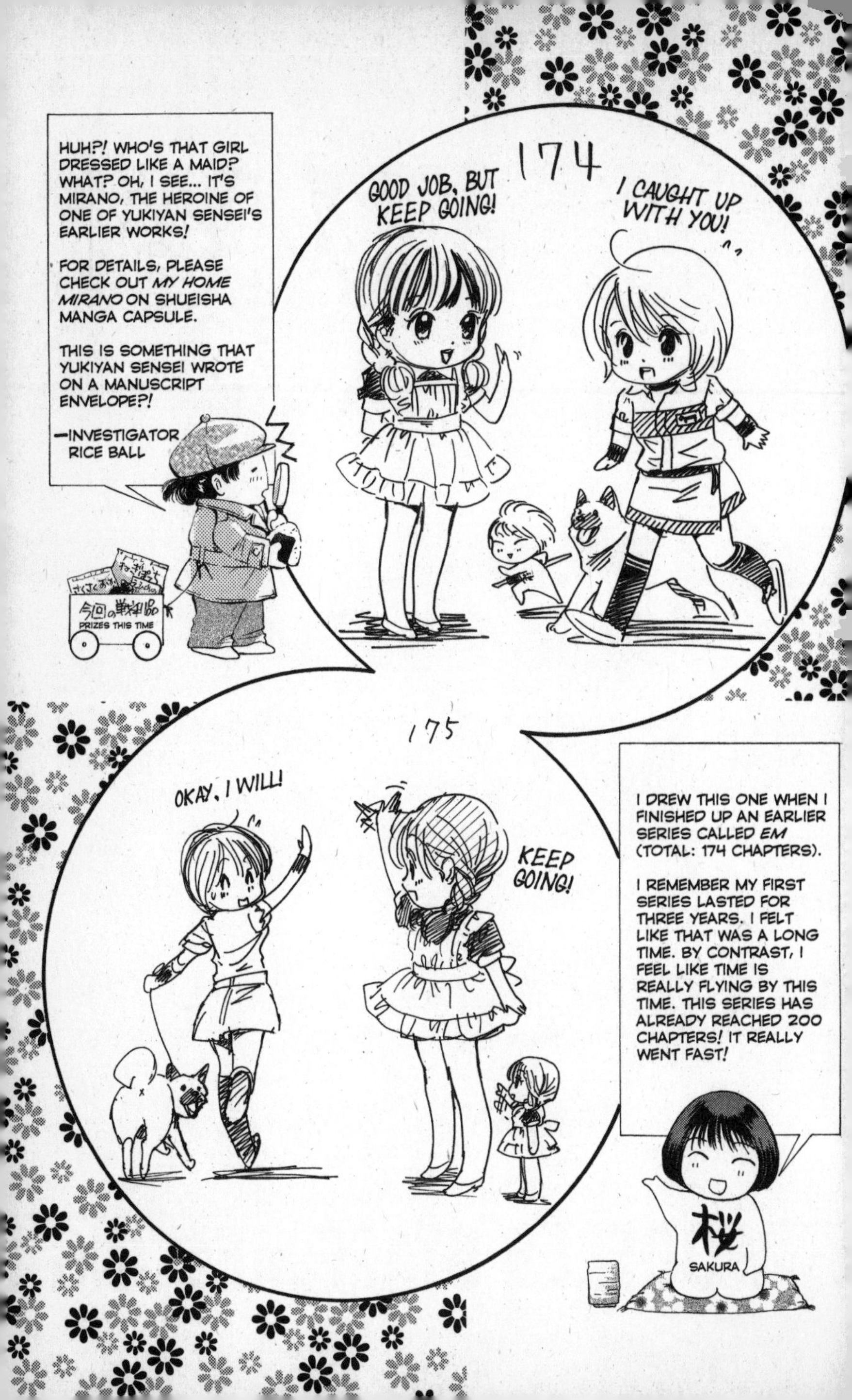
174
I CAUGHT UP WITH YOU!
GOOD JOB, BUT KEEP GOING!
HUH?! WHO'S THAT GIRL DRESSED LIKE A MAID? WHAT? OH, I SEE... IT'S MIRANO, THE HEROINE OF ONE OF YUKIYAN SENSEI'S EARLIER WORKS!
FOR DETAILS, PLEASE CHECK OUT *MY HOME MIRANO* ON SHUEISHA MANGA CAPSULE.
THIS IS SOMETHING THAT YUKIYAN SENSEI WROTE ON A MANUSCRIPT ENVELOPE?!
—INVESTIGATOR RICE BALL
今回の戦利品
PRIZES THIS TIME
I DREW THIS ONE WHEN I FINISHED UP AN EARLIER SERIES CALLED *EM* (TOTAL: 174 CHAPTERS).
I REMEMBER MY FIRST SERIES LASTED FOR THREE YEARS. I FELT LIKE THAT WAS A LONG TIME. BY CONTRAST, I FEEL LIKE TIME IS REALLY FLYING BY THIS TIME. THIS SERIES HAS ALREADY REACHED 200 CHAPTERS! IT REALLY WENT FAST!
桜
SAKURA
175
KEEP GOING!
OKAY, I WILL!

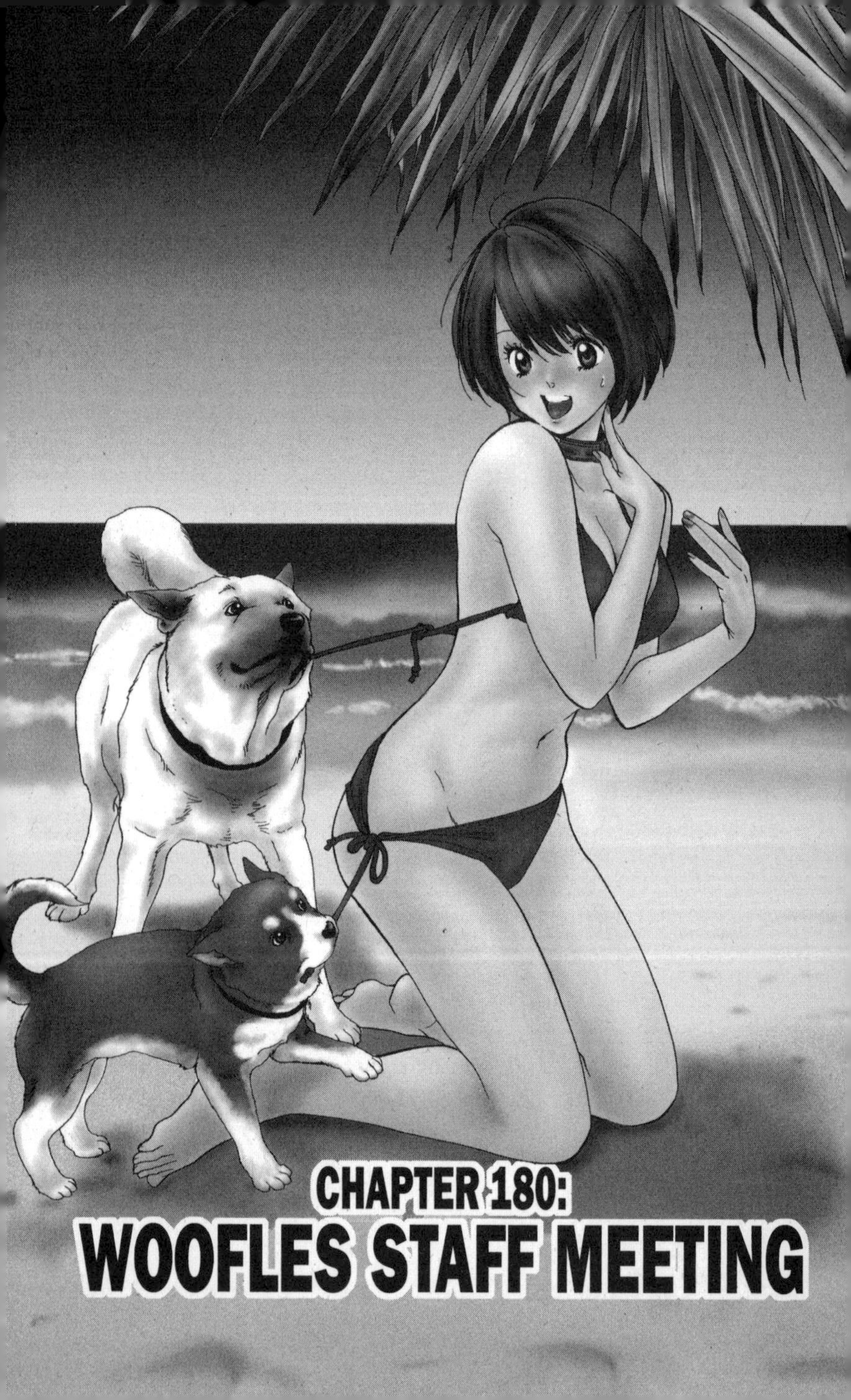

CHAPTER 180:
WOOFLES STAFF MEETING

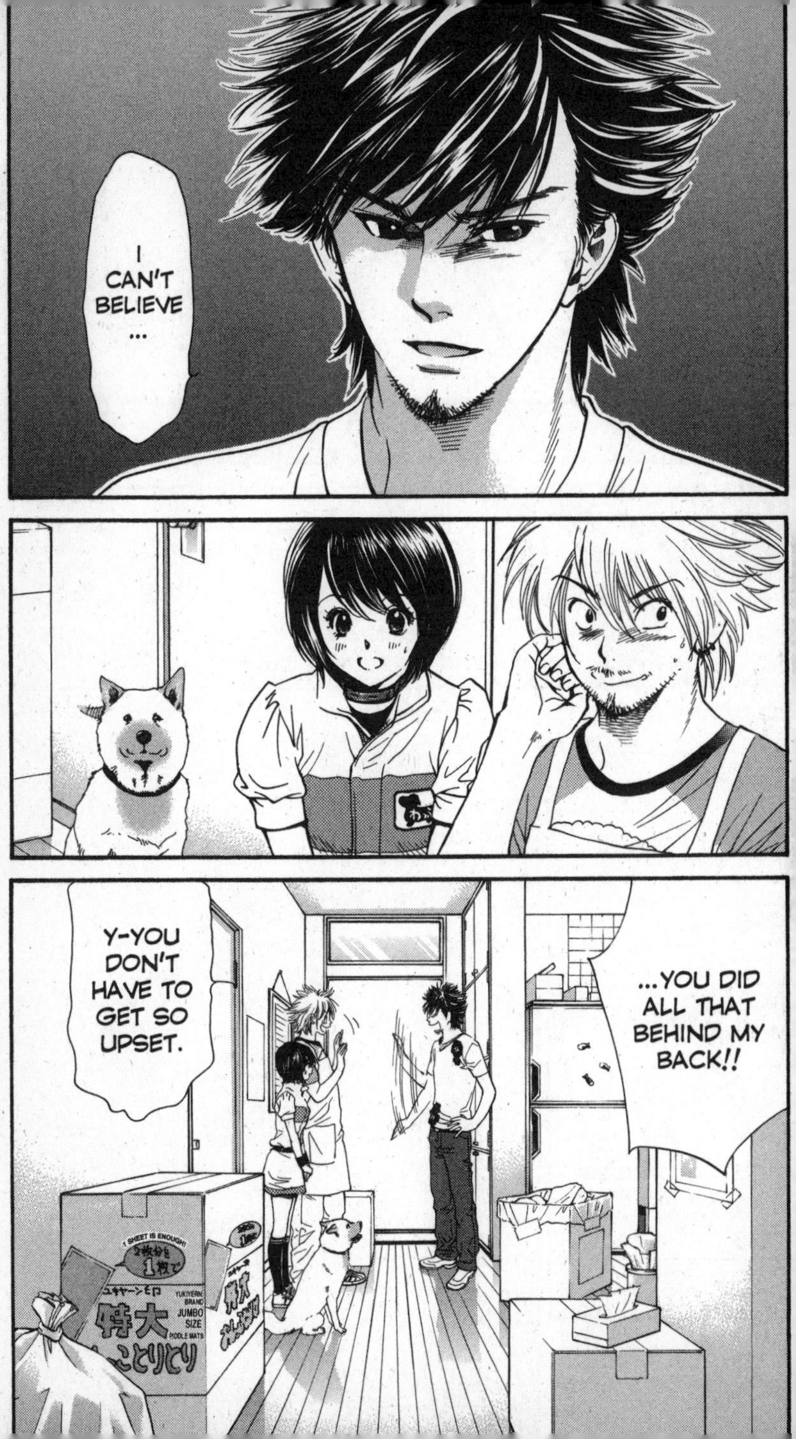
I CAN'T BELIEVE ...
...YOU DID ALL THAT BEHIND MY BACK!!
Y-YOU DON'T HAVE TO GET SO UPSET.
1 SHEET IS ENOUGH!
YUKIYERN BRAND
JUMBO SIZE
PIDDLE MATS

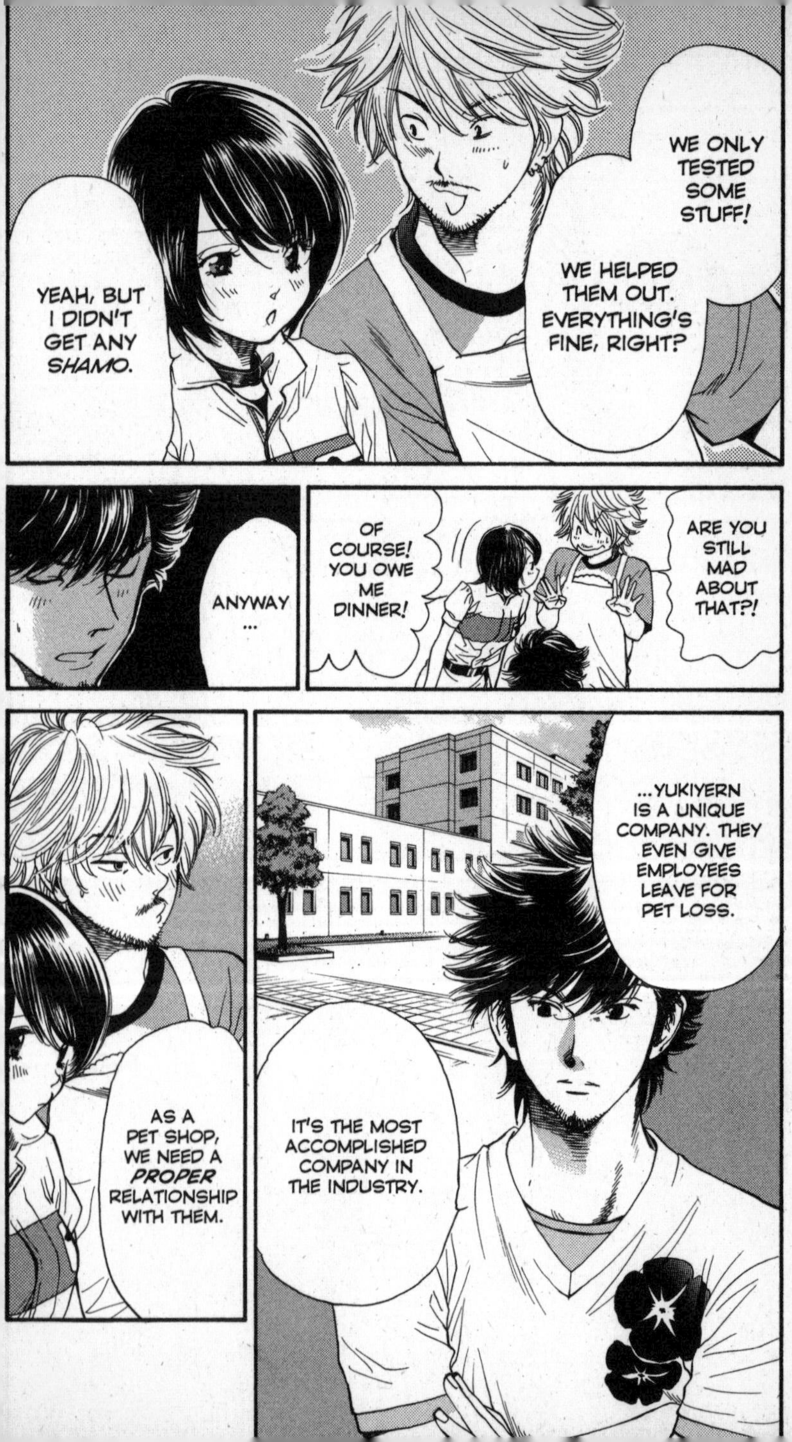
WE ONLY TESTED SOME STUFF!
WE HELPED THEM OUT. EVERYTHING'S FINE, RIGHT?
YEAH, BUT I DIDN'T GET ANY *SHAMO*.
ARE YOU STILL MAD ABOUT THAT?!
OF COURSE! YOU OWE ME DINNER!
ANYWAY ...
...YUKIYERN IS A UNIQUE COMPANY. THEY EVEN GIVE EMPLOYEES LEAVE FOR PET LOSS.
IT'S THE MOST ACCOMPLISHED COMPANY IN THE INDUSTRY.
AS A PET SHOP, WE NEED A *PROPER* RELATIONSHIP WITH THEM.

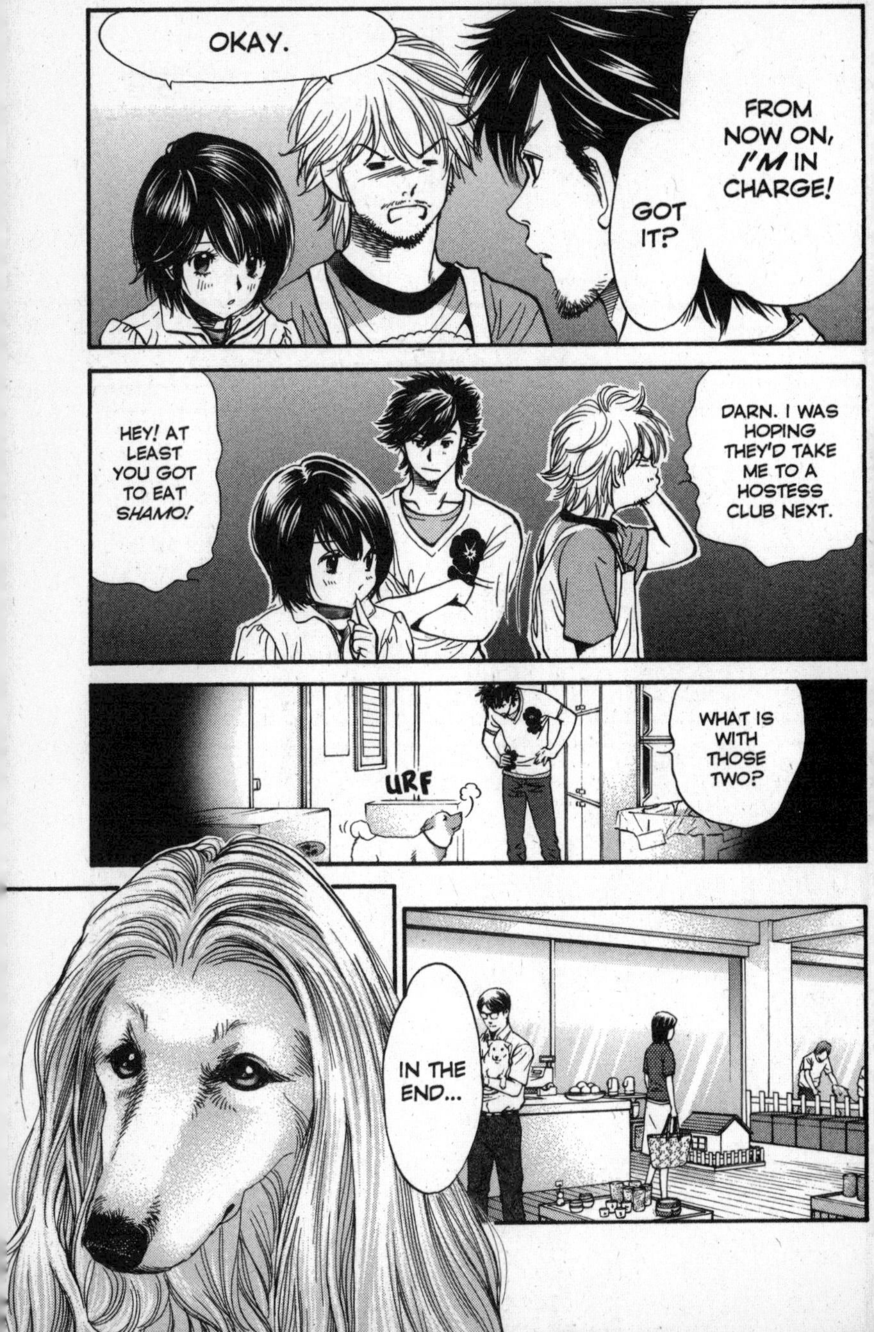
FROM NOW ON, *I'M* IN CHARGE!
GOT IT?
OKAY.
DARN. I WAS HOPING THEY'D TAKE ME TO A HOSTESS CLUB NEXT.
HEY! AT LEAST YOU GOT TO EAT *SHAMO!*
WHAT IS WITH THOSE TWO?
URF
IN THE END...

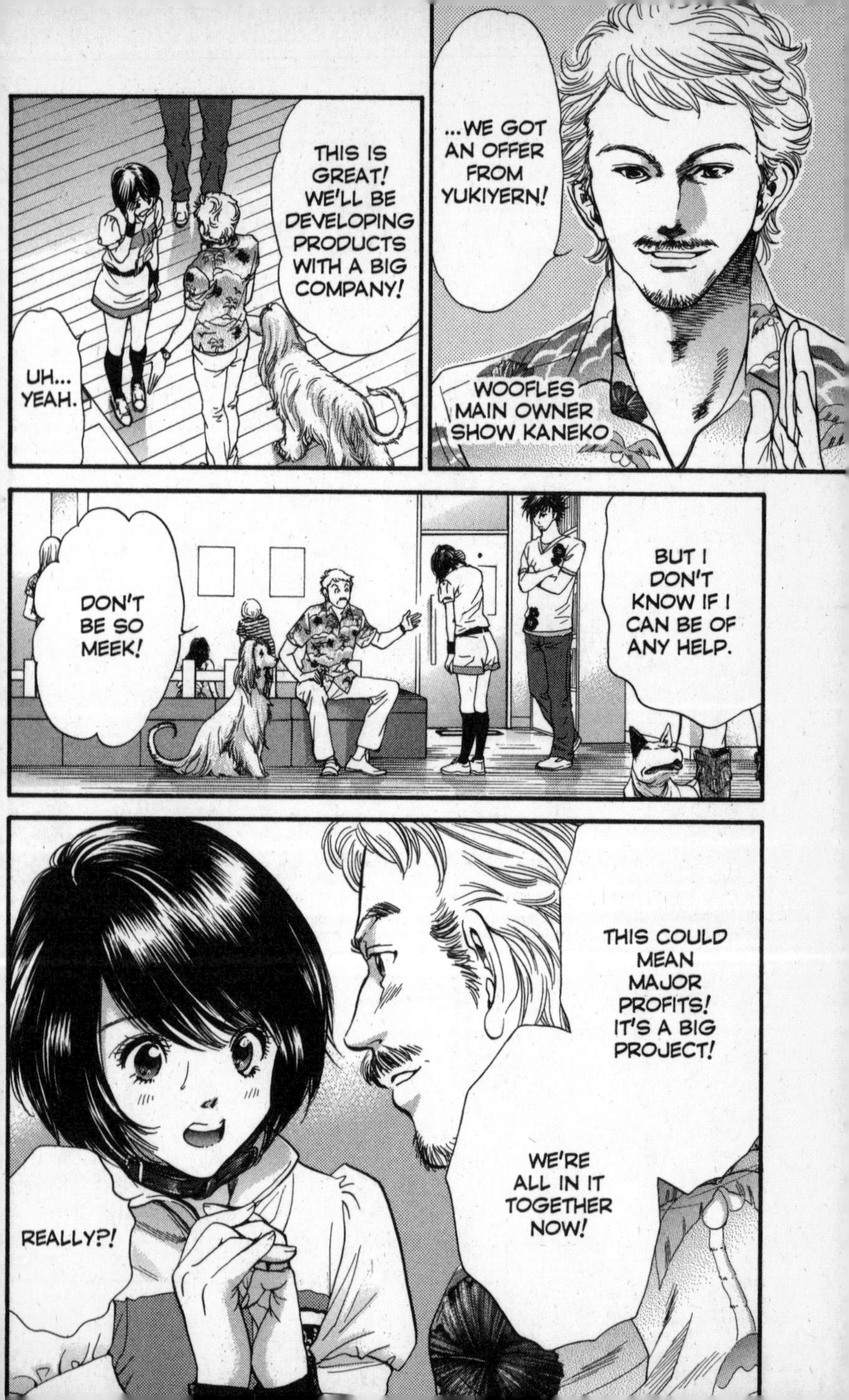
...WE GOT AN OFFER FROM YUKIYERN!
WOOFLES MAIN OWNER SHOW KANEKO
THIS IS GREAT! WE'LL BE DEVELOPING PRODUCTS WITH A BIG COMPANY!
UH... YEAH.
BUT I DON'T KNOW IF I CAN BE OF ANY HELP.
DON'T BE SO MEEK!
THIS COULD MEAN MAJOR PROFITS! IT'S A BIG PROJECT!
WE'RE ALL IN IT TOGETHER NOW!
REALLY?!

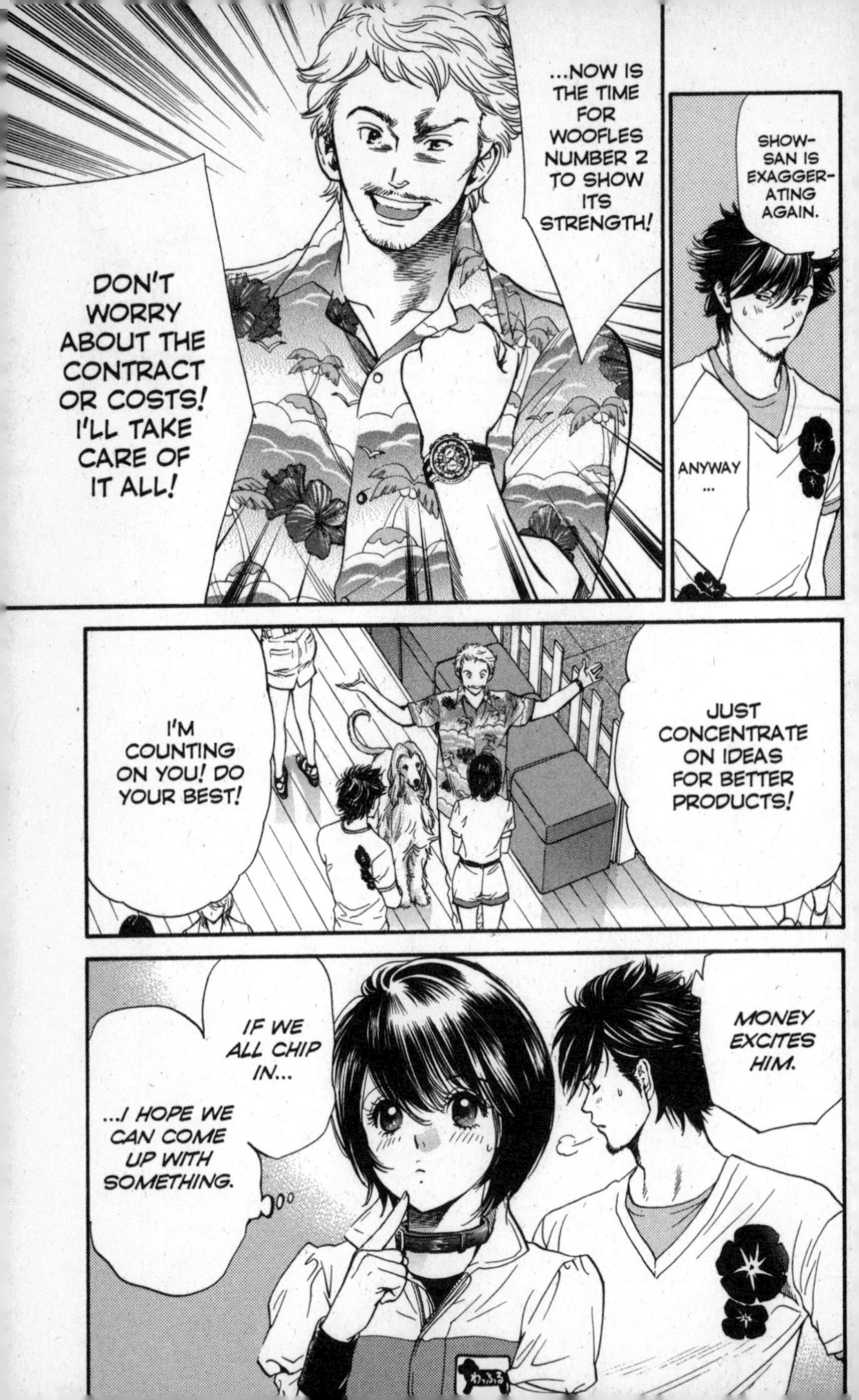
SHOW-SAN IS EXAGGERATING AGAIN.
ANYWAY...
...NOW IS THE TIME FOR WOOFLES NUMBER 2 TO SHOW ITS STRENGTH!
DON'T WORRY ABOUT THE CONTRACT OR COSTS! I'LL TAKE CARE OF IT ALL!
JUST CONCENTRATE ON IDEAS FOR BETTER PRODUCTS!
I'M COUNTING ON YOU! DO YOUR BEST!
MONEY EXCITES HIM.
IF WE ALL CHIP IN...
...I HOPE WE CAN COME UP WITH SOMETHING.

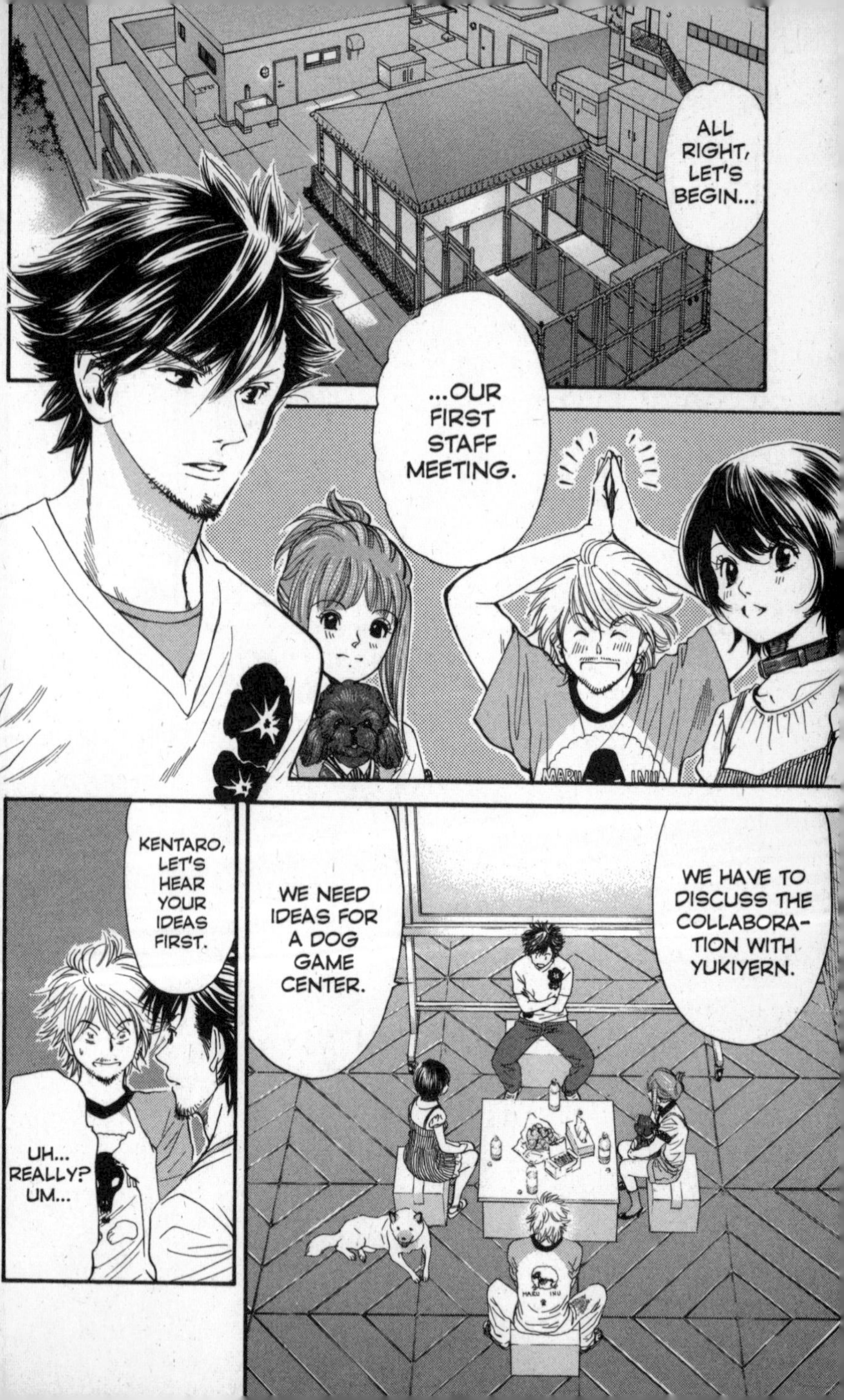
ALL RIGHT, LET'S BEGIN...
...OUR FIRST STAFF MEETING.
WE HAVE TO DISCUSS THE COLLABORA-TION WITH YUKIYERN.
WE NEED IDEAS FOR A DOG GAME CENTER.
KENTARO, LET'S HEAR YOUR IDEAS FIRST.
UH... REALLY? UM...

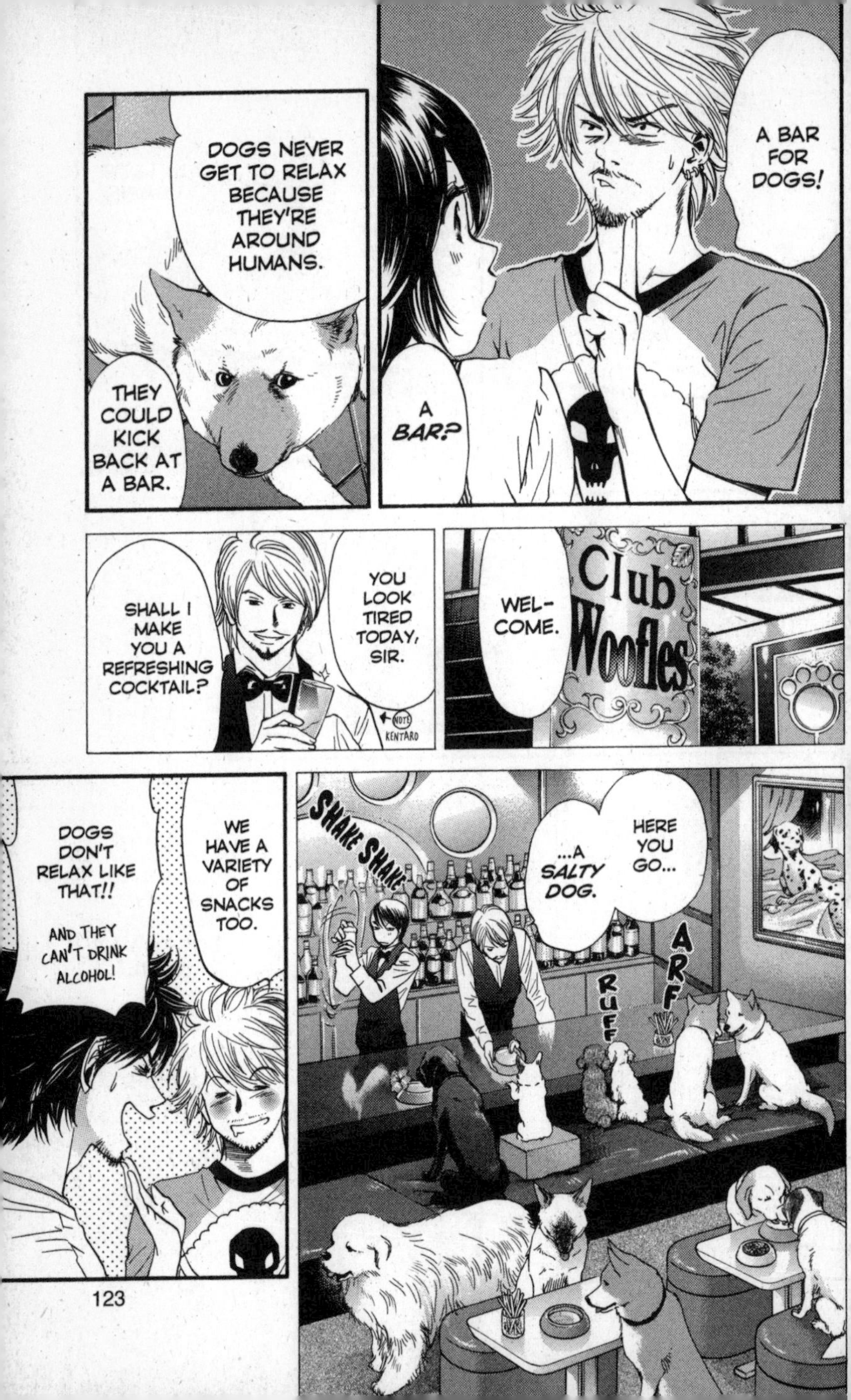
A BAR FOR DOGS!
A BAR?
DOGS NEVER GET TO RELAX BECAUSE THEY'RE AROUND HUMANS.
THEY COULD KICK BACK AT A BAR.
Club Woofles
WEL-COME.
YOU LOOK TIRED TODAY, SIR.
SHALL I MAKE YOU A REFRESHING COCKTAIL?
NOTE KENTARO
SHAKE SHAKE
HERE YOU GO...
...A SALTY DOG.
ARF
ARF
RUFF
WE HAVE A VARIETY OF SNACKS TOO.
DOGS DON'T RELAX LIKE THAT!!
AND THEY CAN'T DRINK ALCOHOL!

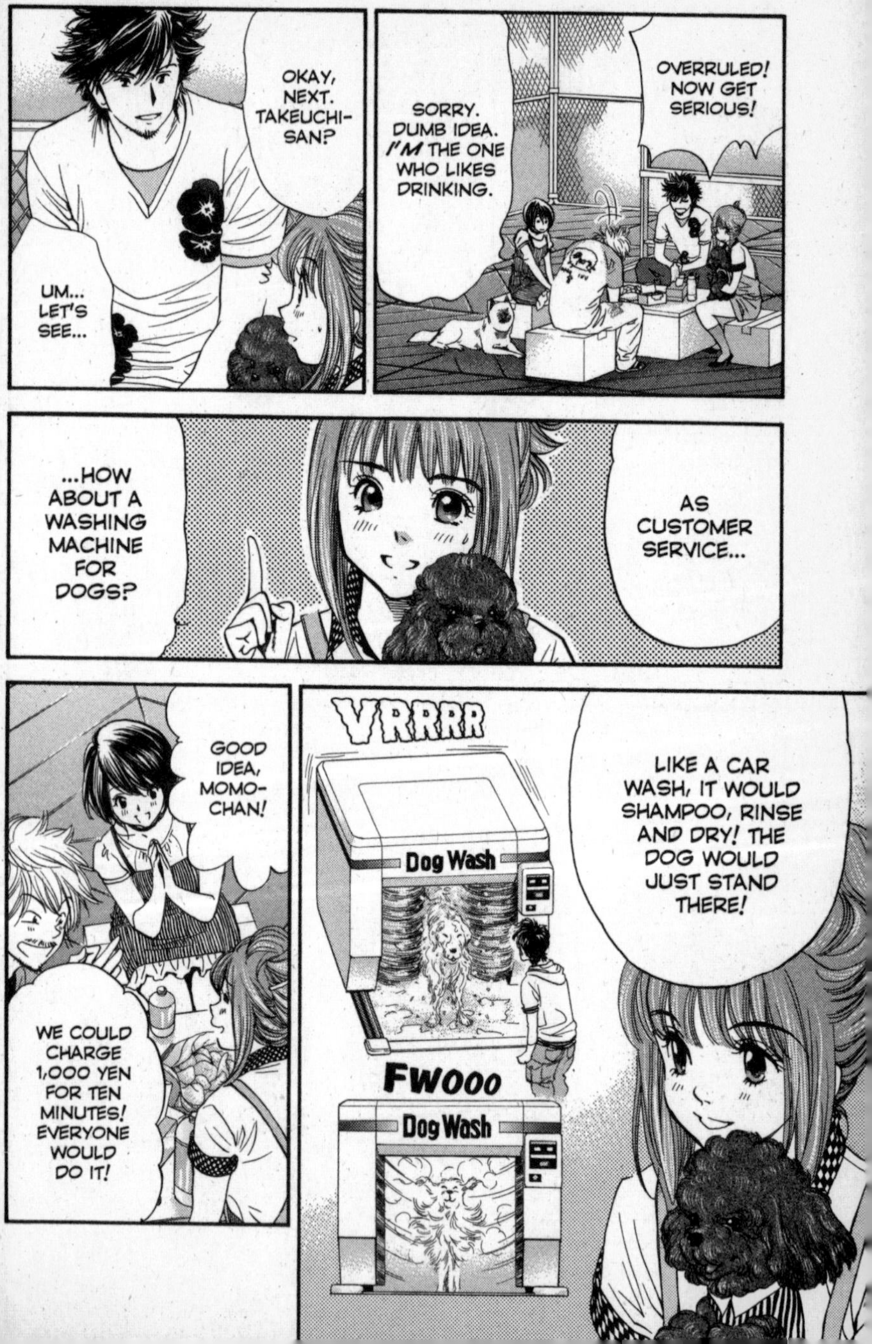
OVERRULED! NOW GET SERIOUS!
SORRY. DUMB IDEA. I'M THE ONE WHO LIKES DRINKING.
OKAY, NEXT. TAKEUCHI-SAN?
UM... LET'S SEE...
AS CUSTOMER SERVICE...
...HOW ABOUT A WASHING MACHINE FOR DOGS?
LIKE A CAR WASH, IT WOULD SHAMPOO, RINSE AND DRY! THE DOG WOULD JUST STAND THERE!
VRRRR
Dog Wash
FWOOO
Dog Wash
GOOD IDEA, MOMO-CHAN!
WE COULD CHARGE 1,000 YEN FOR TEN MINUTES! EVERYONE WOULD DO IT!

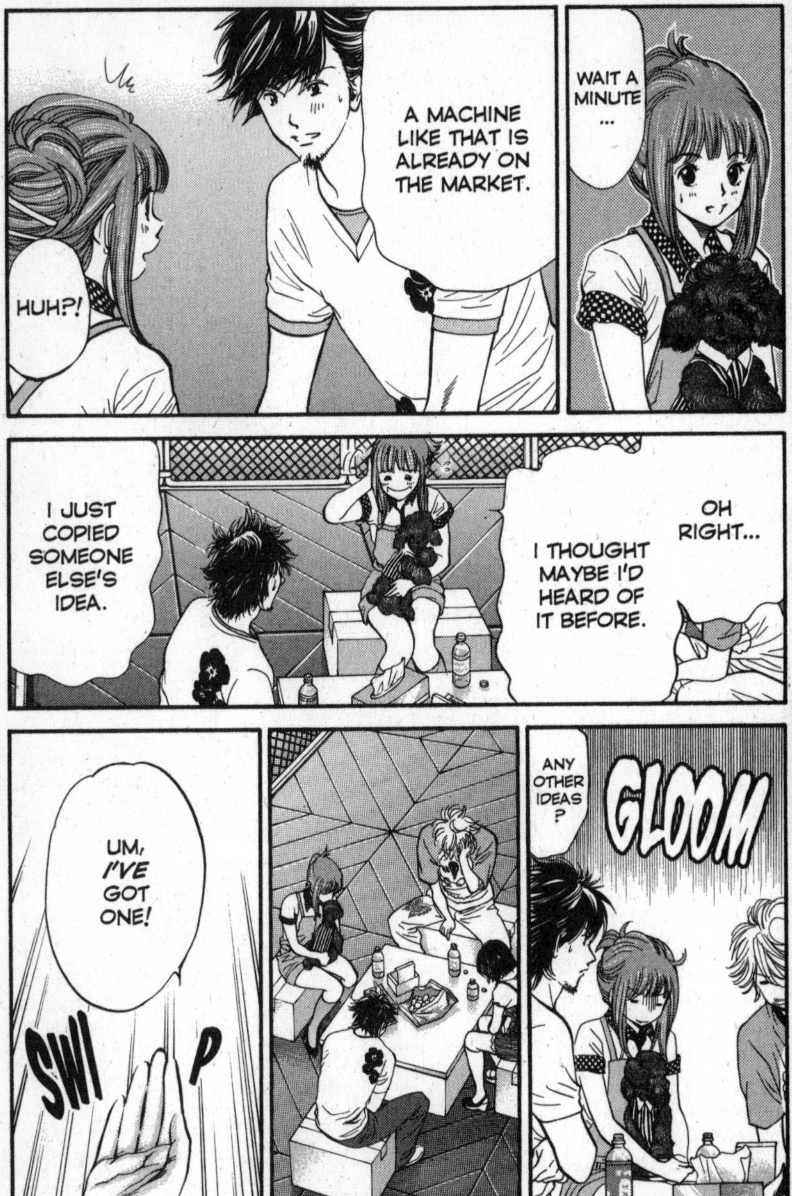
WAIT A MINUTE ...
A MACHINE LIKE THAT IS ALREADY ON THE MARKET.
HUH?!
OH RIGHT...
I THOUGHT MAYBE I'D HEARD OF IT BEFORE.
I JUST COPIED SOMEONE ELSE'S IDEA.
ANY OTHER IDEAS ?
GLOOM
UM, *I'VE* GOT ONE!
SWIP

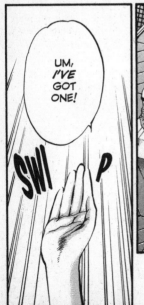

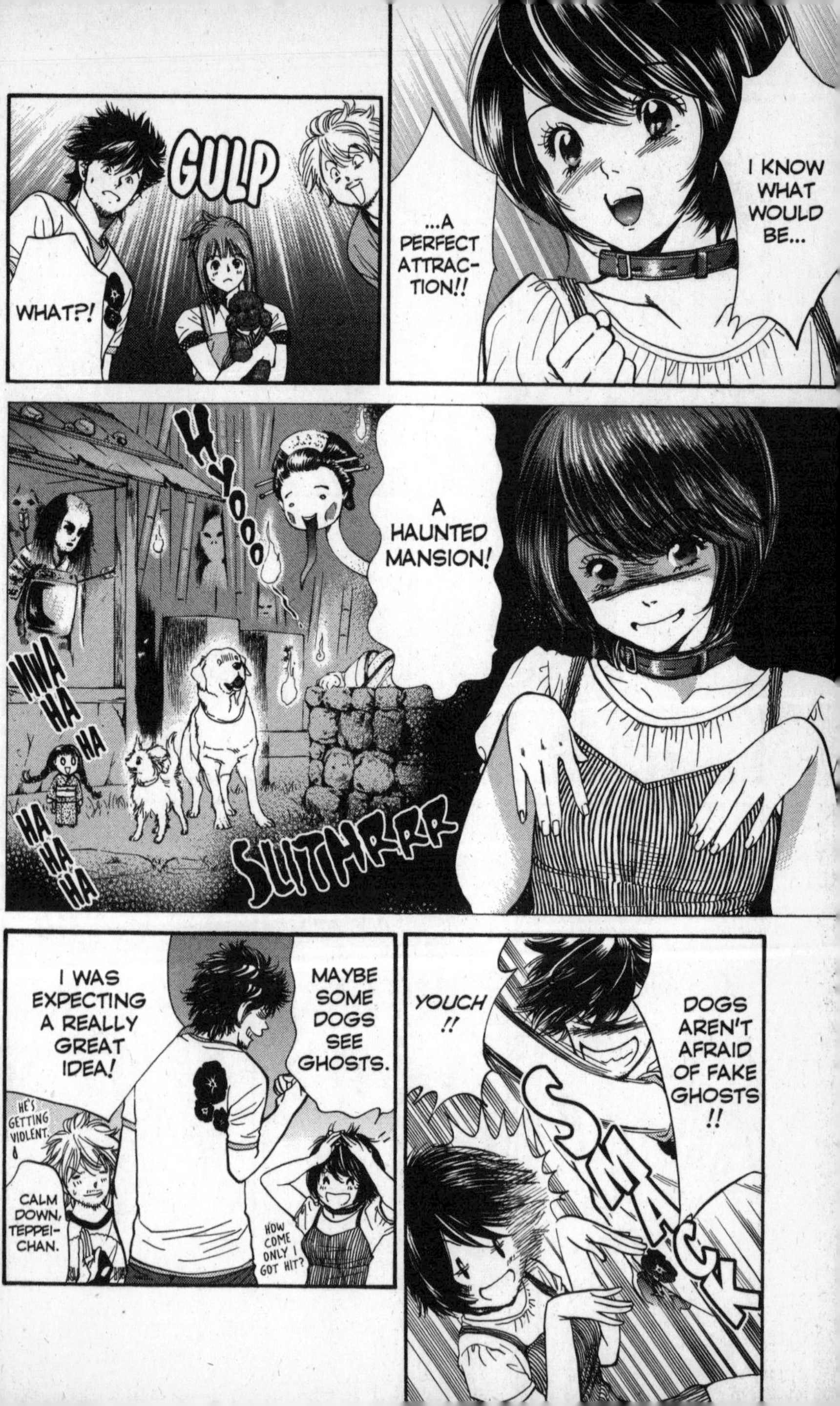
I KNOW WHAT WOULD BE...
...A PERFECT ATTRACTION!!
GULP
WHAT?!
A HAUNTED MANSION!
HYOOO
MWA HA HA
HA HA HA HA
SLITHRRR
DOGS AREN'T AFRAID OF FAKE GHOSTS!!
YOUCH!!
SMACK
MAYBE SOME DOGS SEE GHOSTS.
I WAS EXPECTING A REALLY GREAT IDEA!
HE'S GETTING VIOLENT.
HOW COME ONLY I GOT HIT?
CALM DOWN, TEPPEI-CHAN.

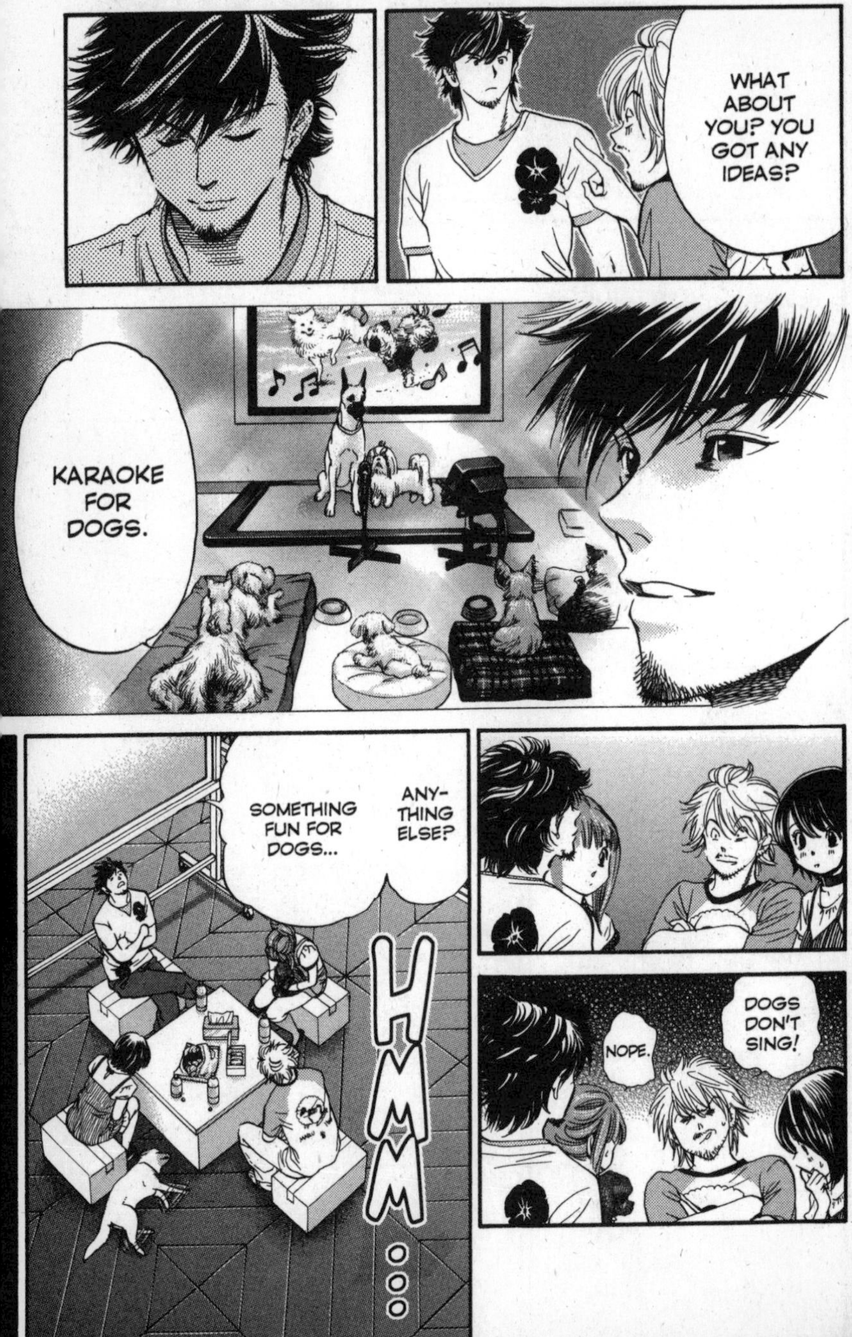
WHAT ABOUT YOU? YOU GOT ANY IDEAS?
KARAOKE FOR DOGS.
DOGS DON'T SING!
NOPE.
ANY-THING ELSE?
SOMETHING FUN FOR DOGS...
HMMM...

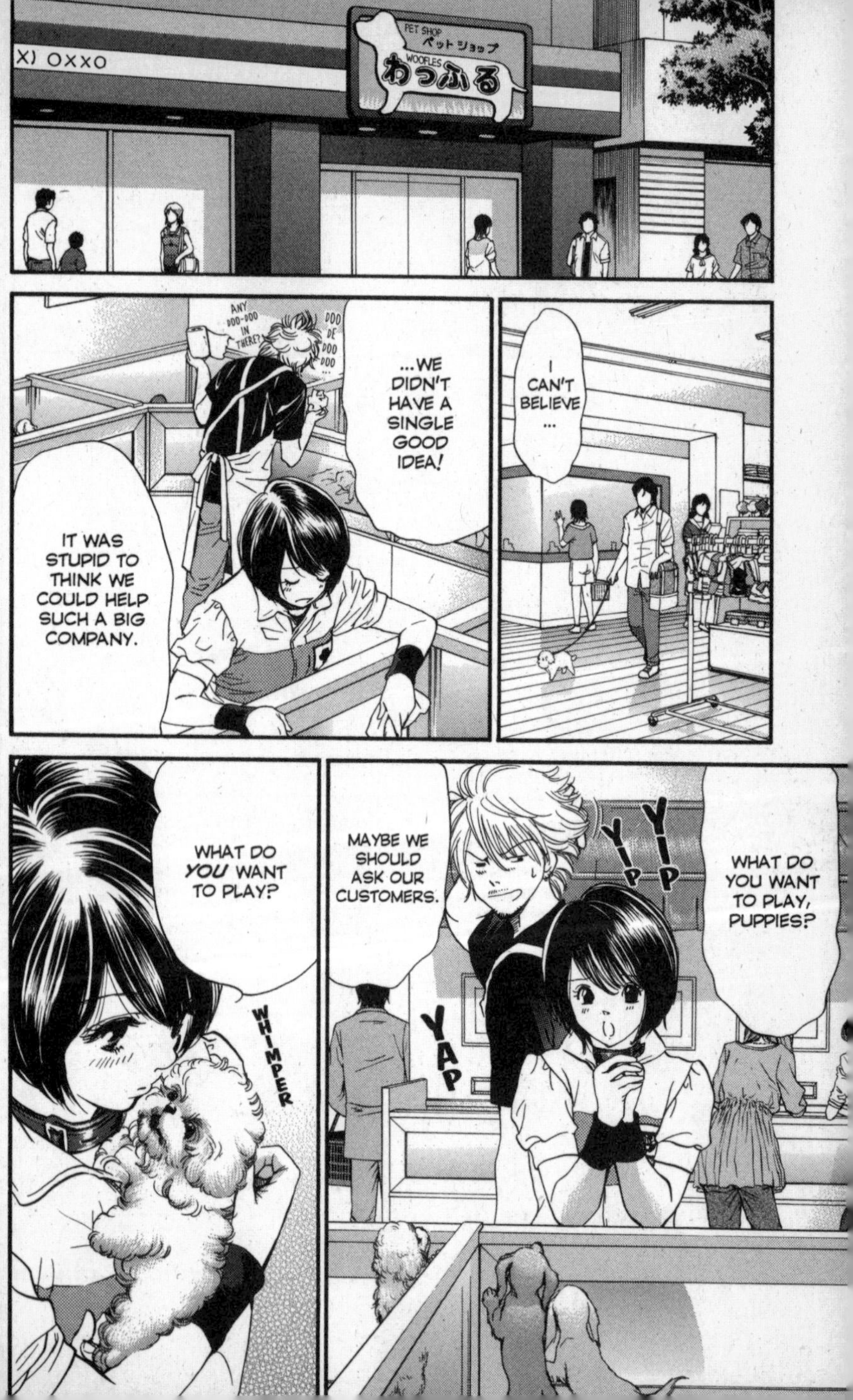

PET SHOP
ペットショップ
WOOFLES
わっふる
X) OXXO
I CAN'T BELIEVE...
...WE DIDN'T HAVE A SINGLE GOOD IDEA!
DOO DE DOO DOO...
ANY DOO-DOO IN THERE?
IT WAS STUPID TO THINK WE COULD HELP SUCH A BIG COMPANY.
WHAT DO YOU WANT TO PLAY, PUPPIES?
YIP
YIP
MAYBE WE SHOULD ASK OUR CUSTOMERS.
YAP
WHAT DO *YOU* WANT TO PLAY?
WHIMPER

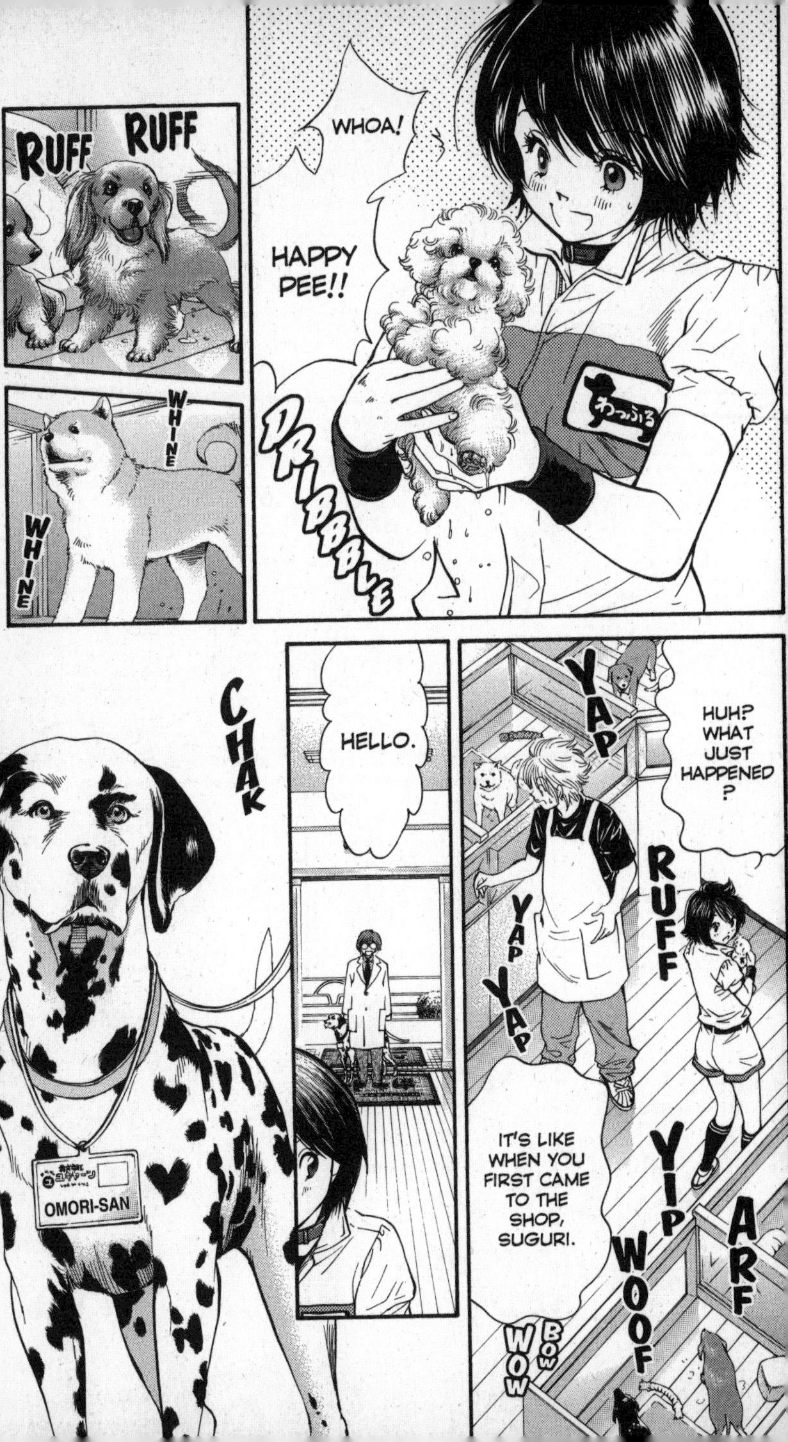
WHOA!
HAPPY PEE!!
わっふる
DRIBBBLE
RUFF RUFF
WHINE WHINE
YAP
HUH? WHAT JUST HAPPENED?
RUFF
YAP YAP YAP
IT'S LIKE WHEN YOU FIRST CAME TO THE SHOP, SUGURI.
YIP
ARF
WOOF
BOW WOW
HELLO.
CHAK
OMORI-SAN

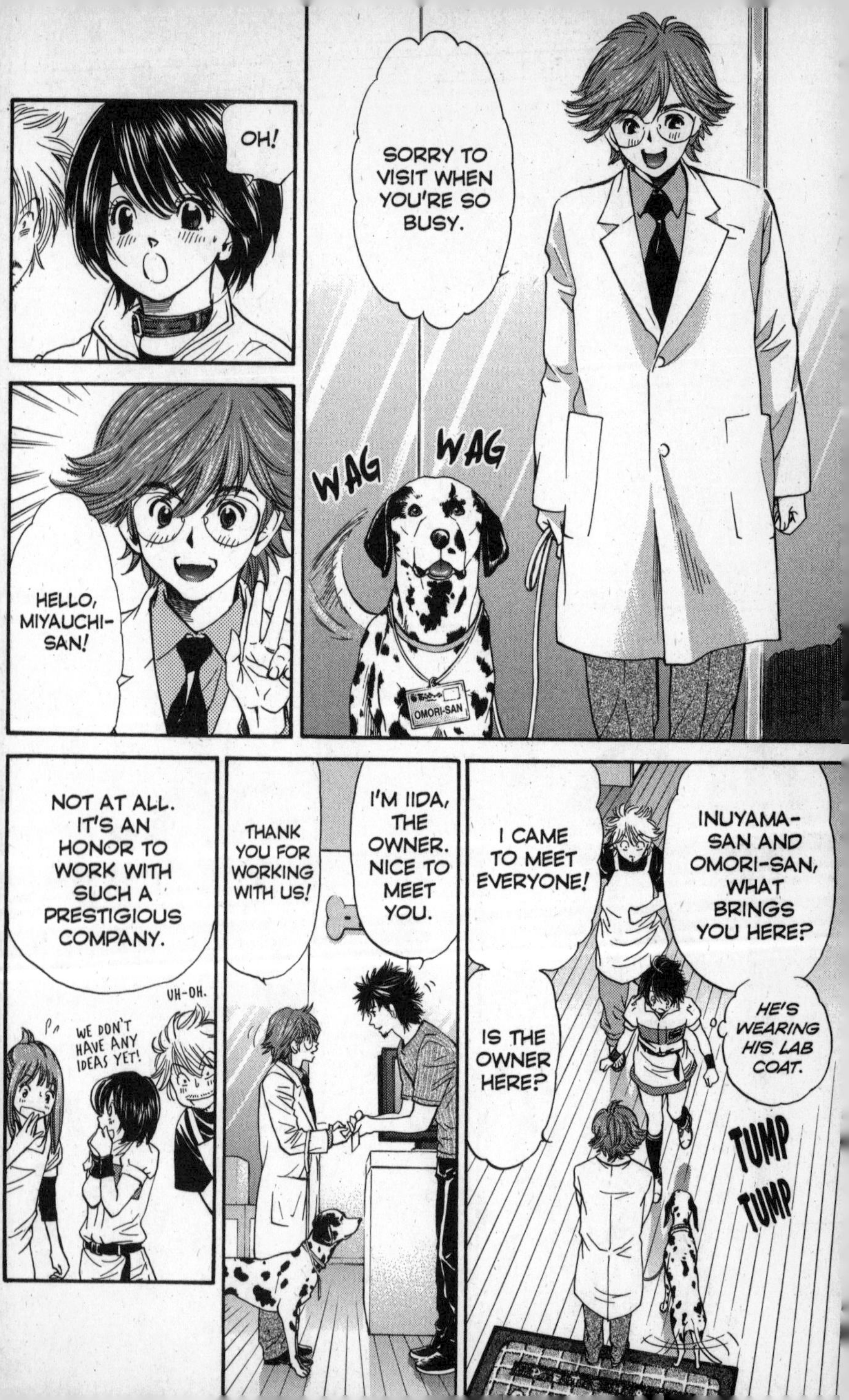
SORRY TO VISIT WHEN YOU'RE SO BUSY.
WAG
WAG
OMORI-SAN
OH!
HELLO, MIYAUCHI-SAN!
INUYAMA-SAN AND OMORI-SAN, WHAT BRINGS YOU HERE?
HE'S WEARING HIS LAB COAT.
TUMP TUMP
I CAME TO MEET EVERYONE!
IS THE OWNER HERE?
I'M IIDA, THE OWNER. NICE TO MEET YOU.
THANK YOU FOR WORKING WITH US!
NOT AT ALL. IT'S AN HONOR TO WORK WITH SUCH A PRESTIGIOUS COMPANY.
UH-OH.
WE DON'T HAVE ANY IDEAS YET!

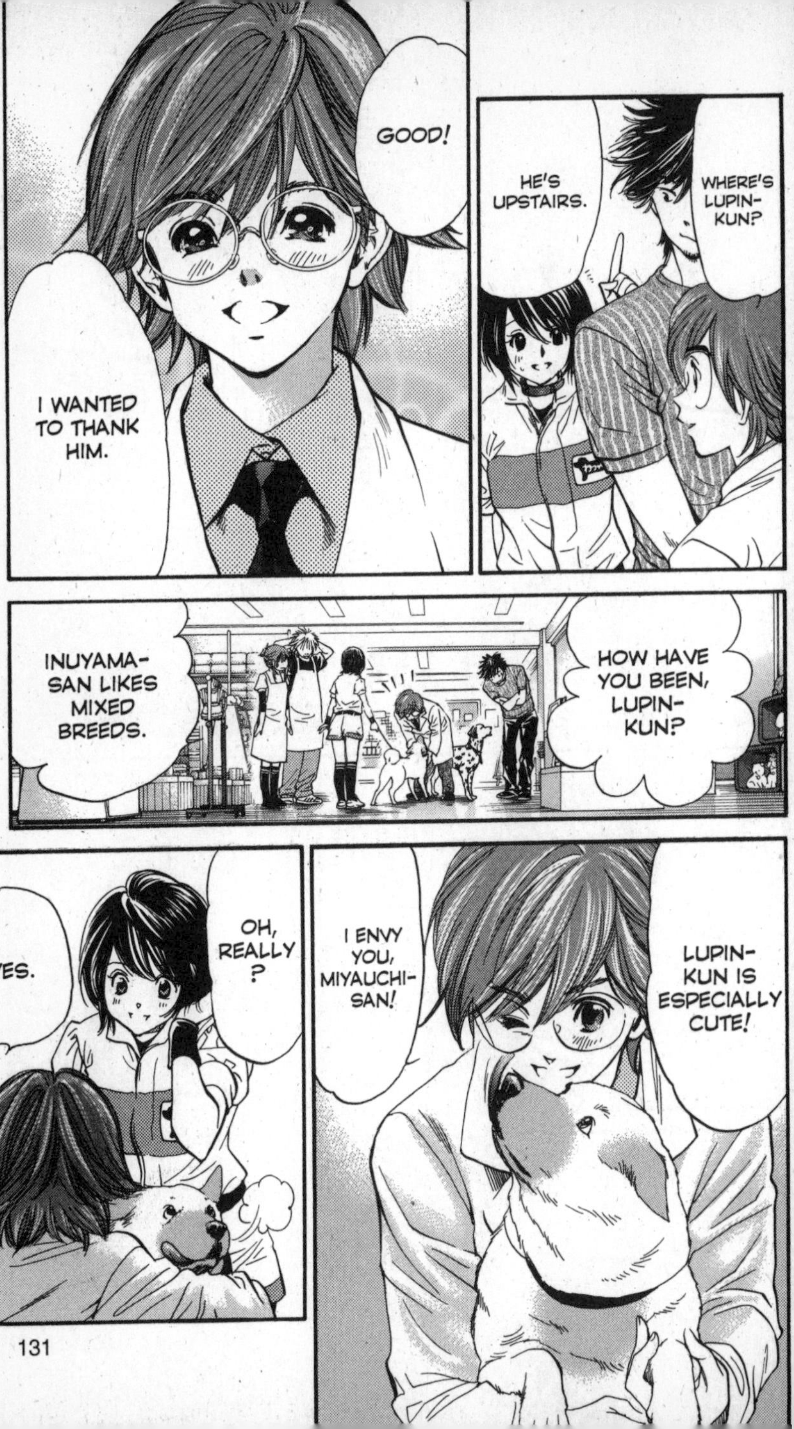
WHERE'S LUPIN-KUN?
HE'S UPSTAIRS.
GOOD!
I WANTED TO THANK HIM.
HOW HAVE YOU BEEN, LUPIN-KUN?
INUYAMA-SAN LIKES MIXED BREEDS.
LUPIN-KUN IS ESPECIALLY CUTE!
I ENVY YOU, MIYAUCHI-SAN!
OH, REALLY?
YES.

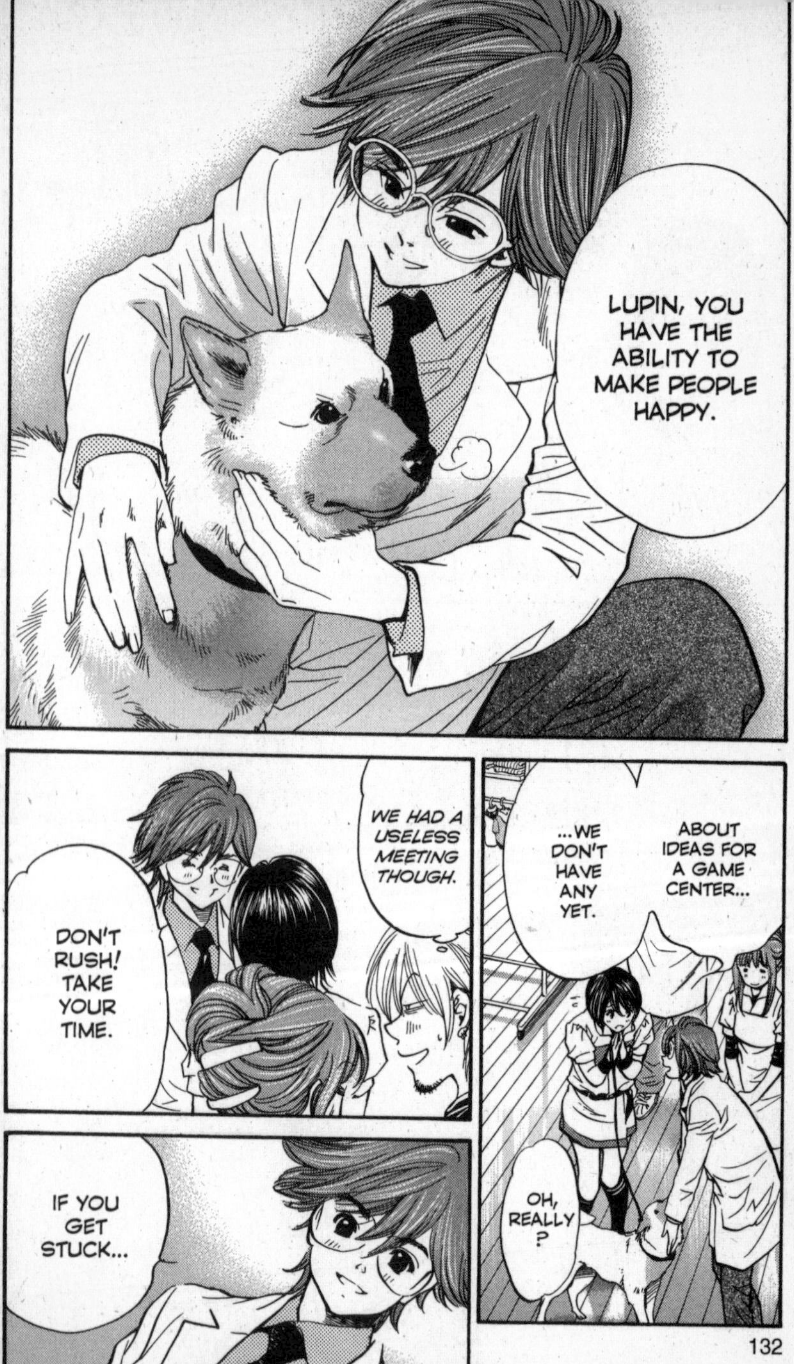
LUPIN, YOU HAVE THE ABILITY TO MAKE PEOPLE HAPPY.
ABOUT IDEAS FOR A GAME CENTER...
...WE DON'T HAVE ANY YET.
OH, REALLY?
WE HAD A USELESS MEETING THOUGH.
DON'T RUSH! TAKE YOUR TIME.
IF YOU GET STUCK...

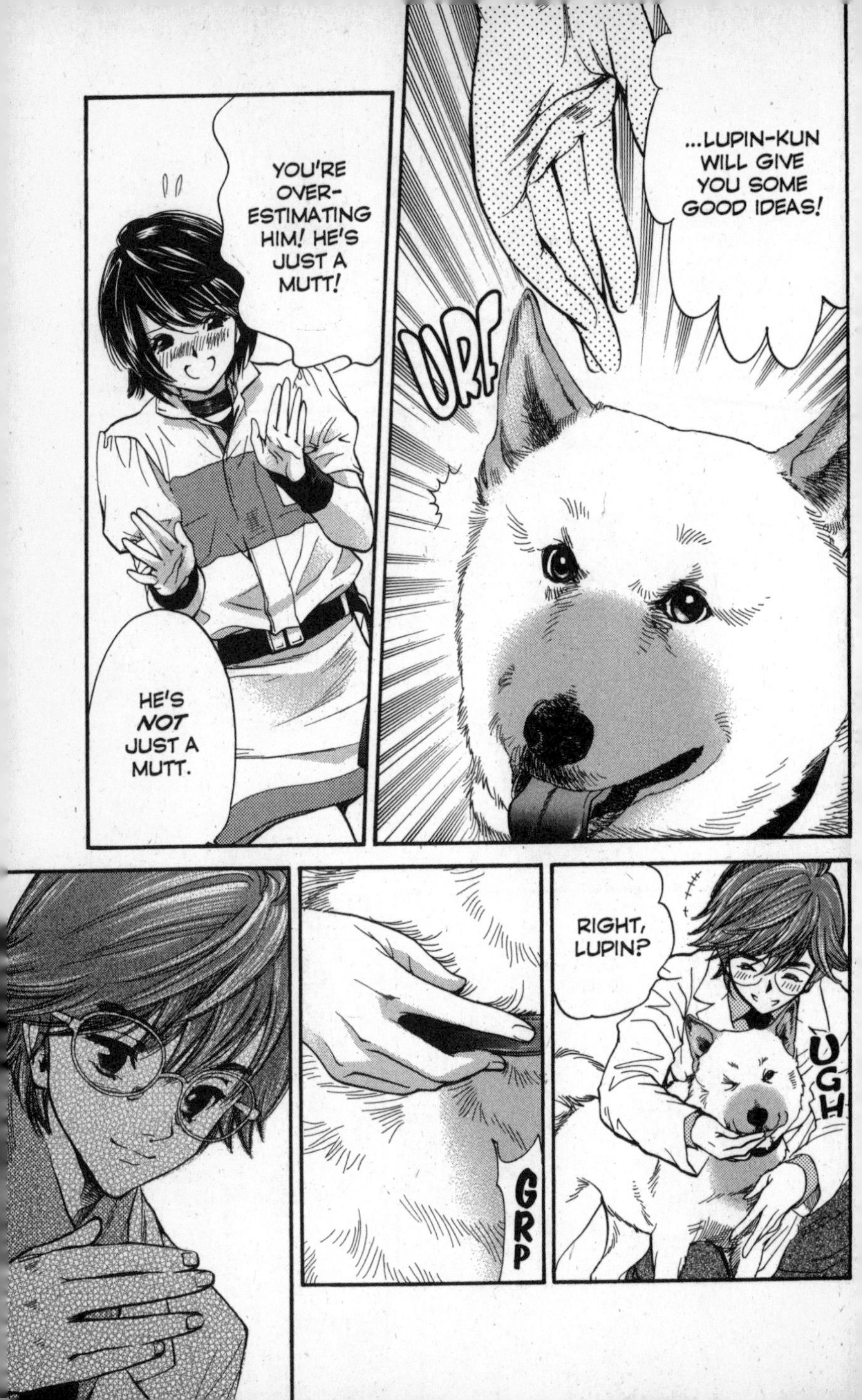
...LUPIN-KUN WILL GIVE YOU SOME GOOD IDEAS!
URF
YOU'RE OVER-ESTIMATING HIM! HE'S JUST A MUTT!
HE'S *NOT* JUST A MUTT.
RIGHT, LUPIN?
UGH
GRP

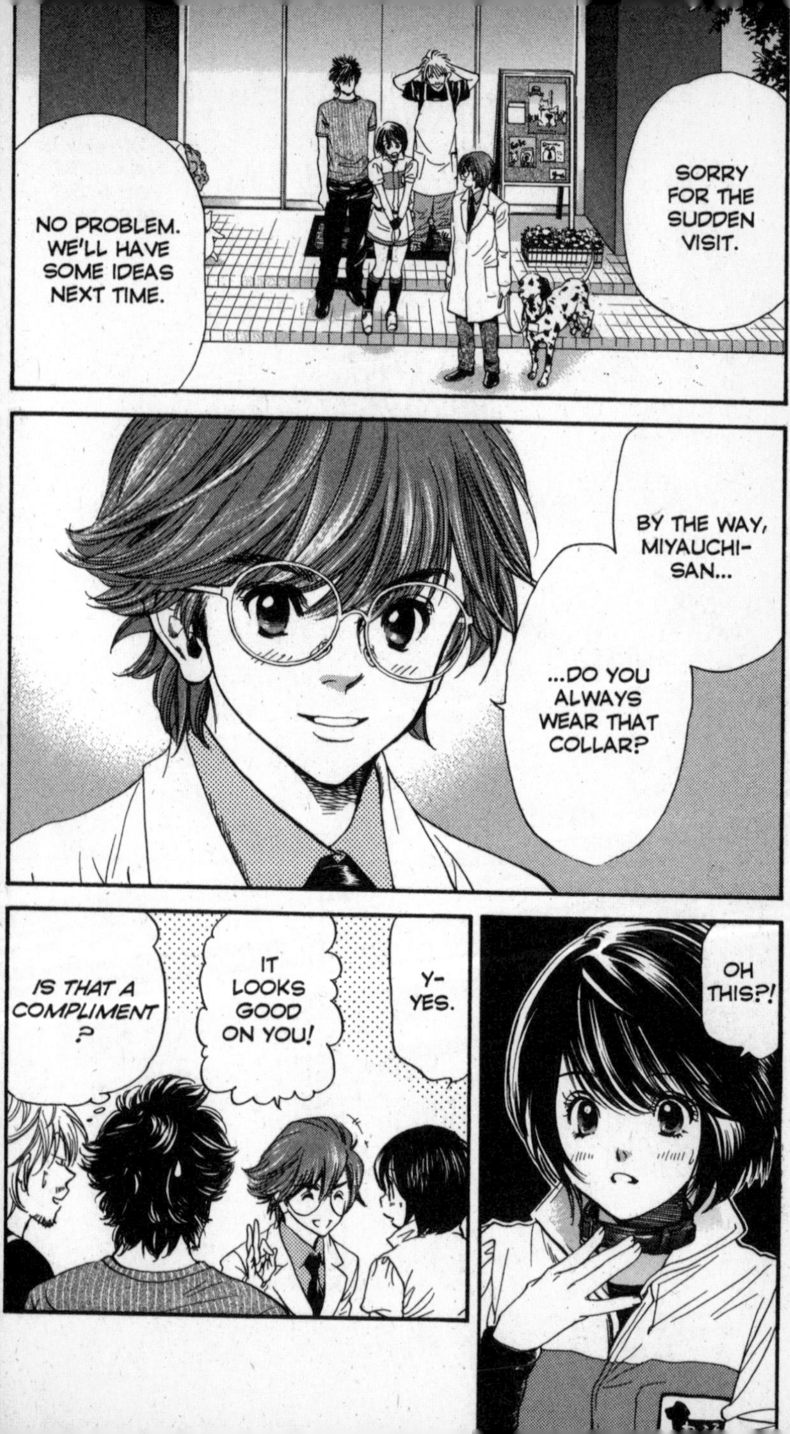
SORRY FOR THE SUDDEN VISIT.
NO PROBLEM. WE'LL HAVE SOME IDEAS NEXT TIME.
BY THE WAY, MIYAUCHI-SAN...
...DO YOU ALWAYS WEAR THAT COLLAR?
OH THIS?!
Y-YES.
IT LOOKS GOOD ON YOU!
IS THAT A COMPLIMENT?

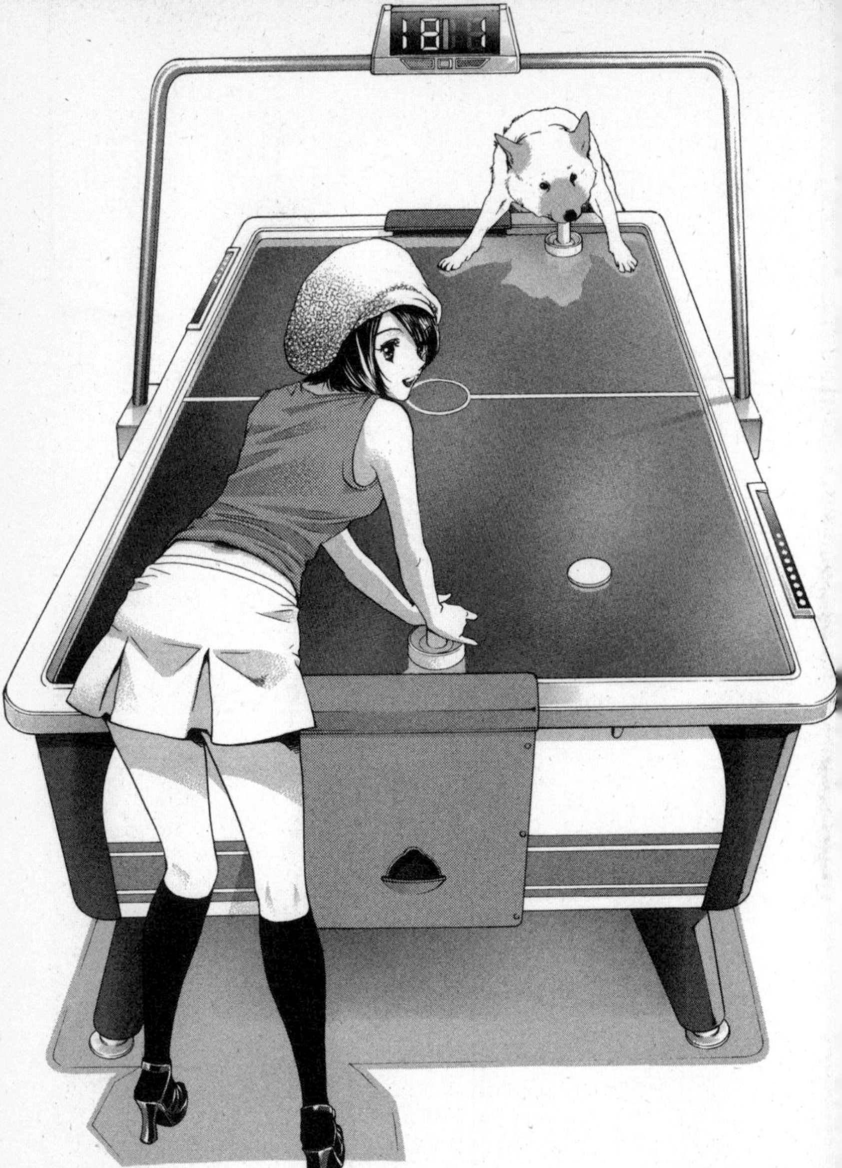

CHAPTER 181:
AWAKEN YOUR HUNTER INSTINCTS!

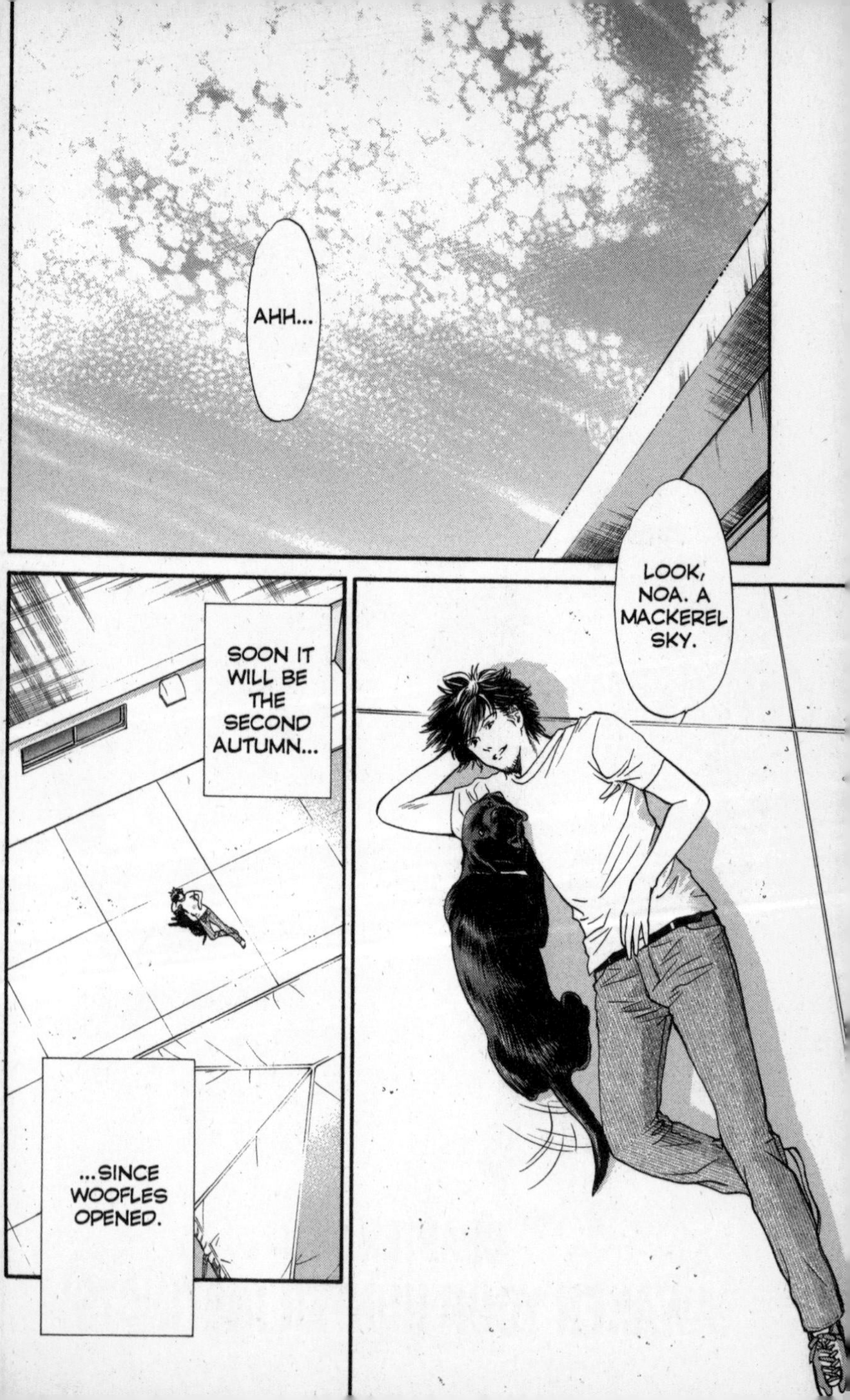
AHH...
LOOK, NOA. A MACKEREL SKY.
SOON IT WILL BE THE SECOND AUTUMN...
...SINCE WOOFLES OPENED.

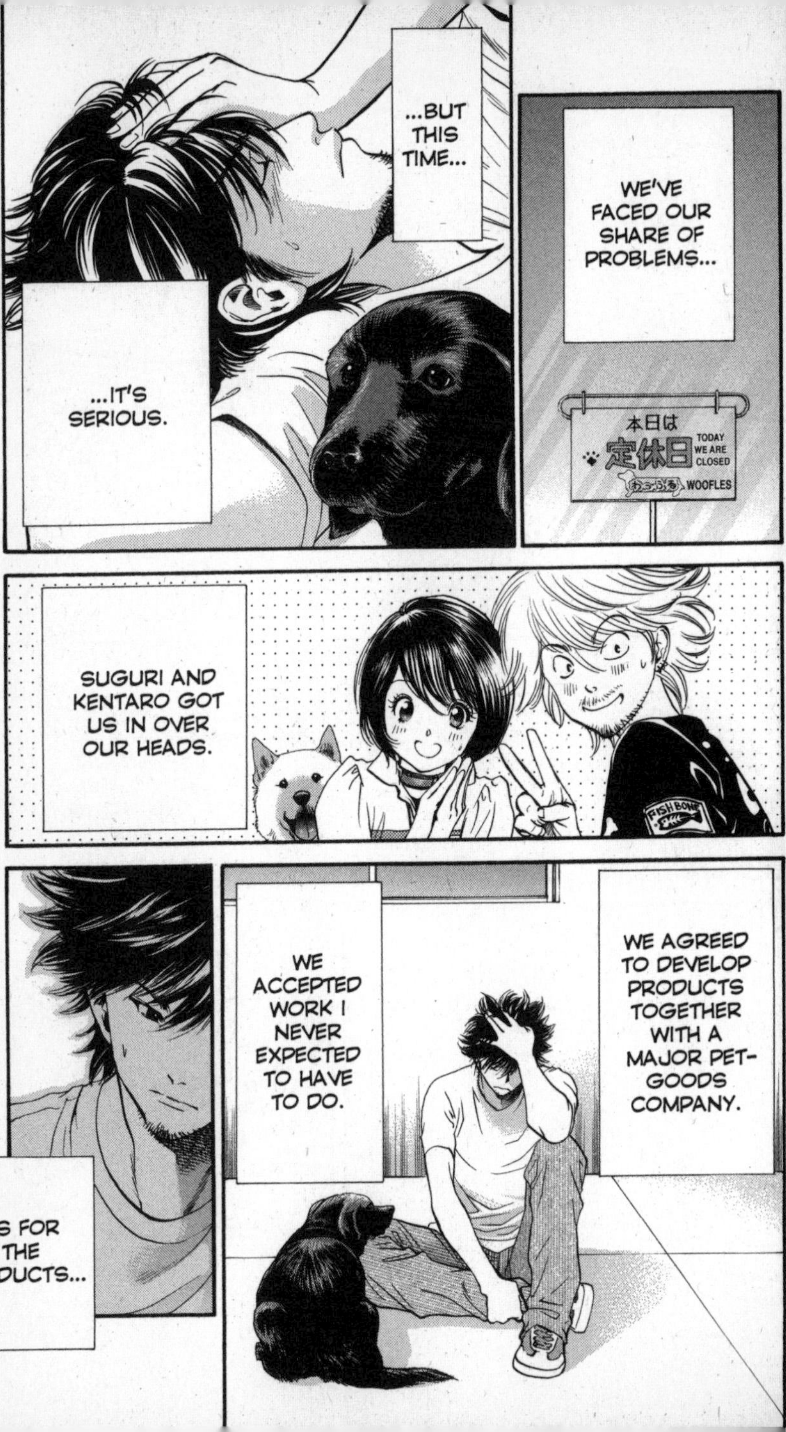
WE'VE FACED OUR SHARE OF PROBLEMS...
本日は 定休日 TODAY WE ARE CLOSED
WOOFLES
...BUT THIS TIME...
...IT'S SERIOUS.
SUGURI AND KENTARO GOT US IN OVER OUR HEADS.
FISH BONE
WE AGREED TO DEVELOP PRODUCTS TOGETHER WITH A MAJOR PET-GOODS COMPANY.
WE ACCEPTED WORK I NEVER EXPECTED TO HAVE TO DO.
AS FOR THE PRODUCTS...

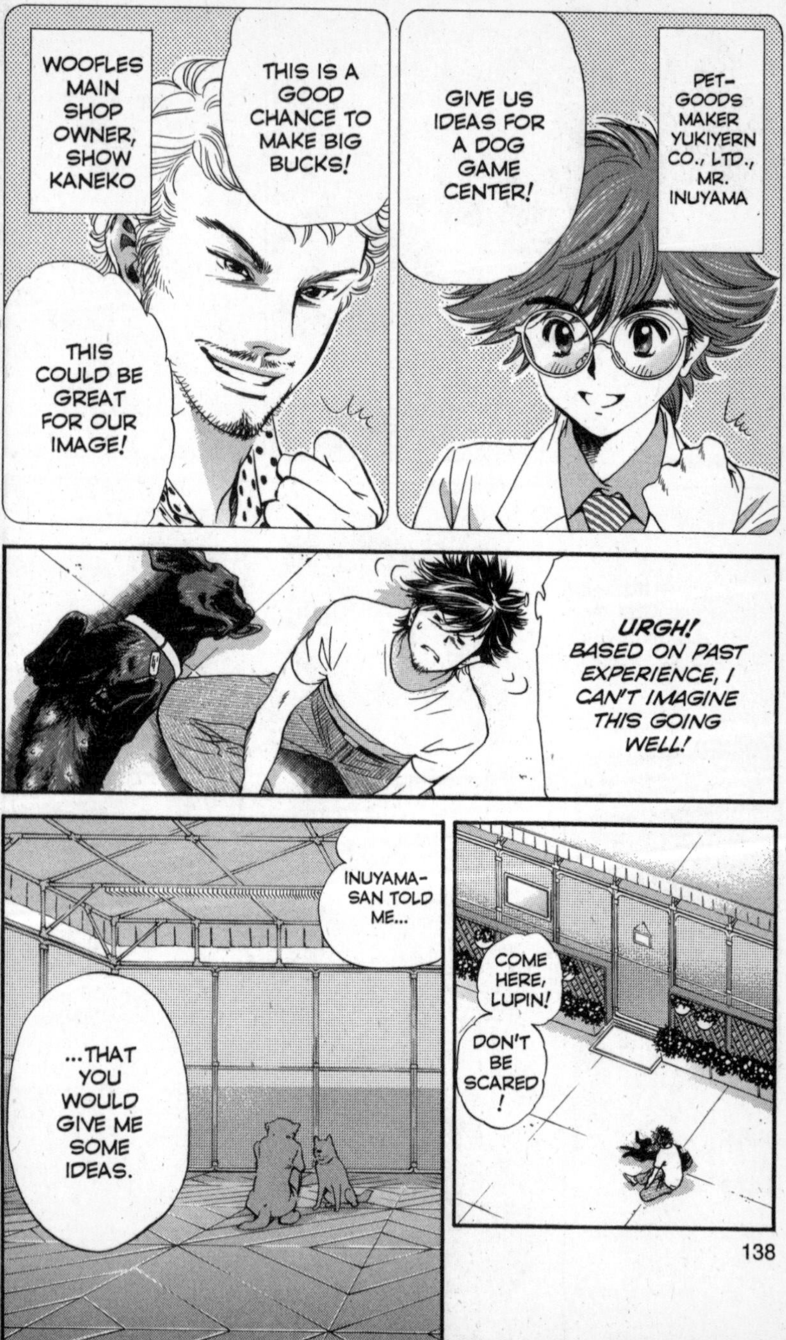
PET-GOODS MAKER YUKIYERN CO., LTD., MR. INUYAMA
GIVE US IDEAS FOR A DOG GAME CENTER!
THIS IS A GOOD CHANCE TO MAKE BIG BUCKS!
WOOFLES MAIN SHOP OWNER, SHOW KANEKO
THIS COULD BE GREAT FOR OUR IMAGE!
URGH! BASED ON PAST EXPERIENCE, I CAN'T IMAGINE THIS GOING WELL!
COME HERE, LUPIN!
DON'T BE SCARED!
INUYAMA-SAN TOLD ME...
...THAT YOU WOULD GIVE ME SOME IDEAS.

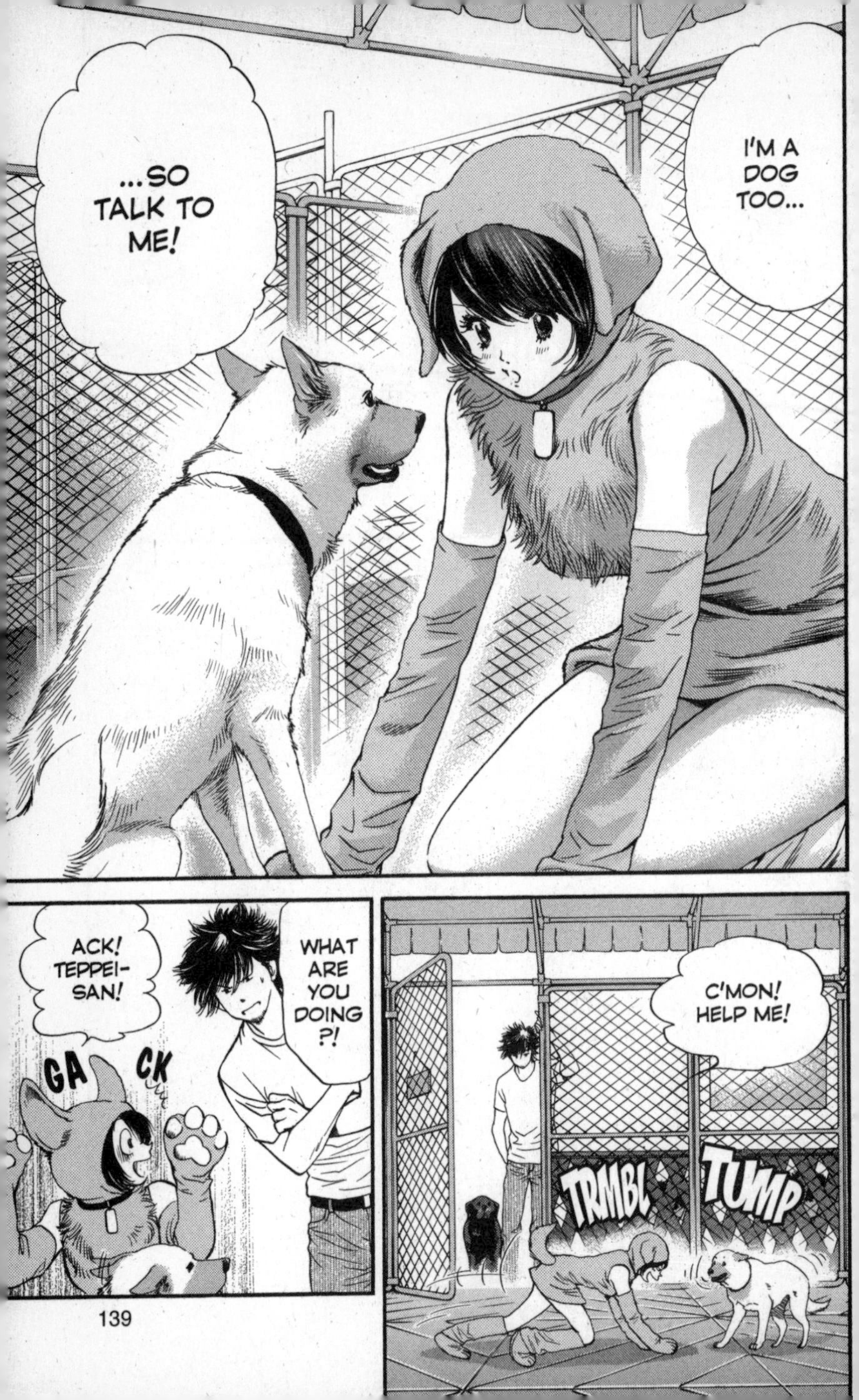
I'M A DOG TOO...
...SO TALK TO ME!
C'MON! HELP ME!
TRMBL TUMP
WHAT ARE YOU DOING?!
ACK! TEPPEI-SAN!
GACK

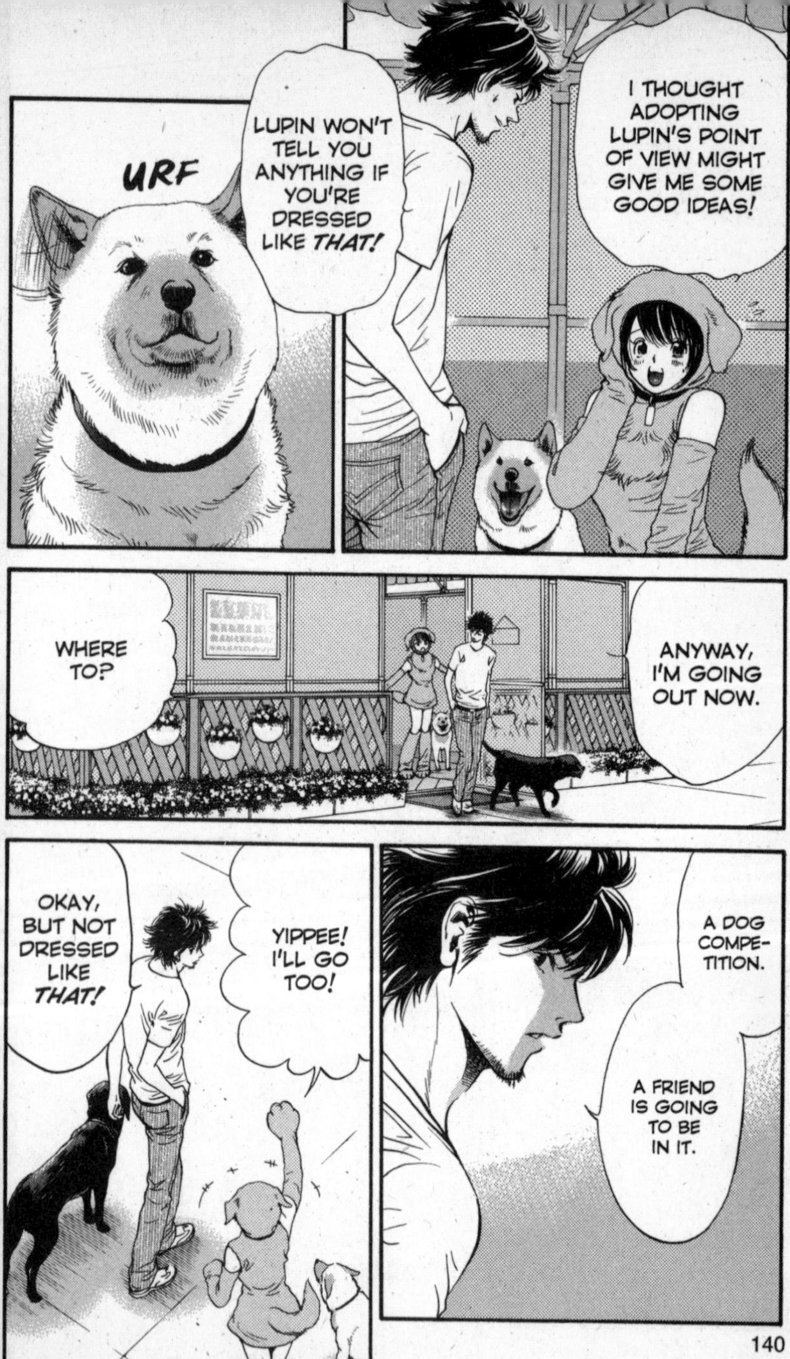
I THOUGHT ADOPTING LUPIN'S POINT OF VIEW MIGHT GIVE ME SOME GOOD IDEAS!
LUPIN WON'T TELL YOU ANYTHING IF YOU'RE DRESSED LIKE *THAT!*
URF
ANYWAY, I'M GOING OUT NOW.
WHERE TO?
A DOG COMPE-TITION.
A FRIEND IS GOING TO BE IN IT.
YIPPEE! I'LL GO TOO!
OKAY, BUT NOT DRESSED LIKE *THAT!*

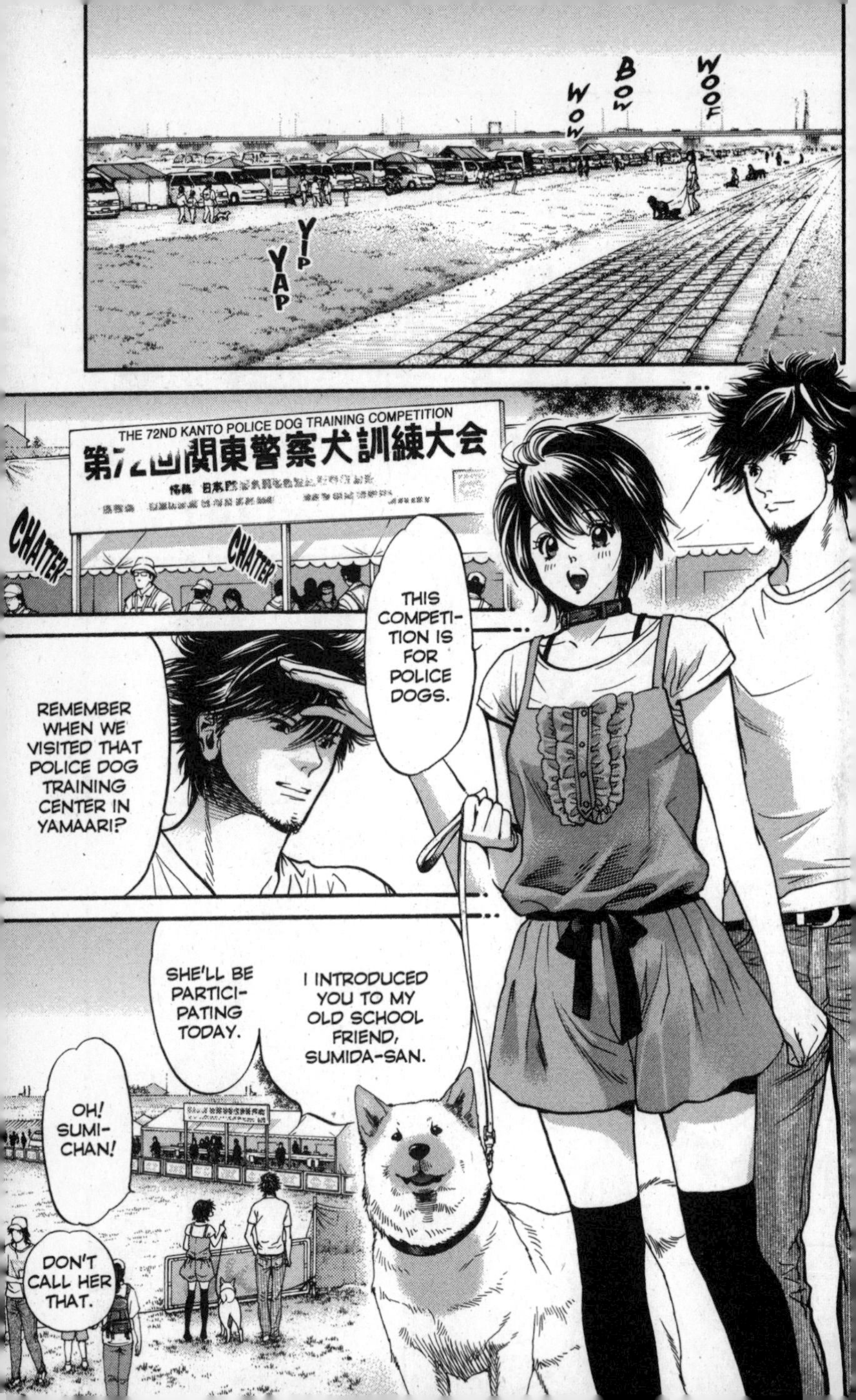
WOOF
BOW
WOW
YIP
YAP
THE 72ND KANTO POLICE DOG TRAINING COMPETITION
第72回関東警察犬訓練大会
CHATTER
CHATTER
THIS COMPETITION IS FOR POLICE DOGS.
REMEMBER WHEN WE VISITED THAT POLICE DOG TRAINING CENTER IN YAMAARI?
I INTRODUCED YOU TO MY OLD SCHOOL FRIEND, SUMIDA-SAN.
SHE'LL BE PARTICIPATING TODAY.
OH! SUMI-CHAN!
DON'T CALL HER THAT.

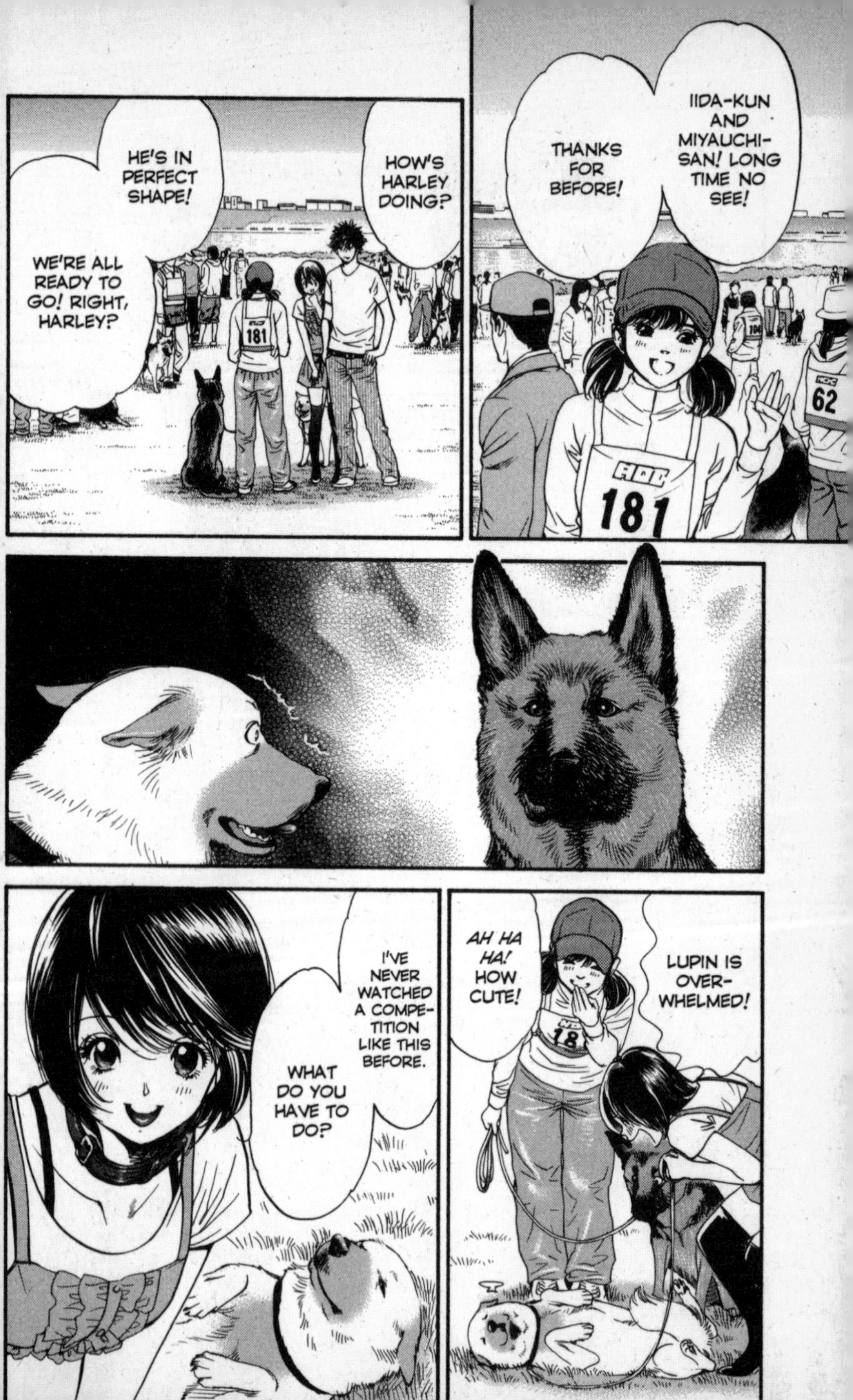
IIDA-KUN AND MIYAUCHI-SAN! LONG TIME NO SEE!
THANKS FOR BEFORE!
181
HOW'S HARLEY DOING?
HE'S IN PERFECT SHAPE!
WE'RE ALL READY TO GO! RIGHT, HARLEY?
LUPIN IS OVER-WHELMED!
AH HA HA! HOW CUTE!
I'VE NEVER WATCHED A COMPE-TITION LIKE THIS BEFORE.
WHAT DO YOU HAVE TO DO?

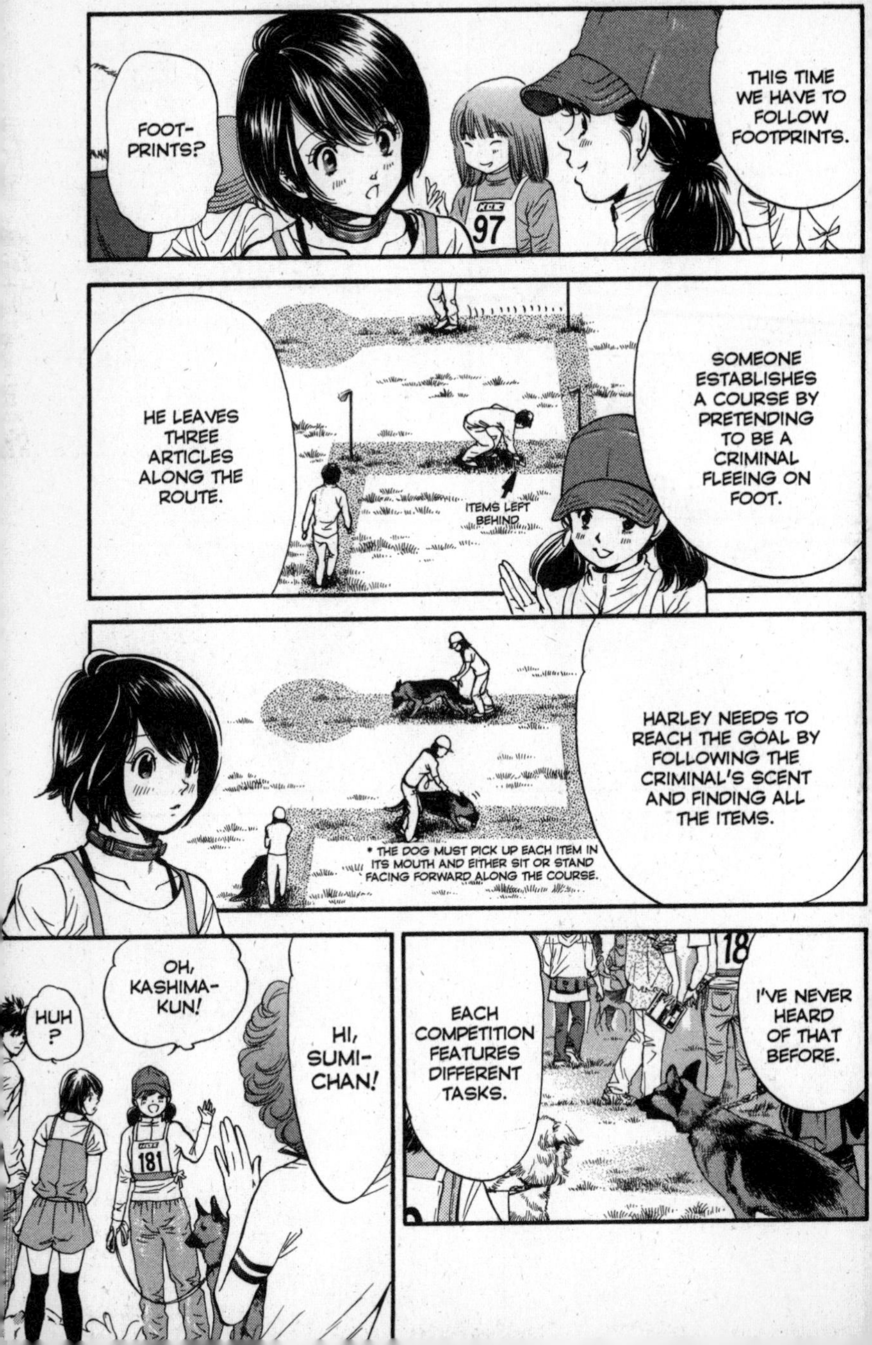
THIS TIME WE HAVE TO FOLLOW FOOTPRINTS.
FOOT-PRINTS?
97
SOMEONE ESTABLISHES A COURSE BY PRETENDING TO BE A CRIMINAL FLEEING ON FOOT.
HE LEAVES THREE ARTICLES ALONG THE ROUTE.
ITEMS LEFT BEHIND
HARLEY NEEDS TO REACH THE GOAL BY FOLLOWING THE CRIMINAL'S SCENT AND FINDING ALL THE ITEMS.
* THE DOG MUST PICK UP EACH ITEM IN ITS MOUTH AND EITHER SIT OR STAND FACING FORWARD ALONG THE COURSE.
I'VE NEVER HEARD OF THAT BEFORE.
EACH COMPETITION FEATURES DIFFERENT TASKS.
HI, SUMI-CHAN!
OH, KASHIMA-KUN!
HUH?
181

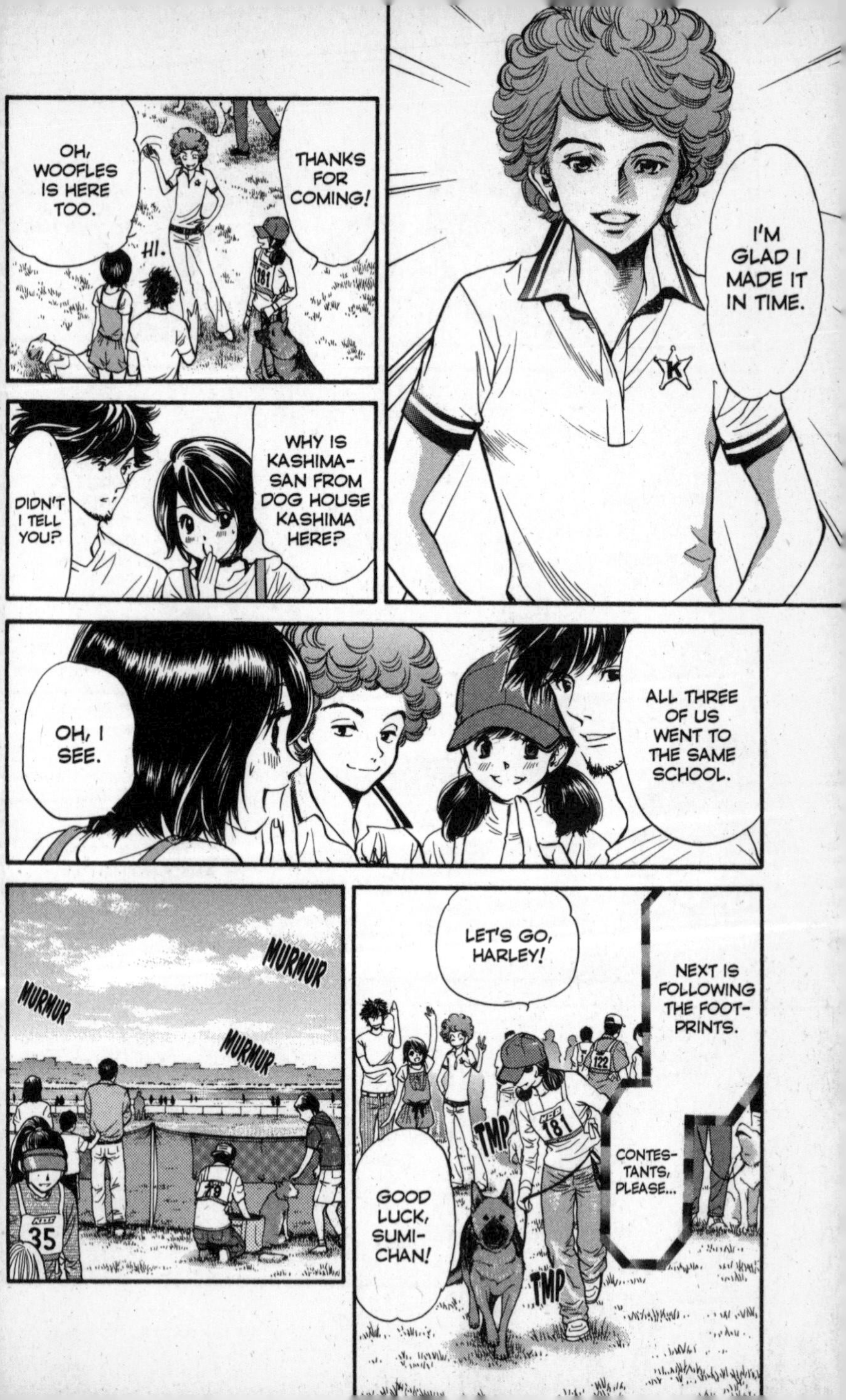
I'M GLAD I MADE IT IN TIME.
THANKS FOR COMING!
OH, WOOFLES IS HERE TOO.
HI.
181
WHY IS KASHIMA-SAN FROM DOG HOUSE KASHIMA HERE?
DIDN'T I TELL YOU?
ALL THREE OF US WENT TO THE SAME SCHOOL.
OH, I SEE.
NEXT IS FOLLOWING THE FOOT-PRINTS.
LET'S GO, HARLEY!
122
181
CONTES-TANTS, PLEASE...
TMP
GOOD LUCK, SUMI-CHAN!
TMP
MURMUR
MURMUR
MURMUR
35

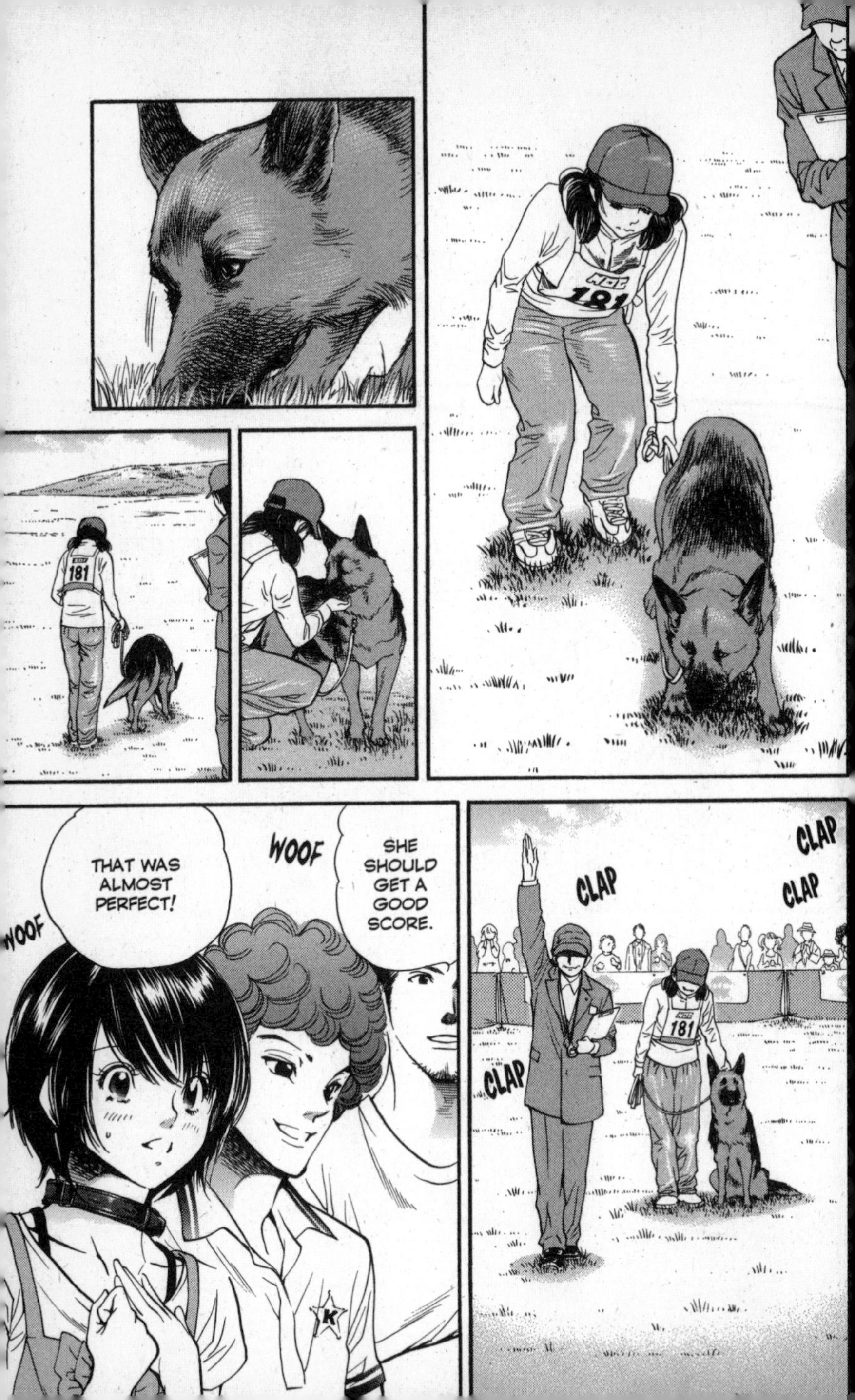
CLAP
CLAP
CLAP
CLAP
SHE SHOULD GET A GOOD SCORE.
WOOF
THAT WAS ALMOST PERFECT!
WOOF

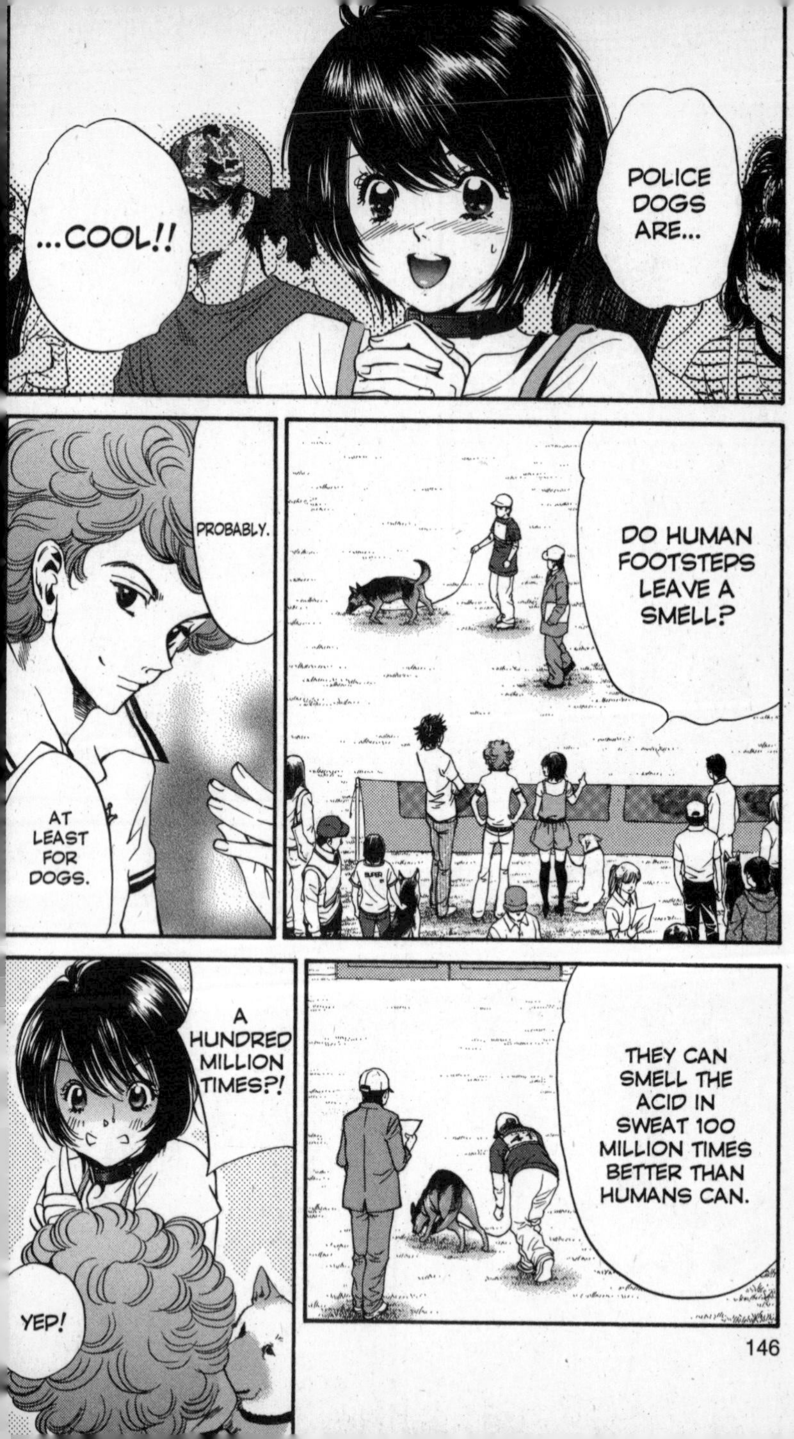
POLICE DOGS ARE...
...COOL!!
DO HUMAN FOOTSTEPS LEAVE A SMELL?
PROBABLY.
AT LEAST FOR DOGS.
THEY CAN SMELL THE ACID IN SWEAT 100 MILLION TIMES BETTER THAN HUMANS CAN.
A HUNDRED MILLION TIMES?!
YEP!

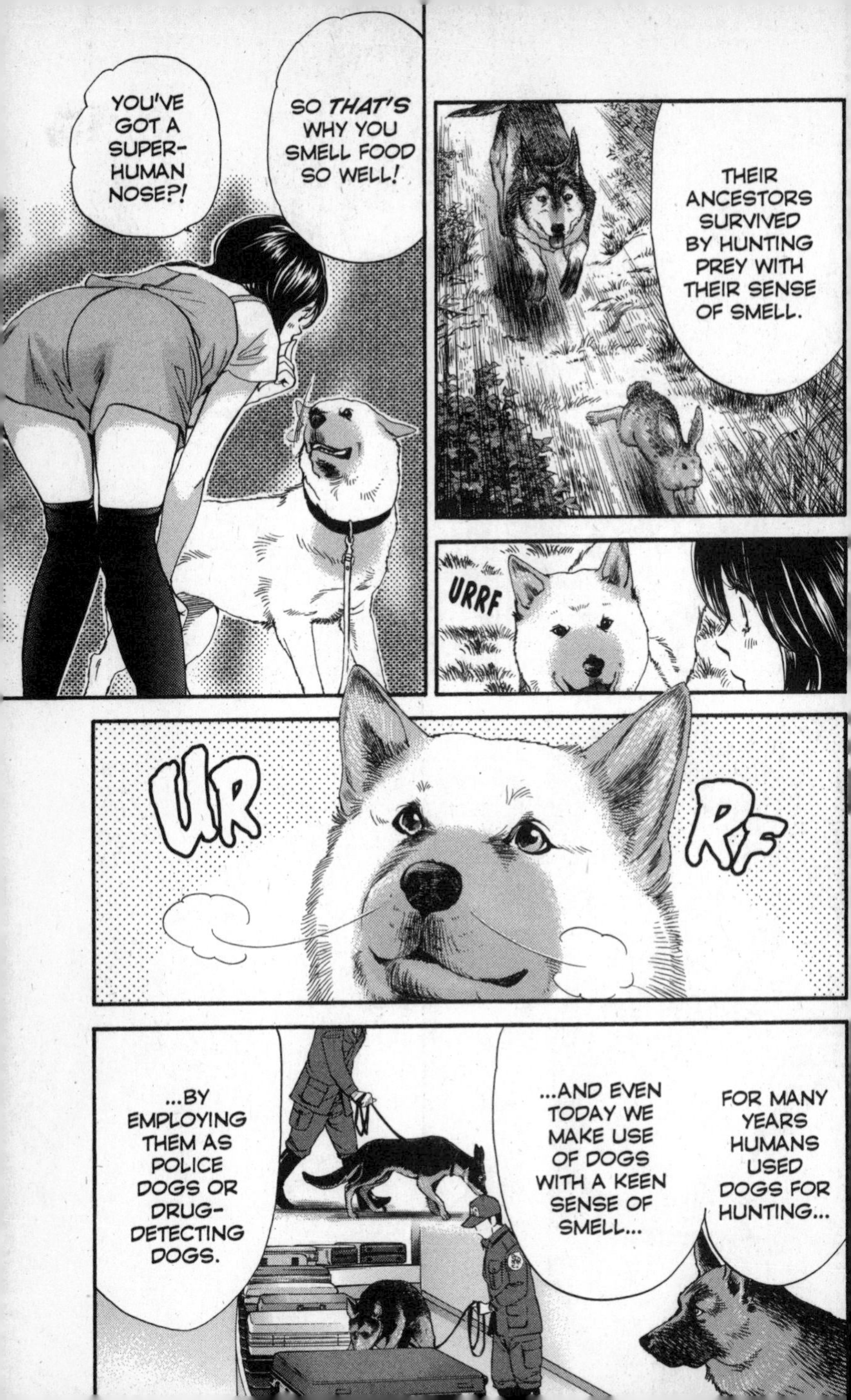
THEIR ANCESTORS SURVIVED BY HUNTING PREY WITH THEIR SENSE OF SMELL.
URRF
SO *THAT'S* WHY YOU SMELL FOOD SO WELL!
YOU'VE GOT A SUPER-HUMAN NOSE?!
UR RF
FOR MANY YEARS HUMANS USED DOGS FOR HUNTING...
...AND EVEN TODAY WE MAKE USE OF DOGS WITH A KEEN SENSE OF SMELL...
...BY EMPLOYING THEM AS POLICE DOGS OR DRUG-DETECTING DOGS.

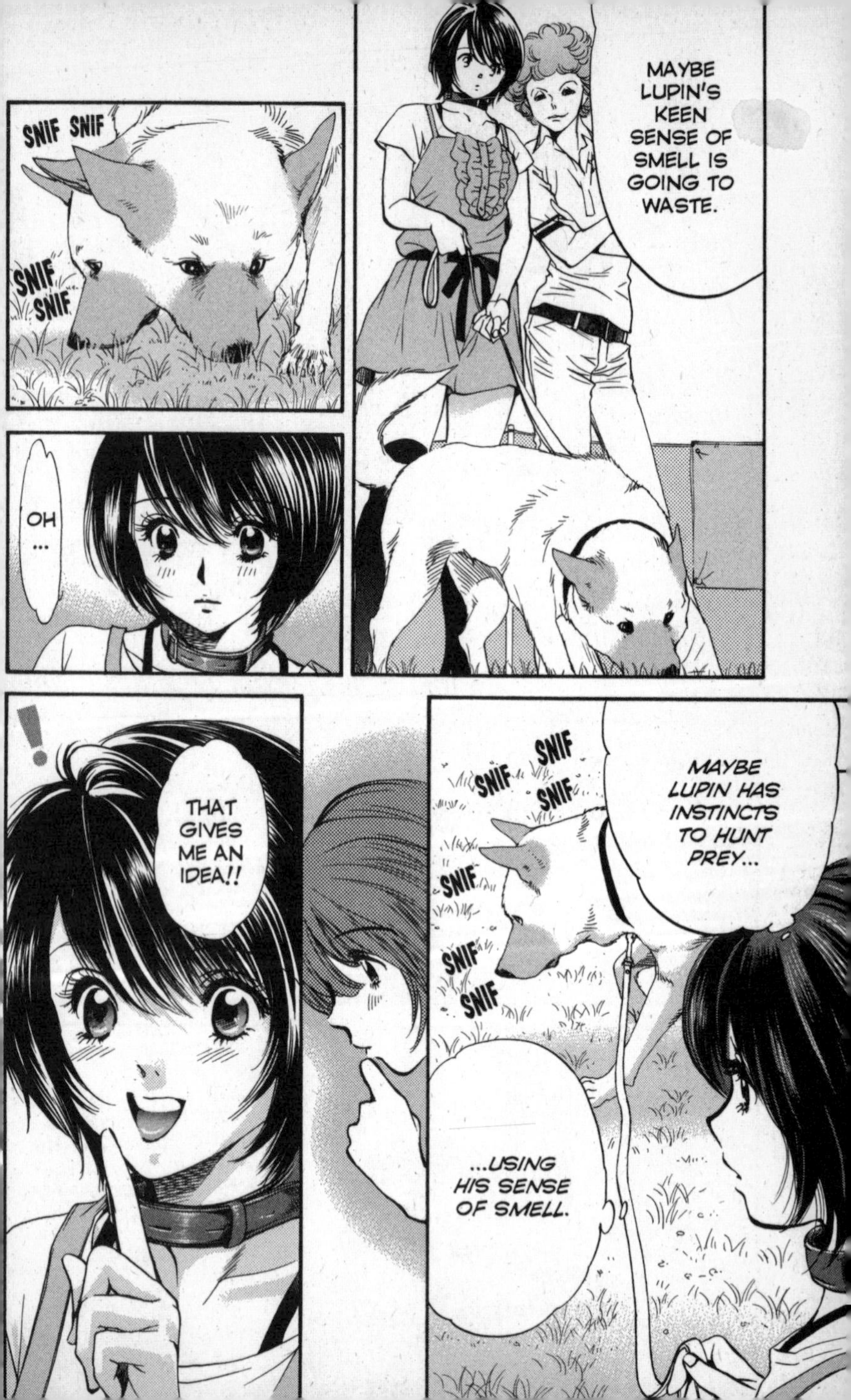
MAYBE LUPIN'S KEEN SENSE OF SMELL IS GOING TO WASTE.
SNIF SNIF
SNIF SNIF
OH ...
MAYBE LUPIN HAS INSTINCTS TO HUNT PREY...
SNIF SNIF SNIF
SNIF
SNIF SNIF
...USING HIS SENSE OF SMELL.
!
THAT GIVES ME AN IDEA!!

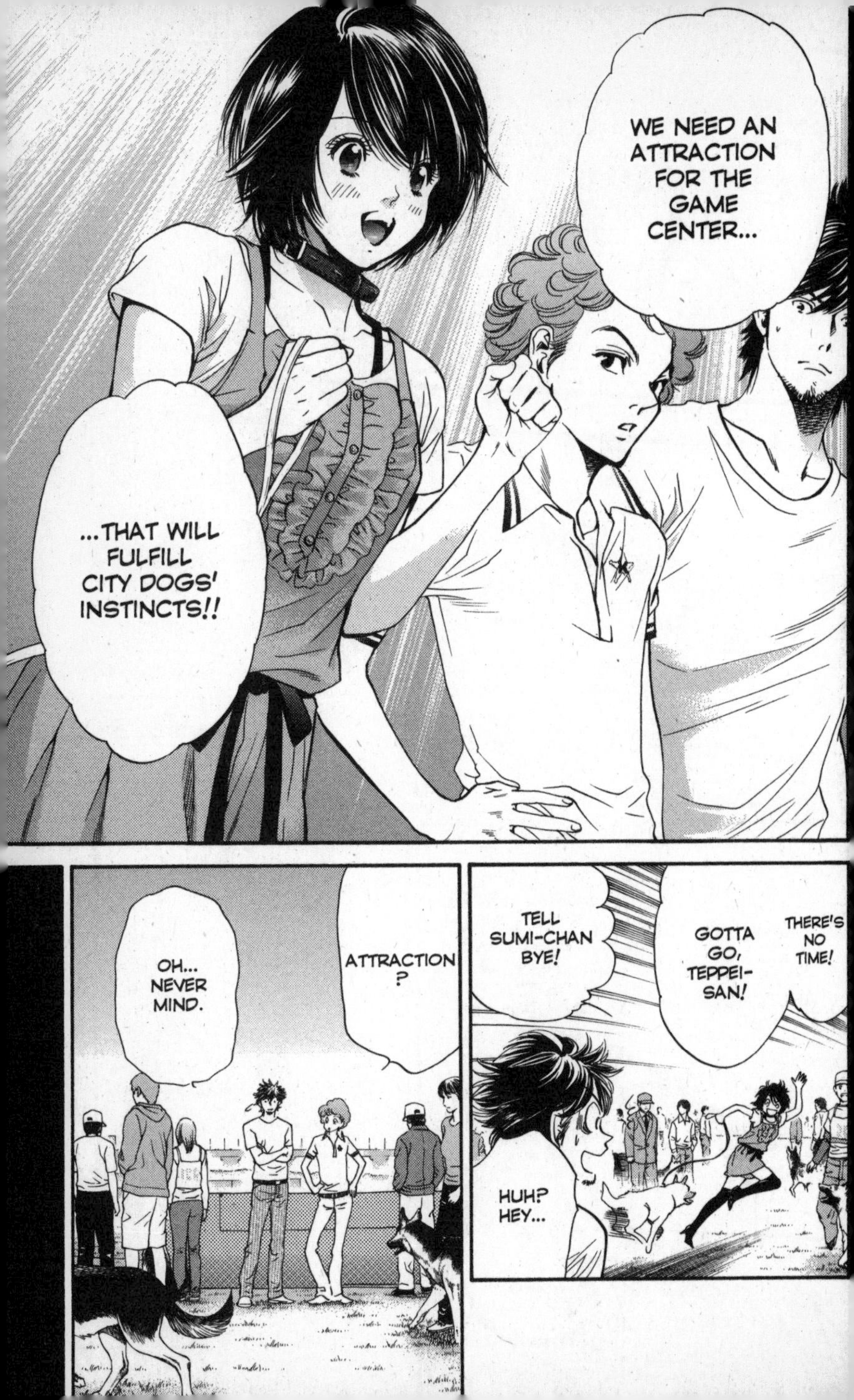
WE NEED AN ATTRACTION FOR THE GAME CENTER...
...THAT WILL FULFILL CITY DOGS' INSTINCTS!!
THERE'S NO TIME!
GOTTA GO, TEPPEI-SAN!
TELL SUMI-CHAN BYE!
HUH? HEY...
ATTRACTION?
OH... NEVER MIND.

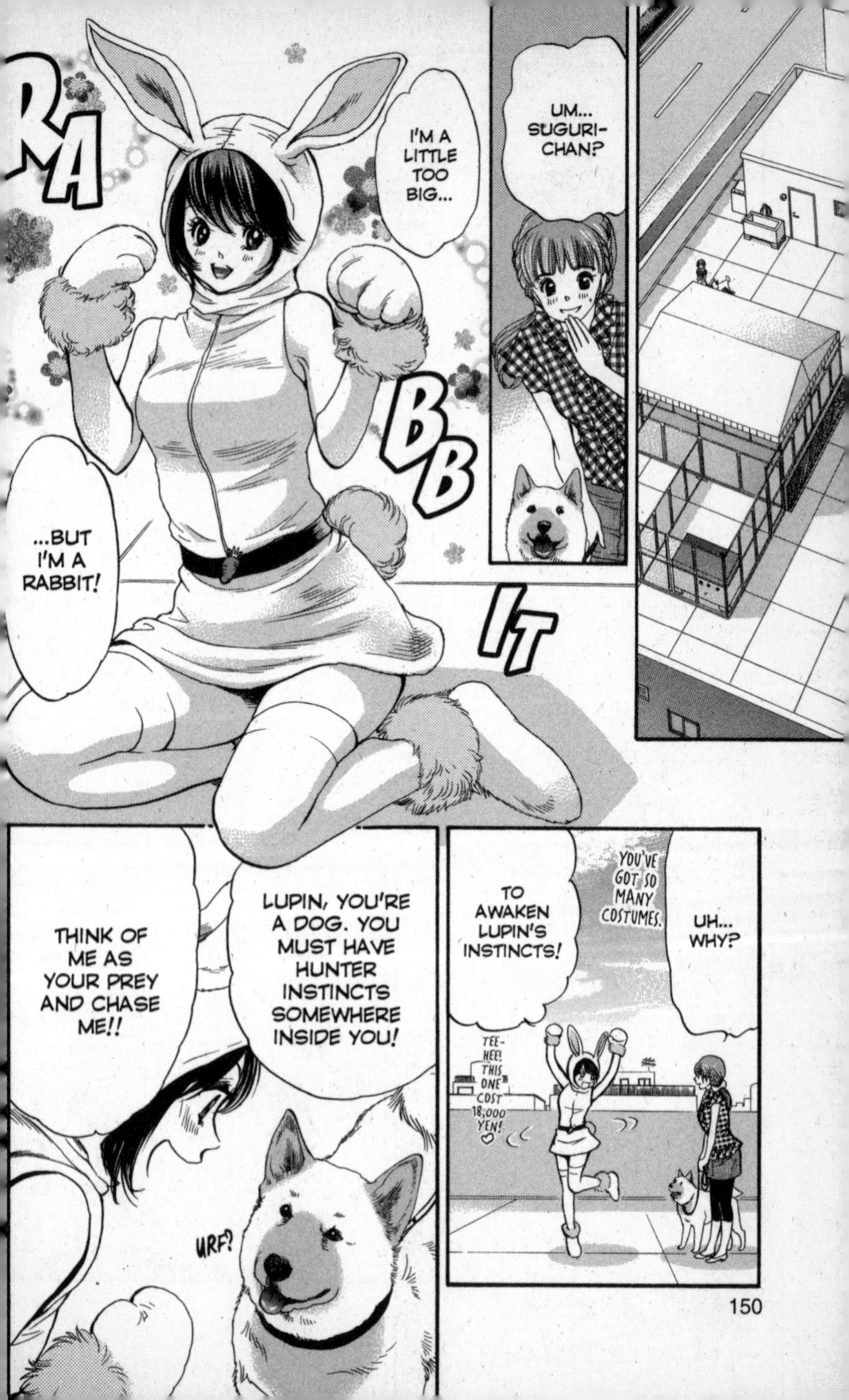
UM... SUGURI-CHAN?
I'M A LITTLE TOO BIG...
RA
BB
IT
...BUT I'M A RABBIT!
UH... WHY?
YOU'VE GOT SO MANY COSTUMES.
TO AWAKEN LUPIN'S INSTINCTS!
TEE-HEE! THIS ONE COST 18,000 YEN! ♡
LUPIN, YOU'RE A DOG. YOU MUST HAVE HUNTER INSTINCTS SOMEWHERE INSIDE YOU!
THINK OF ME AS YOUR PREY AND CHASE ME!!
URF?

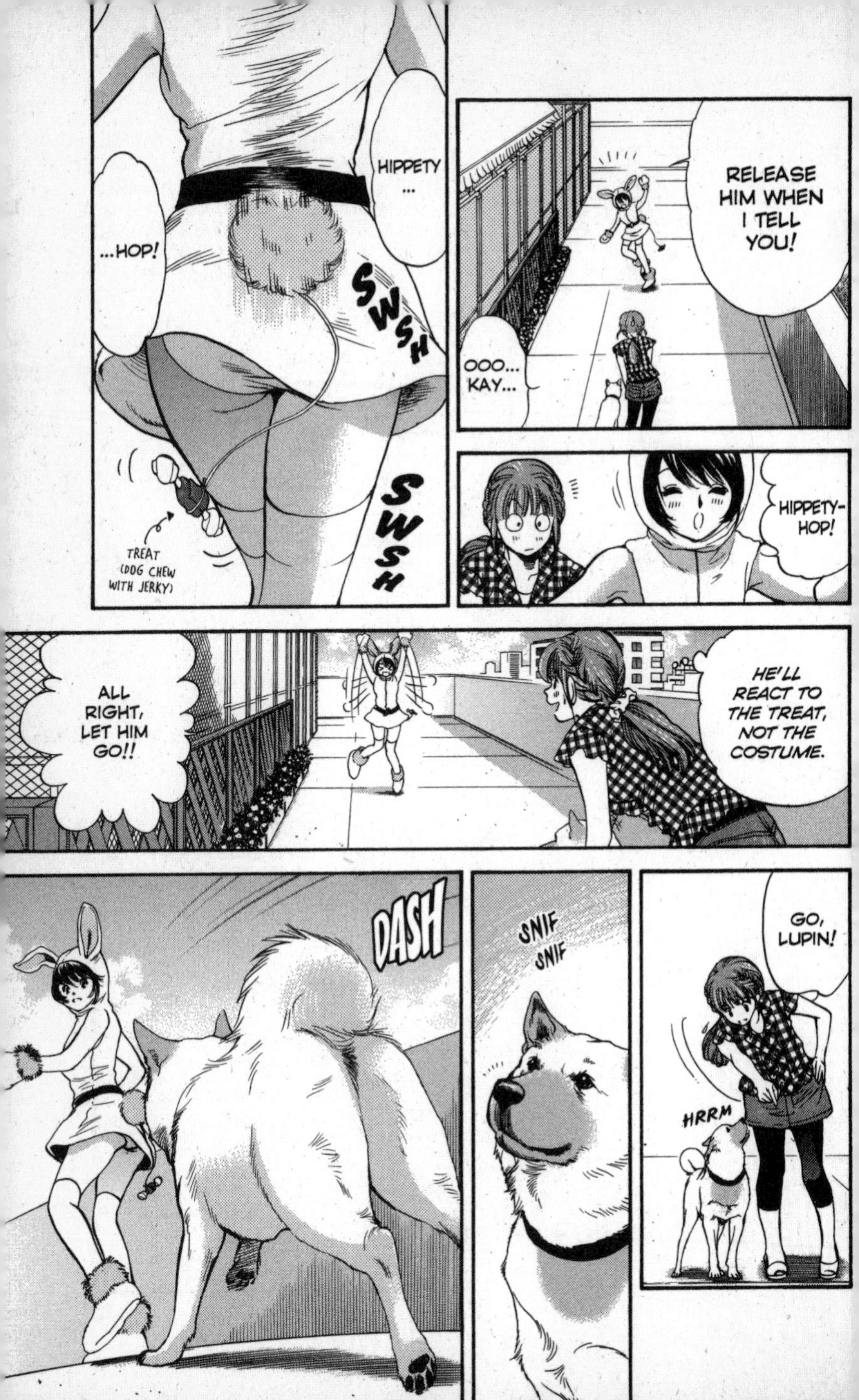
RELEASE HIM WHEN I TELL YOU!
OOO... KAY...
HIPPETY-HOP!
HIPPETY...
...HOP!
SWSH
SWSH
TREAT (DOG CHEW WITH JERKY)
HE'LL REACT TO THE TREAT, NOT THE COSTUME.
ALL RIGHT, LET HIM GO!!
GO, LUPIN!
HRRM
SNIF SNIF
DASH

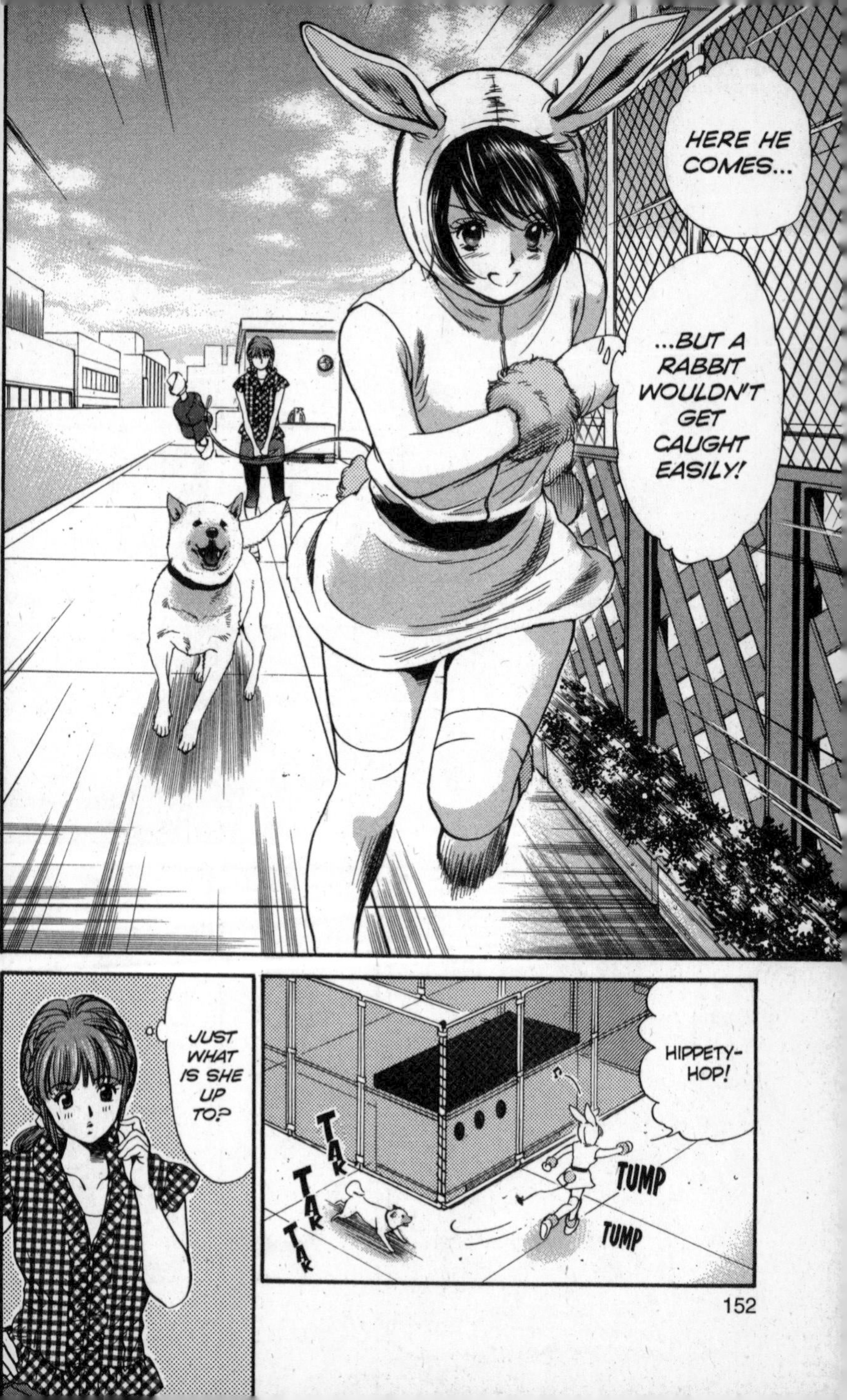
HERE HE COMES...
...BUT A RABBIT WOULDN'T GET CAUGHT EASILY!
HIPPETY-HOP!
TAK TAK TAK
TUMP TUMP
JUST WHAT IS SHE UP TO?

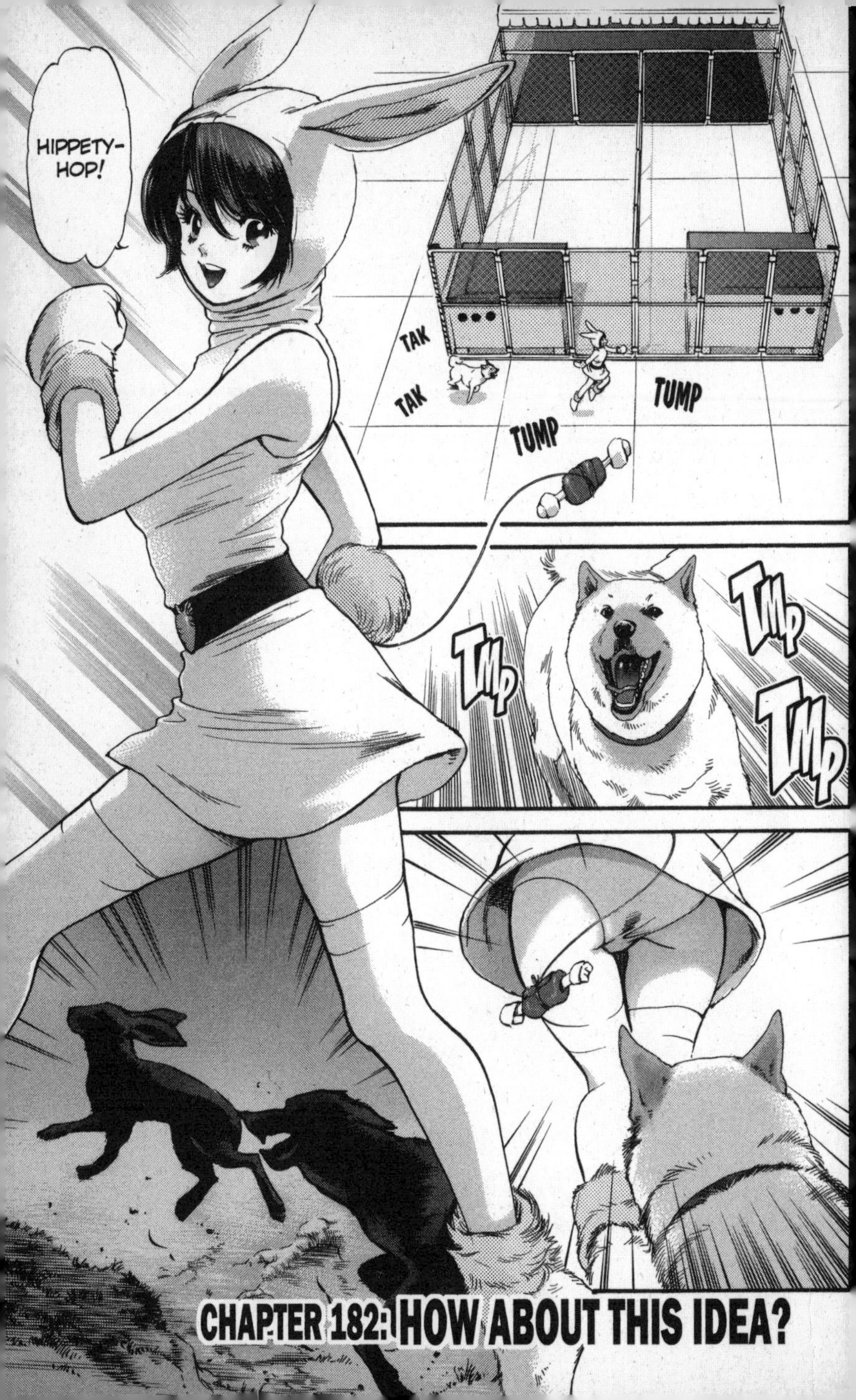
TAK
TAK
TUMP
TUMP
TMP
TMP
TMP
HIPPETY-HOP!

CHAPTER 182: HOW ABOUT THIS IDEA?

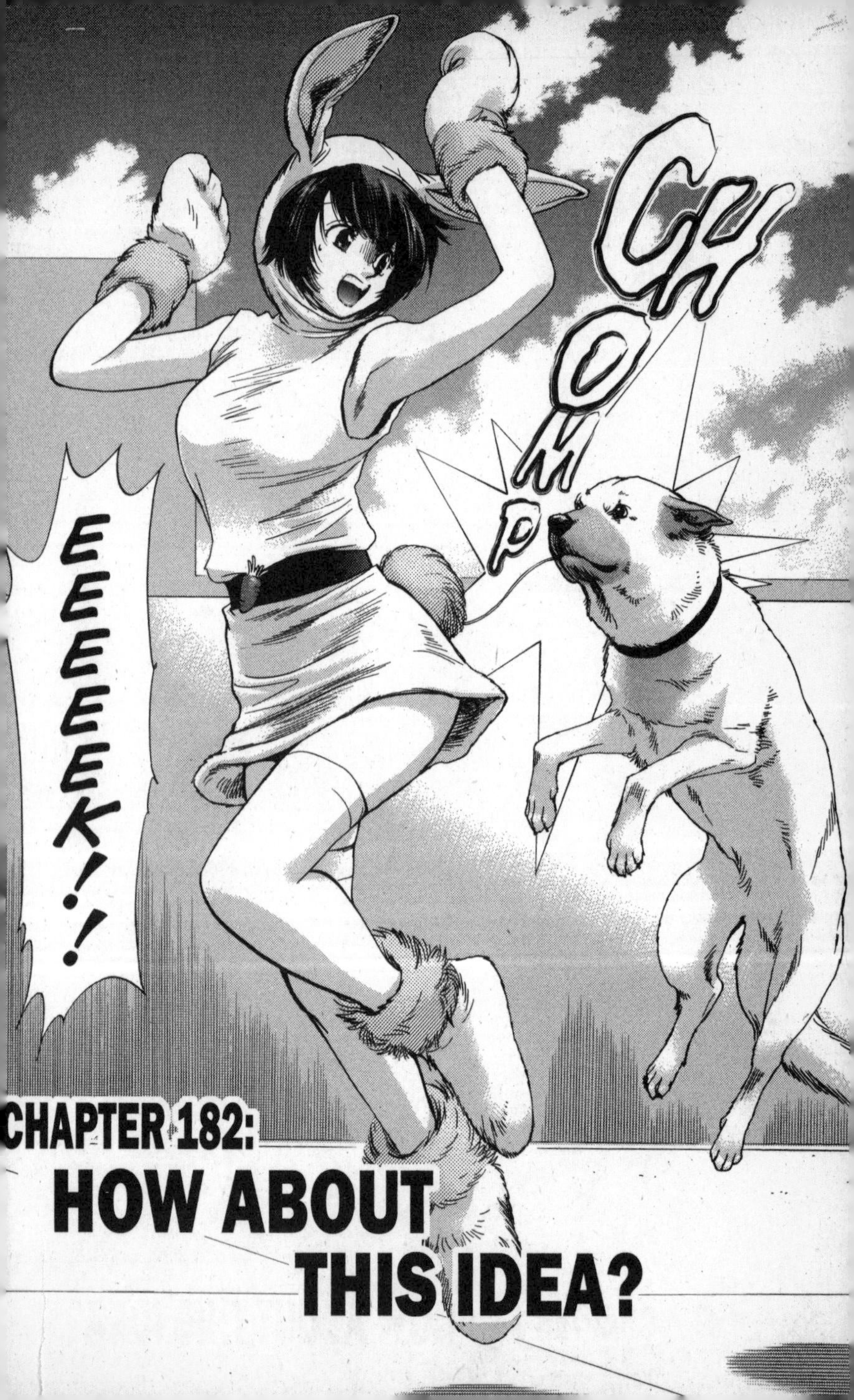
CHOMP
EEEEEEK!!!

CHAPTER 182: HOW ABOUT THIS IDEA?

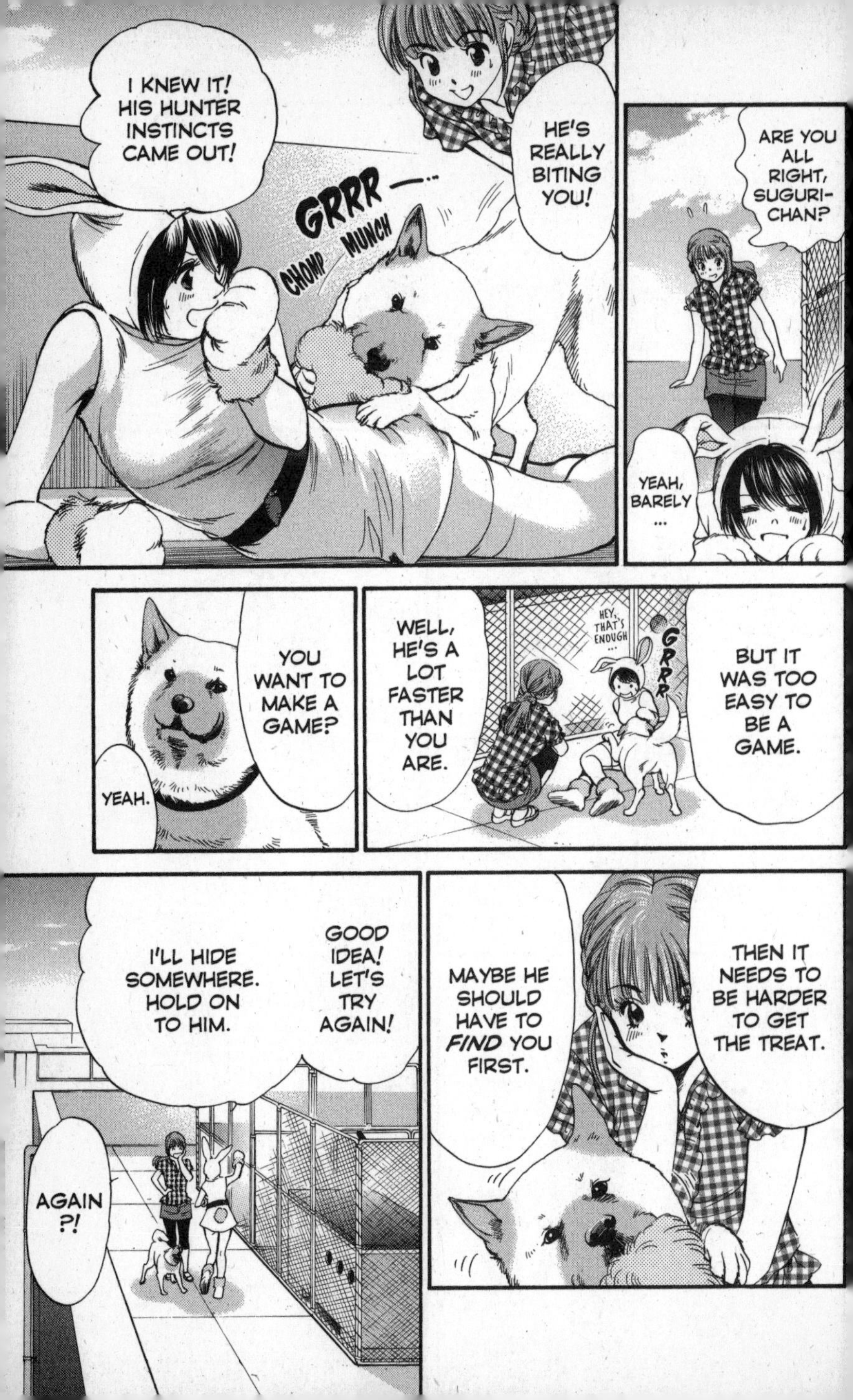
ARE YOU ALL RIGHT, SUGURI-CHAN?
YEAH, BARELY...
HE'S REALLY BITING YOU!
I KNEW IT! HIS HUNTER INSTINCTS CAME OUT!
GRRR—...
CHOMP MUNCH
BUT IT WAS TOO EASY TO BE A GAME.
GRRR
HEY, THAT'S ENOUGH...
WELL, HE'S A LOT FASTER THAN YOU ARE.
YOU WANT TO MAKE A GAME?
YEAH.
THEN IT NEEDS TO BE HARDER TO GET THE TREAT.
MAYBE HE SHOULD HAVE TO *FIND* YOU FIRST.
GOOD IDEA! LET'S TRY AGAIN!
I'LL HIDE SOMEWHERE. HOLD ON TO HIM.
AGAIN?!

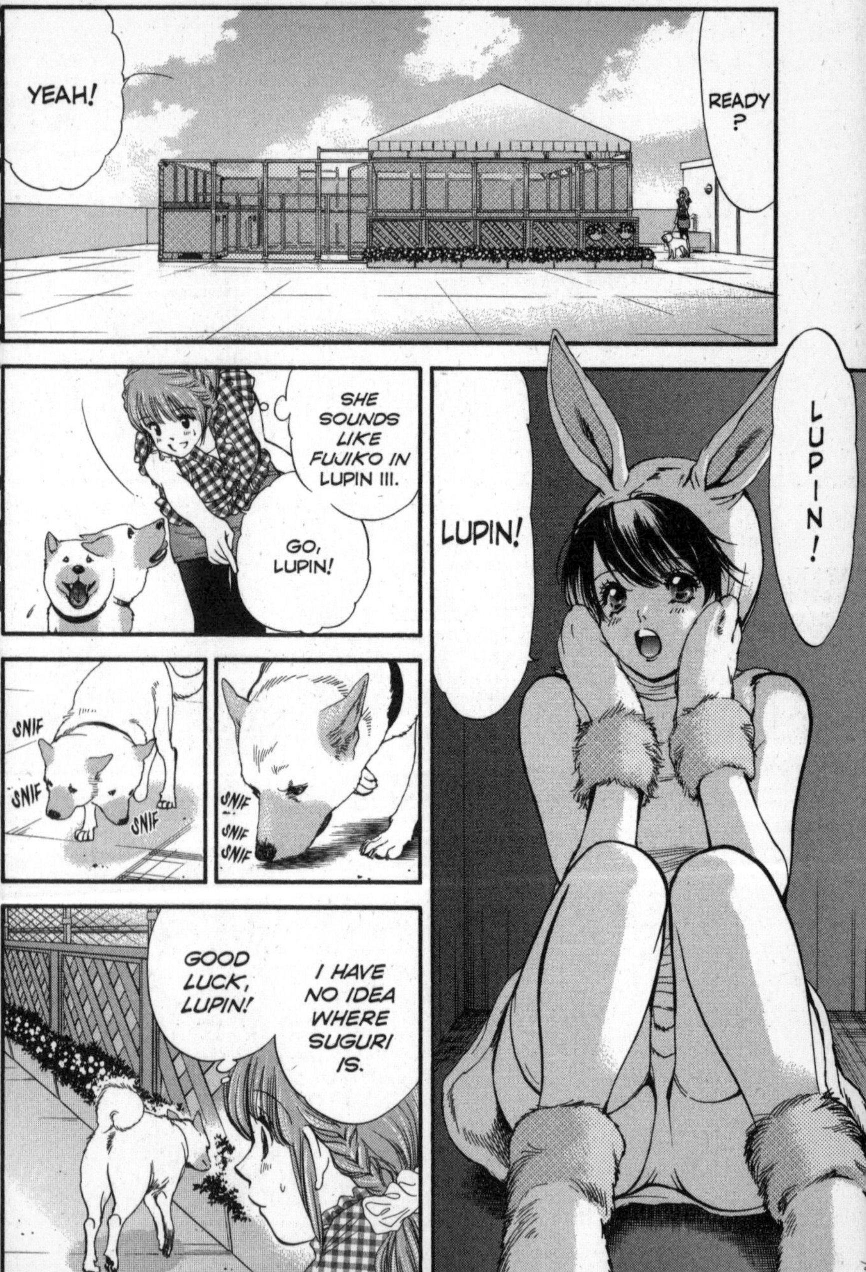
READY?
YEAH!
LUPIN!
LUPIN!
SHE SOUNDS LIKE FUJIKO IN LUPIN III.
GO, LUPIN!
SNIF
SNIF
SNIF
SNIF
SNIF
SNIF
I HAVE NO IDEA WHERE SUGURI IS.
GOOD LUCK, LUPIN!

HIDE-AND-SEEK IS LIKE FOLLOWING FOOT-PRINTS.

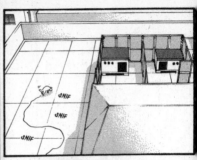

LUPIN DOESN'T HAVE ANY TRAINING THOUGH. MAYBE IT'S TOO HARD.

OH!

PANT

PANT

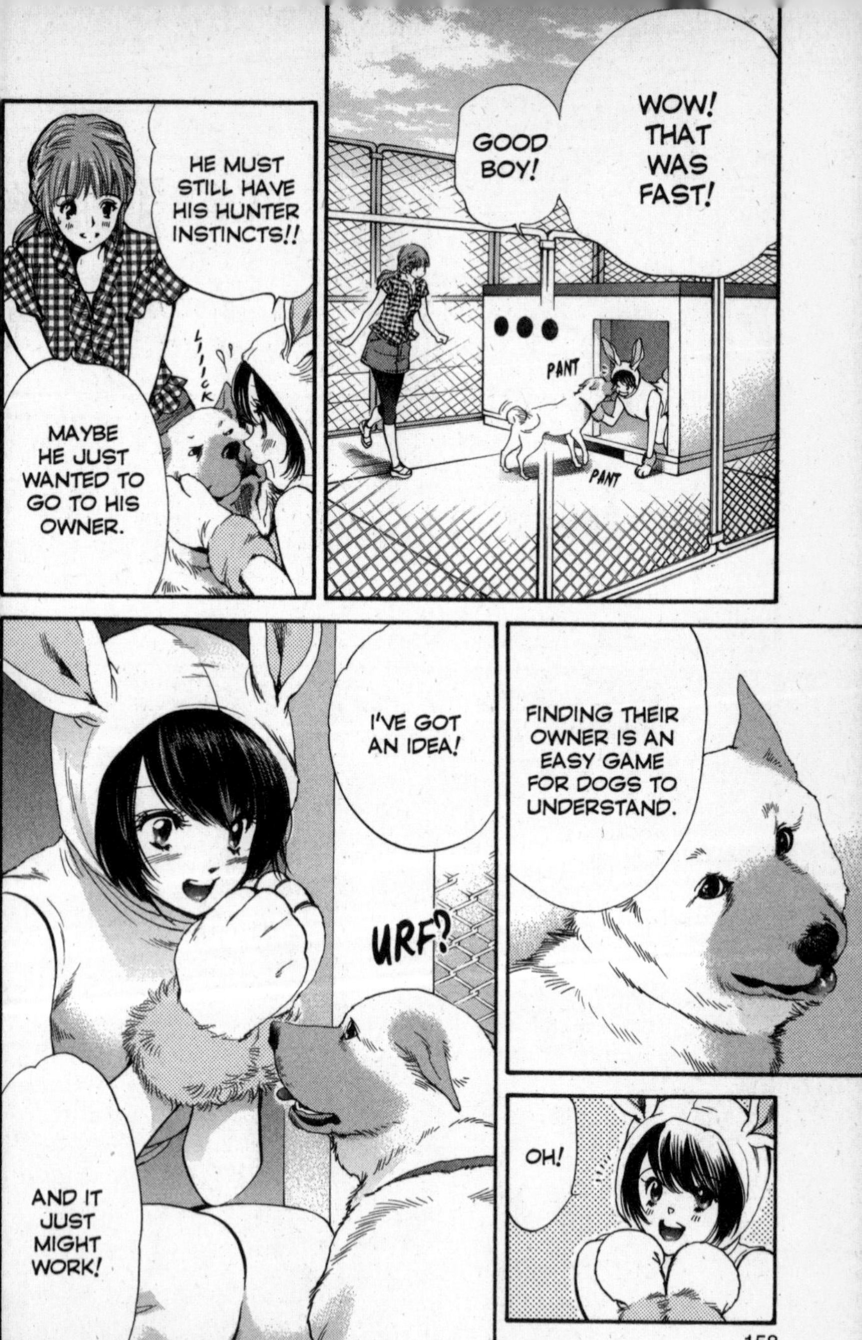
WOW! THAT WAS FAST!
GOOD BOY!
PANT
PANT
HE MUST STILL HAVE HIS HUNTER INSTINCTS!!
LIIICK
MAYBE HE JUST WANTED TO GO TO HIS OWNER.
FINDING THEIR OWNER IS AN EASY GAME FOR DOGS TO UNDERSTAND.
OH!
I'VE GOT AN IDEA!
URF?
AND IT JUST MIGHT WORK!

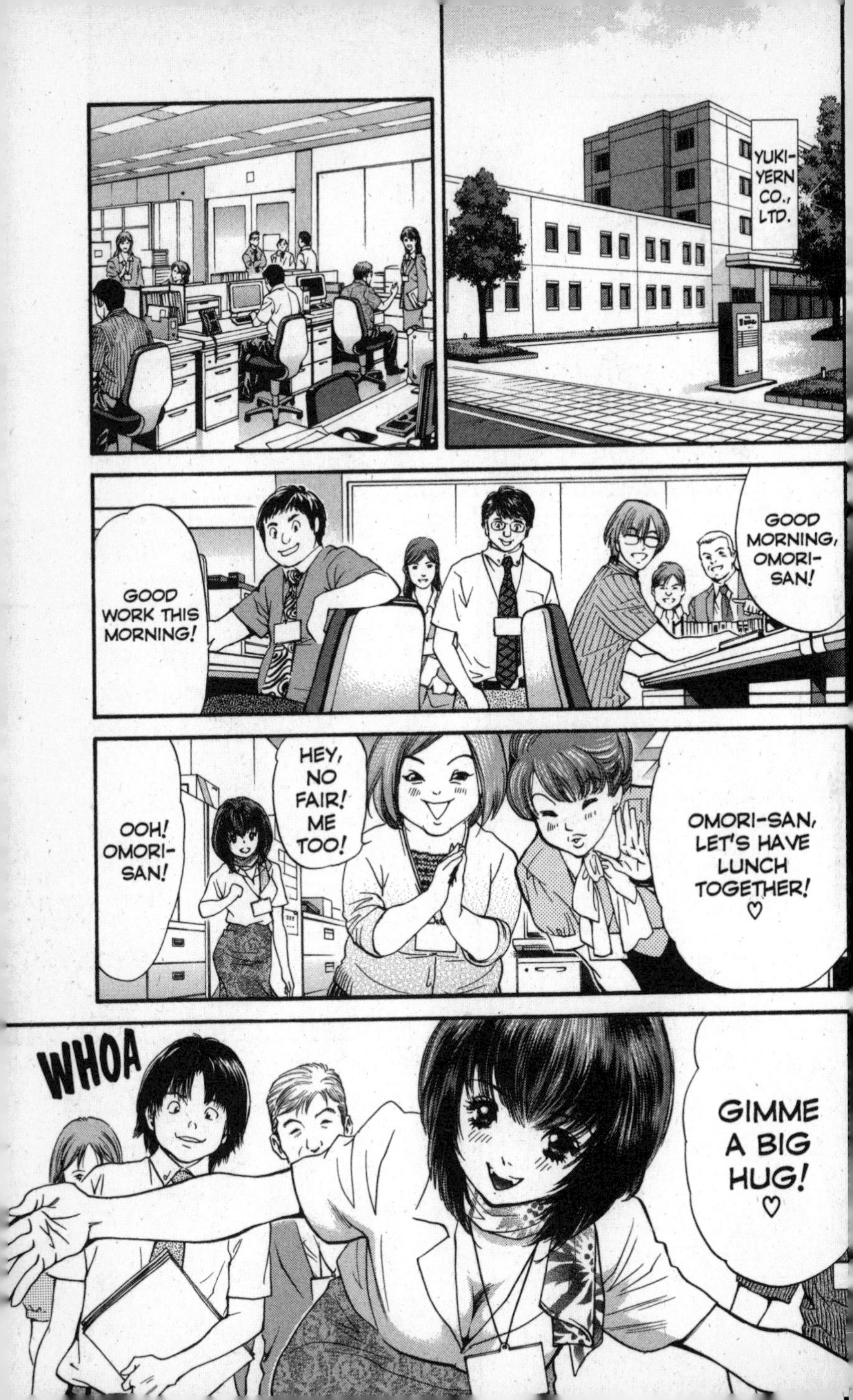
YUKI-YERN CO., LTD.
GOOD MORNING, OMORI-SAN!
GOOD WORK THIS MORNING!
OMORI-SAN, LET'S HAVE LUNCH TOGETHER! ♡
HEY, NO FAIR! ME TOO!
OOH! OMORI-SAN!
GIMME A BIG HUG! ♡
WHOA

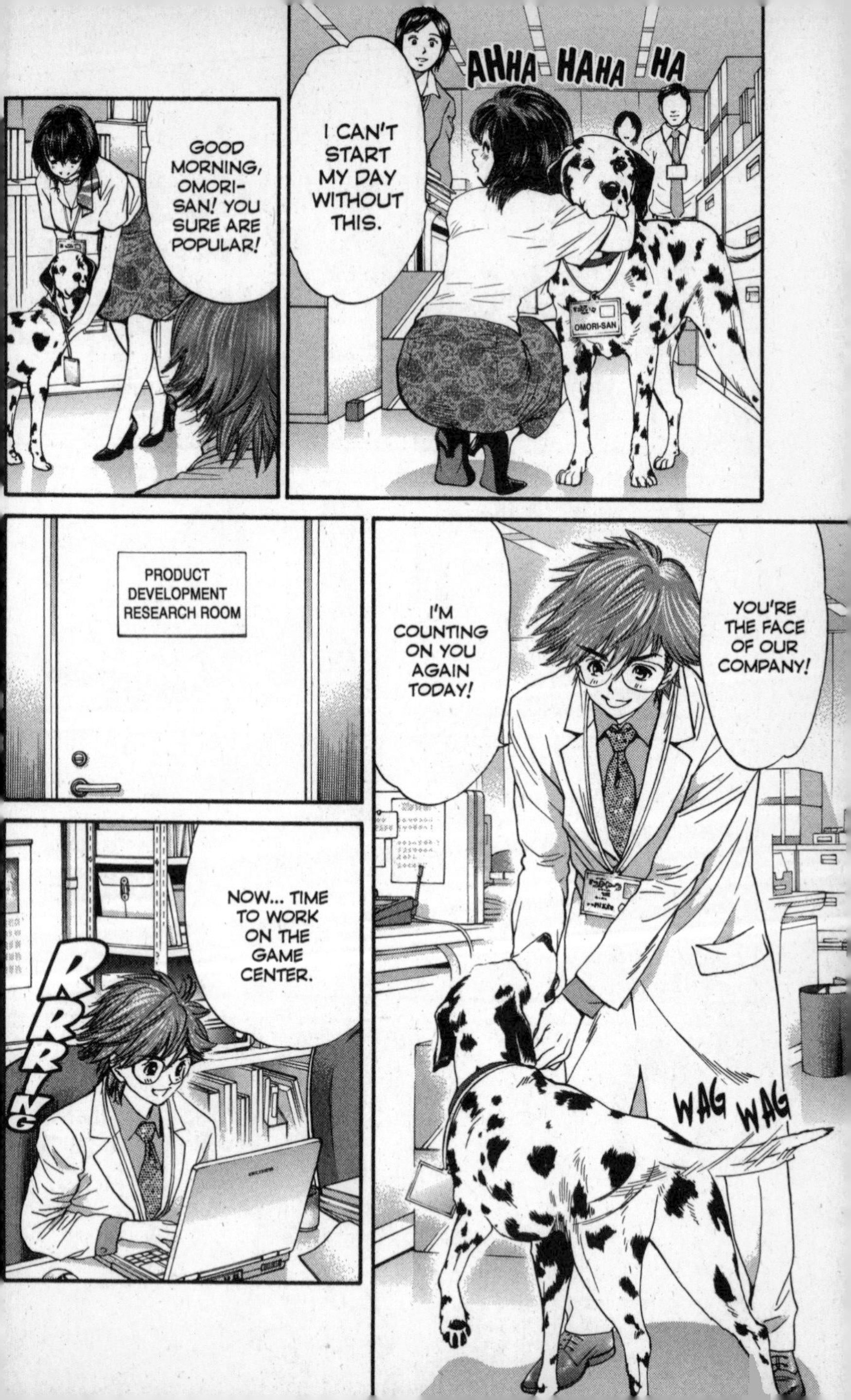
AHHA HAHA HA
I CAN'T START MY DAY WITHOUT THIS.
OMORI-SAN
GOOD MORNING, OMORI-SAN! YOU SURE ARE POPULAR!
YOU'RE THE FACE OF OUR COMPANY!
I'M COUNTING ON YOU AGAIN TODAY!
WAG WAG
PRODUCT DEVELOPMENT RESEARCH ROOM
NOW... TIME TO WORK ON THE GAME CENTER.
RRRING

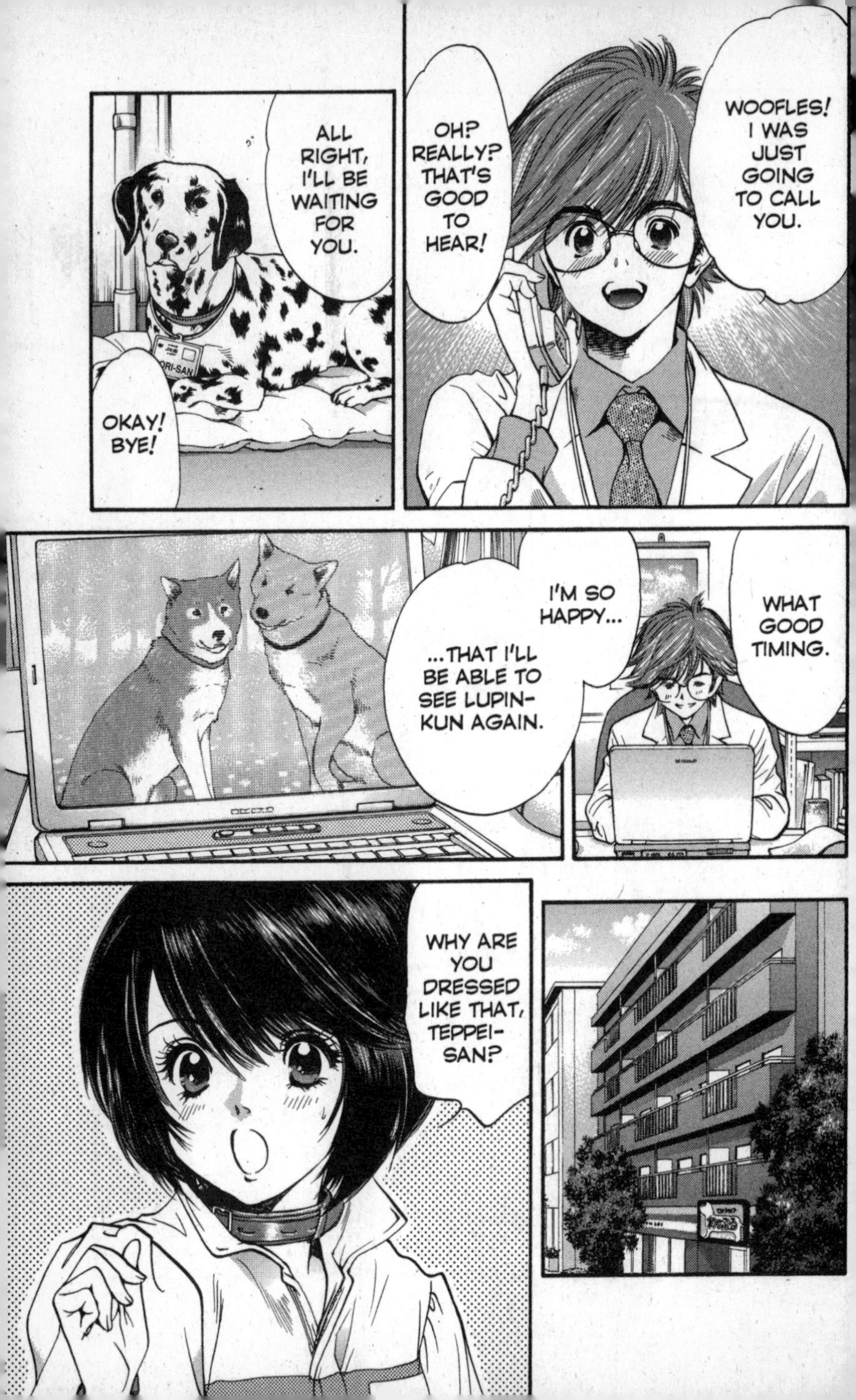
WOOFLES! I WAS JUST GOING TO CALL YOU.
OH? REALLY? THAT'S GOOD TO HEAR!
ALL RIGHT, I'LL BE WAITING FOR YOU.
OKAY! BYE!
WHAT GOOD TIMING.
I'M SO HAPPY...
...THAT I'LL BE ABLE TO SEE LUPIN-KUN AGAIN.
WHY ARE YOU DRESSED LIKE THAT, TEPPEI-SAN?

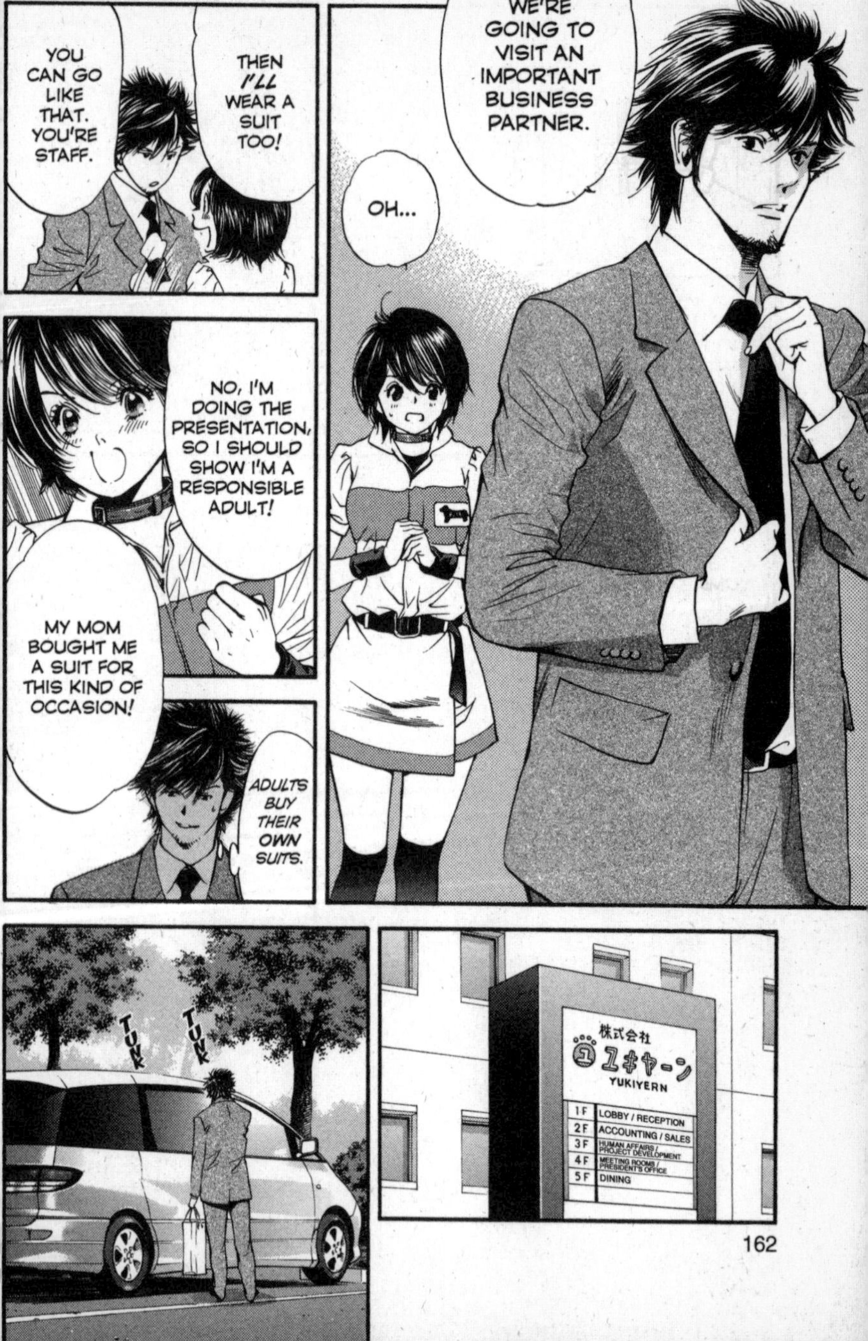
WE'RE GOING TO VISIT AN IMPORTANT BUSINESS PARTNER.
OH...
THEN *I'LL* WEAR A SUIT TOO!
YOU CAN GO LIKE THAT. YOU'RE STAFF.
NO, I'M DOING THE PRESENTATION, SO I SHOULD SHOW I'M A RESPONSIBLE ADULT!
MY MOM BOUGHT ME A SUIT FOR THIS KIND OF OCCASION!
ADULTS BUY THEIR *OWN* SUITS.
株式会社
ユキヤーン
YUKIYERN
1F LOBBY / RECEPTION
2F ACCOUNTING / SALES
3F HUMAN AFFAIRS / PROJECT DEVELOPMENT
4F MEETING ROOMS / PRESIDENT'S OFFICE
5F DINING
TUNK
TUNK

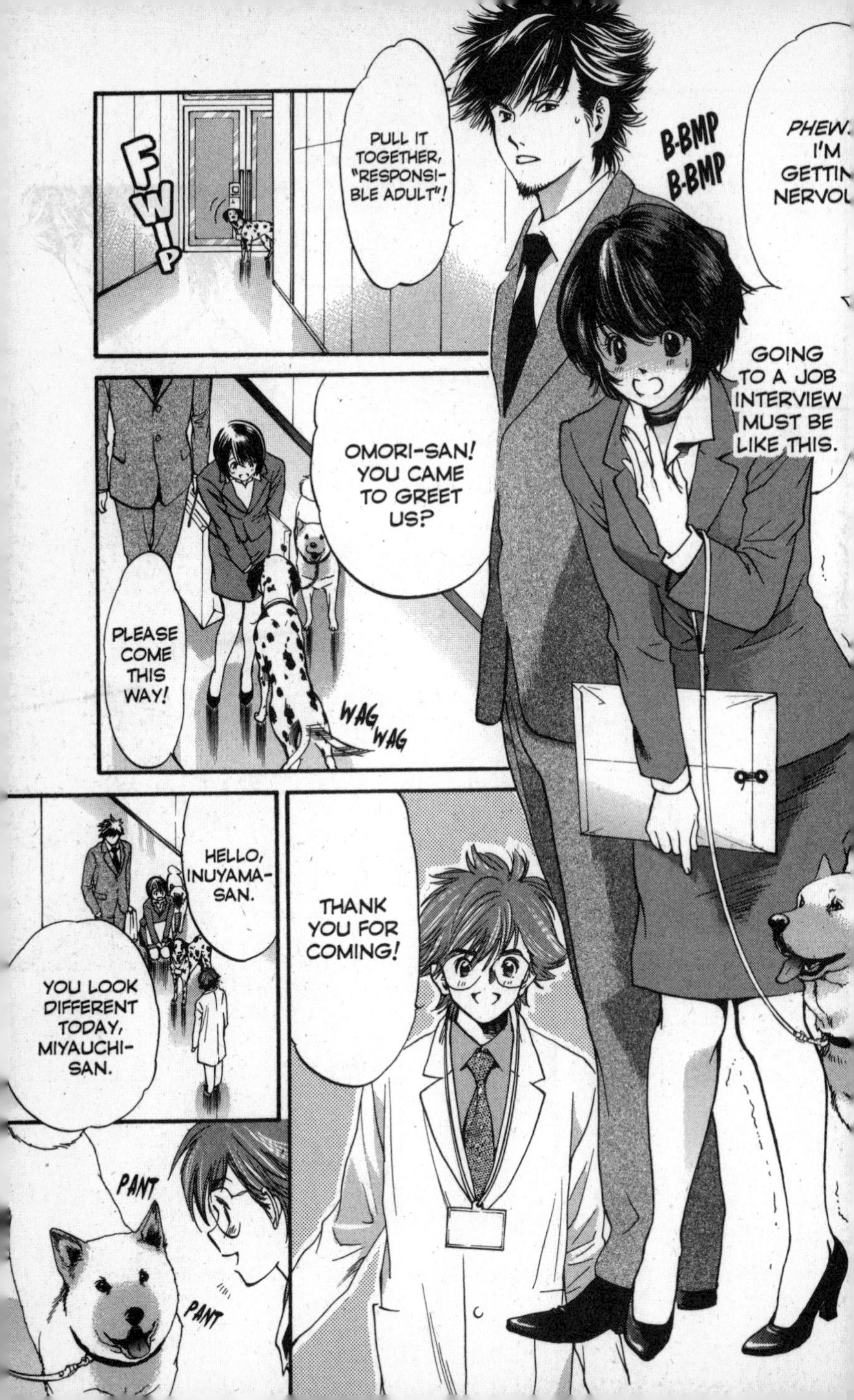
PHEW. I'M GETTIN NERVOU
B-BMP B-BMP
GOING TO A JOB INTERVIEW MUST BE LIKE THIS.
PULL IT TOGETHER, "RESPONSIBLE ADULT"!
FWIP
OMORI-SAN! YOU CAME TO GREET US?
PLEASE COME THIS WAY!
WAG WAG
THANK YOU FOR COMING!
HELLO, INUYAMA-SAN.
YOU LOOK DIFFERENT TODAY, MIYAUCHI-SAN.
PANT
PANT

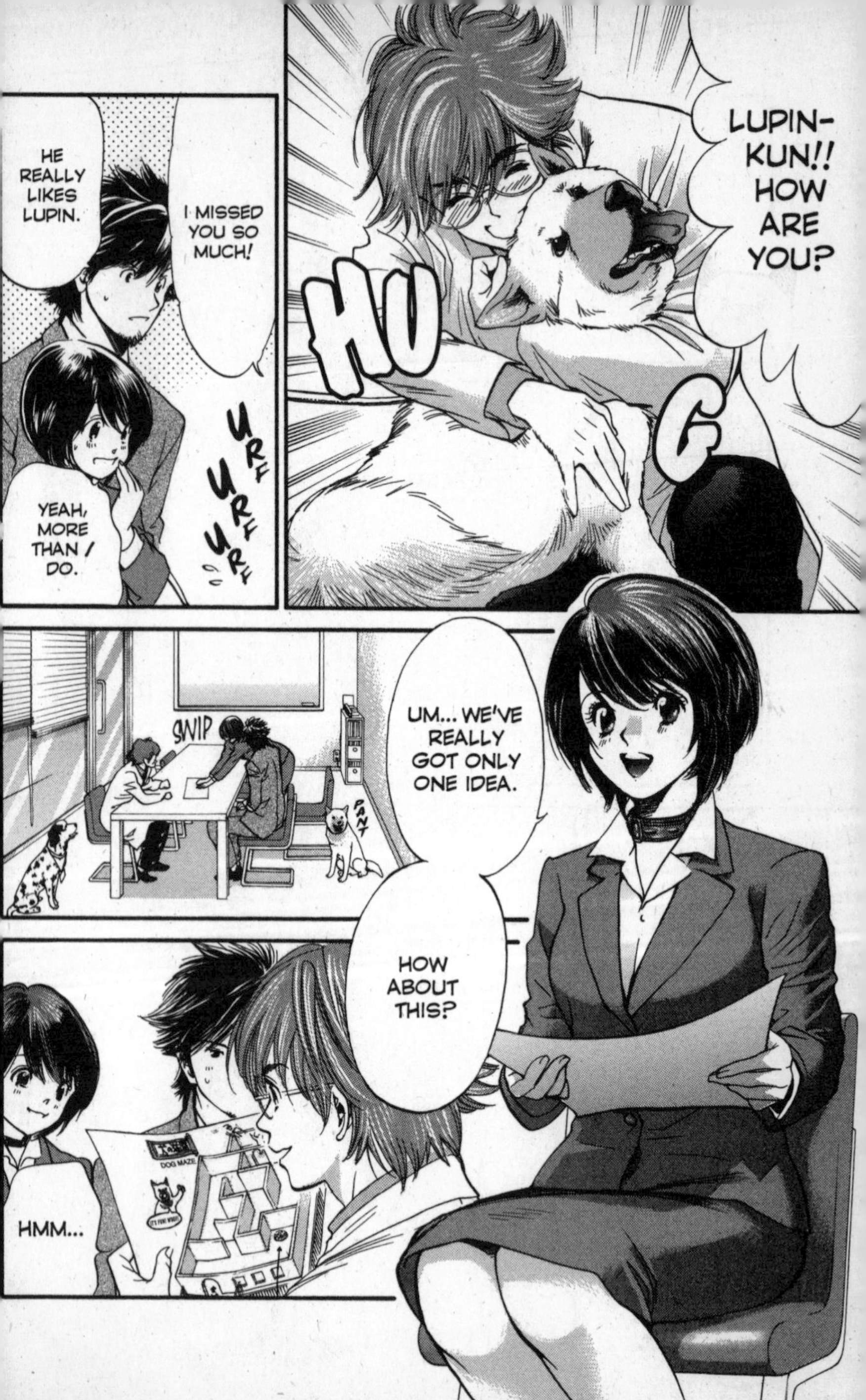

LUPIN-KUN!! HOW ARE YOU?
HUG
I MISSED YOU SO MUCH!
HE REALLY LIKES LUPIN.
URF URF URF
YEAH, MORE THAN I DO.
UM... WE'VE REALLY GOT ONLY ONE IDEA.
HOW ABOUT THIS?
SNIP
PANT
DOG MAZE
HMM...

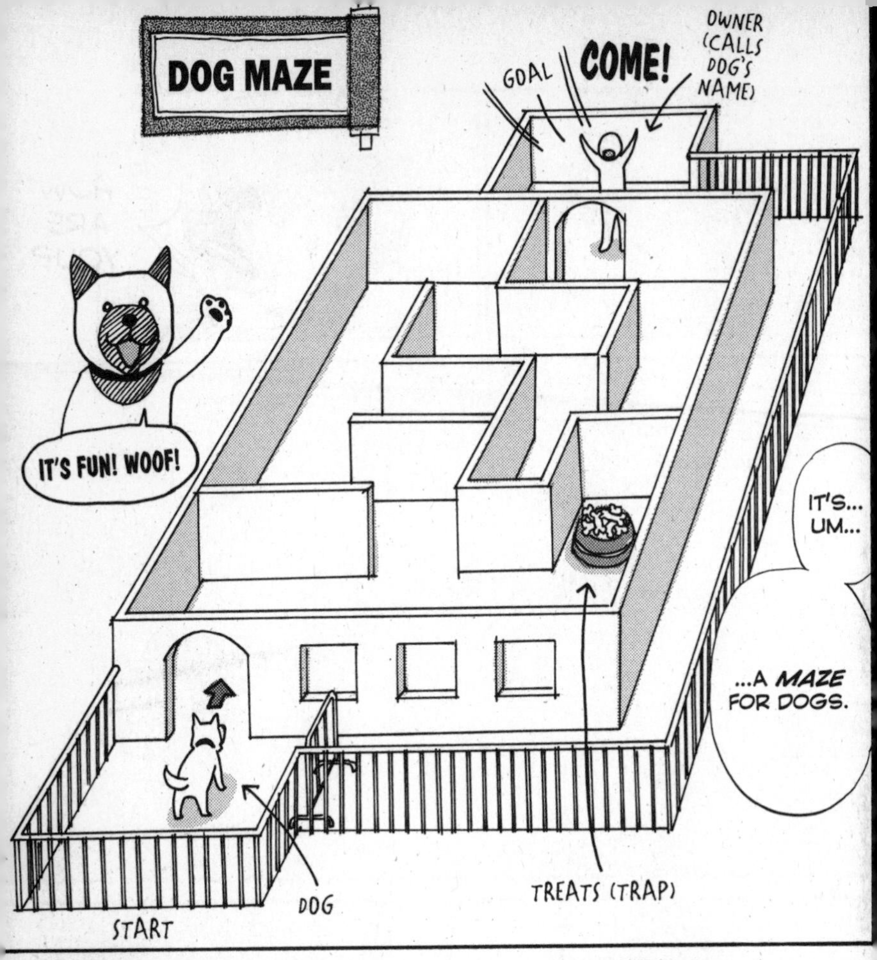
DOG MAZE
OWNER (CALLS DOG'S NAME)
COME!
GOAL
IT'S... UM...
...A *MAZE* FOR DOGS.
IT'S FUN! WOOF!
TREATS (TRAP)
DOG
START

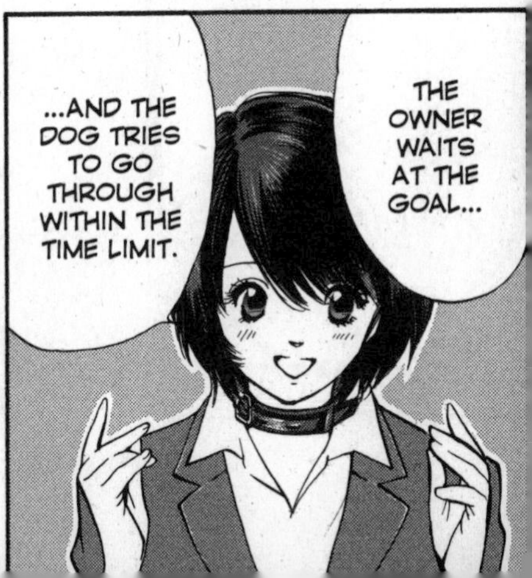
THE OWNER WAITS AT THE GOAL...
...AND THE DOG TRIES TO GO THROUGH WITHIN THE TIME LIMIT.

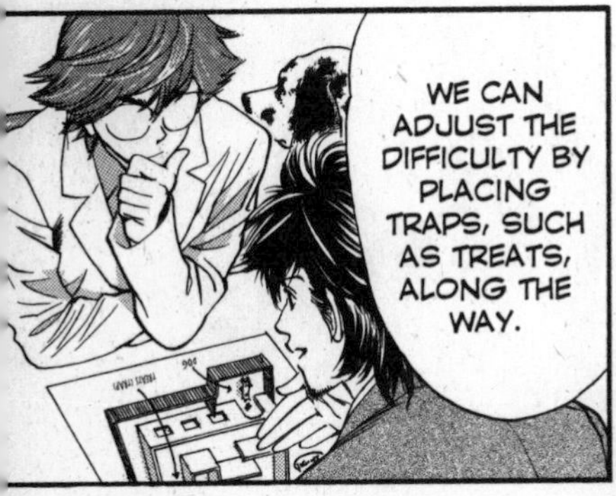
WE CAN ADJUST THE DIFFICULTY BY PLACING TRAPS, SUCH AS TREATS, ALONG THE WAY.

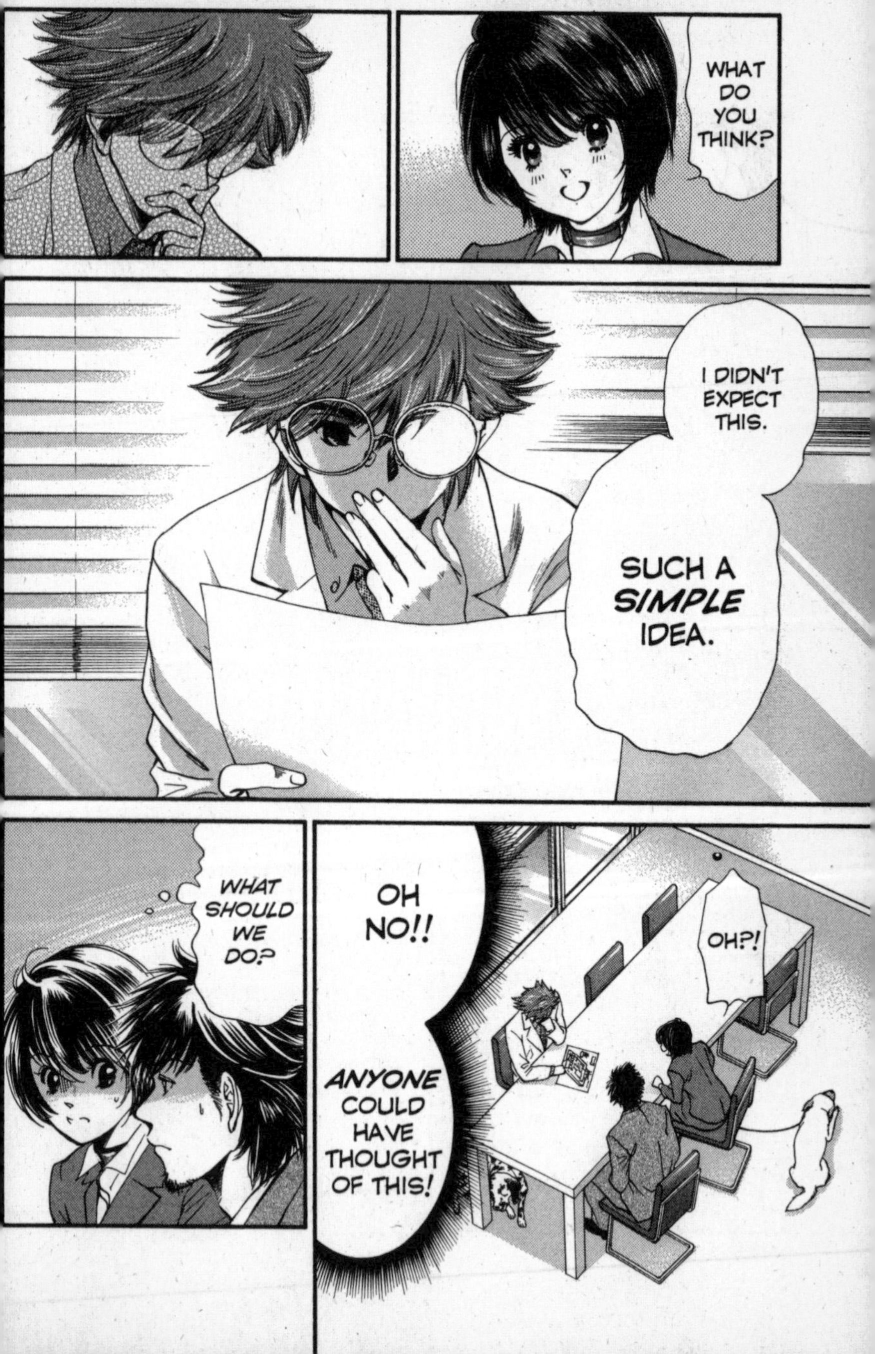
WHAT DO YOU THINK?
I DIDN'T EXPECT THIS.
SUCH A *SIMPLE* IDEA.
OH?!
OH NO!!
ANYONE COULD HAVE THOUGHT OF THIS!
WHAT SHOULD WE DO?

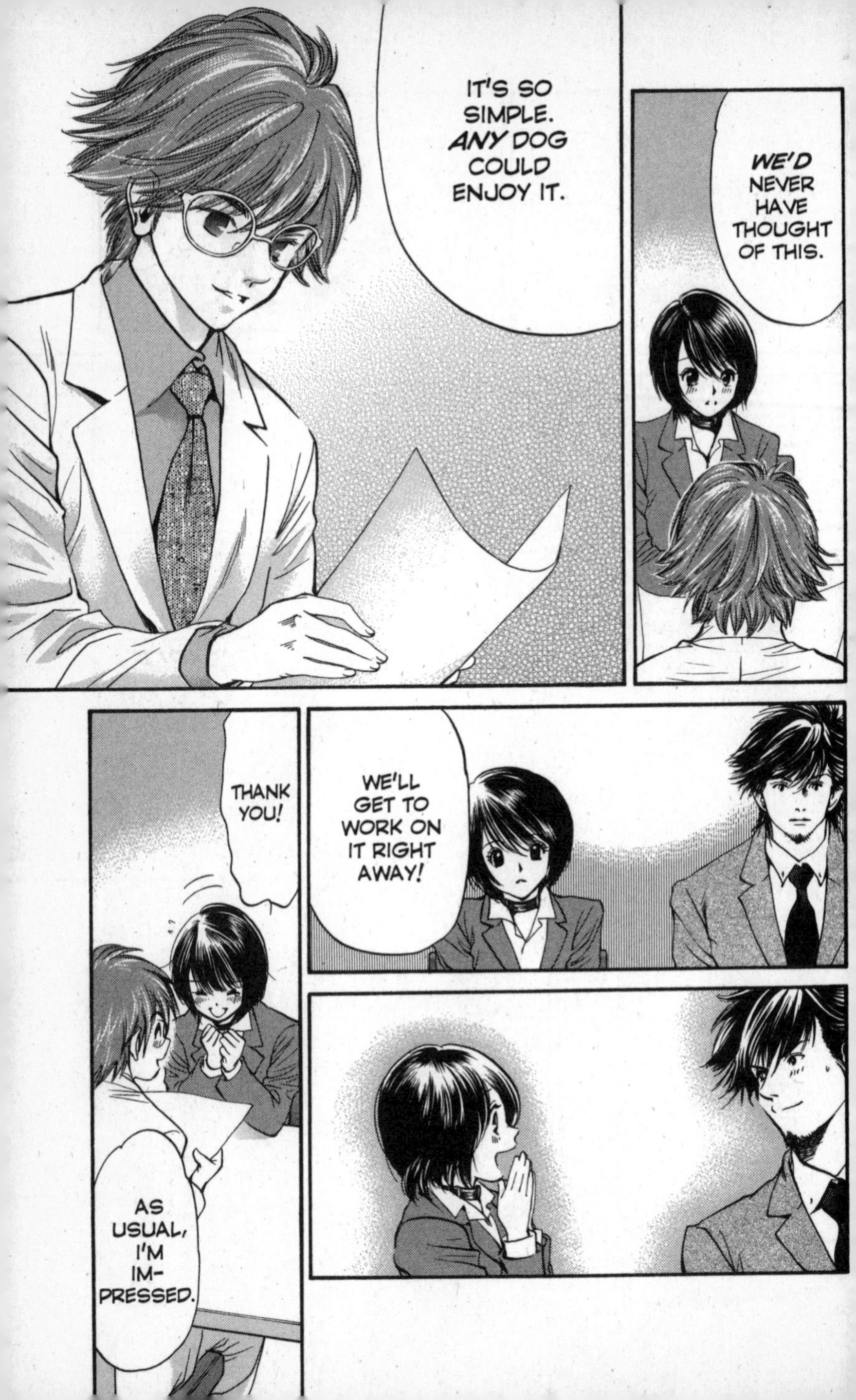
WE'D NEVER HAVE THOUGHT OF THIS.
IT'S SO SIMPLE. ANY DOG COULD ENJOY IT.
WE'LL GET TO WORK ON IT RIGHT AWAY!
THANK YOU!
AS USUAL, I'M IM-PRESSED.

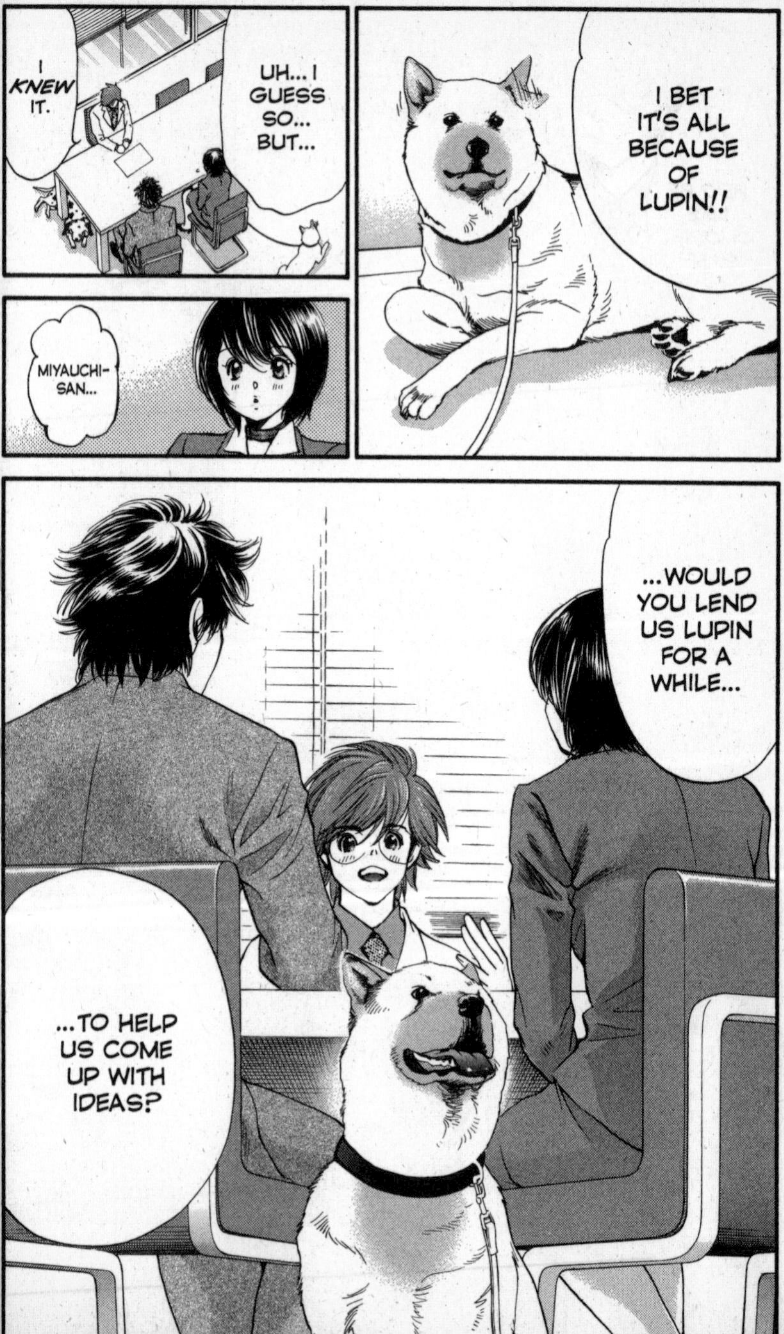
I BET IT'S ALL BECAUSE OF LUPIN!!
UH... I GUESS SO... BUT...
I KNEW IT.
MIYAUCHI-SAN...
...WOULD YOU LEND US LUPIN FOR A WHILE...
...TO HELP US COME UP WITH IDEAS?

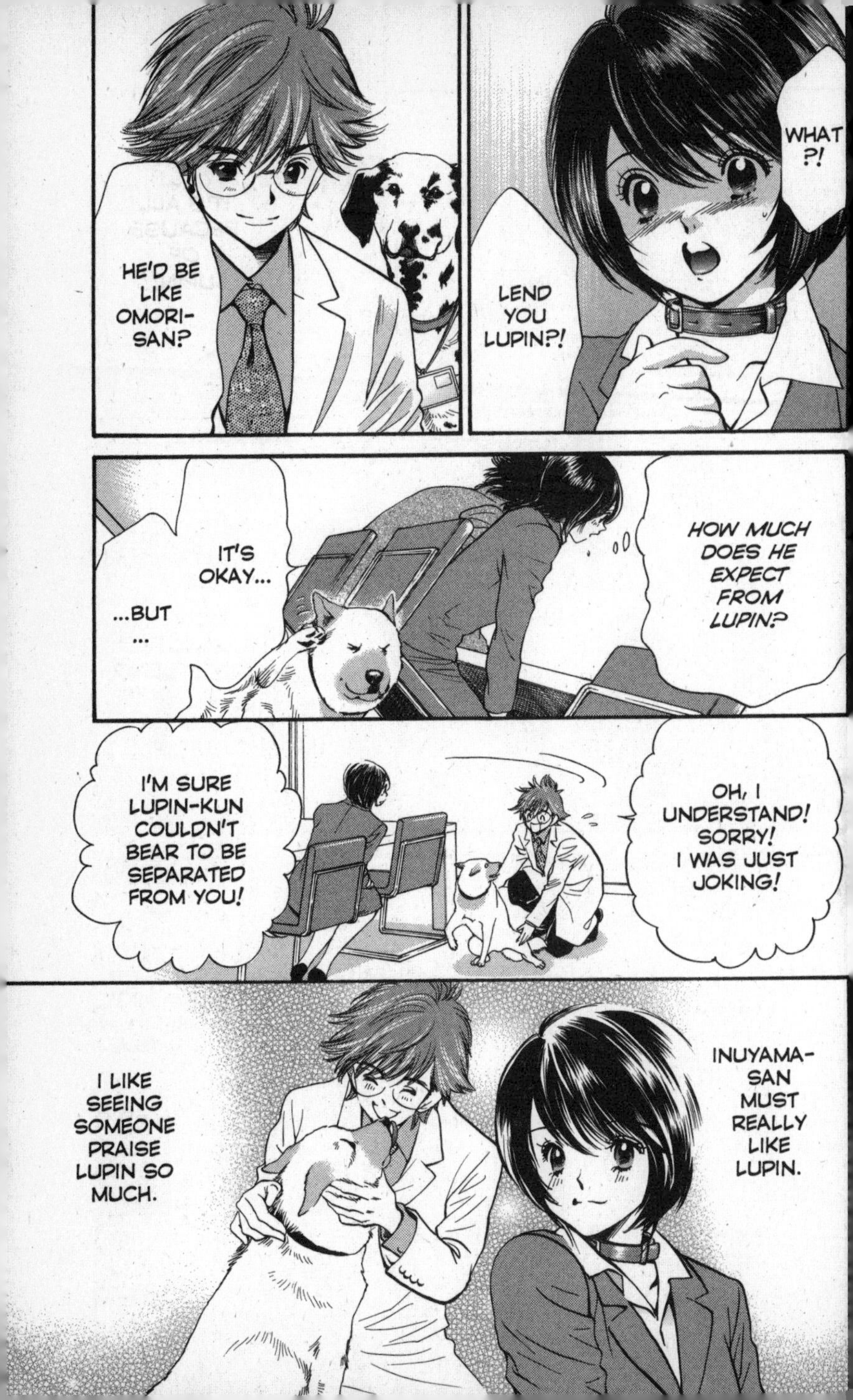
WHAT ?!
LEND YOU LUPIN?!
HE'D BE LIKE OMORI-SAN?
HOW MUCH DOES HE EXPECT FROM LUPIN?
IT'S OKAY...
...BUT ...
OH, I UNDERSTAND! SORRY! I WAS JUST JOKING!
I'M SURE LUPIN-KUN COULDN'T BEAR TO BE SEPARATED FROM YOU!
INUYAMA-SAN MUST REALLY LIKE LUPIN.
I LIKE SEEING SOMEONE PRAISE LUPIN SO MUCH.

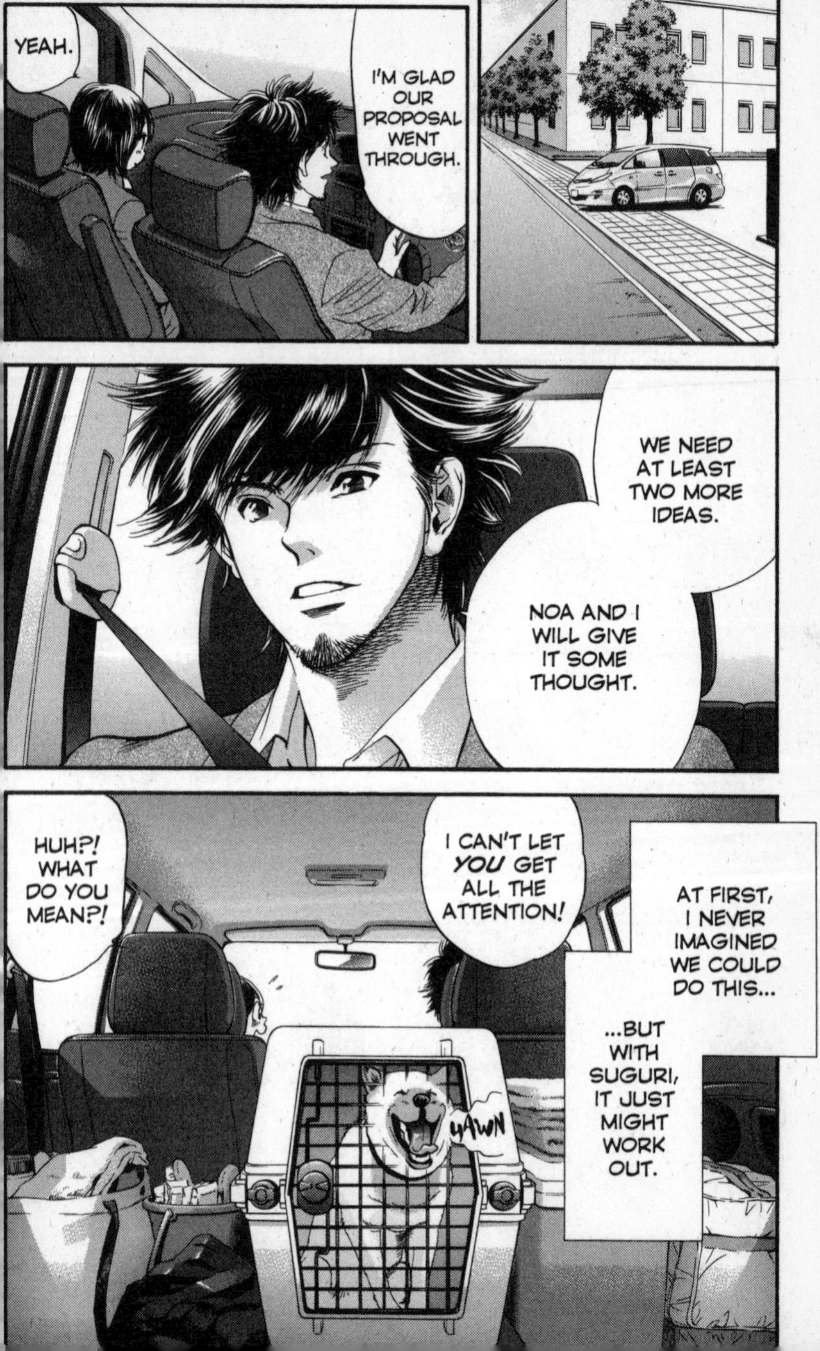
I'M GLAD OUR PROPOSAL WENT THROUGH.
YEAH.
WE NEED AT LEAST TWO MORE IDEAS.
NOA AND I WILL GIVE IT SOME THOUGHT.
AT FIRST, I NEVER IMAGINED WE COULD DO THIS...
I CAN'T LET *YOU* GET ALL THE ATTENTION!
HUH?! WHAT DO YOU MEAN?!
...BUT WITH SUGURI, IT JUST MIGHT WORK OUT.
YAWN

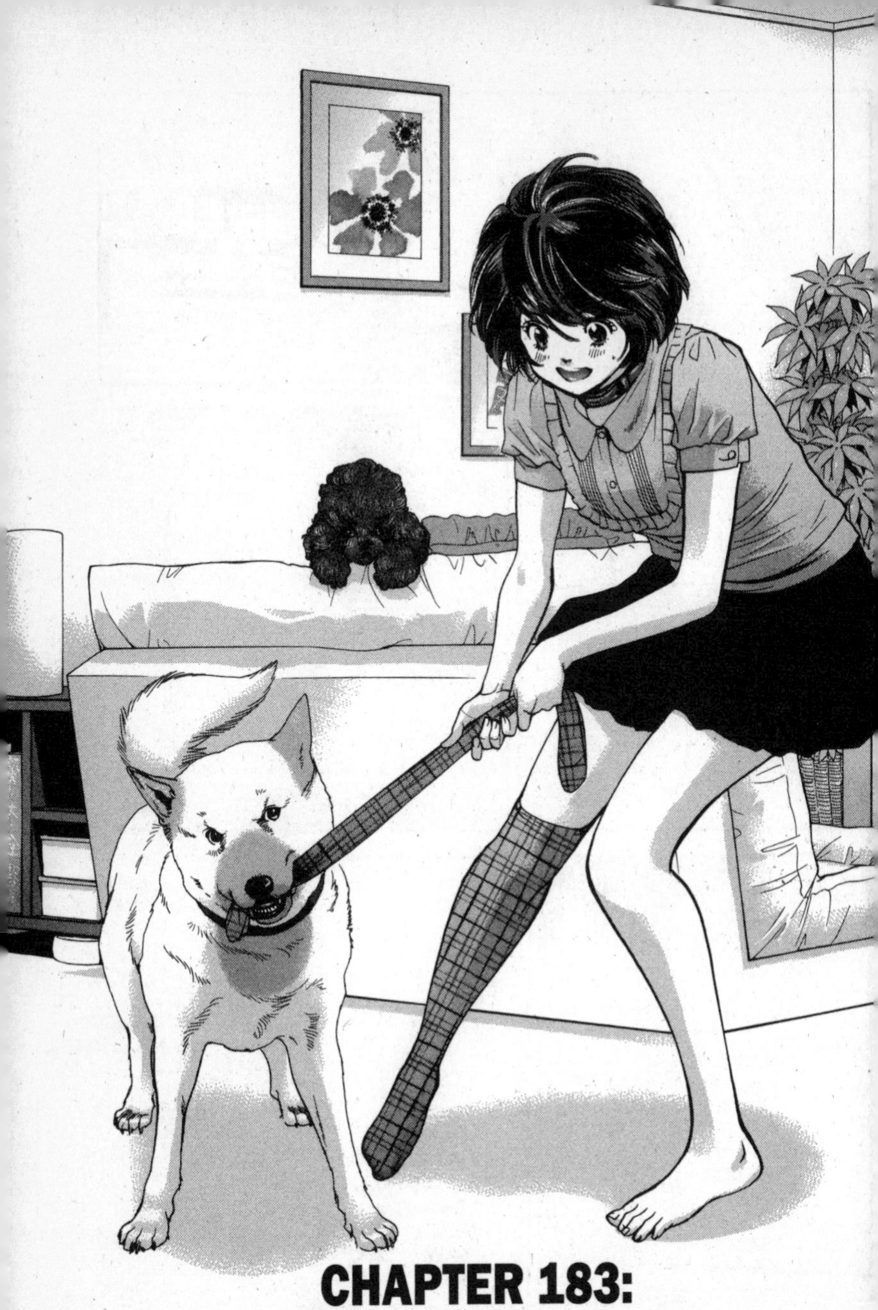

CHAPTER 183:
LET'S PLAY TUG

TAK TAK TAK

TAK TAK

A

PRODUCT SALES (AUGUST)
グッズ売上（8月）

	品　　名ITEM	価PRICE
	リード	¥7
	ング	¥7
	ック	¥8
	ル	¥18
		¥18
	ト	¥18
		¥19

I SEE...

AS USUAL, THAT IS OUR BEST SELLER.

HMM ...

MAYBE MY EXPERIENCE AS A PET-SHOP OWNER WILL LEAD TO SOME GOOD IDEAS.

AT FIRST I DIDN'T THINK IT WOULD WORK...

...BUT AFTER SUGURI CAME UP WITH AN IDEA, I SAW HOPE.

I'LL HAVE TO CONFIRM IT.

WE'RE WORKING TOGETHER WITH YUKIYERN, A PET GOODS COMPANY, TO DEVELOP A GAME CENTER FOR DOGS.

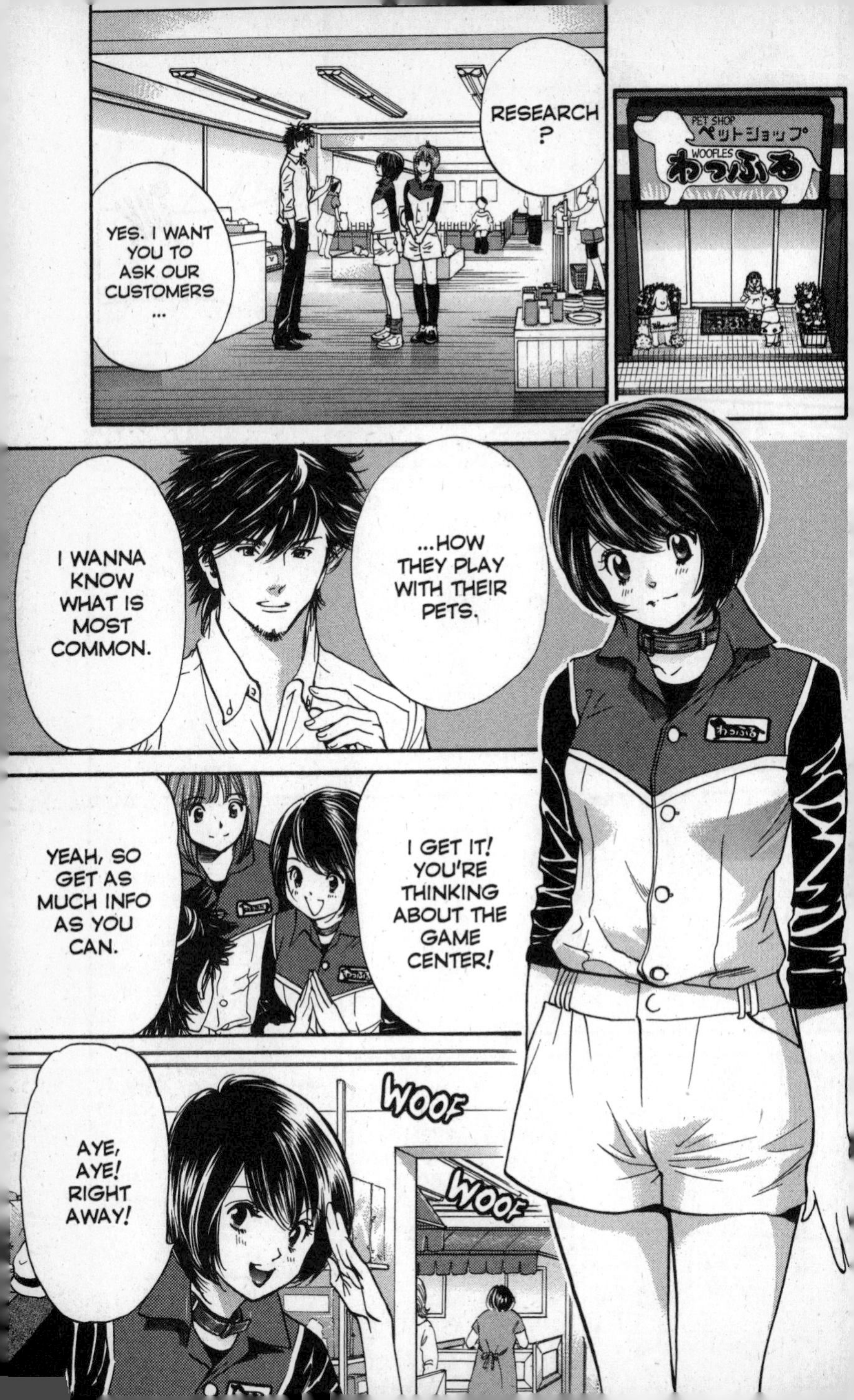
PET SHOP
ペットショップ
WOOFLES
わっふる
RESEARCH?
YES. I WANT YOU TO ASK OUR CUSTOMERS...
...HOW THEY PLAY WITH THEIR PETS.
I WANNA KNOW WHAT IS MOST COMMON.
I GET IT! YOU'RE THINKING ABOUT THE GAME CENTER!
YEAH, SO GET AS MUCH INFO AS YOU CAN.
WOOF
WOOF
AYE, AYE! RIGHT AWAY!

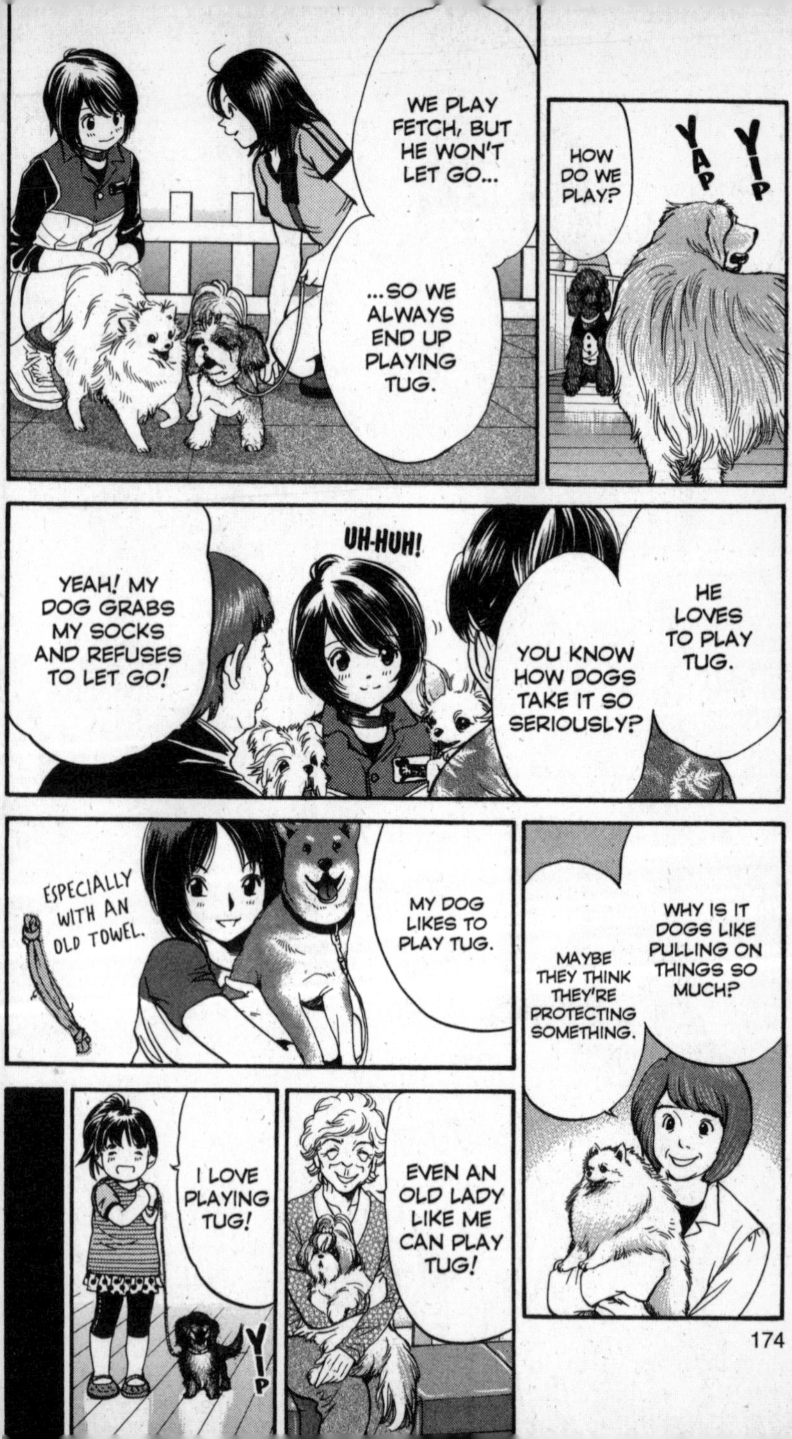
HOW DO WE PLAY?
YAP
YIP
WE PLAY FETCH, BUT HE WON'T LET GO...
...SO WE ALWAYS END UP PLAYING TUG.
HE LOVES TO PLAY TUG.
YOU KNOW HOW DOGS TAKE IT SO SERIOUSLY?
UH-HUH!
YEAH! MY DOG GRABS MY SOCKS AND REFUSES TO LET GO!
WHY IS IT DOGS LIKE PULLING ON THINGS SO MUCH?
MAYBE THEY THINK THEY'RE PROTECTING SOMETHING.
MY DOG LIKES TO PLAY TUG.
ESPECIALLY WITH AN OLD TOWEL.
EVEN AN OLD LADY LIKE ME CAN PLAY TUG!
I LOVE PLAYING TUG!
YIP

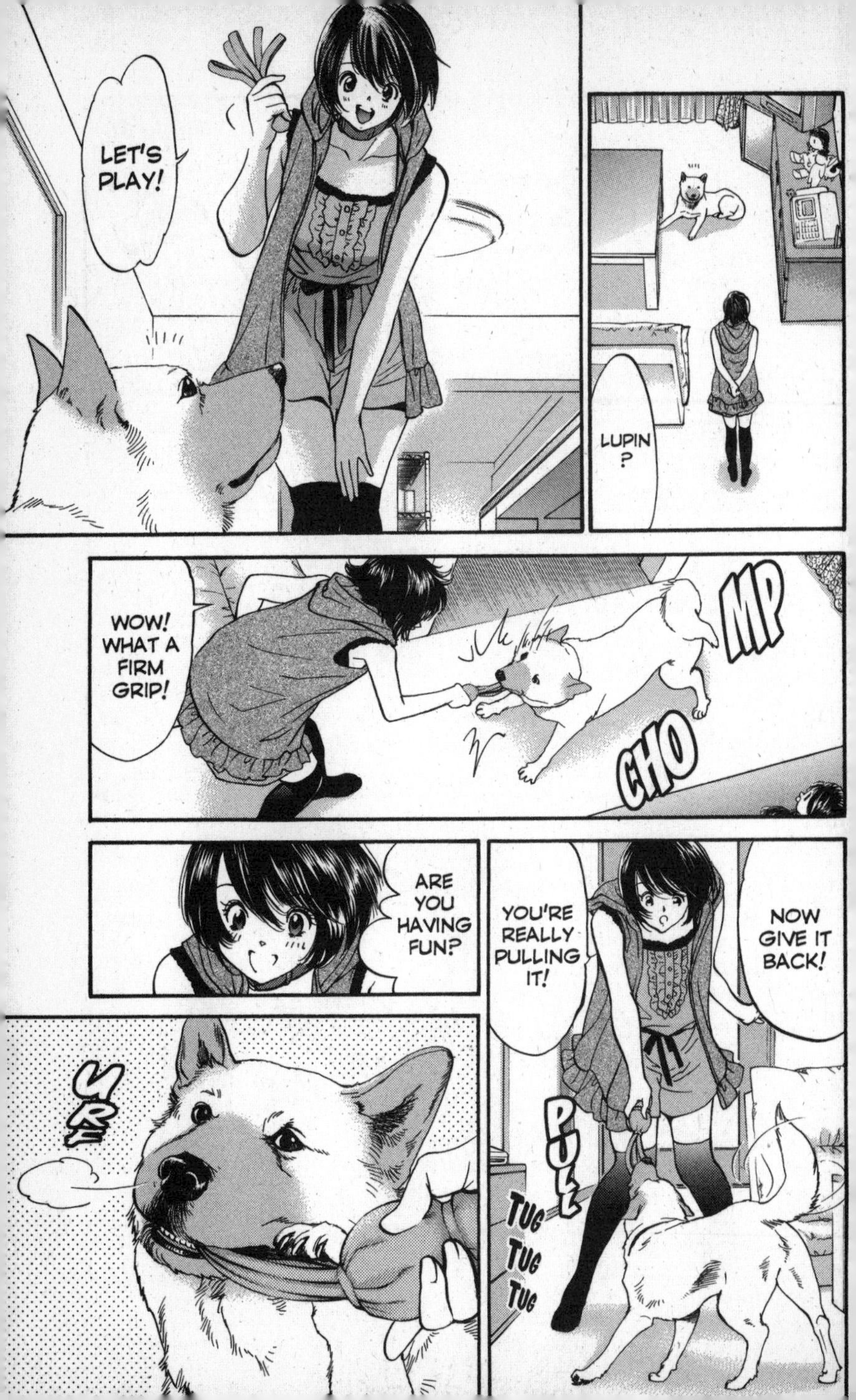
LUPIN?
LET'S PLAY!
WOW! WHAT A FIRM GRIP!
CHO
MP
NOW GIVE IT BACK!
YOU'RE REALLY PULLING IT!
PULL
TUG TUG TUG
ARE YOU HAVING FUN?
URI

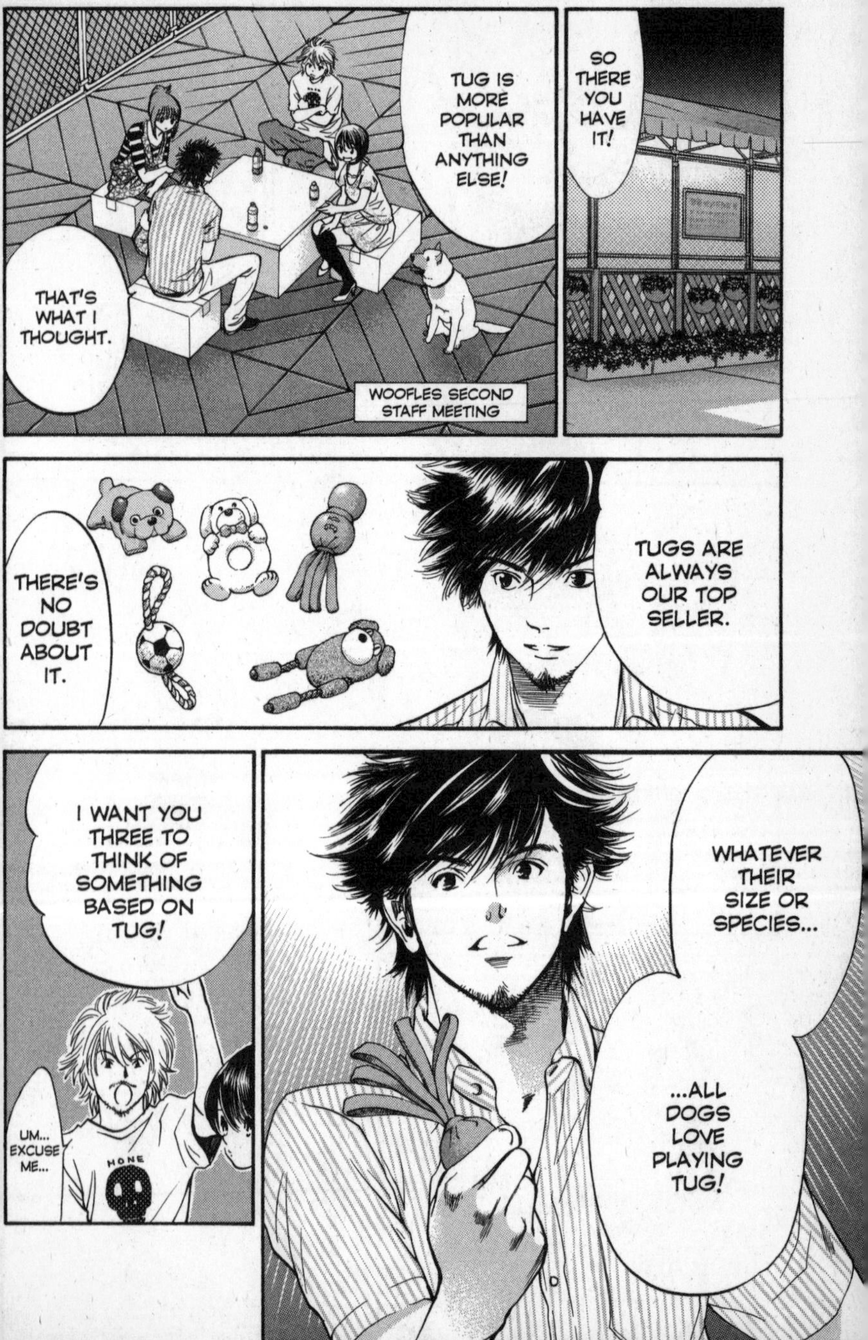
SO THERE YOU HAVE IT!
TUG IS MORE POPULAR THAN ANYTHING ELSE!
THAT'S WHAT I THOUGHT.
WOOFLES SECOND STAFF MEETING
TUGS ARE ALWAYS OUR TOP SELLER.
THERE'S NO DOUBT ABOUT IT.
WHATEVER THEIR SIZE OR SPECIES...
...ALL DOGS LOVE PLAYING TUG!
I WANT YOU THREE TO THINK OF SOMETHING BASED ON TUG!
UM... EXCUSE ME...
HONE

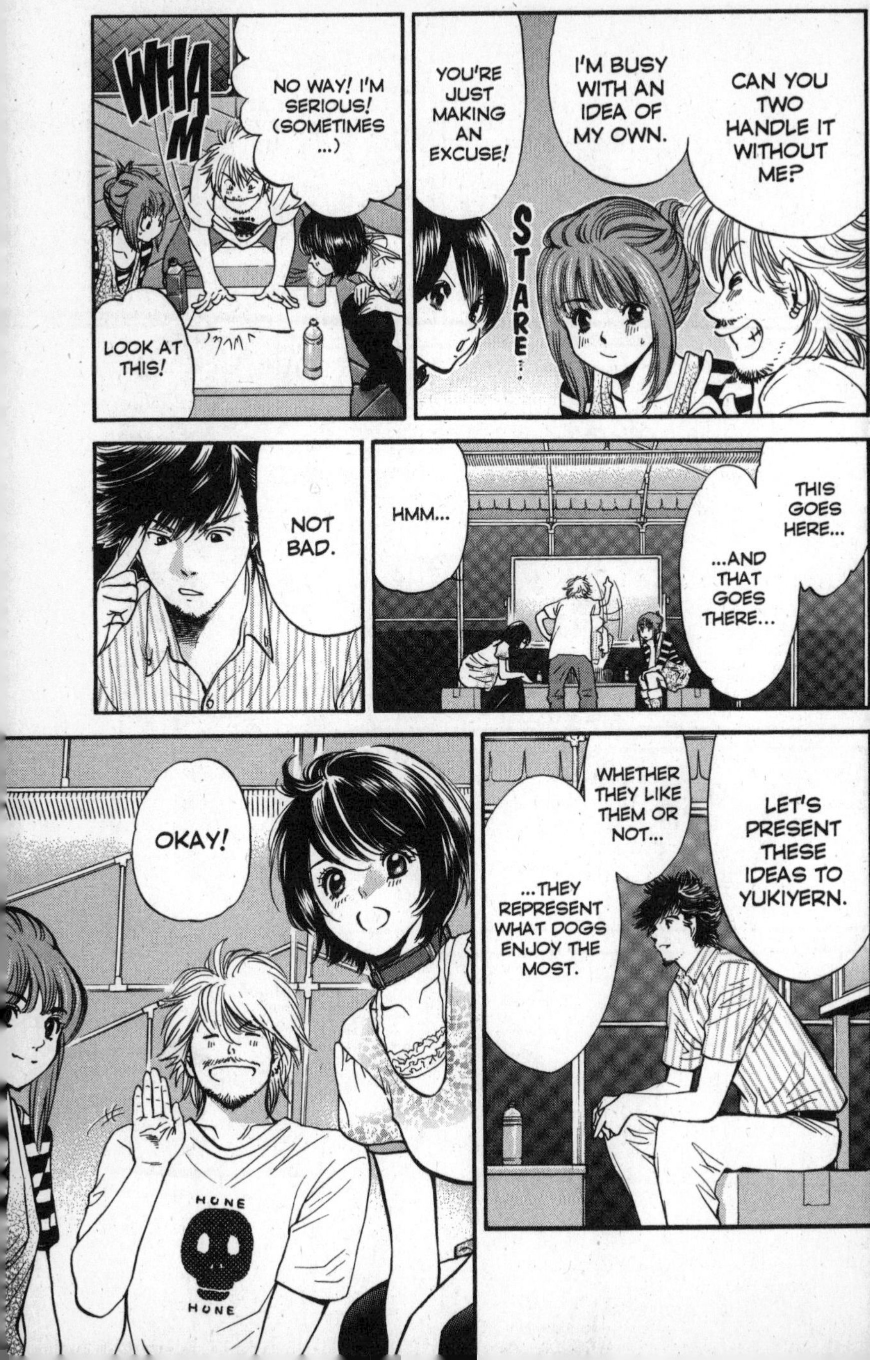
CAN YOU TWO HANDLE IT WITHOUT ME?
I'M BUSY WITH AN IDEA OF MY OWN.
STARE...
YOU'RE JUST MAKING AN EXCUSE!
NO WAY! I'M SERIOUS! (SOMETIMES ...)
WHAM
LOOK AT THIS!
THIS GOES HERE...
...AND THAT GOES THERE...
HMM...
NOT BAD.
LET'S PRESENT THESE IDEAS TO YUKIYERN.
WHETHER THEY LIKE THEM OR NOT...
...THEY REPRESENT WHAT DOGS ENJOY THE MOST.
OKAY!
HUNE
HUNE

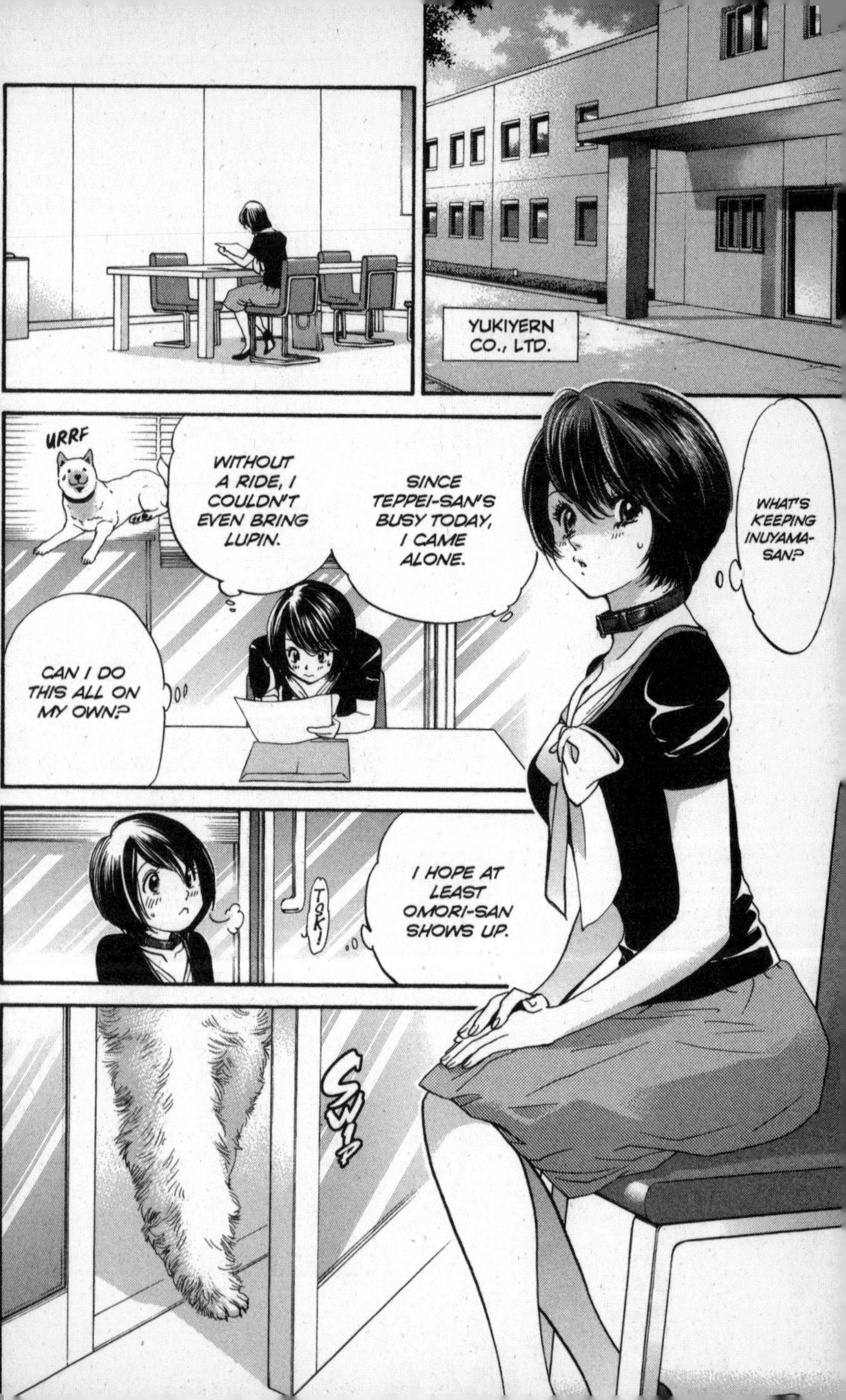
YUKIYERN CO., LTD.
WHAT'S KEEPING INUYAMA-SAN?
SINCE TEPPEI-SAN'S BUSY TODAY, I CAME ALONE.
WITHOUT A RIDE, I COULDN'T EVEN BRING LUPIN.
URRF
CAN I DO THIS ALL ON MY OWN?
I HOPE AT LEAST OMORI-SAN SHOWS UP.
TOK!
SWIP

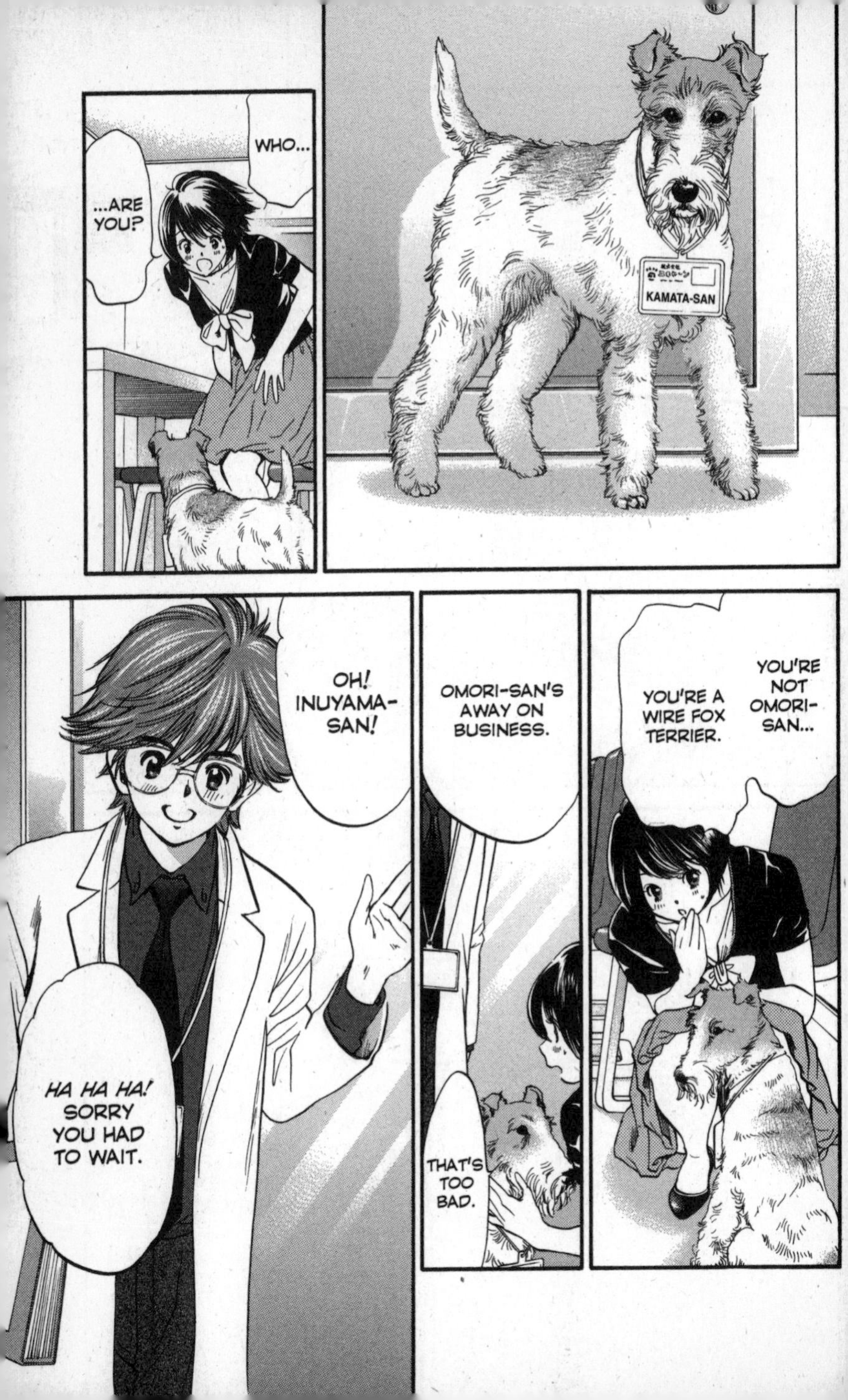
KAMATA-SAN
WHO...
...ARE YOU?
YOU'RE NOT OMORI-SAN...
YOU'RE A WIRE FOX TERRIER.
OMORI-SAN'S AWAY ON BUSINESS.
THAT'S TOO BAD.
OH! INUYAMA-SAN!
HA HA HA! SORRY YOU HAD TO WAIT.

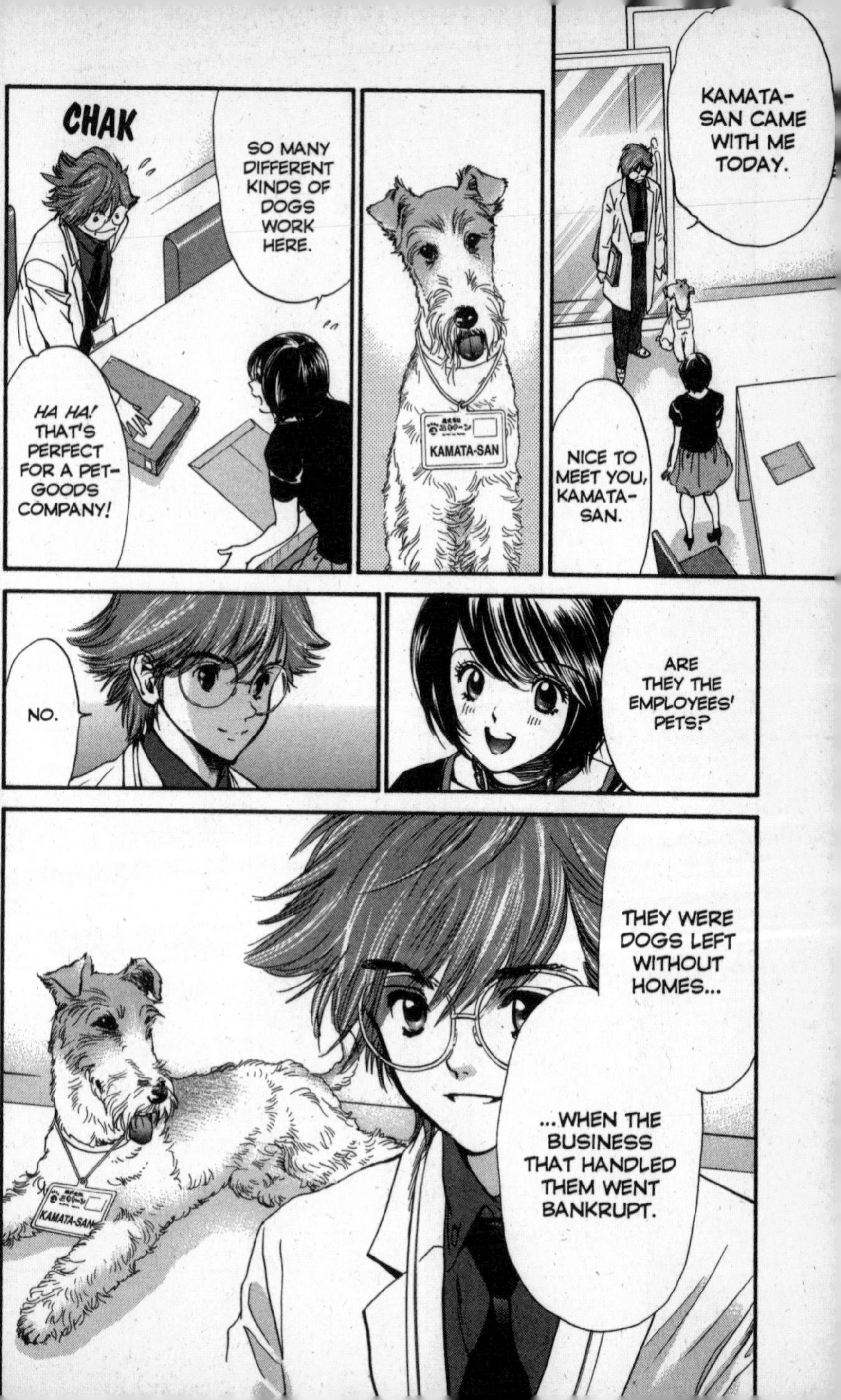
KAMATA-SAN CAME WITH ME TODAY.
NICE TO MEET YOU, KAMATA-SAN.
KAMATA-SAN
SO MANY DIFFERENT KINDS OF DOGS WORK HERE.
CHAK
HA HA! THAT'S PERFECT FOR A PET-GOODS COMPANY!
ARE THEY THE EMPLOYEES' PETS?
NO.
THEY WERE DOGS LEFT WITHOUT HOMES...
...WHEN THE BUSINESS THAT HANDLED THEM WENT BANKRUPT.
KAMATA-SAN

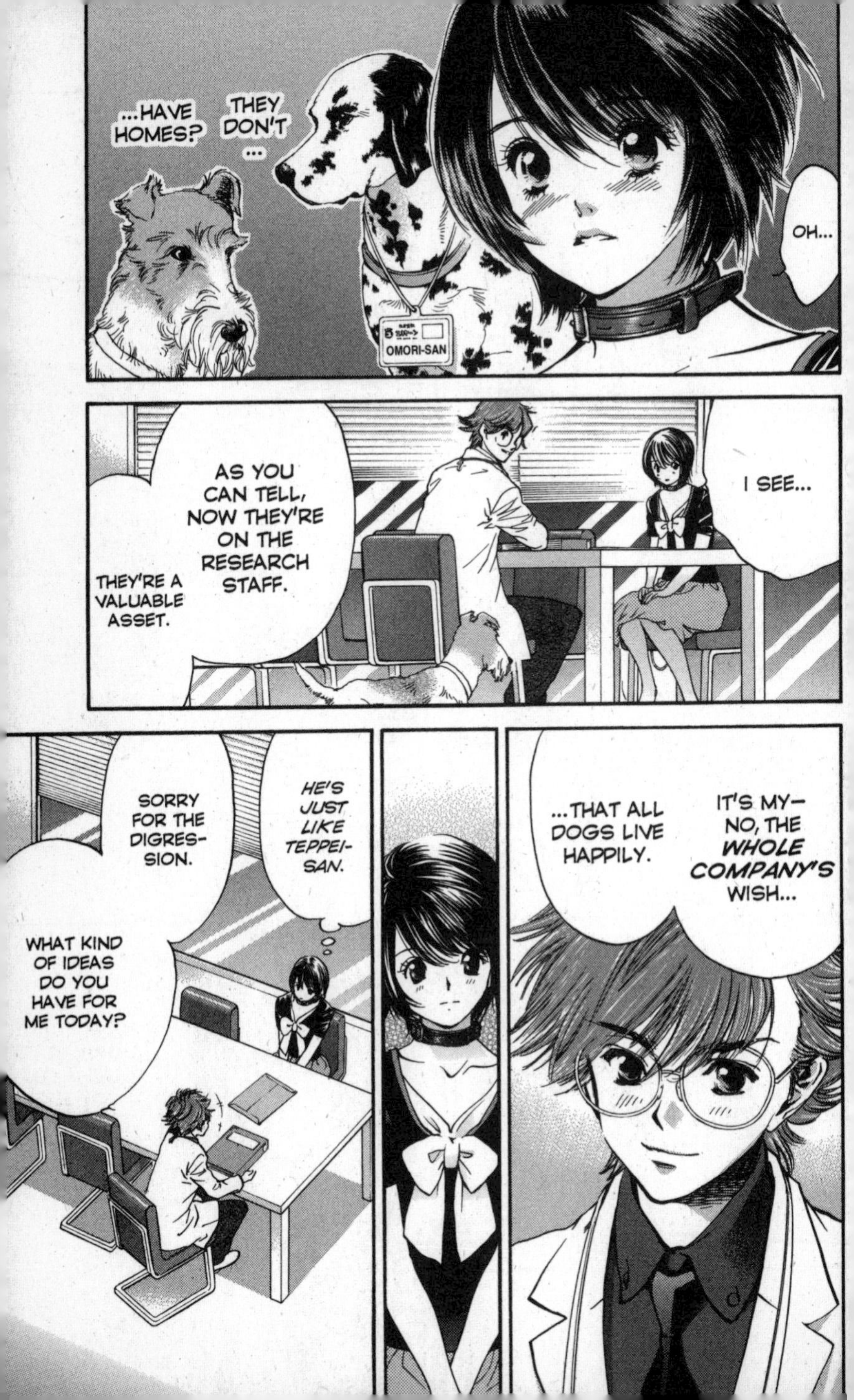
OH...
THEY DON'T ...
...HAVE HOMES?
OMORI-SAN
I SEE...
AS YOU CAN TELL, NOW THEY'RE ON THE RESEARCH STAFF.
THEY'RE A VALUABLE ASSET.
IT'S MY— NO, THE *WHOLE COMPANY'S* WISH...
...THAT ALL DOGS LIVE HAPPILY.
HE'S JUST LIKE TEPPEI-SAN.
SORRY FOR THE DIGRESSION.
WHAT KIND OF IDEAS DO YOU HAVE FOR ME TODAY?

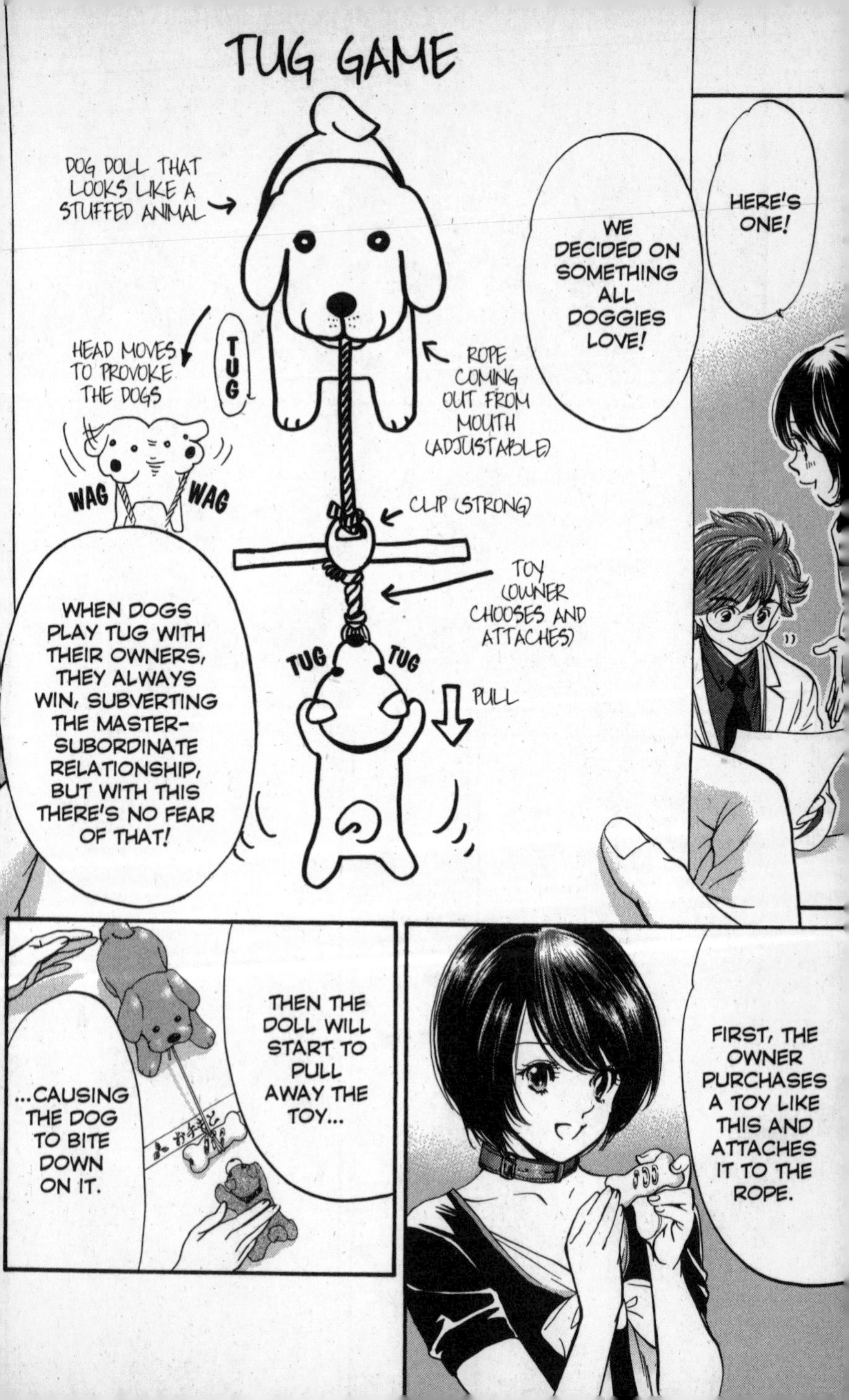
HERE'S ONE!
WE DECIDED ON SOMETHING ALL DOGGIES LOVE!
TUG GAME
DOG DOLL THAT LOOKS LIKE A STUFFED ANIMAL
ROPE COMING OUT FROM MOUTH (ADJUSTABLE)
TUG
HEAD MOVES TO PROVOKE THE DOGS
WAG WAG
CLIP (STRONG)
TOY (OWNER CHOOSES AND ATTACHES)
PULL
TUG TUG
WHEN DOGS PLAY TUG WITH THEIR OWNERS, THEY ALWAYS WIN, SUBVERTING THE MASTER-SUBORDINATE RELATIONSHIP, BUT WITH THIS THERE'S NO FEAR OF THAT!
FIRST, THE OWNER PURCHASES A TOY LIKE THIS AND ATTACHES IT TO THE ROPE.
THEN THE DOLL WILL START TO PULL AWAY THE TOY...
...CAUSING THE DOG TO BITE DOWN ON IT.

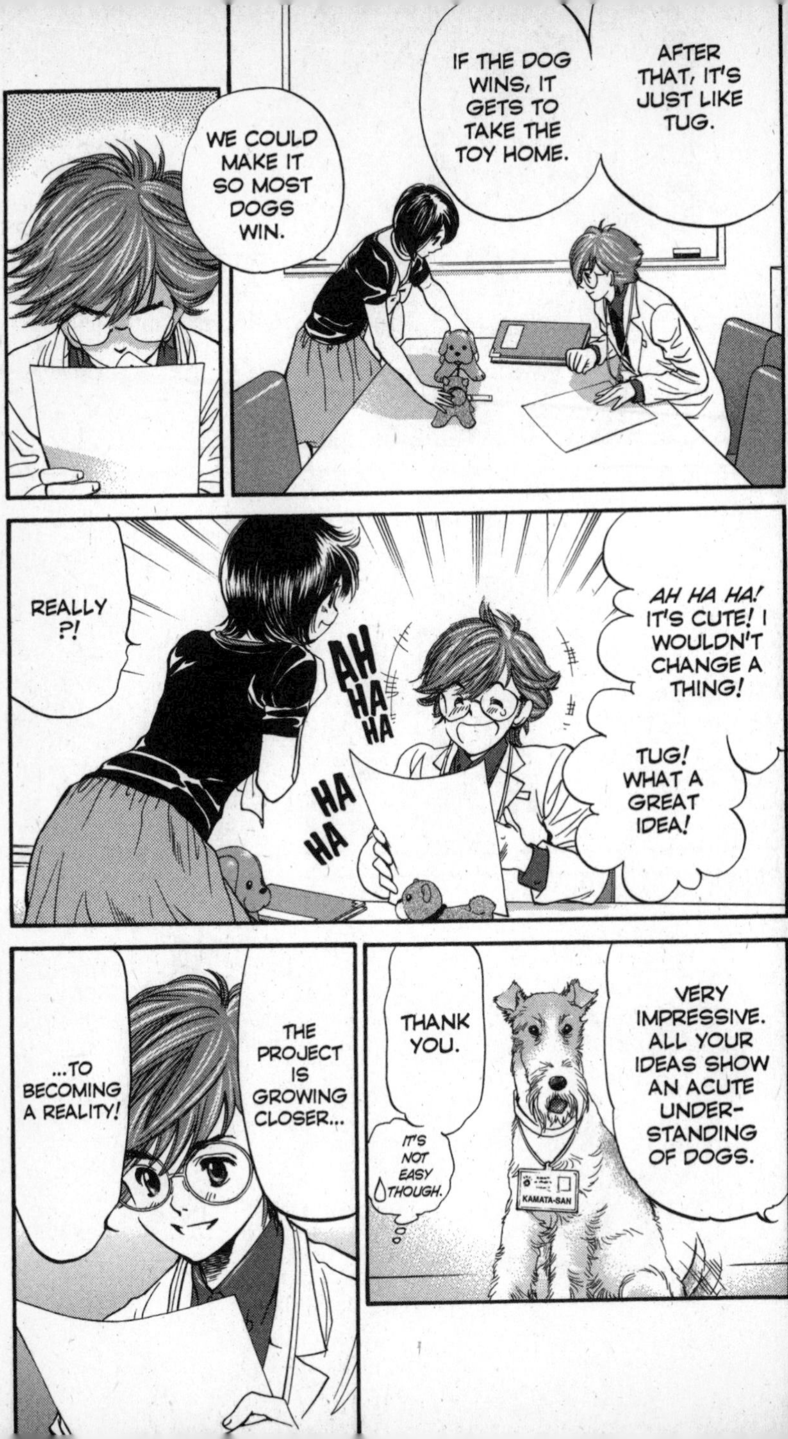
AFTER THAT, IT'S JUST LIKE TUG.
IF THE DOG WINS, IT GETS TO TAKE THE TOY HOME.
WE COULD MAKE IT SO MOST DOGS WIN.
AH HA HA! IT'S CUTE! I WOULDN'T CHANGE A THING!
TUG! WHAT A GREAT IDEA!
AH HA HA
HA HA
REALLY ?!
VERY IMPRESSIVE. ALL YOUR IDEAS SHOW AN ACUTE UNDER-STANDING OF DOGS.
KAMATA-SAN
THANK YOU.
IT'S NOT EASY THOUGH.
THE PROJECT IS GROWING CLOSER...
...TO BECOMING A REALITY!

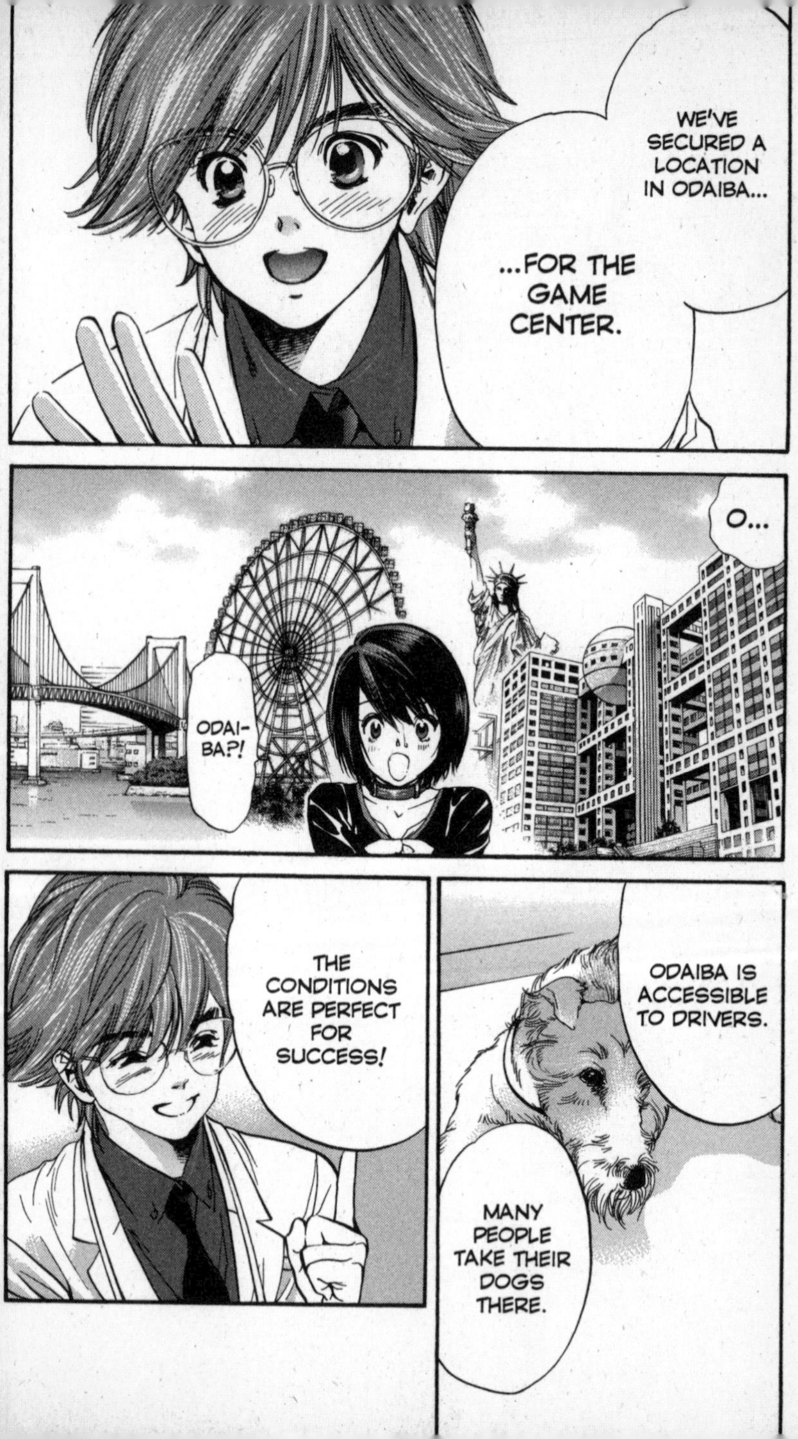
WE'VE SECURED A LOCATION IN ODAIBA...
...FOR THE GAME CENTER.
O...
ODAI-BA?!
ODAIBA IS ACCESSIBLE TO DRIVERS.
MANY PEOPLE TAKE THEIR DOGS THERE.
THE CONDITIONS ARE PERFECT FOR SUCCESS!

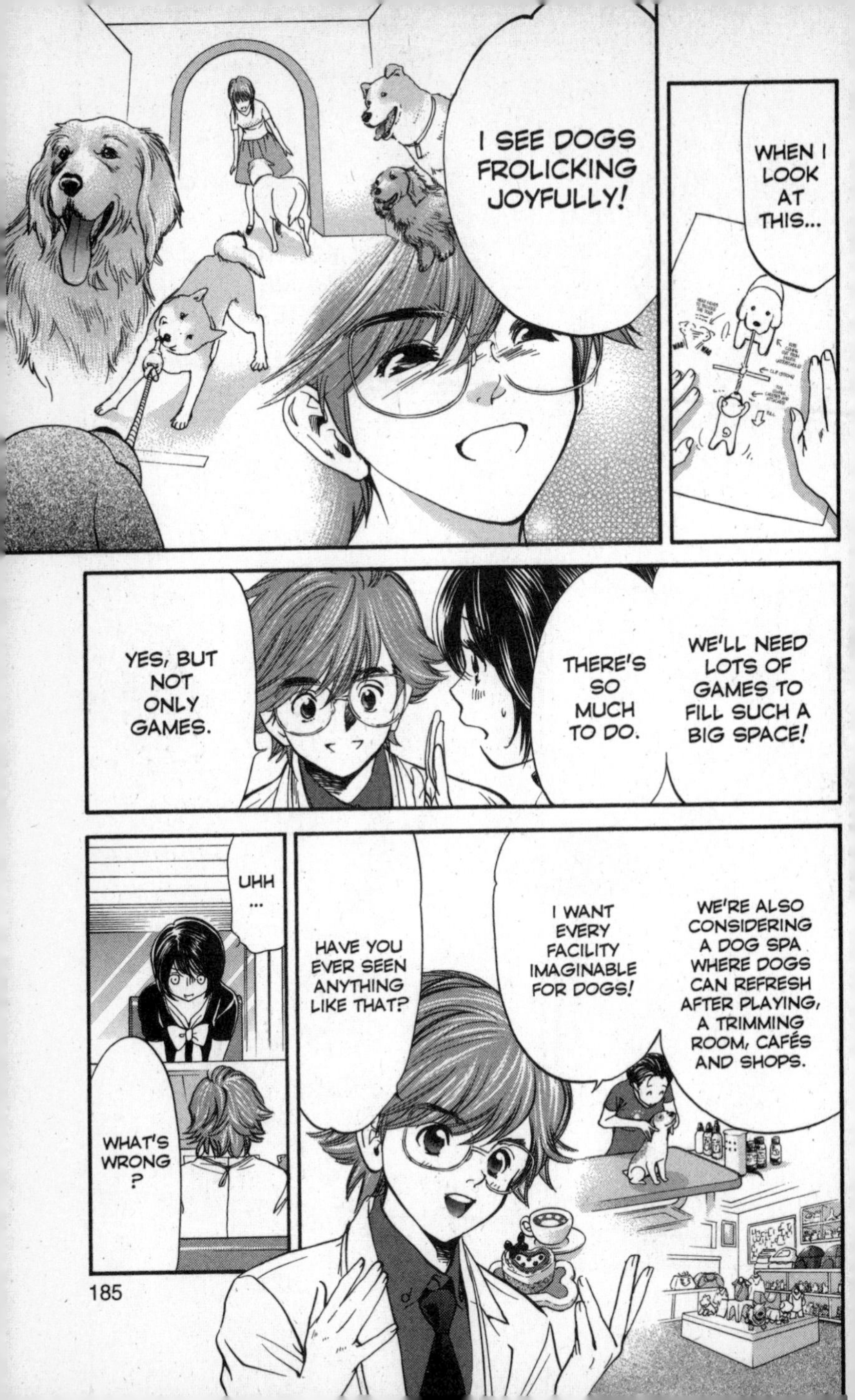
WHEN I LOOK AT THIS...
I SEE DOGS FROLICKING JOYFULLY!
WE'LL NEED LOTS OF GAMES TO FILL SUCH A BIG SPACE!
THERE'S SO MUCH TO DO.
YES, BUT NOT ONLY GAMES.
WE'RE ALSO CONSIDERING A DOG SPA WHERE DOGS CAN REFRESH AFTER PLAYING, A TRIMMING ROOM, CAFÉS AND SHOPS.
I WANT EVERY FACILITY IMAGINABLE FOR DOGS!
HAVE YOU EVER SEEN ANYTHING LIKE THAT?
UHH ...
WHAT'S WRONG ?

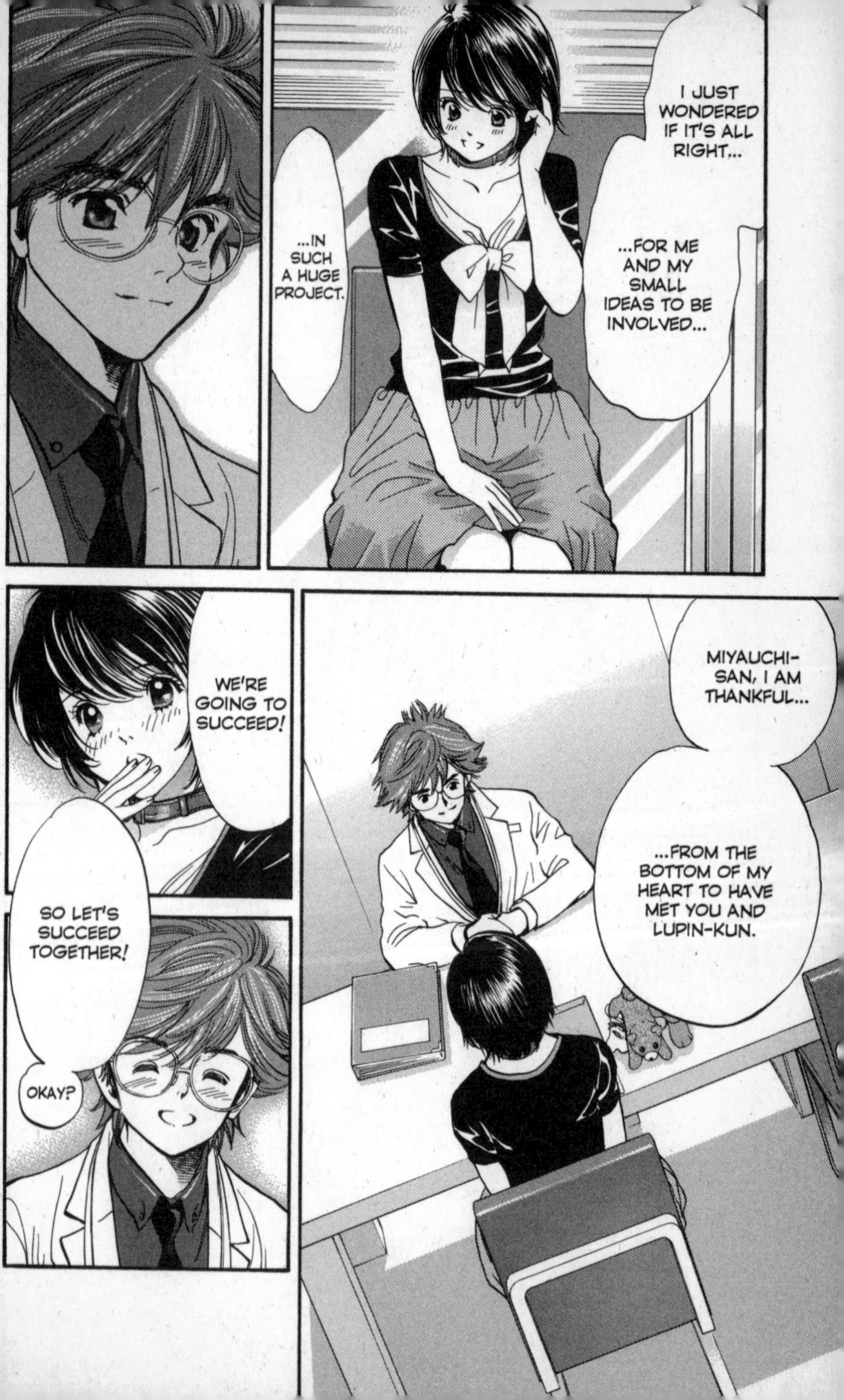
I JUST WONDERED IF IT'S ALL RIGHT...
...FOR ME AND MY SMALL IDEAS TO BE INVOLVED...
...IN SUCH A HUGE PROJECT.
MIYAUCHI-SAN, I AM THANKFUL...
...FROM THE BOTTOM OF MY HEART TO HAVE MET YOU AND LUPIN-KUN.
WE'RE GOING TO SUCCEED!
SO LET'S SUCCEED TOGETHER!
OKAY?

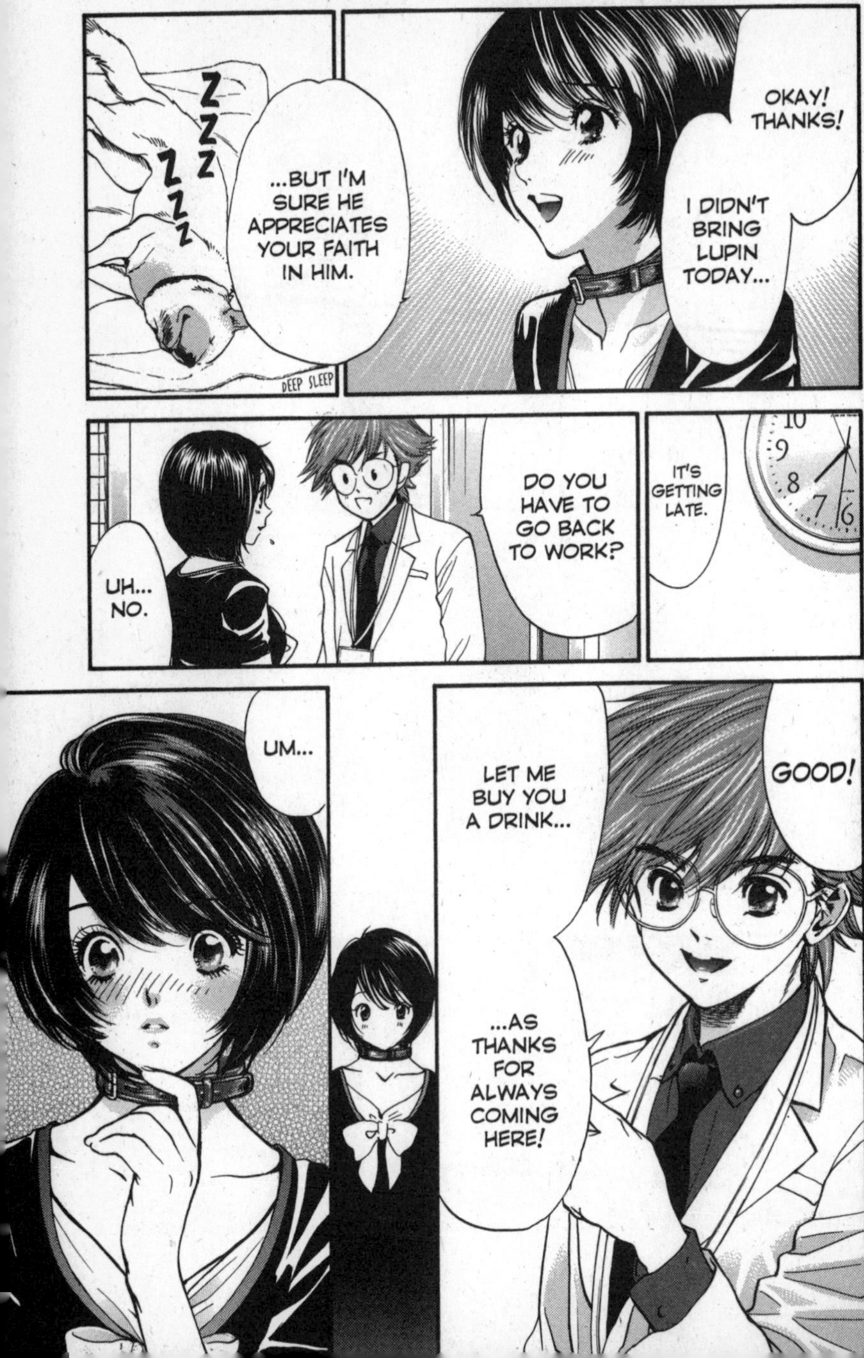
OKAY! THANKS!
I DIDN'T BRING LUPIN TODAY...
...BUT I'M SURE HE APPRECIATES YOUR FAITH IN HIM.
Z Z Z Z Z Z
DEEP SLEEP
IT'S GETTING LATE.
DO YOU HAVE TO GO BACK TO WORK?
UH... NO.
GOOD!
LET ME BUY YOU A DRINK...
...AS THANKS FOR ALWAYS COMING HERE!
UM...

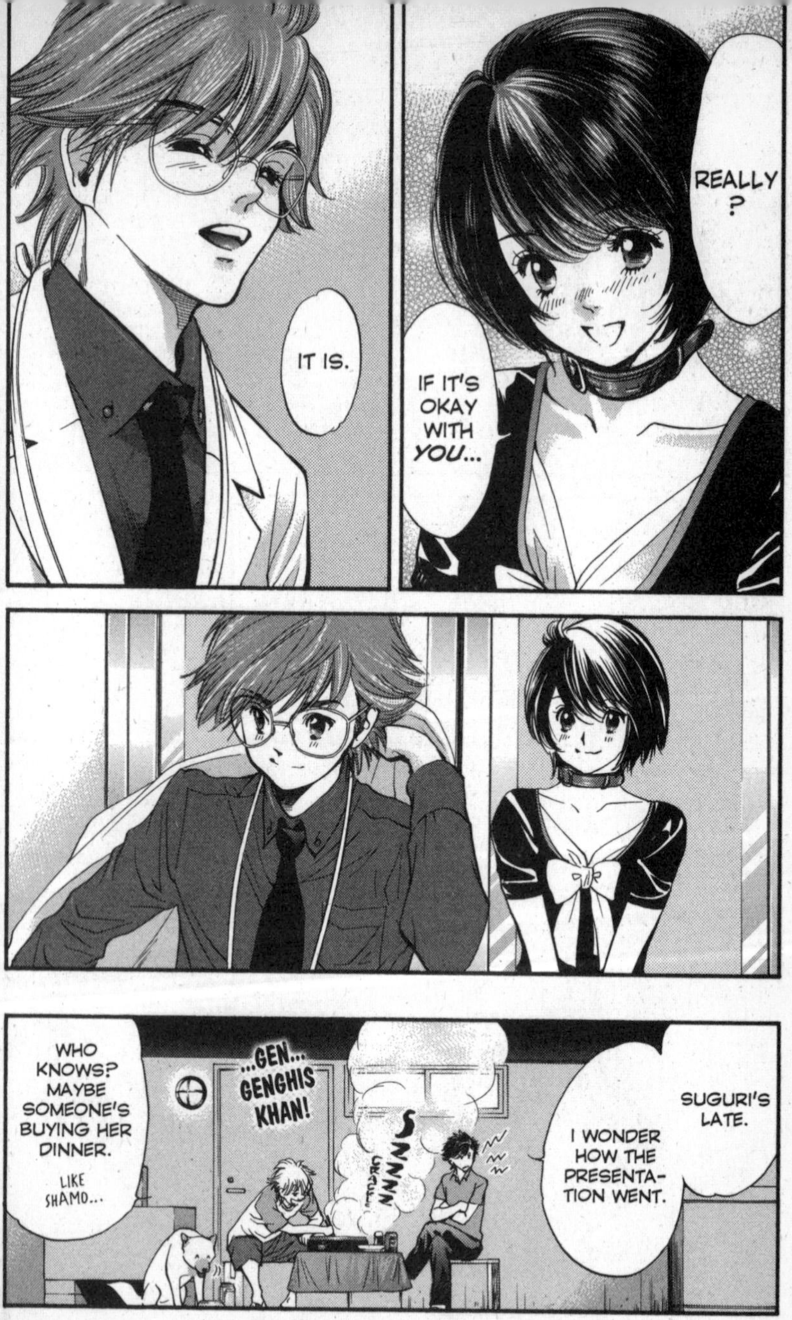
REALLY ?
IF IT'S OKAY WITH YOU...
IT IS.
SUGURI'S LATE.
I WONDER HOW THE PRESENTATION WENT.
SNNNN
...GEN... GENGHIS KHAN!
WHO KNOWS? MAYBE SOMEONE'S BUYING HER DINNER.
LIKE SHAMO...

CHAPTER 184: I LIKE MUTTS

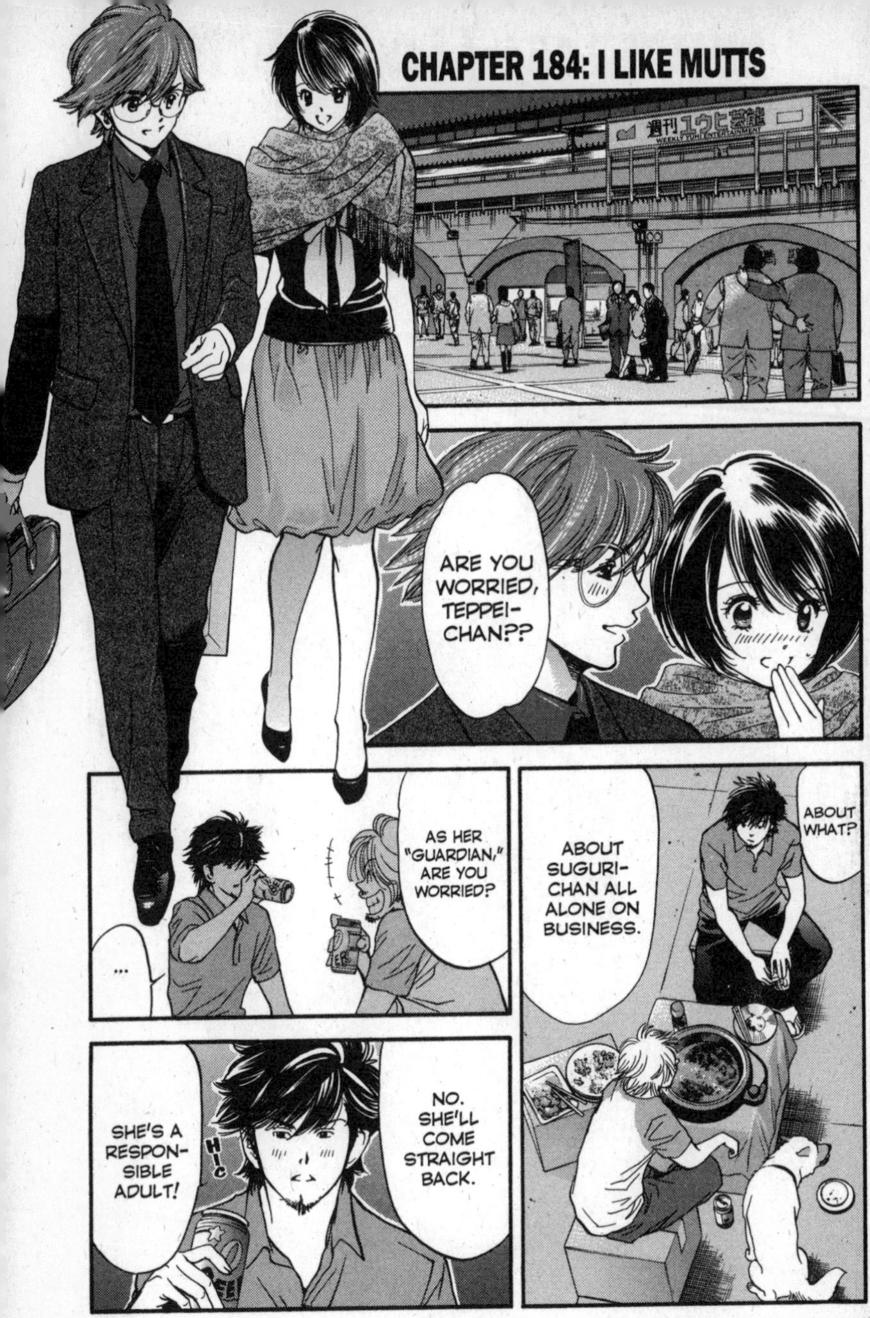

ARE YOU WORRIED, TEPPEI-CHAN??
ABOUT WHAT?
ABOUT SUGURI-CHAN ALL ALONE ON BUSINESS.
AS HER "GUARDIAN," ARE YOU WORRIED?
...
NO. SHE'LL COME STRAIGHT BACK.
HIC
SHE'S A RESPONSIBLE ADULT!

CHAPTER 184: I LIKE MUTTS

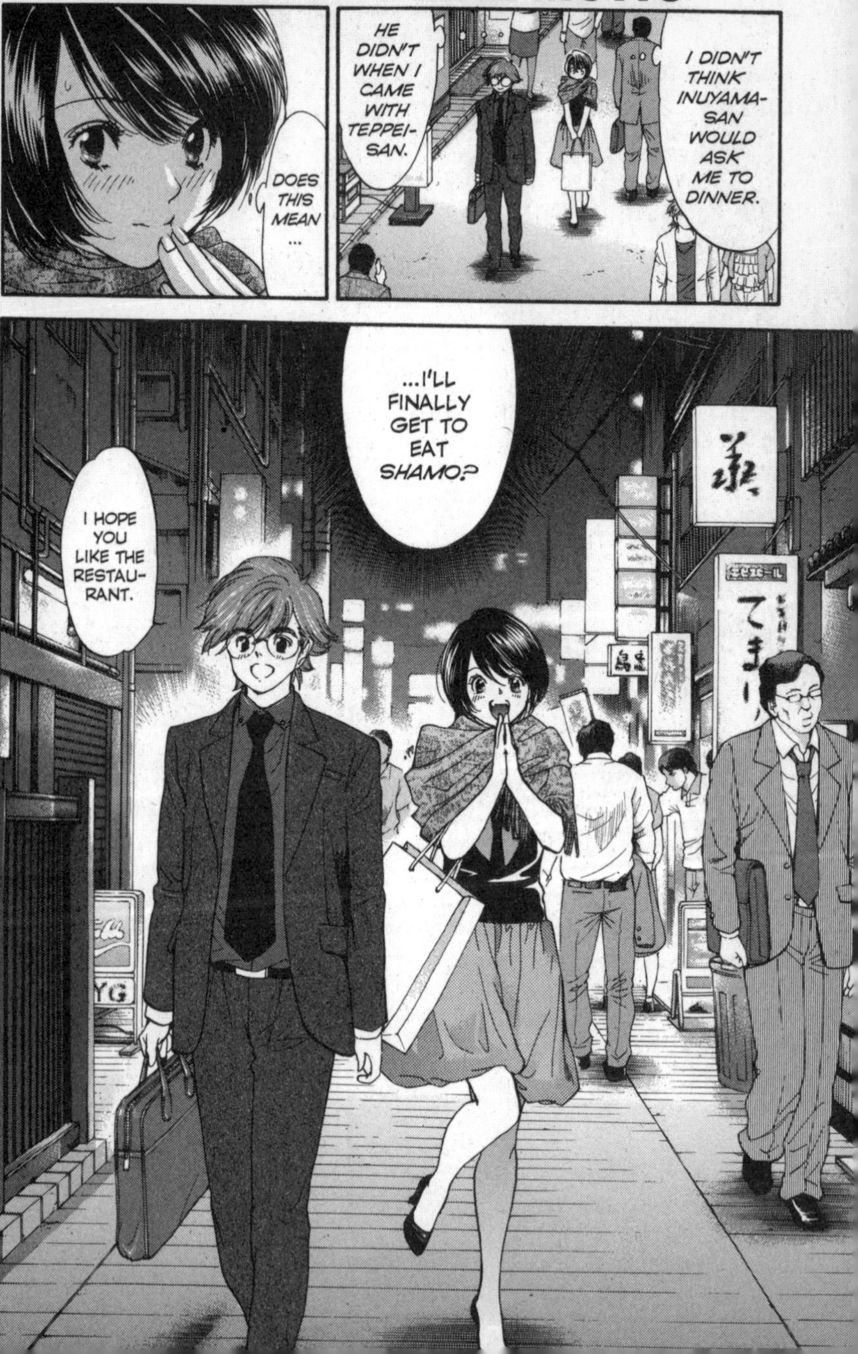
I DIDN'T THINK INUYAMA-SAN WOULD ASK ME TO DINNER.
HE DIDN'T WHEN I CAME WITH TEPPEI-SAN.
DOES THIS MEAN ...
...I'LL FINALLY GET TO EAT SHAMO?
I HOPE YOU LIKE THE RESTAURANT.

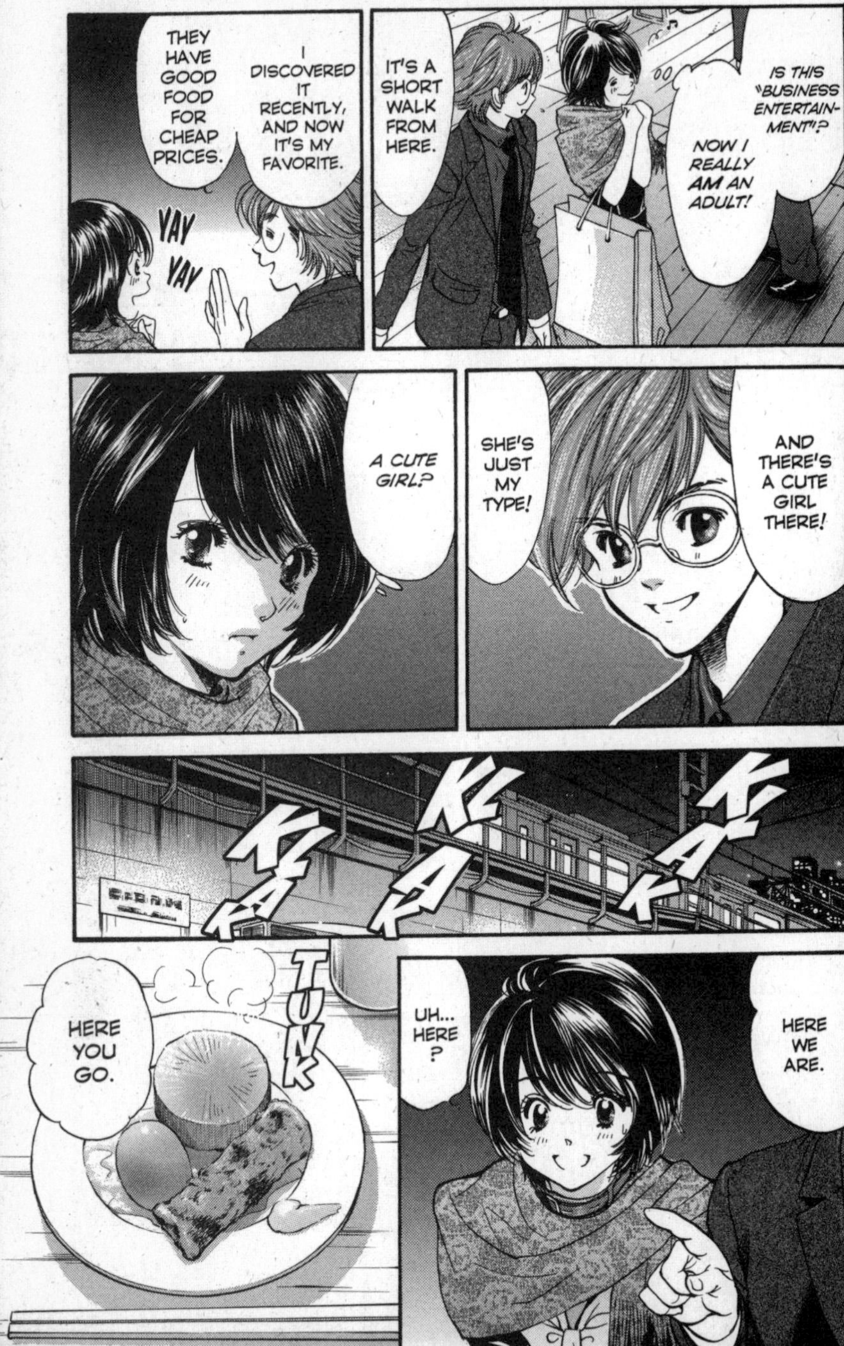
IS THIS "BUSINESS ENTERTAINMENT"?
NOW I REALLY AM AN ADULT!
IT'S A SHORT WALK FROM HERE.
I DISCOVERED IT RECENTLY, AND NOW IT'S MY FAVORITE.
THEY HAVE GOOD FOOD FOR CHEAP PRICES.
YAY YAY
AND THERE'S A CUTE GIRL THERE!
SHE'S JUST MY TYPE!
A CUTE GIRL?
KLAK
KLAK
KLAK
HERE WE ARE.
UH... HERE?
TUNK
HERE YOU GO.

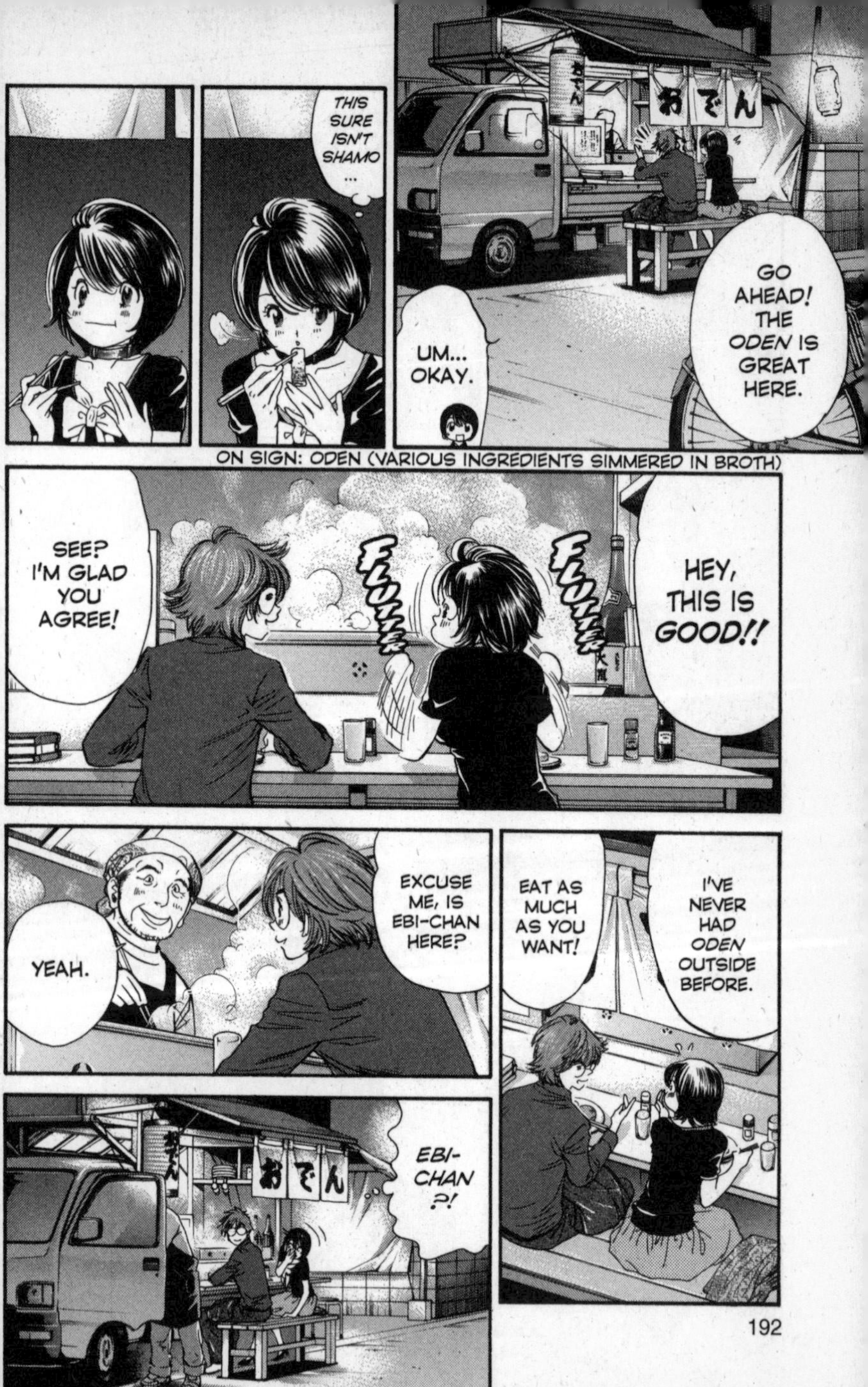
GO AHEAD! THE *ODEN* IS GREAT HERE.
UM... OKAY.
THIS SURE ISN'T SHAMO ...
ON SIGN: ODEN (VARIOUS INGREDIENTS SIMMERED IN BROTH)
HEY, THIS IS *GOOD!!*
FLUTTER
FLUTTER
SEE? I'M GLAD YOU AGREE!
I'VE NEVER HAD *ODEN* OUTSIDE BEFORE.
EAT AS MUCH AS YOU WANT!
EXCUSE ME, IS EBI-CHAN HERE?
YEAH.
EBI-CHAN ?!

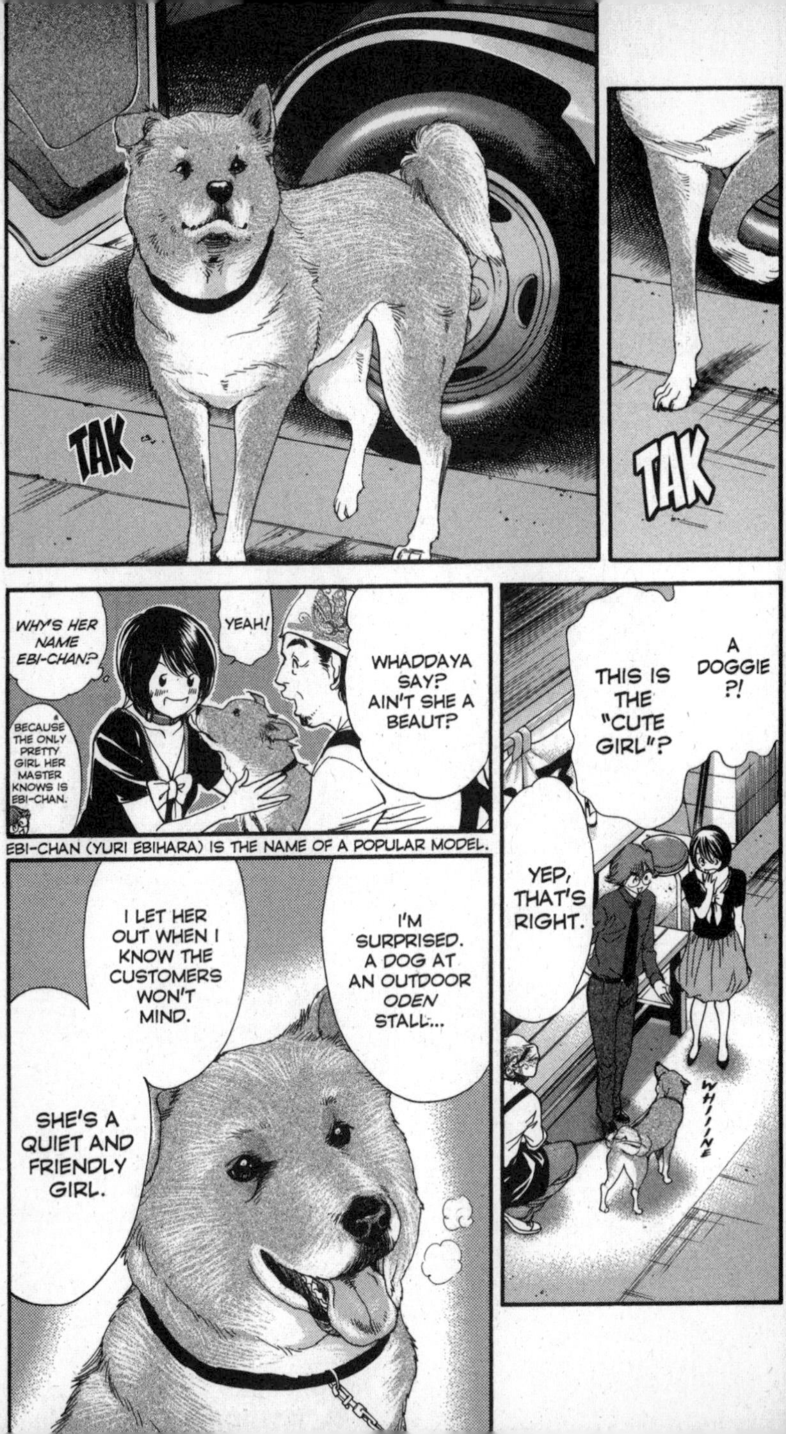
TAK
TAK
A DOGGIE?!
THIS IS THE "CUTE GIRL"?
YEP, THAT'S RIGHT.
WHIIINE
WHADDAYA SAY? AIN'T SHE A BEAUT?
YEAH!
WHY'S HER NAME EBI-CHAN?
BECAUSE THE ONLY PRETTY GIRL HER MASTER KNOWS IS EBI-CHAN.
EBI-CHAN (YURI EBIHARA) IS THE NAME OF A POPULAR MODEL.
I'M SURPRISED. A DOG AT AN OUTDOOR *ODEN* STALL...
I LET HER OUT WHEN I KNOW THE CUSTOMERS WON'T MIND.
SHE'S A QUIET AND FRIENDLY GIRL.

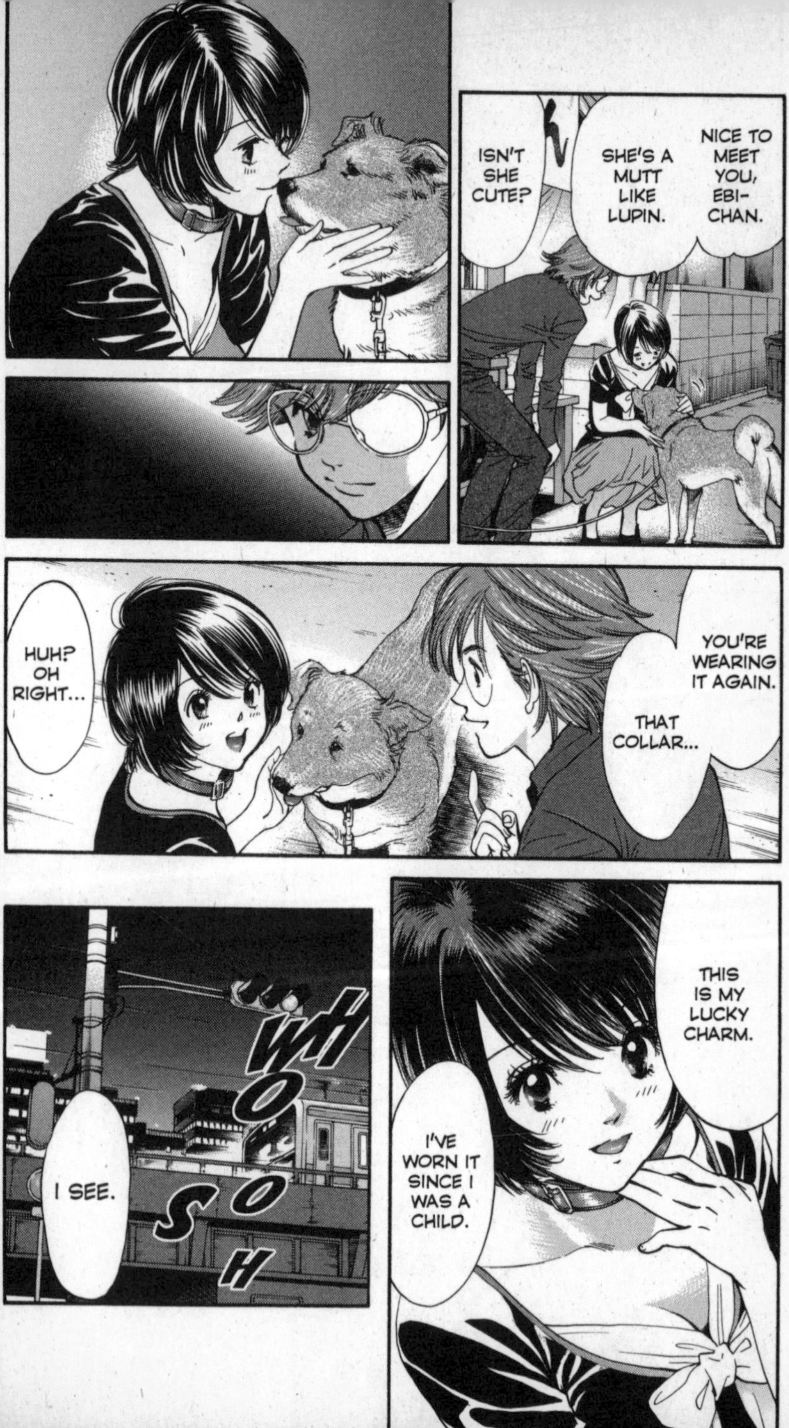
NICE TO MEET YOU, EBI-CHAN.
SHE'S A MUTT LIKE LUPIN.
ISN'T SHE CUTE?
YOU'RE WEARING IT AGAIN.
THAT COLLAR...
HUH? OH RIGHT...
THIS IS MY LUCKY CHARM.
I'VE WORN IT SINCE I WAS A CHILD.
WHOOSH
I SEE.

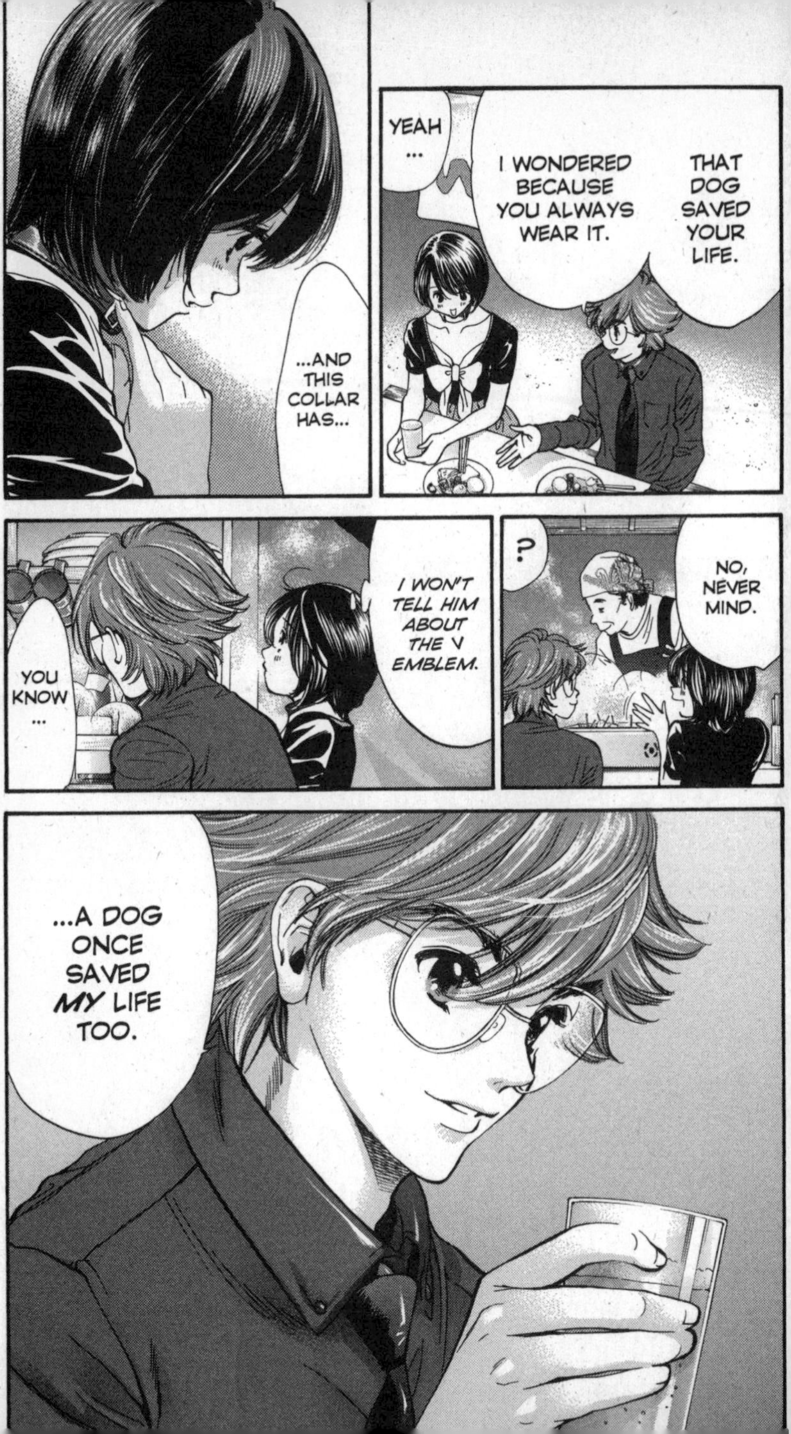
THAT DOG SAVED YOUR LIFE.
I WONDERED BECAUSE YOU ALWAYS WEAR IT.
YEAH ...
...AND THIS COLLAR HAS...
NO, NEVER MIND.
?
I WON'T TELL HIM ABOUT THE V EMBLEM.
YOU KNOW ...
...A DOG ONCE SAVED MY LIFE TOO.

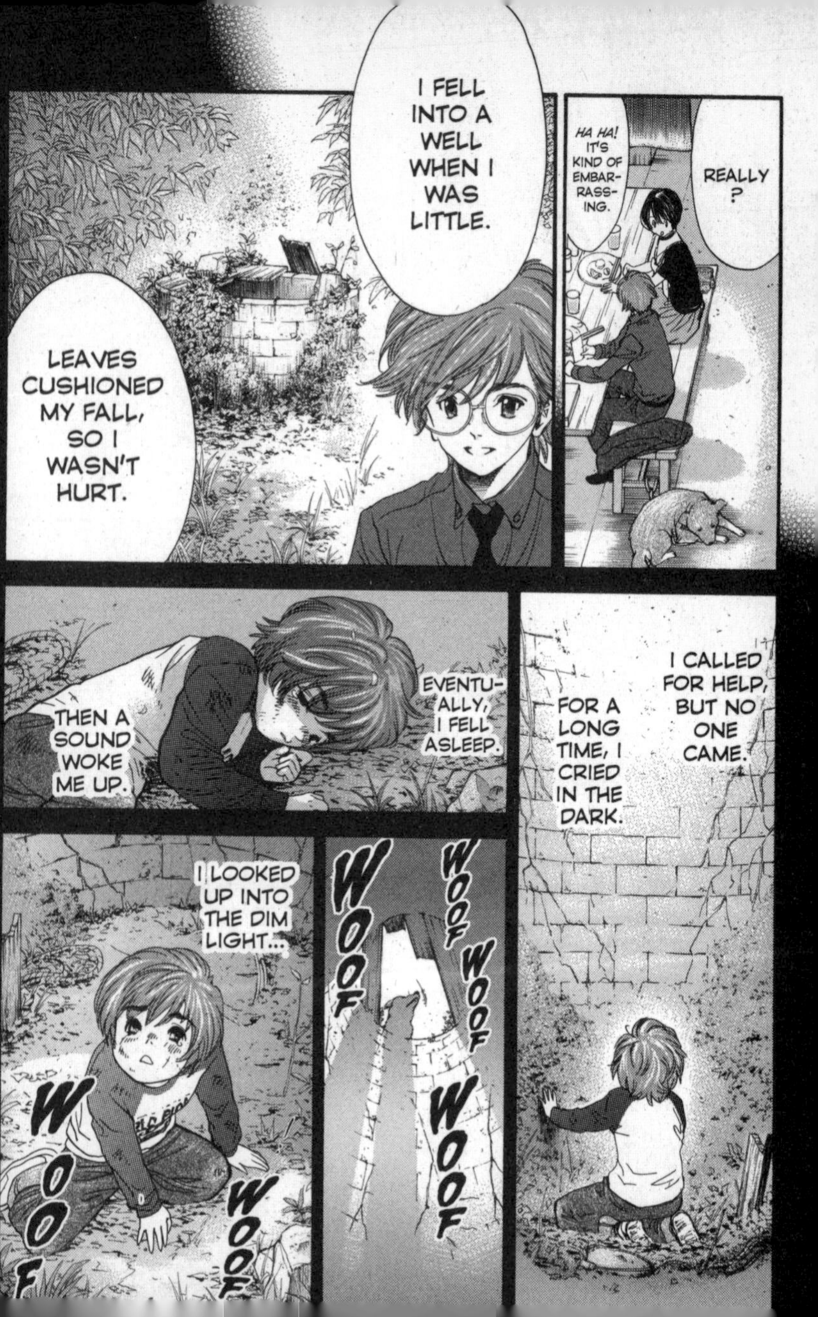
I FELL INTO A WELL WHEN I WAS LITTLE.
REALLY?
HA HA! IT'S KIND OF EMBARRASSING.
LEAVES CUSHIONED MY FALL, SO I WASN'T HURT.
I CALLED FOR HELP, BUT NO ONE CAME.
FOR A LONG TIME, I CRIED IN THE DARK.
EVENTUALLY, I FELL ASLEEP.
THEN A SOUND WOKE ME UP.
WOOF WOOF
WOOF
WOOF
WOOF
I LOOKED UP INTO THE DIM LIGHT...
WOOF
WOOF

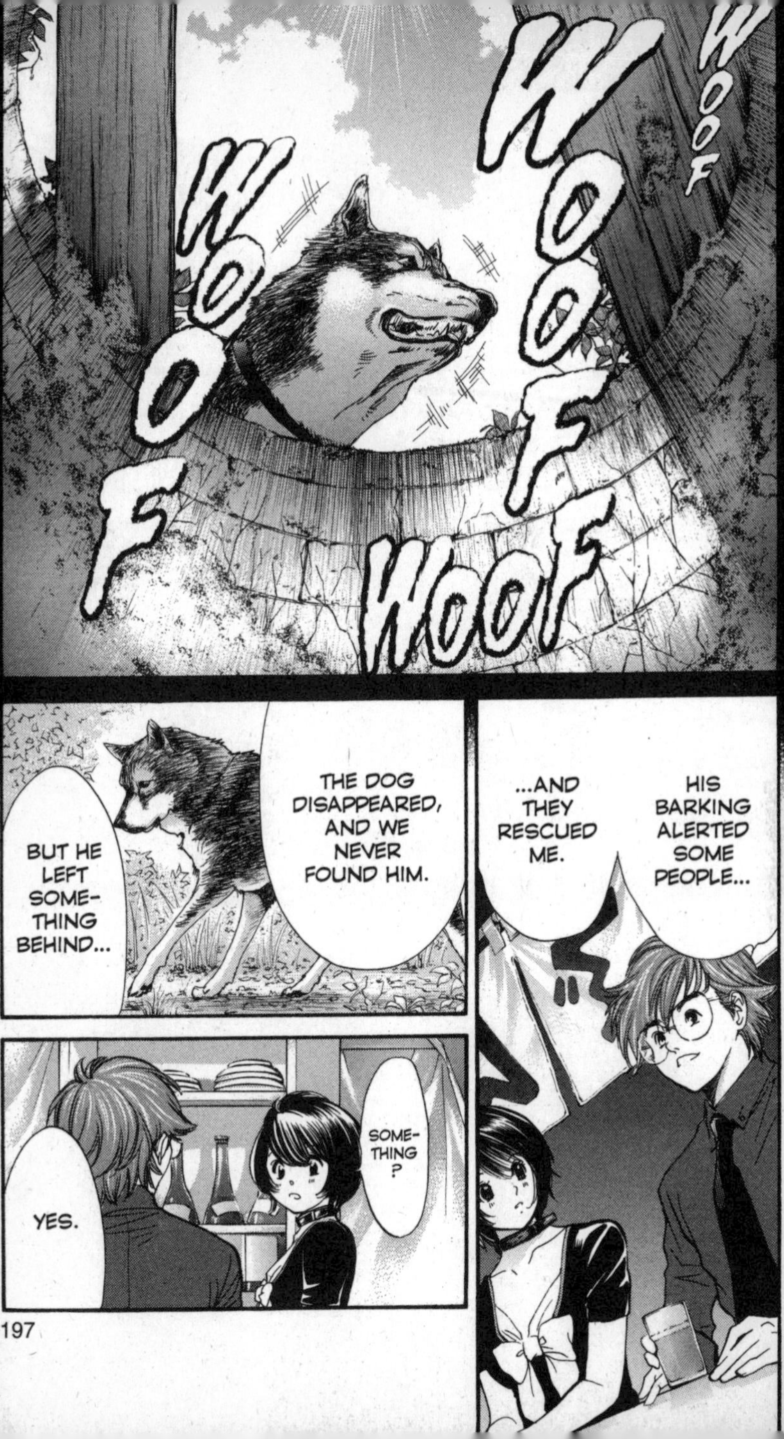

WOOF
WOOF
WOOF
WOOF
HIS BARKING ALERTED SOME PEOPLE...
...AND THEY RESCUED ME.
THE DOG DISAPPEARED, AND WE NEVER FOUND HIM.
BUT HE LEFT SOME-THING BEHIND...
SOME-THING?
YES.

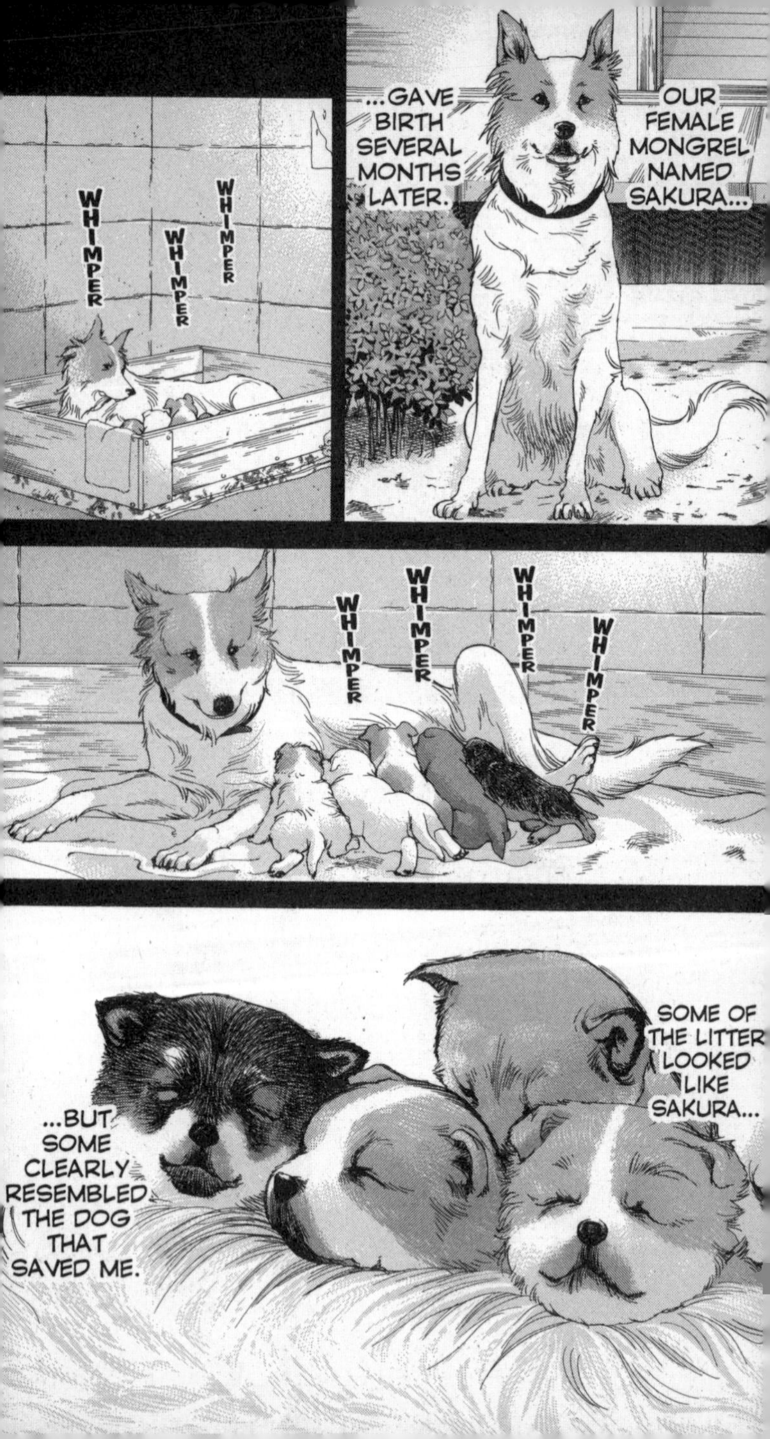

OUR FEMALE MONGREL NAMED SAKURA...
...GAVE BIRTH SEVERAL MONTHS LATER.
WHIMPER
WHIMPER
WHIMPER
WHIMPER
WHIMPER
WHIMPER
WHIMPER
SOME OF THE LITTER LOOKED LIKE SAKURA...
...BUT SOME CLEARLY RESEMBLED THE DOG THAT SAVED ME.

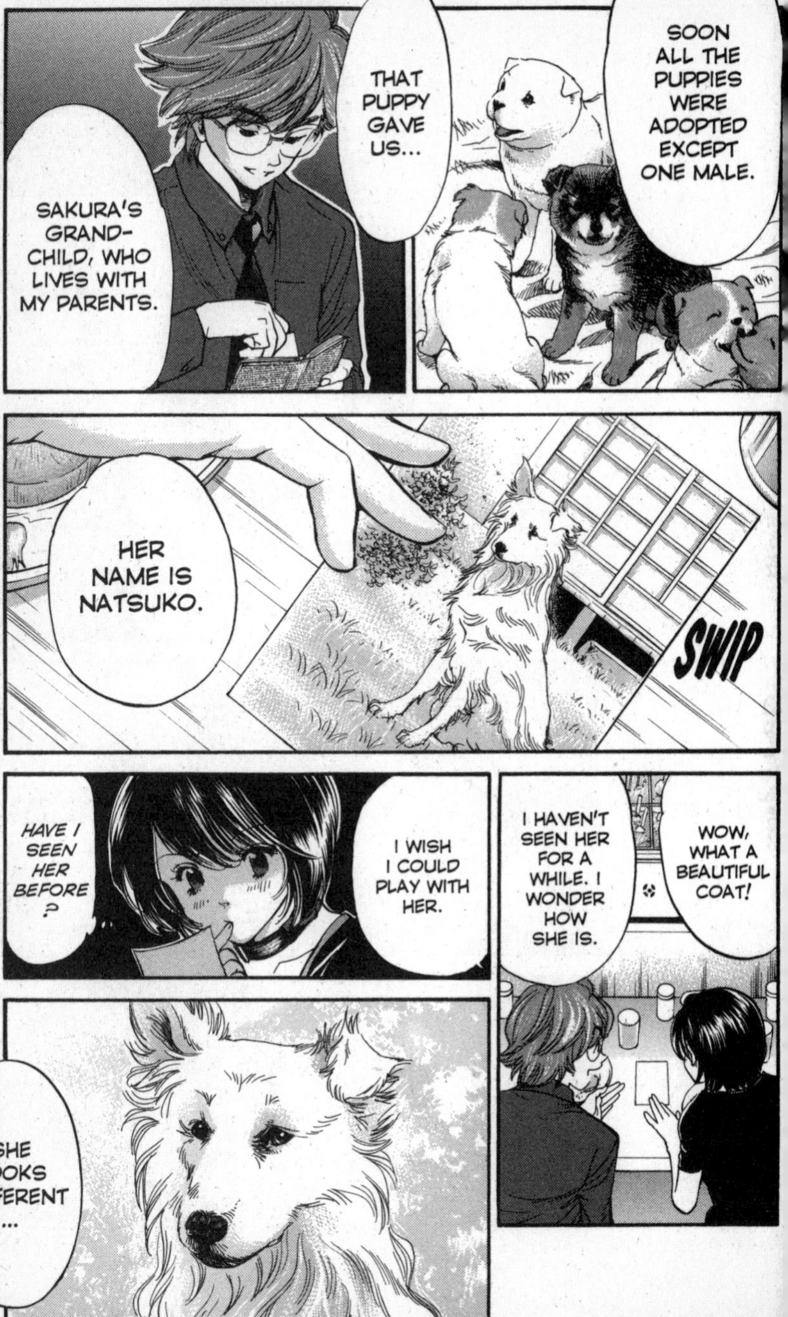
SOON ALL THE PUPPIES WERE ADOPTED EXCEPT ONE MALE.
THAT PUPPY GAVE US...
SAKURA'S GRAND-CHILD, WHO LIVES WITH MY PARENTS.
SWIP
HER NAME IS NATSUKO.
WOW, WHAT A BEAUTIFUL COAT!
I HAVEN'T SEEN HER FOR A WHILE. I WONDER HOW SHE IS.
I WISH I COULD PLAY WITH HER.
HAVE I SEEN HER BEFORE?
SHE LOOKS DIFFERENT...

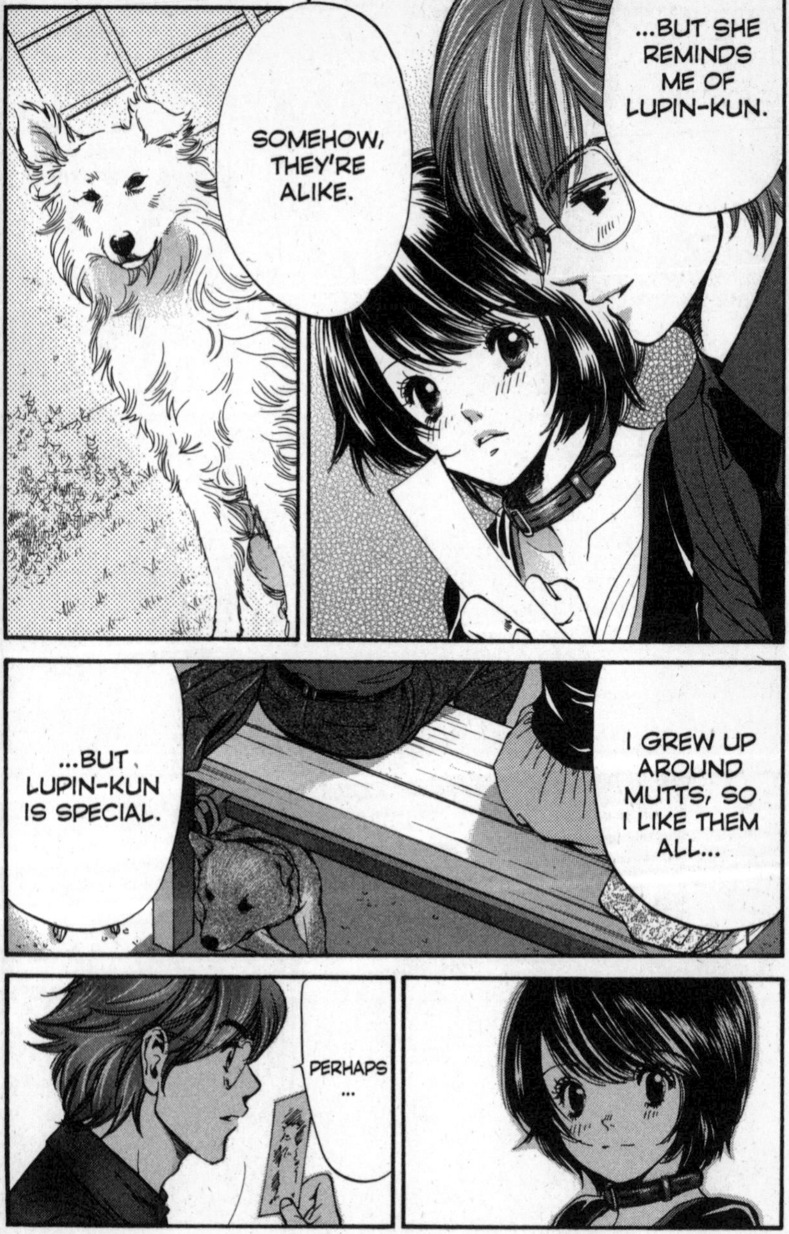
...BUT SHE REMINDS ME OF LUPIN-KUN.
SOMEHOW, THEY'RE ALIKE.
I GREW UP AROUND MUTTS, SO I LIKE THEM ALL...
...BUT LUPIN-KUN IS SPECIAL.
PERHAPS...

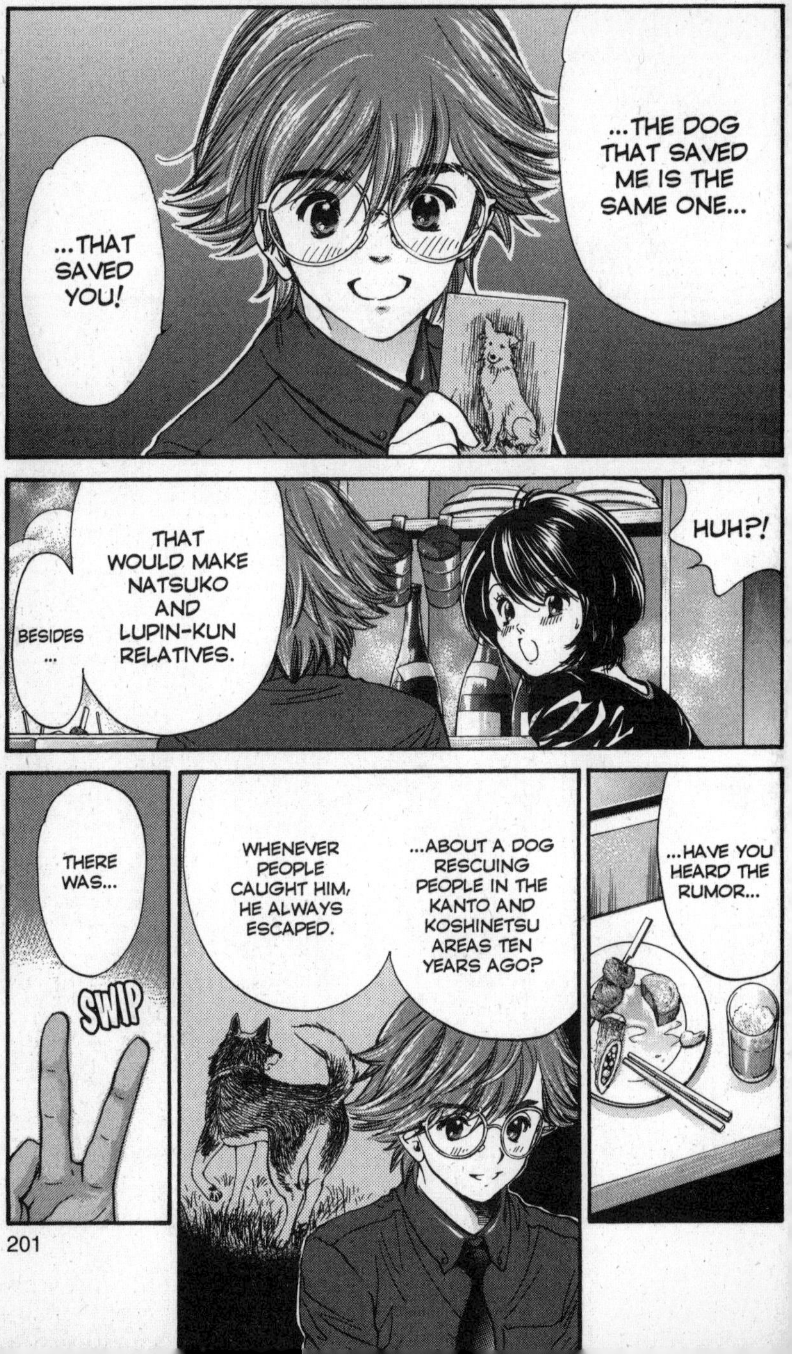
...THE DOG THAT SAVED ME IS THE SAME ONE...
...THAT SAVED YOU!
HUH?!
THAT WOULD MAKE NATSUKO AND LUPIN-KUN RELATIVES.
BESIDES ...
...HAVE YOU HEARD THE RUMOR...
...ABOUT A DOG RESCUING PEOPLE IN THE KANTO AND KOSHINETSU AREAS TEN YEARS AGO?
WHENEVER PEOPLE CAUGHT HIM, HE ALWAYS ESCAPED.
THERE WAS...
SWIP

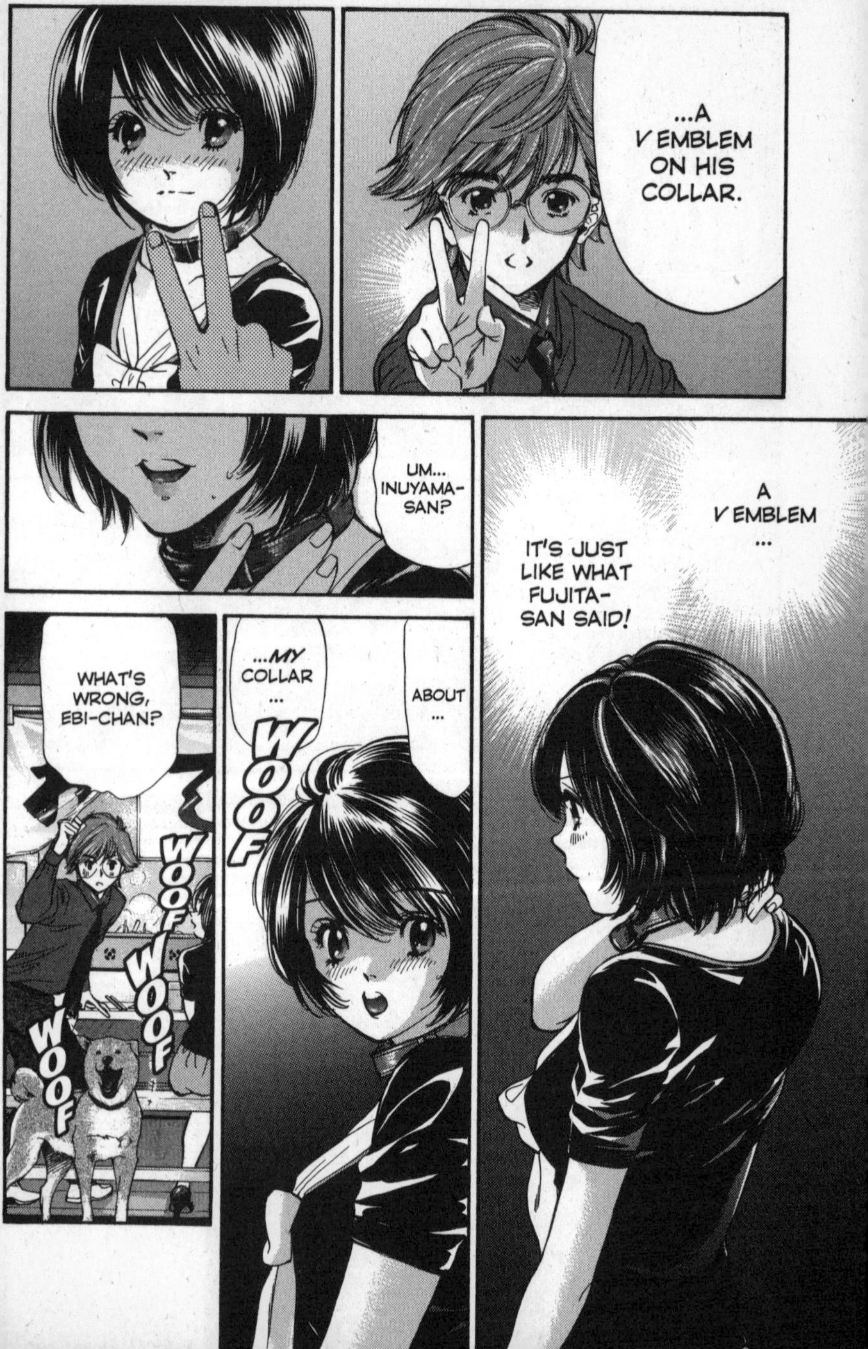
...A V EMBLEM ON HIS COLLAR.
A V EMBLEM ...
IT'S JUST LIKE WHAT FUJITA-SAN SAID!
UM... INUYAMA-SAN?
ABOUT ...
...MY COLLAR ...
WOOF
WHAT'S WRONG, EBI-CHAN?
WOOF WOOF WOOF WOOF

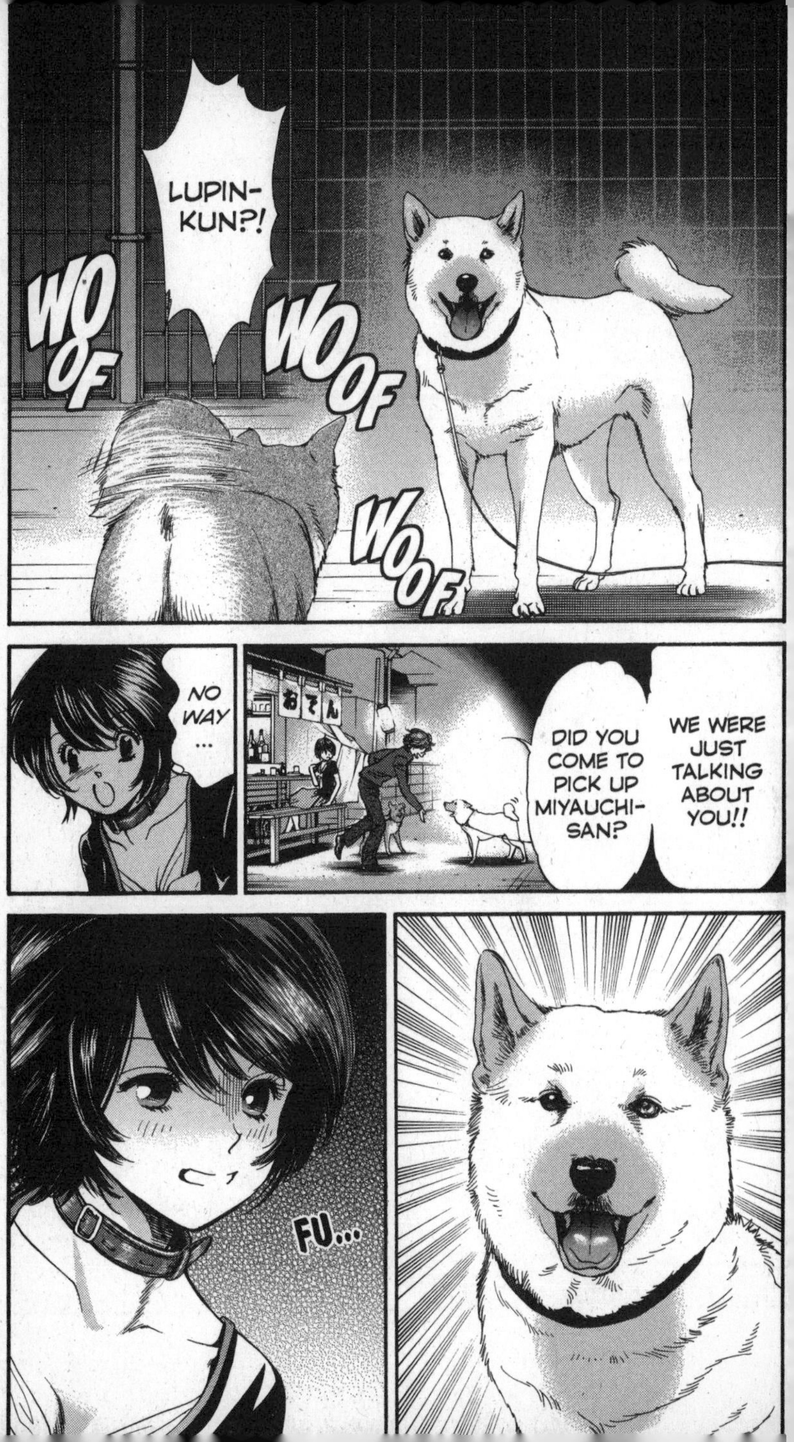
LUPIN-KUN?!
WOOF
WOOF
WOOF
WE WERE JUST TALKING ABOUT YOU!!
DID YOU COME TO PICK UP MIYAUCHI-SAN?
おでん
NO WAY ...
FU...

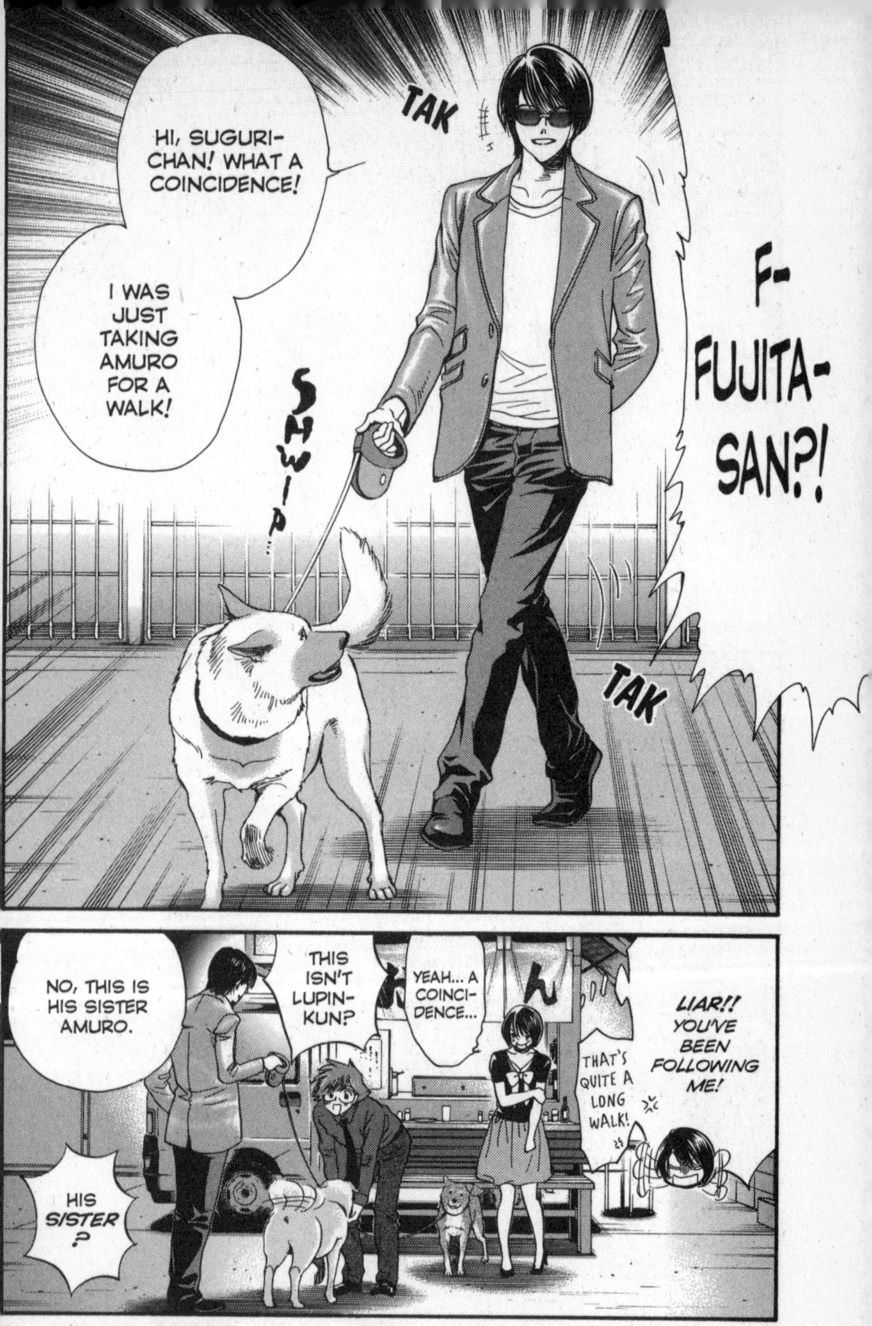
F-FUJITA-SAN?!
TAK
HI, SUGURI-CHAN! WHAT A COINCIDENCE!
I WAS JUST TAKING AMURO FOR A WALK!
SHWIP...
TAK
LIAR!! YOU'VE BEEN FOLLOWING ME!
THAT'S QUITE A LONG WALK!
YEAH... A COINCIDENCE...
THIS ISN'T LUPIN-KUN?
NO, THIS IS HIS SISTER AMURO.
HIS *SISTER*?

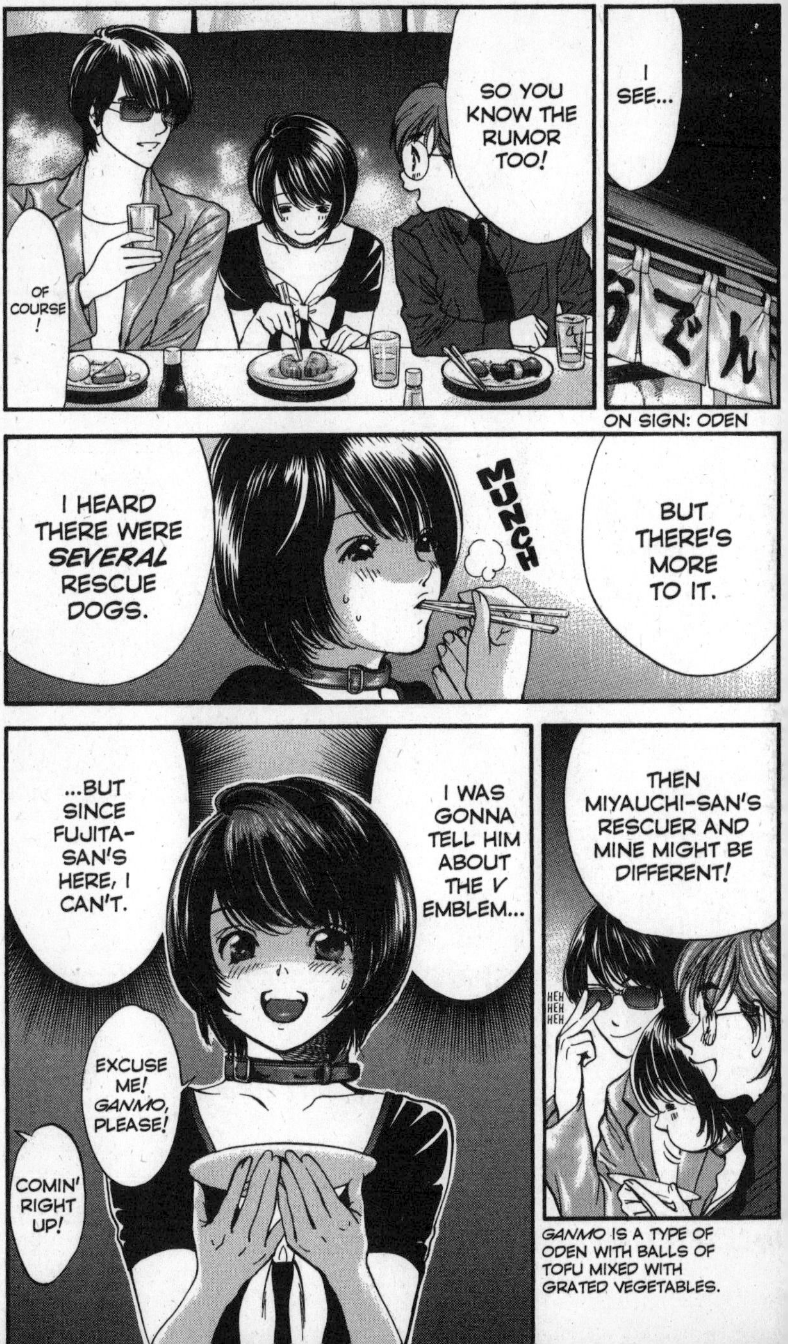
I SEE...
SO YOU KNOW THE RUMOR TOO!
OF COURSE!
BUT THERE'S MORE TO IT.
MUNCH
I HEARD THERE WERE SEVERAL RESCUE DOGS.
THEN MIYAUCHI-SAN'S RESCUER AND MINE MIGHT BE DIFFERENT!
HEH HEH HEH
I WAS GONNA TELL HIM ABOUT THE V EMBLEM...
...BUT SINCE FUJITA-SAN'S HERE, I CAN'T.
EXCUSE ME! GANMO, PLEASE!
COMIN' RIGHT UP!
ON SIGN: ODEN

GANMO IS A TYPE OF ODEN WITH BALLS OF TOFU MIXED WITH GRATED VEGETABLES.

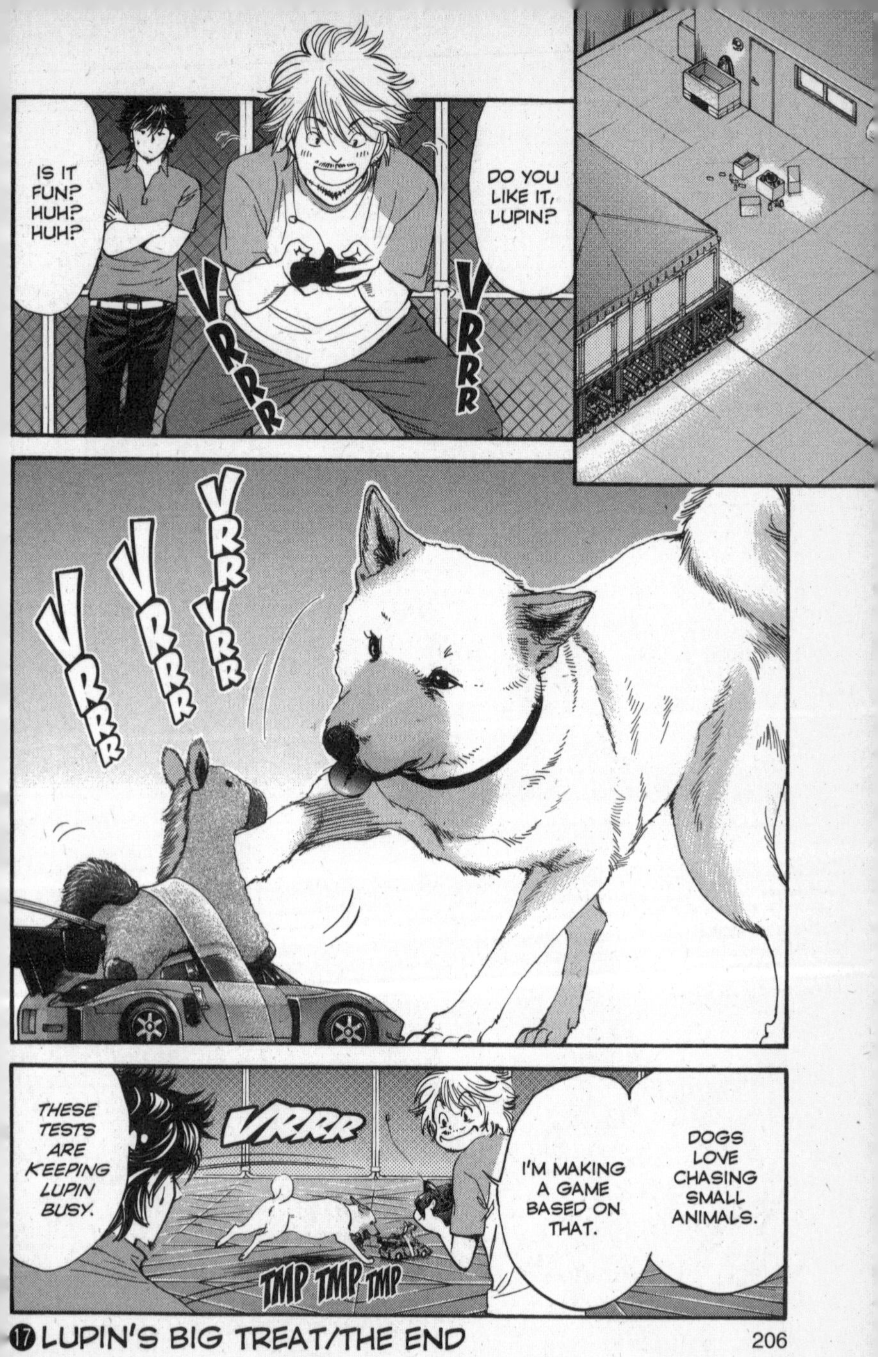
DO YOU LIKE IT, LUPIN?
VRRR
VRRR
IS IT FUN? HUH? HUH?
VRRVRR
VRRR
VRRR
DOGS LOVE CHASING SMALL ANIMALS.
I'M MAKING A GAME BASED ON THAT.
VRRR
TMP TMP TMP
THESE TESTS ARE KEEPING LUPIN BUSY.

INUBAKA

INUBAKA

Everybody's Crazy for Dogs!

From Tam Tam-san in Hokkaido

🐾 Maron-chan (left) & Love-chan (right) (miniature dachshunds)

Although Love-chan has never had babies, once a year she uses a toy to pretend she's giving milk to puppies. She still likes her mother, Maron, a lot.♡ Maron-chan and Love-chan will be a loving mother and daughter forever!

Yukiya Sakuragi

It's too bad this page is black-and-white. (laugh) They look so cute against that background of pink hearts! Those two ladies are quite beautiful! It looks like Maron-chan gets cold easily and sticks close to the heater. My Blanc likes the *kotatsu*...

From Asao-san in Aichi Prefecture

🐾 Jack-kun (left) & Chip-kun (right) (Jack Russell terrier and miniature schnauzer)

These two are close brothers. Jack-kun grooms and cleans Chip-kun's paws. Jack-kun takes care of his brother really well. Chip-kun loves his brother. Today, as ever, they are sticking close by each other!

Yukiya Sakuragi

Although their breeds are different, they get along. Isn't that great? They look so happy in the photo. As you wrote in your message to me, I'll keep writing *Inubaka* in hope that all dogs and pets can live happily!

From Bu-san in Aichi Prefecture

🐾 Gorin-chan (German shepherd)

Gorin-chan is a hyper girl. Currently, her favorite game is to bite down on a soccer ball and use it to play defense against other balls kicked by her owner. Shall we aim for the Japan League, Gorin-chan?☆

Yukiya Sakuragi

Gorin-chan must be happy that she has Bu-san to play with her. Lupin is good at soccer-ball lifting! (laugh) Let him join your team! Gorin-chan's happy face is so cute!

From Chiba-san in Ibaraki Prefecture

🐾 Kaera-chan (Shiba Inu)

When Kaera-chan gets irked, she causes trouble. A foul-tempered girl can be a cute member of the family! May she and her owner have a long and happy life together!☆

Yukiya Sakuragi

Maybe the reason she causes trouble is that she wants attention. (laugh) She looks so ladylike in the picture that I can't imagine her causing trouble. Live the "Inubaka" life together!

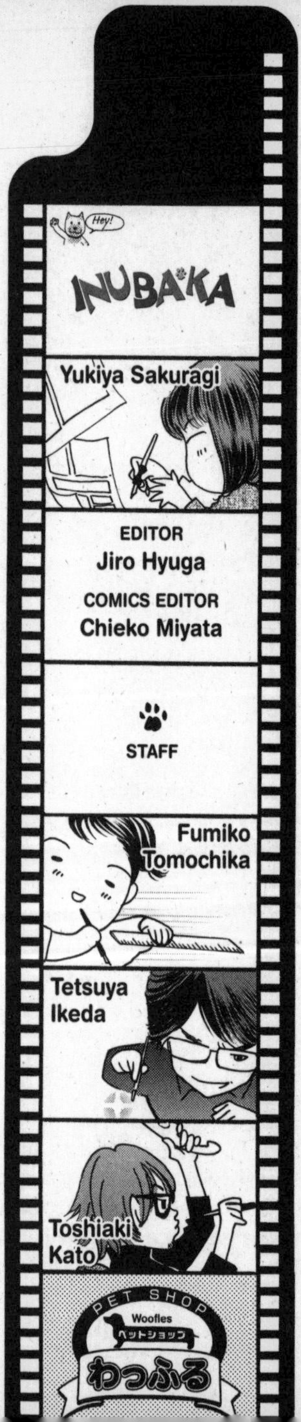
Hey!
INUBAKA
Yukiya Sakuragi
EDITOR
Jiro Hyuga
COMICS EDITOR
Chieko Miyata
STAFF
Fumiko Tomochika
Tetsuya Ikeda
Toshiaki Kato
PET SHOP
Woofles
ペットショップ
わっふる

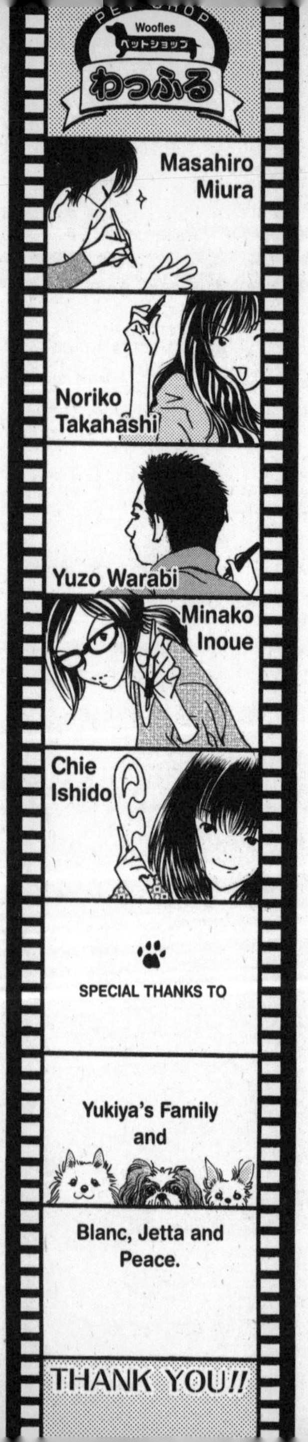
PET SHOP
Woofles
ペットショップ
わっふる
Masahiro Miura
Noriko Takahashi
Yuzo Warabi
Minako Inoue
Chie Ishido
SPECIAL THANKS TO
Yukiya's Family and
Blanc, Jetta and Peace.
THANK YOU!!

Inubaka
Crazy for Dogs
Vol. #17
VIZ Media Edition

Story and Art by
Yukiya Sakuragi

Translation/Ari Yasuda, HC Language Solutions, Inc.
English Adaptation/John Werry, HC Language Solutions, Inc.
Touch-up Art & Lettering/Kelle Han
Cover & Interior Design/Hidemi Dunn
Editor/Carrie Shepherd

INUBAKA © 2004 by Yukiya Sakuragi.
All rights reserved. First published in Japan in 2004 by SHUEISHA Inc., Tokyo.
English translation rights arranged by SHUEISHA Inc.

The stories, characters and incidents mentioned in this publication are entirely fictional.

No portion of this book may be reproduced or transmitted in any form
or by any means without written permission from the copyright holders.

Printed in Canada

Published by VIZ Media, LLC
P.O. Box 77010
San Francisco, CA 94107

10 9 8 7 6 5 4 3 2 1
First printing, November 2010

PARENTAL ADVISORY
INUBAKA is rated T + for Older
Teen and is recommended for
ages 16 and up. May contain
sexual themes.
ratings.viz.com

www.viz.com

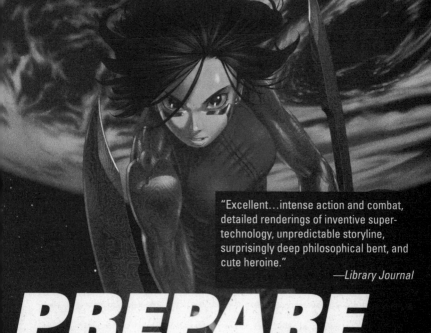

"Excellent...intense action and combat, detailed renderings of inventive super-technology, unpredictable storyline, surprisingly deep philosophical bent, and cute heroine."

—*Library Journal*

PREPARE FOR BATTLE

n this epic story spanning two complete manga series, a powerful cyborg struggles to make sense of her mysterious past. But every answer only leads to more questions. Will she uncover the truth before it's too late?

By Yukito Kishiro

Find out in the *Battle Angel Alita* and *Battle Angel Alita: Last Order* manga—buy yours today!

On sale at **store.viz.com**
Also available at your local bookstore and comic store.

GUNNM © 1991 by Yukito Kishiro/SHUEISHA Inc.
GUNNM LAST ORDER © 2000 by Yukito Kishiro/SHUEISHA Inc.

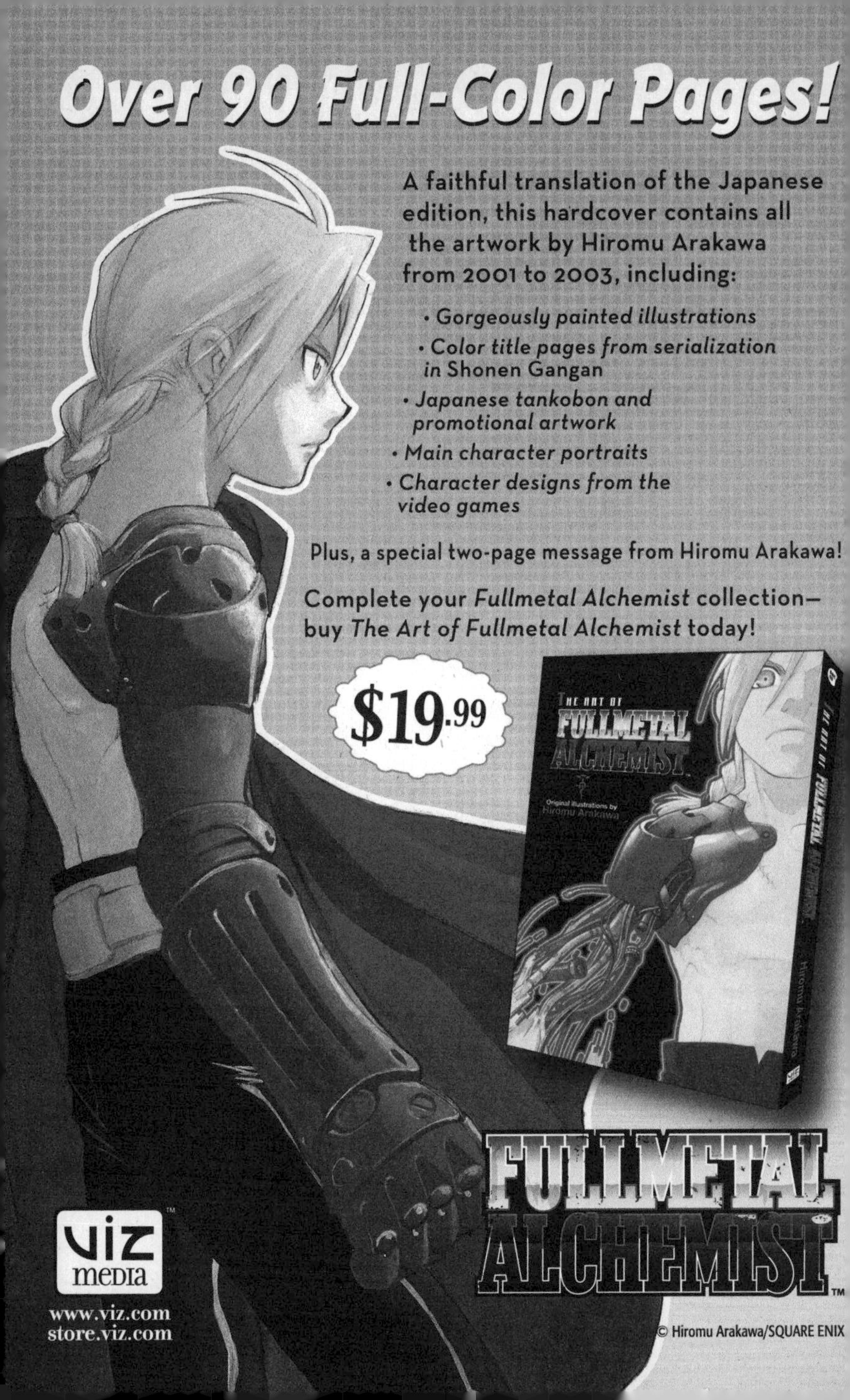
Over 90 Full-Color Pages!
A faithful translation of the Japanese edition, this hardcover contains all the artwork by Hiromu Arakawa from 2001 to 2003, including:
• Gorgeously painted illustrations
• Color title pages from serialization in Shonen Gangan
• Japanese tankobon and promotional artwork
• Main character portraits
• Character designs from the video games
Plus, a special two-page message from Hiromu Arakawa!
Complete your Fullmetal Alchemist collection—buy The Art of Fullmetal Alchemist today!
$19.99
THE ART OF FULLMETAL ALCHEMIST
Original illustrations by Hiromu Arakawa
FULLMETAL ALCHEMIST™
viz media™
www.viz.com
store.viz.com
© Hiromu Arakawa/SQUARE ENIX

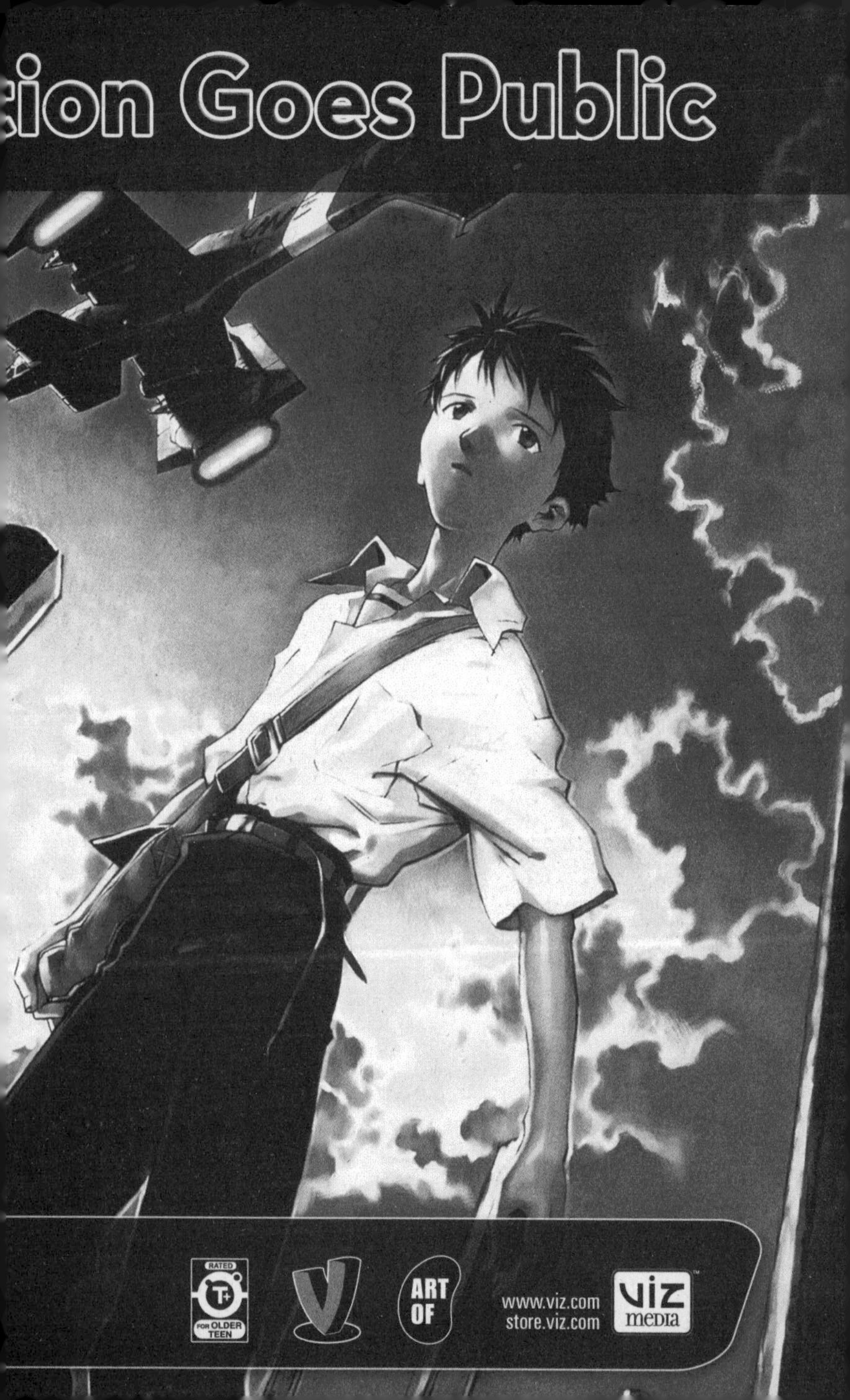
tion Goes Public
RATED
T+
FOR OLDER TEEN
ART OF
www.viz.com
store.viz.com
viz media

A Secret Organiz:

Uncover all the covert operations of NERV
with the complete Neon Genesis Evangelion collection.
Buy yours today at store.viz.com!

NEON GENESIS
EVANGELION

Japan's most controversial anime series
is over…but the manga continues…
Get series co-creator Yoshiyuki Sadamoto's
personal interpretation of the series,
plus bonus content in each volume.

D E R   M O N D

A prestigious hardcover art book featuring 120 pages
of color illustrations, paintings and designs
from Yoshiyuki Sadamoto's most popular series

DER MOND-Collection of Artworks by Yoshiyuki Sadamoto © GAINAX • khara © YOSHIYUKI SADAMOTO © NHK • SOGO VISION © BANDAIVISUAL •
GAINAX • khara © SNK 1992 © 1998 LOVE & POP PRODUCTION GROUP

NEON GENESIS EVANGELEION © GAINAX • khara 1995,1999

A Ninja

Armed with the power to control flame, Recca Hanabishi finds himself in an awkward situation when a mysterious older woman pops into his life one day. Is she good? Is she evil? What exactly does she want with the young ninja firecracker?

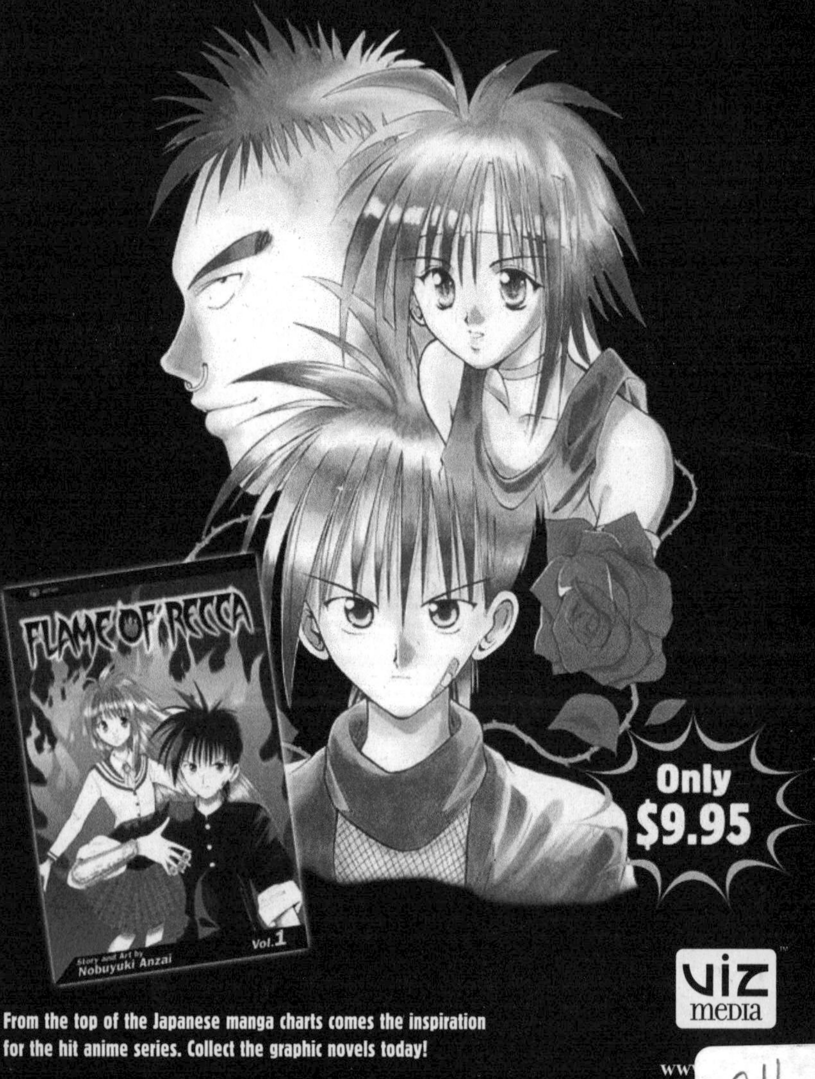
FLAME OF RECCA
Vol.1
Story and Art by
Nobuyuki Anzai
Only
$9.95

VIZ MEDIA

From the top of the Japanese manga charts comes the inspiration for the hit anime series. Collect the graphic novels today!

www
stor